Ball Pest & Disease Manual

2ND EDITION

Disease, insect, and mite control on flower and foliage crops

Charles C. Powell, Ph.D.
Richard K. Lindquist, Ph.D.

Ball Publishing

Batavia, Illinois USA

Ball Publishing
335 North River Street
Batavia, Illinois 60510 USA
630/208-9080

Library of Congress Cataloging-in-Publication Data

Powell, Charles C.
    Ball pest & disease manual : disease, insect, and mite control on
flower and foliage crops / Charles C. Powell, Richard K. Lindquist.
    —2nd ed.
        p.   cm.
    Includes bibliographical references and index.
    ISBN 1-883052-13-0

    1. Plants, Ornamental—Diseases and pests—Handbooks, manuals,
etc. 2. Plants, Ornamental—Diseases and pests—Control—Handbooks,
manuals, etc. 3. Pesticides—Handbooks, manuals, etc.

I. Lindquist, Richard Kenneth, 1942– . II. Title.

SB608.07P69 1996   96-46954
635.9'2—dc21   CIP

All photos in this book were supplied by the authors unless otherwise noted.

Front cover: Melon/cotton aphids in chrysanthemum flower, *top*; powdery mildew on poinsettia, *bottom*.

Contents

Preface

There were three primary motivations for preparing this second edition of the *Ball Pest and Disease Manual*. Most important was the fact that the first edition was so overwhelmingly received by the industry. This indicated that our efforts had indeed filled a need. The improvements in this second edition should help fill the need even more adequately. But filling a need means that the information must be kept up to date. Thus, the second motivation for producing this second edition. Finally, we wanted to reorganize the information so that it would better fit the curriculum development needs of educators in our industry. This guide is unique and popular with teachers in that it combines disease and pest management in one book. Practical information of disease and pest management on flower and foliage crops, along with a bit of information that gives the reader an understanding of "why" as well as "how," is rare in our industry.

After a short introduction defining the holistic approach to plant health management, this edition of the *Ball Pest and Disease Manual* presents detailed information on pest and disease detection methods. The color photo section has been enlarged to further assist the reader in detection and diagnosis. Since successful management depends on "knowing all the players," the disease and pest management chapters are prefaced with chapters on the biology of the pathogens and pests encountered on flower and foliage crops.

The chapters on pesticide use have been updated and enlarged in response to new safety regulations, new products, and a general need to know more about pesticides. Pesticide toxicity is presented from a use perspective, centering on reducing exposure during and following applications. New application methods are also brought into the work.

Readers of the first edition commented repeatedly on the usefulness of the address lists, math tables, and other appendices included at the end of the book. This information has been updated for our second edition. Take some time to become familiar with what is there. When you need a math conversion or the address of a plant clinic, you need it quickly. You may find it in the back of the new *Ball Pest and Disease Manual.*

There was no authors' preface in the first edition of the *Ball Pest and Disease Manual.* This did not give us the opportunity to thank those who helped us so much. First and foremost are our spouses, Penny Powell and Linda Lindquist. The creative effort that has to go into any book to make it good often runs upon hard ground. Penny and Linda helped us get through those times. Next, Liza Sutherland and her team at Ball Publishing have been most helpful. They often have the unpleasant task to having to push us on deadlines and having to tell us there is no room for this or that! Our thanks to them for understanding why we sometimes were at odds with their well-intentioned suggestions and needful scheduling. The work is now finished and ready for you, the ultimate critic!

Charles C. Powell   Richard K. Lindquist
President   Professor
Plant Health Advisory Services   The Ohio State University

PLANT HEALTH MANAGEMENT AND PROBLEM DIAGNOSIS OF FLOWER AND FOLIAGE CROPS

Chapter 1

Holistic Approach to Health Management of Flower and Foliage Crops

T he maintenance of plant health is the primary objective of much of the work you do as a grower of flower and foliage crops in the field or greenhouse. People reach this objective by understanding the linkages of one problem with another, of one environmental stress or change with another and one plant process with another— by practicing holistic plant health management (fig. 1.1).

Holistic management is an outgrowth of the older concepts of integrated pest management and integrated health management. Success in pest management involved capitalizing on a pathogen's or pest's weaknesses, perhaps by using

Fig. 1.1. Good plant health management is a holistic concept, involving integrated management practices.

3

a particular insecticide at the right time and frequency. Good growers might also have kept their plants healthy and pest-free by using a well-drained planting mix.

Holistic plant health management involves not only knowing the pathogen's or pest's weaknesses, but also knowing the particular host plant's strengths. With the holistic approach, a grower might make use of the fact that a plant becomes more resistant to damping-off as it matures, employing growing conditions that promote rapid seedling maturation and thereby managing damping-off diseases.

The holistic management approach is not new to health sciences. Practitioners of the holistic view have long been successful in dealing with human health. Its use in horticulture goes back to experienced growers who were guided by a lot of common sense. Some scientists and researchers currently work in this area. Work that is often called "environmental stress management research" is best done in a holistic framework. Even with such things as testing pesticides in the field under varying conditions, the holistic viewpoint comes into play (fig. 1.2).

This chapter will discuss some holistic ideas and how they fit together. By studying these concepts you will begin to make total plant care approaches work for you. You will see good plant health management as intertwined with good horticulture. The detailed methods in the rest of this book will become clearer. You will become a holistic plant health manager!

Fig. 1.2. Nutritional, pesticide, cultivar development, and other experiments are best evaluated by holistic testing in the greenhouse.

Plant health balance

What is a healthy plant? Is it the same as a plant in good health? Not necessarily! Good health involves a balance. If all of the environmental elements influencing the plant are within reasonable ranges—both by themselves and in relation to each other—the result is a plant that can balance its internal processes to satisfy its needs (fig. 1.3), and the need with the highest priority in any living system is the need to remain healthy.

This balanced plant, then, is a plant in continuing good health. The environmental variables are always in some sort of relationship to one another. The internal plant processes are likewise always in a relationship to one another, as well as to the environmental factors. This external and internal balancing makes plant health a holistic concern—one, according to *Webster's Ninth New Collegiate Dictionary*, "relating to or concerned with wholes or with complete systems rather than with the analysis of, treatment of, or dissection into parts."

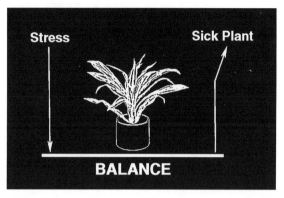

Fig. 1.3. Balanced processes within plants lead to plant health; plant stresses cause imbalance and poor health.

It all starts with a balanced environment

The holistic approach to plant health management views the plant and the environment as one continuing system. The basic environmental elements that promote plant health are simple: friable soil, a proper balance of nutrients, balanced soil acidity, enough root and crown space, ample water, optimum temperature and light, pure air, and freedom from pests and diseases (fig. 1.4). When one or more of these elements are out of the healthful range, however, there is an environmentally induced stress situation, and the health balance of the plant itself is at risk.

Fig. 1.4. These crops are healthy because no environmental stresses are present.

A plant's internal balance follows the environmental balances. Flower and foliage crops growing in a field or a greenhouse have a remarkable ability to balance their internal processes and maintain health. They must—they cannot move to escape an inhospitable environment like humans and most other animals. A good example of balance is how plants stop growing when subjected to droughty conditions. The plant is indeed balanced, but not in a way that we horticulturists would want.

As plant health managers and horticulturists, we must plan and conduct activities that will enable plants both to balance their internal processes and to perform to our expectations. This, then, becomes our definition of holistic plant health management.

In many cases, environmental factors that lead to plant stress are not defined precisely in regard to plant health, but this does not make the environment less important as a concept. Remember that a healthful environment for plants contains many elements that occur in optimum ranges. Too much or too little of such things as light (fig. 1.5), temperature, or water can cause stress.

Fig. 1.5. Lighted roses are under less stress in the winter months.

Acute versus chronic stress

Stresses can be of different types. There are acute stresses and chronic stresses. Acute stress occurs suddenly and causes damage soon after it occurs. Improper sprays (fig. 1.6), frosts or freezes, and injuries from farm implements are examples of acute stress. Chronic stress, on the other

Fig. 1.6. Pesticide burns are an acute stress that may lead to other problems.

hand, includes nutritional imbalances, weed competition, a buildup of certain insect pests, and improper soil pH (leading to nutrient unavailability). Chronic stress takes time to make a plant unhealthy.

Dealing with chronic stress is sometimes easier than dealing with acute stress. There is some time to reverse an imbalance if you have learned to recognize the signs soon after the chronic stress has begun. Acute stress, on the other hand, gives you little time to correct the condition before serious harm occurs. About all you can do is learn from the experience and make sure it is not repeated in the future. The common rapid infection and rotting of a root system by *Pythium* after an overwatering is an example of acute stress.

Understanding plant decline

Chronic stresses that work on a plant over a period of time will eventually cause a sick plant. The time it takes to make the plant sick is called the period of plant decline. There are all degrees of plant health, from magnificently healthy to pathetically diseased. The longer a plant has to endure stress, the more it slips along the continuum from health to disease. An important key to holistic health management is to recognize early when decline is beginning, then take quick measures to reverse it.

Good environmental awareness can help you recognize more easily when plant stress is apt to occur. When confronted with an unhealthy plant, your first job should be to identify chronic stresses, even though you already might have noted the presence of a particular acute stress, such as an infectious disease or an insect pest. Put yourself in the place of the plant. You might want to investigate the soil water situation, light or temperature extremes, or soil aeration and compaction. For instance, soil dryness does not become stressful until temperatures climb. Such situations have often been called disease or stress complexes.

Noninfectious and infectious diseases and pests

A diseased plant shows obvious signs of an imbalanced health condition. Sometimes these symptoms can be due to acute stress, such as pesticide phytotoxicity. Symptoms caused by acute stress have been called injuries in the past, but now some authors are using the term disease even for this type of plant problem. In a sense, this is correct, because it is only the time involved that makes an acute condition different from any other kind of plant problem.

Pathogenic organisms and many insect pests commonly attack and infect a plant that has been stressed and may already show symptoms of a noninfectious disease condition. When the pathogen or pest becomes involved, the health imbalance and stress of infection is added to the previously existing noninfectious stress. In such cases, remember that the two types of disease imbalance exist in the plant or crop simultaneously. Stress management can do a lot toward managing the infectious as well as the noninfectious parts of this picture. However, this is not always true. There are some pests and disease organisms that will attack even vigorously growing, healthy plants.

It is difficult to provide general guides for stress management in an industry as diverse as growing flowers and foliage plants! For the most part, attention to the growing principles given later on in this book will provide for adequate stress management. If you do get into a problem, attention to the proper diagnosis—the subject of the next chapter—should help you make proper stress management decisions.

As you read about various pests and diseases of flower and foliage crops, remember the bottom line of holistic plant health management: are you truly willing to commit yourself to the time, labor, and expense of managing the problem? In the following chapters on insect and disease control, references are often made to the sorts of stresses that may be contributing to a problem, for holistic stress management is basic to the production of healthy flower and foliage crops.

Chapter 2

Diagnosing Problems on Flower and Foliage Crops

M uch of the skill of the good flower or foliage crop production specialist involves quickly determining the causes of plant problems. This is the business of diagnosis. Actually, identifying problem causes is only part of the diagnostic process, which consists of three general areas: perception of a problem, determination of the cause or causes, and planning a solution. An important part of the diagnostic procedure is to organize one's thinking at each step.

A diagnostic overview

The following questions are often used to illustrate the flow of a diagnostic procedure. Notice how they move through the three general diagnostic areas. Their usefulness lies in how they keep your thinking orderly.

1. What kind of plant are you dealing with? What are its cultural requirements? Are these requirements being met in this situation? Knowing the plant type will also enable you, before a problem develops, to anticipate specific diseases or insect pests and the times they may appear.

2. What is wrong? Exactly what symptoms are of concern? What is the condition of the surrounding plants? List all the symptoms you can see.

3. How long has the problem been going on? Be careful here! Many people sincerely believe plants get sick overnight. Such is possibly the case with some acute stresses, but it is rare.

4. What are the possible problem causes that initially come to mind? Be sure to list them all, including environmental conditions. There will generally be more than one item on your list if you have thought the situation through. If necessary, have a plant disease clinic assist you (more about this later).

5. What remedies or health management practices can be applied? Next to the list of causes, list all possible remedies—regardless of cost or practicality at this point.

6. Of the possible remedies, which are practical? This is a crucial step! Doing nothing and merely tolerating the situation may in fact turn out to be the most practical thing to do.

7. Of the practical remedies, when would be the best time (of year, in the crop production cycle, of the day) to apply them?

8. Are you truly willing to commit yourself to the time, labor, and expense of managing the problem?

Perception of problems

The first diagnostic stage, problem perception, generally starts with the appearance of a symptom, which is defined as a noticeable abnormal condition. A good diagnostician can recognize specific symptoms before the untrained eye can see any problem at all!

There are four perspectives to consider to increase your ability to perceive a symptom. The detailed or close-up view, the most common way people look for symptoms, can be very rewarding. Often a hand lens magnifier is used to view plant tissue (fig. 2.1). Spider mites or powdery mildews can be quickly diagnosed this way.

In many cases, however, the general view of many plants or an entire crop may be just as important as close-up views of individuals (fig. 2.2). For instance, a general view might enable you to determine where the mites or mildew came from.

Fig. 2.1. Hand lens magnification helps with proper diagnosis of plant problems.

Another useful perspective is to get some idea as to the amount of time a certain symptom or set of symptoms have been present. Plants cannot directly tell you how long they have been sick, but you can evaluate a period of decline by using indirect diagnostic methods and knowledge. For instance, experienced growers routinely keep records of plant conditions, which they can trace

Fig. 2.2. A general view is often needed for proper diagnosis of problems. This, for example, is a dry spot created by the fan.

back through when problems arise. Perhaps lower leaf browning is noticed on a crop of geraniums in March. A review of irrigation procedures may reveal that a new watering procedure or fertilization program began in February. This would suggest that the leaf condition may relate to poor root health initiated by stresses associated with the earlier changes.

Finally, we must not forget the perspective that our knowledge and experience can give us regarding our initial perception. The more we study plants, the more things we learn to look for with particular situations and plants. Scheffleras, for example, are particularly susceptible to mites. Grape leaf ivy often is seen with powdery mildew. Geraniums can easily get *Botrytis* diseases.

Determining causes of problems

Generally, a plant problem does not arise from one isolated cause. There may be a primary, most obvious cause, such as spider mites or powdery mildew fungus disease. However, there may be some associated environmental stress conditions that need to be diagnosed as well. We need to sort out causes by using correct perspectives and orderly thinking. Formulate a series of questions about the plant material. You may need to write out a list of symptoms, then related questions (fig. 2.3). The key is to keep thinking orderly. Do not repeat yourself or go off on a tangent unnecessarily.

One of the most difficult diagnostic areas for the production manager is determining the causes of problems that result in nonspecific symptoms, such as leaf yellowing, leaf drop, or browning of the tips or edges of leaves. Although such symptoms may be serious and easily detected, hundreds of things can go

Fig. 2.3. Writing down your observations will keep your diagnosis process orderly.

wrong with the root environment to result in such symptoms. Some of these may be infectious diseases, and others may be noninfectious environmental problems. (Table 2.1, at the end of this chapter, gives some examples of nonspecific symptoms and possible causes.)

When beginning with a nonspecific symptom, the only way to work toward a correct determination of the cause of a plant problem is to find more symptoms. Gather more data. Produce a set of symptoms. Even if your set of symptoms includes nothing more than a group of individually nonspecific conditions, it might still lead to a correct diagnosis. Let's suppose you start with yellow leaves (fig. 2.4). We could increase our symptom set by noting *where* on the plant the yellow leaves are; *when* they first showed up; *what* unusual cultural things might have happened; *what* other leaf conditions are seen (browning? leaf drop? leaf size change?); and *what* soil conditions are present (wet? dry? compacted? acidic? salty?). Perhaps an outside diagnostic clinic or a soil-testing service will be needed, but the end result of all of this investigation will be an increased ability to correctly diagnose the cause and plan a correct solution.

Fig. 2.4. Yellow leaves are a nonspecific symptom. You must find other symptoms to go along with yellowing.

Recognizing infectious diseases

Recognizing infectious diseases on flower, leaf, and stem parts is sometimes more difficult than recognizing insect or mite pests because the pathogens cannot be viewed directly. You may be unfamiliar with what the pathogens and the damage they cause look like!

Most often, the pathogens you are looking for will be fungi. Many different fungal pathogens can occur on the leaves, flowers, and stems of greenhouse-grown ornamentals. They produce different sizes, shapes, and colors of lesions. A fungus often grows on a leaf similar to the way mold grows on bread or a rotted spot develops on a fruit or vegetable. Look for a circular spot of growth. Sometimes one circular spot overlaps another, giving a blotchy appearance. Look for concentric rings in the spot, making a bull's-eye. Sometimes you can see evidence of fungal spore production or moldy growth on the leaf or stem surface, such as you see in powdery mildews. Also, look for black pinpoint pustules within the damaged tissue (fig. 2.5). These pustules are actually fungal formations in which many spores are produced and pushed to the outside.

Fig. 2.5. Pustules from white rust have formed on chrysanthemum.

Bacterial diseases sometimes appear as oily, greasy, or water-soaked spots on leaves (fig. 2.6). These lesions are often visible by viewing the underside of the leaf. Some bacterial diseases are systemic in nature and cause branch blighting, wilting, and blackening. A common bacterial problem seen in greenhouses causes a soft rot of plant stems.

Fig. 2.6. Oily leaf spots are often caused by bacterial blight.

Virus diseases often show up as yellowish or lighter green ringed patterns on foliage (fig. 2.7). Leaf distortions may be associated with virus diseases as well. Impatiens necrotic spot virus can produce a variety of symptoms of leaves, often resembling a fungal or bacterial leaf spot.

Fig. 2.7. Light green ring spots often indicate a virus infection.

Infectious root rots cause general plant yellowing and wilting. They can be diagnosed more specifically by directly observing the root system (fig. 2.8). Off-color or brownish to blackish roots often indicate root rot. Being able to pull off outer root tissue with your fingers (leaving the stringlike root cortex behind) is a good sign of root rot. To determine the health of a root system, you should know what a healthy root system looks like. Healthy roots are firm to the touch and usually white.

Fig. 2.8. Rotted roots showing outer tissue sloughed off from the inner core tissue.

One of the most common areas of diagnostic difficulty is root health problems. This is largely because the top symptoms that we see are basically nonspecific, although resulting from poor root health. Wilting, yellowing, stunting, leaf scorch, leaf drop, or general dying of plants may be about all that we have to deal with regarding root problems. How-ever, as you know, there can be hundreds of things wrong with the root environment to cause health problems.

We need to take our symptomatology further and get closer to the root environment problem to see if we can find any inadequacy. Soil tests, soil probing, drainage determination, investigation of the soil mix, actual visual observation, and laboratory culturing of pieces of root tissue are all helpful methods to diagnose the problem correctly.

Scouting techniques

The most critical part of any pest and disease management program is detecting and identifying problems before they cause serious injury. This basic principle of plant health management has not changed for many decades. For insects and mites, scout, or inspect, plants on a regular basis for the pests or their injuries, or use traps to detect flying insects. Usually, both tactics must be used for best results. For plant diseases and pathogens, plant inspections must be done as discussed above.

Sticky traps

Flying adult insects of several species are attracted to certain colors. A sticky trap has material of an attractive color, covered with a sticky material to trap the insects that alight (fig. 2.9). Most sticky traps are particular shades of yellow or blue. These are in common use in greenhouses. Yellow sticky traps catch winged aphids, leafminers, thrips, whiteflies, fungus gnats, and shoreflies. Some blue traps are more attractive to western flower thrips than yellow traps, but yellow is satisfactory in most cases and attracts more pest species.

Fig. 2.9. Sticky traps are widely used to detect types and numbers of insects on greenhouse crops.

Sticky traps should supplement plant inspection as a pest detection method, but traps should not replace inspection. Insects already on greenhouse plants may be quite content to remain on their host plants, as long as the plants are in good condition and the pest population is not too high. For example, whiteflies occur in localized infestations that traps may not detect. Nonwinged aphids and spider mites are not caught on traps.

Sticky traps can be purchased from many greenhouse equipment and supply outlets or pesticide formulators, or they can be made in-house. Traps can be made out of almost anything that either is or can be painted bright yellow. Rust-Oleum No. 659 Yellow is a bright yellow paint that works quite well. The sticky substance can be as simple as a thin layer of cooking oil, other oils (automatic transmission fluid has been used), a mixture of mineral oil and petroleum jelly, or commercially prepared materials such as Sticky Stuff (Olson Products Inc., P.O. Box 1043, Medina OH 44256) or Pestick (Phytotronics, Inc., 2760 Chouteau Avenue, St. Louis, MO 63103). Sometimes the sticky substance is applied to clear plastic wrap, and the wrapping material placed over the yellow or blue surface, for easier removal and trap changing.

Place traps vertically at or just above plant height (fig. 2.10). This is where most insect flight activity occurs. However, fungus gnats, shoreflies, thrips, and leaf-miners can also be trapped quite well just above the potting mix or bench surface. Fungus gnat monitoring is much better with horizontal traps. Also, silverleaf whitefly adults are detected more easily early in a crop with horizontal traps.

Fig. 2.10. Sticky traps must be distributed properly to be useful as diagnostic aids.

Be certain to place some traps near side vents, doors, and known susceptible varieties.

The number of traps to use will depend on the pest group and the ability of the grower, manager, or pest scout to inspect them. A minimum should be one per 10,000 square feet (about 1,000 square meters), but more will be better. Whitefly monitoring requires a minimum of one trap per 1,000 square feet (100 square meters), but one trap per 250 square feet (25 square meters) will be more effective. As you can see, trap purchase, deployment, and inspection can become a major operation.

Once trapped, the insects must be identified to determine whether they are problems. Recognizing insects and determining their pest or non-pest status will require some training and a 10X or 15X hand lens for magnification. Perhaps even a microscope will be needed. It is important to learn the general outlines and colors of the different pest groups. Publications can help with identification.

For species determination to be completely accurate, you may need to send the trapped insects to a specialist. This is especially true in the case of thrips, where accurate identification is very important when working out management programs. The same is true for insects found on plants (as discussed later).

Inspect sticky traps at least weekly, and make counts or estimates of pest numbers. Sometimes traps are deployed for only a few hours or a day, giving a better picture of insect activity at that period. This provides more of a snapshot of insect activity, compared with weekly inspections.

Number the sticky traps and have a greenhouse outline map, which can be used to keep records of trap locations and insect infestations. If used properly, traps will not only provide some information on when to apply pesticides or release beneficial insects or mites; they may provide information on the effectiveness of your pest management program.

Larva detection

Insect larvae are more difficult to sample because they do not fly, making sticky traps nearly useless (except in the case of western flower thrips: horizontal traps placed below plants will trap thrips larvae as they drop off the plants). With most pests, proper use of sticky traps or plant inspection combined with biological knowledge will provide adequate information on larvae. For example, Lepidoptera larvae (caterpillars) or their injuries to plants can usually be seen quite easily by inspecting plants.

In the case of an insect whose larvae feed on plant roots, it is very useful to know something about larval numbers and growth stages to properly time pest management procedures. That is the case with fungus gnat (*Bradysia* species) larvae. Adults can be trapped on yellow sticky traps, but this provides just general information about fungus gnat population trends. To obtain information about specific larval development stages in the growing media, potato slices or wedges placed on, or inserted into, the growing media may be useful (fig. 2.11). The potato pieces are left in place in the flats or pots for about 72 hours to attract larvae, then lifted and inspected. Both the numbers and the growth stages of the larvae are observed and noted.

Fig. 2.11. A potato wedge on the growing media will attract fungus gnat larvae and permit their detection.

Indicator plants

Using plants that are more attractive to pests or that show symptoms of pathogen infection more quickly than the main production crop is an old idea that is making a comeback (fig. 2.12). Indicator plants must meet one or more of the following criteria: they must be more attractive to the pest than the producing crop; the pests or pathogen must develop faster on the indicator plants; the indicator must show feeding damage (or virus symptoms) more readily.

Fig. 2.12. These petunias are being used as a trap crop. Petunias attract thrips and will show symptoms if virus-carrying thrips are present in the greenhouse.

Indicator plants, or IPs, are now used mainly for western flower thrips and virus detection, but they can also be used to detect spider mites, whiteflies, and aphids. The IPs are placed among the production crop, or outside the greenhouse, in a manner similar to sticky traps. Sometimes a nonsticky yellow or blue card is placed behind the IP to attract more pests.

Plant inspection

Properly inspecting plants for accurate information on pest abundance or disease occurrence is always an interesting topic. How many plants should be inspected? Where should the plants be located within the crop? The answers are not clear-cut. Of course, to get the most accurate information, *all* the plants should be sampled. This is obviously unrealistic, so you need to make compromises.

Much of the sampling procedure depends on the pest. Thrips, for example, are relatively easy to sample for in flowering plants (if you can see these tiny insects!). If thrips are found in a few flowers, chances are quite good that they are everywhere in the crop. If thrips are not found in some flowers, however, are they absent from the entire crop? If not absent, are they at least at low numbers? Probably, but keep looking.

Whitefly infestations tend to be localized, particularly in the initial stages. There are numerous sampling plans for these insects, including sampling a certain number of plants at random (e.g., 50 poinsettias in every 2,000). Sequential sampling is done when some upper and lower limits have been set on pest numbers to enable the sampler to decide on whether to apply pest controls, not to apply pest controls, or to continue sampling (up to a predetermined maximum number of plants) because a decision cannot be made with the available data.

To make sampling useful, you must establish economic injury levels, or action thresholds, for one or more pests. If the sampled pest levels are below these levels, then no controls need to be applied. You need to continue sampling throughout the crop at regular intervals. The general outdoor and greenhouse environment must be considered, as well. Temperature and humidity are two environmental factors that greatly affect pest and disease development.

One of the best ways to obtain information on pest or disease problems is to get reports from the people working among the plants every day. A little pest identification training will be a great help here. If the workers are trained properly (and this certainly is a key point), problems will be identified quickly.

Another excellent way to keep track every day is to give the pest and disease scouting responsibilities to certain interested employees or to hire somebody to do the scouting. Regardless of how it is accomplished, the inspection procedure must provide data useful for pest and disease management. Keep records of pest infestations and plant disease occurrence. Over time, these records will provide valuable information on pest and disease cycles.

Pest and disease scouting may not reduce the cost of crop production. Sticky traps must be purchased, and someone may have to be hired specifically to do the plant inspections and monitor the sticky traps (or indicator plants, potato pieces). Even if the persons are from within the company, pest monitoring keeps them away from other regular duties. However, most growers who develop and use systematic inspection or trapping programs find that either fewer pesticide applications are needed or that the pesticide applications actually made are more effective.

Diagnostic field-testing kits

In recent years, there has been considerable advancement in the field of immunologically based field testing. Kits can detect minute quantities of certain fungal or viral pathogens associated with symptomatic plant tissue (fig. 2.13). They are generally quite specific, which enables the grower to take, say, a generally rotted root and determine quickly whether certain pathogens are present. It is almost like having a laboratory right in the greenhouse.

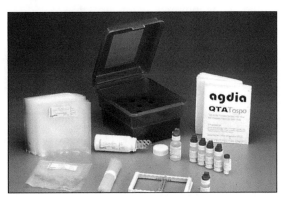

The key to using these kits properly is to realize that a negative result may still mean the pathogen in question is present! You should keep in mind that there are many reasons why any

Fig. 2.13. Field-testing kits can be used to detect viruses, root rots, and bacterial diseases.

particular test is not working and is giving a false negative, such as not following directions closely enough, using old, improperly stored test components, and not testing from symptomatic tissue. Field-test kits are not designed to work with tissue that does not show symptoms because the amount of pathogen present is too small to be detected. False positives are also possible, but not that common.

How to work with diagnostic laboratories

What are we to do when we have a sick plant but cannot tell exactly what the cause of the problem is? As you will note with table 2.1 (at the end of this chapter), there are many such situations, the most common being when we are dealing with root rots and viruses.

To plan and carry out corrective action, we need more information. This is where the services of a diagnostic plant laboratory come into play. A diagnostic laboratory employs a number of techniques to reveal the association of pathogens with symptomatic plant tissue (fig. 2.14). These techniques usually involve micro-scopic examination of tissue or getting the pathogen to grow over the tissue or on laboratory media. There are many more exotic diag-nostic techniques, such as DNA probes, coming into use now as well. Such techniques require expensive equipment and trained technicians, but they are usually highly specific and are well worth the added costs that must be

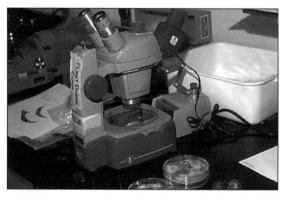

Fig. 2.14. Samples can be sent to diagnostic labs or clinics for more detailed examination.

passed on to the grower. These new techniques make diagnostic laborato-ries even more useful to us.

However, there are still concerns about working with such a service to best advantage. In fact, the actual technique used is often of no concern to the grower. What is found is of paramount importance. Here is a list of para-meters to keep in mind when working with a plant diagnostic laboratory:

1. Do you know what kind of sample to send in? Generally, send recently symptomatic, whole plants. Do not attempt to use a diag-nostic laboratory to determine if a healthy-looking plant is actually free of pathogens. That is the business of an indexing service, and there has been much confusion about this of late. A plant diagnos-tic laboratory is set up to work with symptomatic plant material, whereas an indexing service approaches its task from another direction, going through tedious tests to confirm the cleanliness of plant material.

2. Do you know how to send the sample in? Do not pack the sample with too much water. Shake the growing medium from the roots. Ship the sample using a one- or two-day service (UPS, FedEx, Priority Mail) at the beginning of the week. Most labs have instruc-tion sheets they will send you. There is nothing more frustrating for a laboratory technician than receiving a sample in poor condition!

3. Do you communicate with the laboratory, and is the laboratory willing to communicate with you? This is a major problem in

many areas of the country. Growers get upset because they think clinics are slow or not interested in them. However, phone calls generally correct these troubles. If they do not, change clinics.

4. Do you realize that you do not have to use a clinic at your particular state university? There are certain clinics that are particularly good at, say, diagnosing problems on greenhouse crops or virus problems. Some of these labs are private. You may have to pay more than at your state laboratory, but the extra cost is usually well worth it. Find out about and use the best diagnostic service that you can.

5. Does the clinic reply to you promptly? Is the laboratory willing to fax you the results? Will they give you results over the phone? Again, these are communication issues, vital to success in using a diagnostic laboratory. Because of the value of greenhouse crops, a clinic's reply promptness is crucial. If the clinic does have a delay for some technical reason, it should call you. Again, change clinics if you are having problems in this area.

6. Does the reply contain management suggestions? Be careful here! Remember, the clinic personnel are not in your greenhouse. They will be giving you general corrective suggestions centered on the pathogens or pests detected. If they are not experienced with greenhouse problems, their suggestions may not be economical or practical, or they may actually worsen the problem. If they are not competent, they may not even have found the right pathogens. Holistic plant health management requires a careful look at all the factors contributing to a problem. The grower, with or without an experienced consultant, needs to take the lead in planning solutions.

Planning solutions to problems

Formulating solutions would be much easier if the diagnostics have been done carefully and correctly up to this point. Again, we can start by thinking generally about solutions, then sort out a specific plan from the array of plant cures and doctoring techniques used by many practitioners.

There are really only four general approaches toward health mainte-nance or the correction of a problem. First of all, prevent problems from showing up in the first place by proper health management techniques. This, of course, is by far the best method. An example would be excluding insects by installation of microscreening over greenhouse vents and doors.

Another general approach is to cure the sickness by the correct use of a pesticide or by pruning or removing the diseased plant part. Root sys-tems where the drainage is poor can sometimes be cured by repotting and reestablishing the roots in a more hospitable environment. Generally, curatives are difficult to employ because cures are typically applied to only one of the many causes of the problem. For instance, spider mites may be occurring on a plant because it is being kept too hot and dry. Spraying the plant with a miticide will kill the mites but will not cure the whole problem, because you have not taken care of the underlying hot and dry conditions.

Another general approach to a plant health problem is simply to tol-erate the situation. In many instances, toleration is the only alternative. Generally, however, in commercial greenhouses, problem toleration is not a suitable alternative.

Finally, simply start over. Plant material can be removed and discarded, and new material can be brought in. This will be an expensive general plant health management approach. It will work if some sort of correction of the problem causes has also been carried out.

Testing and evaluating planned solutions in an ordered manner

Many growers lose sight of the diagnostic process as they begin correc-tive measures, since a clear, ordered plan has not been drawn up and fol-lowed precisely. There are many reasons for this, the most compelling is that growers want to fix problems as soon as possible. The high value of greenhouse crops produces a feeling of anxiety, leading to what is known as the shotgun approach, as seen most commonly with pesticide use (fig. 2.15). If a product is applied and does not work immediately, anoth-er is applied, or the dose is raised, and so on until the plants are "gasping for air."

The result of the shotgun approach is that problems may not be solved, proper evaluation of the plan of action is impossible, and other problems could arise. The problem may be solved, but there will be no clue as to which shotgun blast did it. Draw up a plan of action, have confidence in it, and carry it out long enough so that it can be tested.

Fig. 2.15. Only after proper diagnosis can the right management strategies be carried out.

Conclusions

Remember, diagnosis of problems on ornamentals grown in the greenhouse is a three-step process. First, you must correctly perceive the problem in its entirety. Second, you must correctly determine the causes of the problem. Be sure and look for environmental stresses as well as the presence of a pathogen or pest. Third, you must plan your course of action to solve the problem and prevent it from happening again.

Proper attention to each of these areas requires ordered thinking, data gathering, and careful planning. Whereas experience and knowledge can help a lot, good greenhouse production professionals know that they can always sharpen their diagnostic skills, which are an important part of their continued success as plant health managers.

Table 2.1   General diagnostic guide for plants exhibiting nonspecific leaf symptoms

Symptoms	Possible causes
Brown or scorched leaf tips	• Poor root health from overwatering, excessive soil dryness (especially between waterings), or excessive fertilizer or other soluble salts in the soil • Specific nutrient toxicities (such as fluoride, copper, or boron) • Excessive heat or light • Pesticide or mechanical injury • Air pollution
Leaf spots or blotches	• Excessive soil dryness coupled with high temperatures • Chemical spray injury • Fungal or bacterial infections
Foliage yellow-green: older leaves	• Insufficient fertilizer, usually nitrogen • Poor root health due to poor drainage • Insufficient light from shading • Root rot diseases
Foliage yellow-green: newer leaves	• Soil pH (acidity) imbalance • Trace element imbalance
Foliage generally yellow-green	• Too much light • Insufficient fertilization • High temperatures, especially when associated with dryness • Insect infestation or root rot disease
Foliage of one branch yellowing	• Fungal or bacterial canker • Injury • Fungal infection of vascular system

Table 2.1   continued

Symptoms	Possible causes
Leaf drop	• Poor root health from overwatering, excessive dryness, or excessive fertilizer or other soluble salts in the soil • Sudden change in light, temperature, or relative humidity • Insect or mite infestation
Wilting or drooping of foliage	• Poor root health from overwatering, excessive dryness, excessive fertilizer or other soluble salts in the soil, or poor soil drainage • A toxic chemical poured into soil • Root rot disease • Fungal or bacterial cankers
Yellowed leaves with a tiny speckled spotting; leaves later bronzed and drying	• Spider-mite infestation • Air pollution • Insect infestation
Deformed or misshapen leaves	• Herbicide injury • Virus infection • Insect or tarsonemid mite infestation

Note: To more correctly determine causes of greenhouse plant problems, compile lists or sets of symptoms. Look for specific symptoms associated with these nonspecific symptoms. In later chapters, specific symptoms will be noted for many pests and diseases of floral and foliage crops.

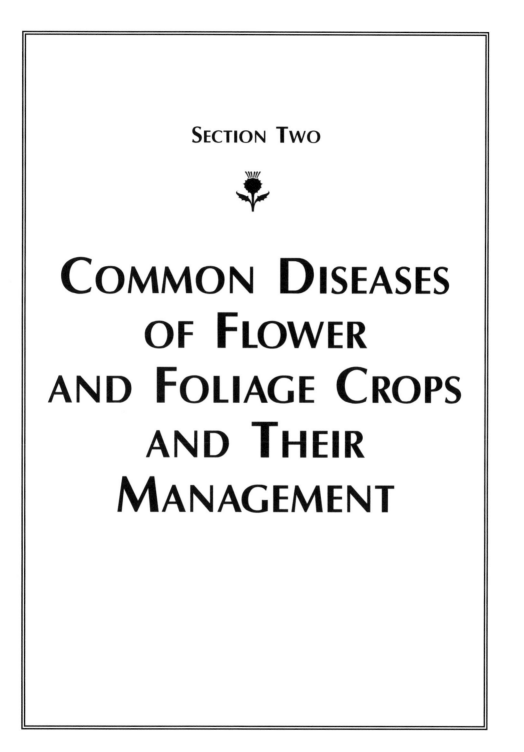

SECTION TWO

COMMON DISEASES OF FLOWER AND FOLIAGE CROPS AND THEIR MANAGEMENT

Chapter 3

Biology and Management of Plant Pathogens and Diseases They Cause

A ll species of plants, both wild and cultivated, are subject to attack by pathogens causing diseases. More than 80,000 different diseases have been recorded in the world; more than 50,000 occur in the United States. Each species of plant is subject to only a small number of these diseases. The kinds of diseases a particular plant might get depend on the type of plant and the cultural or environmental conditions present.

Cultivated plants are usually more susceptible to disease than their wild relatives, partly because large numbers of the same plant are often grown closely together in pure stands. Disease-causing organisms (pathogens) often get established under such conditions. Once this happens, the pathogens may spread rapidly. In addition, many of our valuable varieties of ornamental plants are basically very susceptible to disease and would have difficulty surviving in nature. Finally, constant cultivation—be it of roses, cabbages, or sycamores—is disturbing nature and tends to create environmental stresses. Stresses often weaken plants and subject them to pathogenic infections.

Plant diseases are not new. Fossils have been found that prove plants had pathogen enemies 250 million years or more before people appeared on earth. Plant diseases undoubtedly arose and developed along with other forms of life. Many injurious pests, including rusts, smuts, mildews, blights, and blast, are mentioned in the Bible and other ancient writings. These diseases and others have plagued human beings, causing famine and unrest, since the dawn of recorded history. Plant diseases contributed to the defeats of Alexander the Great and the fall of the Roman Empire. Potato late blight caused the great Irish potato famine and emigration to the United States in the mid-1800s. The American chestnut tree has for all practical purposes been eliminated from our country because of a disease called chestnut blight. The southern corn leaf blight epidemic of 1970 cost U.S. farmers more than 700 million bushels of corn.

What is a plant disease?

When a plant is *continuously* disturbed over a fairly long period of time by some environmental factor or group of factors that interfere with its normal structure, growth, or functional activities, it is said to be diseased. Diseases can be infectious or noninfectious, depending on the living or nonliving status of the causal factors. It is important to remember that infectious diseases are caused by pathogens, to be discussed in detail later on. Diseases do not spread; pathogens do spread. Diseases don't infect; pathogens do.

There is often no sharp distinction between healthy and diseased plants. Disease, in some of its aspects, may merely be an extreme case of poor growth. Knowledge of normal growth habits, variety (cultivar) characteristics, and normal variability of plants within a species is required for recognition of a disease condition. The development of disease in a plant parallels the development of the pathogen or the intensity of the disturbance. Diseases do not happen overnight. In addition, they do not go away overnight.

Diseases are commonly named after the most obvious symptom. Some diseases result in plugging of the plant's water-conducting vessels, producing a wilting condition similar to drought. Root rots destroy the feeding roots, which absorb water and nutrients from the growing medium. Leaf spotting or blighting diseases reduce photosynthesis, resulting in less food being manufactured. Seeds, corms, bulbs, seed pieces, fruits, and flowers may be destroyed by rots, scabs, or blights. Diseases of these types reduce the reproductive ability of a species.

Infectious and noninfectious plant diseases and their causes

Some plant diseases are caused by unfavorable growing conditions (called nonparasitic, noninfectious, abiotic, or physiogenic diseases), others by living pathogens (called infectious or parasitic diseases). Living pathogens include bacteria, fungi, viruses, viroids, mycoplasmas, nematodes, and parasitic seed plants. Symptoms resulting from diseases in these two groups are often similar. The cause of the disease must be known because control measures vary widely from one group to the other.

Unfavorable growing conditions. Noninfectious diseases can be caused by extremes in temperature; an excess or deficiency of light, water, or essential growing medium elements (such as nitrogen, phosphorus, potassium, calcium, iron, magnesium, manganese, boron, copper, molybdenum, zinc, or sulfur); unfavorable growing medium moisture or oxygen relationships; extreme growing medium acidity or alkalinity; pesticide or fertilizer injury; toxic impurities in the air or growing medium; mechanical and electrical agents, fire; growing medium compaction; plus unfavorable preharvest or postharvest storage conditions (fig. 3.1).

Fig. 3.1. The patchy growth, flat by flat, indicates a media/fertilizer mixing problem.

Plants in poor health because of unfavorable growing conditions are more commonly encountered than are plants attacked by disease-producing organisms. Noninfectious or physiogenic troubles *do not spread* from sick to healthy plants. However, they often arise, sometimes very suddenly, at about the same time on a number of plants growing in a given area or environment (fig. 3.2).

Pathogens. Infectious diseases are generally caused by parasitic microorganisms—bacteria, fungi, nematodes, mycoplasmas, viruses, and viroids. These organisms or agents attack plants and live in or on and at the expense of the host plant. These pathogenic parasites cause infectious diseases that often spread easily from diseased to healthy plants.

Fig. 3.2. This leaf mottling occurred on all the plants of one variety overnight following a spraying. It is a pesticide reaction.

Bacteria. Most of the 4,000 species of bacteria that have been described are harmless or even beneficial to people. However, more than 100 species are known to cause human and animal diseases, and almost 200 species incite diseases in plants. Bacteria, one-celled microorganisms found in all types of air, growing media, and water, are common on and in all plants, animals, and man. They can be seen only with a good microscope. Placed end to end, 10 to 20 thousand bacteria would be needed to make a 1-inch line.

Bacteria enter plants through wounds (produced by adverse weather, man, insects, or nematodes) and small natural openings, such as stomates, lenticels, hydathodes, nectaries, and leaf scars. Bacteria multiply rapidly inside a plant, where they can cause death of cells (necrosis) or leaf spots, abnormal growth (tumors), blockage of water-conducting tissues (wilting), or breakdown of tissue structure (soft rot). The bacteria often migrate throughout the plant. Some produce toxins that poison the plant and produce yellowing (chlorosis), water-soaking, and other symptoms.

Bacteria are spread by man through cultivating, harvesting, grafting, pruning, and transporting diseased plant material, such as seed, tubers, corms, bulbs, nursery stock, and transplants. Animals (including insects, mites, and nematodes), splashing rain, flowing water, and wind-blown dust are other common disseminating agents.

The most common bacterial diseases of plants are soft rots, angular leaf spots or blotches, leaf and stem blights, stem cankers, wilts, and galls. Most bacterial diseases are favored by warm, rainy weather. They are common on greenhouse-grown crops subject to overhead irrigation, especially in southern regions of the United States.

When conditions are unfavorable for growth and multiplication, bacteria lay dormant on or inside perennial plants, seeds, storage organs (such as potato tubers, flower bulbs, corms, rhizomes), plant refuse, garden tools and farm implements, or growing media. A few types are known to live for several months or longer in the bodies of living insects, as with Stewart's disease of corn, where the causal bacterium overwinters in the corn flea beetle.

Most bacteria that cause plant diseases are quickly killed by high temperatures (10 minutes at 125F, 53C), dry conditions, and sunlight. Many pathogenic bacteria in growing media are eaten by protozoa and other minute animal life forms in the growing media. Some are inhibited by antibiotic substances liberated by other media-inhabiting organisms, chiefly bacteria, actinomycetes, and fungi.

Fungi. Like bacteria, fungi are simple, usually microscopic organisms that lack chlorophyll (green pigments) and hence cannot make their own food. More than 100,000 species of fungi have been described, probably less than half of the total number in the world. Approximately 20,000 different species of fungi produce disease in plants. Fungi that grow on or in another living plant and obtain nourishment from it are *parasites*, and the living plant is called the *host*. Fungi that feed on manure, dead leaves, stems, wood, and other nonliving organic matter are called *saprophytes* (fig. 3.3). Many fungi are able to parasitically attack living plants at certain times, yet live as saprophytes in plant debris or in growing media at other times. Some fungi are *obligate parasites*, living only on living plants.

Fig. 3.3. These "toadstools" are from a harmless, saprophytic fungus growing in the potting medium. They will soon die down and disappear.

A typical fungus begins life as a microscopic spore, comparable in function to the seed of a higher plant. Under moist conditions the spore may germinate and produce one or more branched, tubular threads called *hyphae*. The hyphae grow and branch to form a *mycelium*, a fungus body. The mycelium may be an interlacing tangle of hyphae, a loose woolly mass, or even a compact, solid body. A parasitic mycelium may grow on the surface of its plant host, appearing as delicate, whitish, cobweblike threads (powdery mildew) or as sooty brown to black filaments. The mycelium may be completely within the host plant (as with wilt-producing and wood-rotting fungi) and not evident on the plant surface.

Fungus hyphae may penetrate a plant by (1) growing into a wound made by a tool or farm implement, hail, wind, blowing sand, insects, nematodes, or other fungi; (2) growing through a natural opening; or (3) by forcing their way through the plant's epidermis by a combination of pressure and enzyme action.

Spores play an important role in the multiplication, dissemination, and survival of fungi (fig. 3.4). Spores are easily carried by air currents; splashing or flowing water; insects, mites, birds, slugs, spiders, and other animals; plant parts (seeds, bulbs, transplants, nursery stock); and cultivating, harvesting, and pruning equipment. Man also spreads spores on hands, clothing, and shoes.

Certain fungus spores have been known to blow a thousand miles or more, sometimes at altitudes up to 90,000 feet, before descending (frequently in a rainstorm) and infecting plants. Foliage that is wet, sticky, hairy, or rough traps more spores than plant surfaces that are dry and smooth.

Some fungal spores, *resting* or *resistant spores*, allow certain fungi to withstand unfavorable growing conditions, such as extreme heat, cold, drying, and flooding (fig. 3.5). Spores of certain fungi may lie dormant in growing media for many years and are extremely difficult to kill.

Certain fungi do not produce spores. They multiply and overseason by forming compact masses of hyphae called *sclerotia*, or the fungus body divides into fragments that are broken off and spread by water, wind, man, and other agents.

Fig. 3.4. Most leaf-spotting fungi are spread by microscopic spores, such as the one seen here on a powdery mildew stalk on a rose.

Fungal diseases, like bacterial diseases, are more prevalent in damp areas or seasons than in dry ones. Fungi that infect leaves, stems, flowers, or fruit generally require that the host surface be wet during spore germination and penetration. Moisture is also essential to their rapid reproduction and spread. Soil-inhabiting fungi may or may not require a wet growing medium for infection and development.

Fungi cause the majority of infectious or parasitic plant diseases, including all rusts, smuts, and mildews; most leaf spots, cankers, scabs, and blights; root, stem, and fruit rots; wilts; galls; and others.

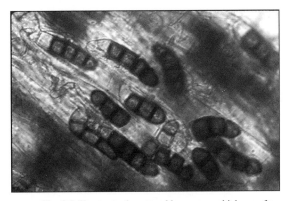

Fig. 3.5. Root rots also spread by spores, which are often embedded in old, dead roots.

Fungi, like bacteria, survive apart from host plants on and in plant refuse, growing media, perennial plants (weeds), seeds, tubers, bulbs, corms, and occasionally in insects. Knowledge of the habits of fungi guides the development of effective control measures. For example, some root-rotting fungi are growing medium invaders and cannot survive in a growing medium for long periods without a host plant. These can often be controlled by clean cultivation and crop rotation.

Other root-rotters are growing medium inhabitants and cannot be controlled by these cultural practices. They can live for a long time in a growing medium without the host plant being there. Sanitation or chemical protection of seeds, bulbs, tubers, corms, transplants, and plant roots is needed to manage these pathogens and the diseases they can cause.

Viruses. The 300 or more plant-infecting viruses are complex macro-molecules that infect, replicate, mutate, and otherwise act like living organisms *only* when in living plant cells (fig. 3.6); they are obligate parasites. With few exceptions, viruses are composed of infectious ribonucleic acid (RNA) with a protective protein "overcoat." They are much smaller than bacteria (perhaps 1/200,000 of an inch long) and can be seen only with an electron microscope. Viruses resemble the genes of chromosomes present in all living plant and animal cells.

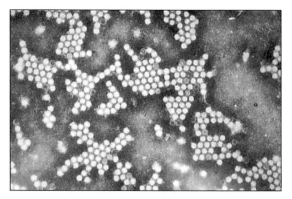

Fig. 3.6. Viruses can cause severe plant damage, but they can only be seen inside living plant cells with the aid of an electron microscope.

Viruses cause plant disease by imposing a different set of genetic information on the biosynthetic apparatus of host plant cells. The nucleic acid portion of the virus causes invaded plant cells to reproduce more virus particles like itself. This results in altered and detrimental host metabolism.

Symptoms induced by a given virus may differ between varieties or cultivars of the same species or even in the same plant (as in stone fruits). Moreover, two unrelated viruses may induce identical symptoms in a given plant variety. Solely for convenience, virus diseases are often grouped together generally by symptoms, regardless of true molecular relationships.

The most common types of virus-caused diseases, classified by symptoms, are mosaics, yellows, spotted wilts, ringspots, stunts, mottles, and streaks. Depending on environmental conditions, many crop plants and weeds may harbor viruses but show no external symptoms, particularly at temperatures above 85F (29C). Virus diseases are often confused with nutrient deficiencies and imbalances, pesticide injury, insect-induced toxemias, mite feeding, and even some genetic conditions.

A few plant viruses, such as tobacco mosaic virus (TMV), are quite infectious, spreading easily from diseased to healthy plants by mere contact (workers' hands or clothing). Others are transmitted in nature only by insects (primarily by over 100 species of leafhoppers and 200 species of aphids; a few by thrips, mealybugs, whiteflies, plant-hoppers, grasshoppers, scales, and certain beetles). Some 50 to 60 viruses are disseminated by infected seed, and a few by mites, pollen, slugs and snails, fungi, nematodes, and possibly other minute animal life in growing media.

Practically all viruses can be spread by vegetative propagation (grafting or budding, cuttings [fig. 3.7], seed pieces, root and rhizome divisions, tubers, corms, bulbs) or by parasitic plants (such as dodder). Virus diseases are generally most serious in crops that are vegetatively propagated, such as Irish potato, many ornamental flowers, bulbs, trees, and cane or bush fruits.

Viruses often overwinter in biennial and perennial crops and weeds, in the bodies of insects, and in plant debris. Once infected with a virus, plants normally remain so for life. Most plant-infecting viruses can "live" in a number of different plant hosts; many of these may be symptomless.

Fig. 3.7. The lesion on this impatiens stem indicates that a cutting from the stem would be infested with virus.

Viroids. Several diseases (including chrysanthemum stunt, potato spindle tuber, citrus exocortis) previously thought to be caused by viruses have been found to be caused by a new class of infectious particles named viroids. The potato spindle tuber viroid is 80 times smaller than the smallest known virus. It is a fragment of double-stranded ribonucleic acid (RNA) and has no protective protein coat. Like viruses, viroids invade plant cells and disrupt their functions.

Mycoplasmas. More than 60 of what used to be considered "yellows" or "witches'-broom" type viruses are now known to be peculiar, one-celled, free-living organisms. Known as mycoplasmas, these are the simplest and smallest known organisms that can be grown in laboratory media free of living tissue. Mycoplasmas discovered in plants are saclike, without rigid cell walls. Mycoplasmas are smaller than bacteria but within the size range of large virus particles. They reproduce by budding (like yeasts) or binary fission (like bacteria).

Plant-infecting mycoplasmas have also been found in leafhoppers, the principal or only vectors of certain yellows-type diseases. In the future, we will probably discover more leafhopper-transmitted diseases to be caused by mycoplasmas.

Nematodes. More than 9,000 species of nematodes have been described. They are probably the most numerous multicellular animals on earth. A pint of growing medium may contain 20,000 nematodes or more. Most types are harmless, feeding primarily on decomposing organic material and other growing medium organisms. Several hundred are even beneficial to man since they are parasitic on root-infecting pests. Plant-parasitic nematodes cannot be easily seen with the naked eye because of their transparency and small size (practically all forms fall within the range of one-tenth to one-hundredth of an inch in length).

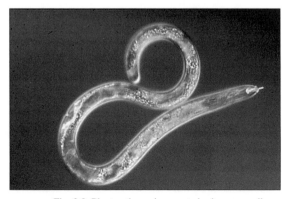

Fig. 3.8. Plant pathogenic nematodes have a needle or stylet as a mouth.

Plant-parasitic nematodes obtain food by sucking juices from living plants through a hollow, needlelike mouth part called a *stylet* (fig. 3.8). When feeding, the nematode pushes the stylet into plant cells and injects a mixture of enzymes that predigests plant cell contents. The liquefied contents are then drawn back into the nematode's digestive tract through the stylet. Nematode feeding lowers the plant's natural resistance, reduces its vigor and yield, and affords easy entrance for wilt- or root rot-producing fungi and bacteria, as well as for other nematodes. Nematode-damaged plants are often more susceptible to winter injury, drought, disease, and insect attack.

Plant-parasitic nematodes may live part of the time free in growing media around roots or in fallow gardens and fields. In causing disease, the nematodes may tunnel inside plant tissue (*endoparasites*) or feed externally on the root surface (*ectoparasites*). They may enter plants through wounds or natural openings, or by penetrating roots and pushing in between cells.

All plant-parasitic nematodes (about 1,800 species) require living plant tissues for reproduction, which is done by laying eggs in or on plant tissues, especially roots, or in growing media. The eggs hatch, sometimes after months or even years, releasing young wormlike larvae (more accurately called juveniles), which usually are born ready to start feeding.

Most plant-parasitic species require 20 to 60 days to complete a generation from egg through four larval stages to adult and back to egg again. Some nematodes have only one generation a year but still produce several hundred or more offspring.

Soil populations and the developmental rate of plant-parasitic nematodes are affected by many environmental factors. Certain nematodes live strictly in light, sandy growing media. Some build up high populations in mucky growing media. High populations of nematodes, as well as greater crop damage, are much more common in the light, sandy media than in heavy clay.

Many plant-infecting nematodes become inactive at temperatures of about 40 to 60F (4 to 16C) and over 85 to 105F (29 to 41C). The optimum temperature for most nematodes is 60 to 85F (16 to 29C), varying greatly with the species, stage of development, activity, growth of the plant host, and other factors.

Many species of nematodes are easily killed by air-drying the growing media after harvest or before planting. Other types remain alive but in a dormant state under the same conditions. When dormant (as cysts or eggs, or when embedded in plant tissues), they are much more difficult to kill by chemicals or heat than when moist and actively moving.

Losses due to nematodes can be reduced by watering during droughts, fertilizing to promote vigorous growth, clean cultivation, fall and summer fallowing, resistant varieties, plowing out the roots of susceptible plants right after harvest to expose them and nematodes to the drying of sun and wind, heavy organic mulches or cover crops, and nematode-free planting materials. Crop rotation is often an important control measure. Because complete control is impossible or unlikely, periodic checks of nematode populations are most desirable whenever troublesome types have been found in large numbers in the past.

Nematodes are easily spread about by any agency that moves infested growing media, plant parts, or contaminated objects. These include all types of tools and machinery, bags and other containers, flowing water, wind, clothing and shoes, land animals and birds, and movement of infested nursery stock (especially plants with growing media around the roots).

Most plant-parasitic nematodes cause the same general symptoms in plants as those resulting from poor root health. Root-knot nematode, the best known nematode, produces galls, or knots, on the roots of more than 2,000 kinds of plants (fig. 3.9). Most root-feeding species, however, cause no specific symptoms. Infested plants are weakened and often appear as if suffering from drought, excessive media moisture, sunburn or frost, a mineral deficiency or imbalance, insect or mite injury to the leaves, roots, or stem, or diseases (such as wilt, dieback, crown rot, or root rot). Other common symptoms of nematode injury include stunting; loss of green color and yellowing; dieback of twigs and shoots; slow

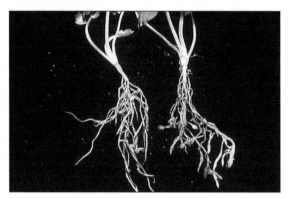

Fig. 3.9. Some nematodes cause galls, cysts, or knots on the roots of plants.

general decline; temporary wilting on hot, bright days; and lack of normal response to water and fertilizer. Feeder root systems are reduced, perhaps stubby or excessively branched, and often shallow, discolored, and decayed. Many times the first indication of nematode injury in a field or garden is the appearance of scattered circular to oval or irregular areas of stunted plants with yellow or bronzed foliage.

Parasitic seed plants. A number of flowering, seed-producing plants are important as parasites of ornamental plants. Among the more important are American, or true, and dwarf mistletoes, broomrapes, witchweed, and dodder. Like most higher plants, they reproduce by seed and are spread from place to place by land animals, birds, wind, water, growing media, or by man as contaminants in seed lots.

Dodder (*Cuscuta* species) is the most common parasitic seed plant on greenhouse plants. All 170 species of dodder are orange to yellow, "leafless," threadlike vines that occur in tangled, yellowish orange patches in fields and gardens. The vines twine around field-crop, vegetable, and ornamental host plants, drawing them together and downward. A dodder-infested area is usually less than 9 or 10 feet (3 meters) in diameter the first year but spreads more rapidly in succeeding years. Dodder seeds, which are rough, irregularly round and flat-sided, and gray to reddish-brown, are widely distributed as a contaminant in clover, alfalfa, sugar beet, and flax seed.

Dodder is controlled by planting certified, properly cleaned seed and by mowing infested areas well before the plants flower. Upon drying, the patches should be sprinkled with fuel oil and burned. Spot treatment with a selective herbicide or growing medium fumigant is often recommended by extension weed specialists. Planting known dodder-infested areas with resistant plants (such as corn, cereals or grasses, soybeans, garden beans, and peas) is another method of control.

Conditions necessary for infectious disease

Infectious diseases vary greatly in prevalence and severity from year to year and from one area to another. At least three conditions are necessary for disease to develop.

1. The air and growing medium environment (principally the amount and frequency of rains, irrigation, or heavy dews; relative humidity; air and growing medium temperatures; and plant nutrient balance) must be favorable for the pathogens' activity.

2. The host plant must be susceptible.

3. A virulent, disease-producing agent or pathogen must be present.

All three of these basic ingredients, commonly called the *disease triangle,* must be present for an infectious disease to develop (fig. 3.10).

Notice that this disease triangle is not merely conceived from the point of view of the development of the pathogen in or on the host. The other two sides of the triangle are also important. Favorable conditions for the interaction of the host and the pathogen are often conditions of stress as far as the host is concerned. They may also be conditions that favor spread or growth

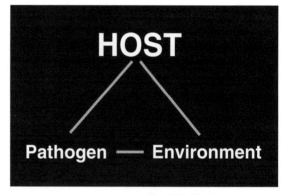

Fig. 3.10. The disease triangle.

of the pathogen. The bottom line is successful infection of the pathogen, development of the pathogen in the host, and expression of symptoms—disease development!

Environmental factors and infectious disease development

Some important environmental factors that commonly affect the development, prevalence, and severity of infectious plant diseases include temperature, relative humidity, growing medium moisture, growing medium reaction (pH), growing medium type, and growing medium fertility.

Temperature. Each pathogen has an optimum temperature for growth. The different growth stages of a fungus (such as spore production and germination, growth of the mycelium) may have different optimum temperatures. Knowing these temperatures, usually combined with certain moisture conditions, permits forecasting the development of such diseases as late blight of potato and tomato, downy mildews of vine crops and lima beans, fire blight of pome fruits, and sycamore anthracnose. Most seed rots and seedling blights are favored by low growing medium temperatures after planting. High temperatures (above about 85F, 29C) commonly mask the symptoms of certain virus and mycoplasma diseases, making them difficult or impossible to detect. Warm, dry weather favors the buildup of such insects as aphids, leafhoppers, and thrips. Some virus diseases spread by these insects are more severe during warm, dry seasons.

Relative humidity. High humidity (88 to 100 percent) fosters development of practically all leaf, stem, fruit, and flower diseases caused by fungi and bacteria. Moisture from rain, irrigation, or dew is generally needed for germination of fungal spores, the multiplication and penetration of bacteria, and initiation of the infection process.

Soil moisture. High or low medium moisture may limit the development of certain root rot diseases. "Water mold" root-rotting fungi, such as *Aphanomyces*, *Phytophthora*, and *Pythium*, thrive where the growing medium is saturated or nearly so. Excessive watering lowers the oxygen level and raises the carbon dioxide content of the medium, making the roots more susceptible to root-rotting organisms. Diseases that are most severe under low moisture levels include *Rhizoctonia* damping-off of bedding plants and stem rot of poinsettia.

Soil reaction (pH). The acidity or alkalinity of the growing medium greatly influences a few diseases, such as black root rot on pansies. Some growers add sulfur or an acid fertilizer to keep the pH around 5.0.

Soil type. Certain pathogens are favored by growing media high in loam or clay, or media that are light (warming up quickly). For example, *Fusarium* wilt diseases and nematodes are most damaging in lighter, coarser growing media that warm up quickly on outdoor-grown crops in the spring.

Soil fertility. Raising or lowering the levels of certain nutrient elements essential to plant growth influences the development of certain infectious diseases. Excessive nitrogen fertilizer increases the destructiveness of *Botrytis* blights, bacterial soft rots, *Septoria*, many other leaf-spotting fungi, and numerous other diseases.

Growing media maintained at highly productive levels by the proper use of fertilizers (based on a growing medium test), incorporation of organic matter, and good micronutrient balance tend to produce vigorous plants. These will be more resistant to many infectious diseases.

How diseases are managed in general

Effective disease control measures are aimed at breaking or preventing the formation of the environment–pathogen–host plant triangle. For example, the plant can be made less susceptible by breeding a resistant variety. The environment can be changed to favor growth of the host plant and inhibit development, reproduction, and spread of the disease-causing agent or pathogen. These basic control concepts can be expanded into numerous particular practices.

Successful disease management is based on accurate diagnosis of the cause; thorough knowledge of the pathogen, its disease cycle, and how the host and pathogen interact with various environmental factors; ease of implementing new practices, if need be; and the costs of these practices. Management of plant diseases should start with the purchase of the best varieties, seed, and planting stock available. It should continue throughout the season in the field or greenhouse, and after harvest until the crop is fully utilized.

The most important point in managing a plant disease is *choosing the best method for a given situation.* The best management method for one type of disease on a certain host may not be the best method for another disease on the same plant. Also, several management measures (integrated control) are often needed. For example, several cultural management practices can be combined with a protective fungicide spray program. Disease management practices should be integrated into a broader program of biological or cultural and chemical methods needed to control the various pests—insects, mites, rodents, weeds—that attack a given crop.

Infectious diseases are managed by one of four basic strategies: exclusion, protection, resistance, and eradication. The best disease management program, *disease prevention*, is built on the first three.

Exclusion. Disease-causing organisms and agents can be excluded from certain areas or countries by quarantines and embargoes; inspection and certification of seed and other plant materials; disinfection of plants, seeds, and other propagative parts by using heat or chemicals; and other methods to prevent movement of pathogens into areas where they are absent or rare.

Plant diseases can be excluded by selecting practices unsuited to disease development. Examples of such exclusion practices include managing storage and moisture conditions for cut flowers, crop rotation with unrelated plants, sowing seed early or late, sticking cuttings at the proper depth, and propagating and planting only disease-free material.

Sanitation in and around propagating beds, greenhouses, gardens, and fields is an excellent pathogen exclusion measure as well. Clean and disinfect potting benches, growing media bins, head houses, greenhouse benches, tools, and equipment (fig. 3.11). Disinfecting tools and equipment is most valuable if they have been used in handling diseased plants or around general debris.

Protection. Plants can be protected by uniform, timely applications of recommended, disease-control chemicals (fungicides, bactericides, nematicides); through suggested cultural practices (proper spacing; proper time of planting and harvest; careful handling during harvest, grading, and

Fig. 3.11. Between crops you can easily see the potential for pathogen contamination of the greenhouse.

packing; proper pruning, watering, and fertilization); and by altering the air and growing medium environment to make them unfavorable for the pathogen to infect, develop, reproduce, or spread. When applying fungicides, it is important to have the fungicide on the plant surface or in the growing medium where and *before* infection takes place (fig. 3.12). Most fungicides are protectants, not eradicants.

Resistance. The ideal disease-management measure is the growing of resistant or immune varieties, cultivars, or species. Unfortunately, there are no plants resistant to all diseases. The development of resistant or immune varieties is an ever-continuing process, one critically important for low-value crops where other controls are either unavailable or their expense makes them impractical. The development of resistant varieties and cultivars is greatly complicated by pathogens having several to hundreds of physiological races. Most "resistant" cultivars or varieties ward off only one pathogen or race of pathogens.

Fig. 3.12. Spraying plants with fungicides is a commonly used protection practice.

Eradication. Plant pathogens can be eliminated (eradicated) and insect vectors can be managed by pesticides—such as growing medium fumigants—by heat treatment, or by removal and destruction of diseased plants (*roguing*) or plant parts (*surgery*). These plants may be weeds or alternate host plants. Other eradication methods include crop rotation, which "starves" out medium-invading pathogens.

Management practices for pathogens attacking leaves, stems, and flowers of greenhouse crops

Many common pathogens attack stems, leaves, and flowers of plants, including floral and foliage crops. These pathogens include those that cause powdery mildew diseases, *Botrytis* diseases, rust diseases, *Alternaria* leaf spots, *Septoria* leaf spots, bacterial leaf spots and wilts, virus diseases, and *Fusarium* stem rots. The numbers of different kinds of organisms and the different kinds of plants involved are truly large when we speak of diseases of these plant portions!

Management strategies for disease of stems, leaves, and flowers can be confusing if you think constantly about the many kinds of fungi, bacteria, and host plants involved. We must look for common denominators concerning the diseases. Begin by thinking about the basic definition of a plant disease. To have a plant disease, we must have a host, a pathogen, and an environment that allows the action of the pathogen on the host. All three of these elements must be present at the same time, in the same place. As mentioned, disease management strategies are designed to prevent the establishment of this triangle of necessary elements.

Finally, do not forget that since plant health is a holistic concept, the management of plant health must be holistic, as well. Using many different approaches to manage a disease will always be better than using only one.

Sanitation

Sanitation is partly effective in controlling these kinds of diseases. Many pathogens attacking stems, leaves, and flowers have airborne spores or inoculum. Thus, they can come in from fields or yards near your fields or greenhouse. On the other hand, many pathogens depend on splashing water to spread about. Thus, ridding your area of diseased plants is effective to some degree. For instance, *Botrytis* is a fungus that will proliferate and produce spores on crop debris. Plant material should never be dumped under the greenhouse bench or at the side of a greenhouse and allowed to sit there and rot (fig. 3.13).

Many diseases of stems, leaves, and flowers are introduced into a crop via the use of infested stock. This is particularly important for bacterial diseases, *Fusarium* wilt diseases, virus diseases, downy mildews, and the rust diseases. The pathogens are difficult to control once they are within the plant and within the greenhouse. Thus, try and get only pathogen-free material. The extensive movement of greenhouse plant

Fig. 3.13. Crop debris, like these old geranium leaves, should never be left in a greenhouse.

material around the world has made this of increasing concern of late. There is not much growers can do if they get healthy-looking material that turns out to be diseased a few weeks later!

Avoiding leaf wetness

Environmental control of diseases of stems, leaves, and flowers of floral and foliage crops primarily involves preventing situations that allow moisture on leaves. In the first place, splashing water can spread the inoculum of many pathogens. Drops of water that remain on the leaves, stems, or flowers allow many pathogens to infect host plants.

The time that the leaf must stay wet will vary according to the organism and disease involved. For instance, with powdery mildew and bacteria, a very short period of leaf dampness is all that is necessary, in most cases. On the other hand, with diseases such as *Botrytis* blight, downy mildew, or *Alternaria* leaf spots, several hours of leaf wetness are needed to allow infection of the fungal spores.

Always try to avoid moisture on the leaves of floral and foliage crops. There are many ways to accomplish this. First of all, it may be possible to alter your irrigation system to avoid overhead irrigation, especially late in the day. The bacterial blights of foliage plants have largely been eliminated in many greenhouses through altered irrigation. Never water a greenhouse crop late in the day, which may lead to a long period of wetness at night.

High humidity or dampness in a greenhouse (especially as the temperatures drop toward nightfall) may cause dew, or condensation of moisture, to form on the crops. This may allow the development of diseases on stems, leaves, and flowers.

We have also seen condensation of moisture on leaves when temperatures are allowed to drop too suddenly at other times during the day. For instance, in greenhouses that have very efficient fan-and-pad cooling, if the vents and pads are opened too wide or too quickly in the midmorning and a blast of cool air hits the warmer greenhouse air, a short but sometimes damaging moisture-condensation episode will occur! We have seen this sort of thing lead to bad powdery mildew infestations in many new or modern greenhouses. Also, with double-layer plastic coverings becoming popularly accepted, condensation drips can produce moisture on the leaves and flowers of many crops.

As mentioned, it is especially important to control the humidity or dampness in a greenhouse at night. The best way to do this is to ventilate at the end of the day. Heat the incoming air slightly during ventilation.

With a little heating, the air can be dried out even though it may come in saturated with humidity because of an outdoor rainy period. Of course, this is difficult to do in the heat of the summer, especially after a day in which we have used evaporative cooling pads for several hours!

Good fan-jets, horizontal airflow, or air turbulator systems—all of which move the air around the foliage within a plant's canopy—will help control dampness on the greenhouse crop. Finally, proper crop spacing on the bench will allow good air circulation around the leaves and prevent pockets of dampness from occurring in the leaf canopy. All this is done to control high relative humidity and leaf wetness.

Resistant plants

It is possible to take advantage of certain plants' resistance to some of the diseases of leaves, flowers, and stems. There are not a great deal of reliable published data on this point. Nevertheless, many growers have made good observations over the years about which plants are more prone to powdery mildew or rust or *Botrytis* than other plants. They have altered their cultivar selection lists accordingly. Also, the stem rot and wilt diseases, such as bacterial wilt and *Fusarium* stem rot, can be managed through careful observations and alteration of your plant cultivar selection list.

Fungicides

Many different pesticides and fungicides are used for diseases of leaves, stems, and flowers of floral and foliage crops. The information given in chapter 18 will provide needed detail.

Many growers of diversified crop types in greenhouses or outdoors are turning to fungicide mixes to create broad-spectrum tank mixtures. These can be used on a variety of hosts for several diseases. Here are some mixtures in use today:

- Inexpensive and fairly good, especially when bacterial diseases are present: a fixed copper plus mancozeb

- Better than the above, but no bactericidal activity: thiophanate-m plus mancozeb

- The best tank mix for general fungal diseases: thiophanate-m plus mancozeb plus a DMI systemic product

- The best for powdery mildews: piperalin plus thiophanate-m plus a DMI product

Fungicide application procedures. Many growers fail to achieve proper pesticide control of a disease on leaves, flowers, and stems because they do not apply the products properly. "Wet-down," or high-volume, spraying continues to be the most effective method to get good performance from a chemical. It is important to get complete coverage of all plant surfaces that can be infected. Most importantly, this includes the

leaf undersurfaces (fig. 3.14). A sweeping, up-and-over motion with a hydraulic applicator that produces reasonably fine droplets with good momentum will achieve proper plant coverage. Plan on using anywhere from 100 to 300 gallons (379 to 1,135 l) of dilute spray per acre, however!

Low-volume applicators are being used by many growers to save time, labor, and chemicals. We have found in our research

Fig. 3.14. Spraying foliage to get complete wetting ensures the best performance from fungicides.

that many low-volume methods are quite effective. However, you must know precisely what you are doing and be fairly knowledgeable about the biology of the system with which you are working. Low-volume application methods involve careful calibration and delivery techniques to avoid undue plant phytotoxicity. Also, certain products work better than others in a low-volume applicator.

Management practices for pathogens attacking roots and crowns of greenhouse plants

There are many root rot diseases on floral and foliage crops, including those caused by *Pythium*, *Phytophthora*, *Rhizoctonia*, *Fusarium*,

Thielaviopsis (Charala), and *Cylindrocladium*. Many of these fungal pathogens also cause crown rots and damping-off on floral and foliage crops.

With many diseases on many crops caused by many different organisms, planning how to manage root rots can seem quite complicated. As with the diseases of leaves, stems, and flowers, we figure out management strategies by thinking about the common denominators of root rot diseases. We also must continue to think in an integrated and holistic manner.

Sanitation

Root rots generally result from the presence of medium-borne pathogens. A single, tiny grain of growing medium can be contaminated with many pathogenic fungi (fig. 3.15)! Therefore, we can begin planning root rot management by thinking about the pathogen elimination via sanitation of planting media and media-associated items. Planting media sanitation is successful if equal attention is given to two aspects, the initial cleansing and preventing recontamination.

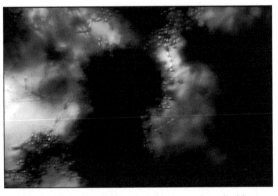

Fig. 3.15. This single grain of sand is contaminated with many particles of *Rhizoctonia*, each capable of causing disease.

To properly understand growing media sanitation, let's begin with a bit of microbiology. To serve as a medium for plant growth, any medium must contain living microbes. Truly sterile soils or growing media will not support plant growth for very long, at least in a practical sense. There are many beneficial soilborne animals and plants (fungi, bacteria, protozoans, nematodes). Mycorrhizal fungi even infect plants and work their good from within the plant roots! Thus, the concept of complete soil or growing media sterilization is faulty, and sanitation methods can sometimes do more harm than good!

Yet, there are harmful microbes that can invade, live in, and spread in soils or growing media. They will cause root, stem, and crown rot diseases if, and only if, two situations exist: their numbers must be high enough, and the particular environmental conditions for plant tissue infection must exist for a certain length of time. Plant pathologists often refer to this as the *inoculum potential* of the growing medium or soil.

If you are going to place plants in ground beds or if you will be using field-growing media or topsoil in potting mixes, you should sanitize with steam, steam-air mixtures, other types of heat, or fumigants to ensure that you do not start off with high numbers of harmful, or pathogenic, microbes in the growing media. If you are using soilless or bagged media, it is usually not necessary to sanitize it prior to the plant installation. Most soilless media will have pathogenic microbes, but only in small numbers. The good aeration and drainage characteristics of soilless media are not conducive to pathogen development.

Heat sanitization. Sanitization methods using heat are usually more foolproof and safer than chemical methods, but they are also more difficult to do properly in greenhouses or nurseries without a source of steam.

- Oven heating. For small batches of growing media, you can use an oven or other type of heating chamber. Spread out the growing medium in a shallow pan and slightly moisten it. Place it in the oven set at 200F (93C), with a small potato (2 inches [5 cm] in diameter) on the medium surface. When the potato is done, the medium has been sufficiently heated to be rid of pathogenic microbes.

- Steam pasteurization. Many professional growers use steam under pressure to sanitize growing media. With steam, 180F (82C) for 30 minutes is required for sufficient killing of microbes, insects, nematodes, and weed seed. The bed or batch of growing media must be tightly tarped, and steam delivery hoses must be run under the tarp to the media.

  The greatest shortcoming of steam pasteurization is that desired temperatures may not be reached throughout the medium mass for the required time. The batch or bed may be hot enough in general, but there may be a corner that is not. The additional steaming that must be done to heat the entire batch tends to make the procedure expensive and time-consuming. You may actually be oversteaming the majority of the medium, which can create an overkill situation in which beneficial microbes are wiped out. Monitor the temperature with a long-stemmed thermometer. Make no assumptions as to the thoroughness of the job.

- Electric pasteurization. Electric pasteurizers are being used by many growers to sanitize batches of growing media (fig. 3.16). This is merely another way of pasteurizing with heat, but it can be economical and effective. Because the electric process is time consuming, most growers will heat the growing media at night. Lower nighttime electric rates can also provide savings. Most of the devices on the market are sufficiently insulated to hold heat for enough time

Fig. 3.16. An electric growing media pasteurizer.

once it reaches 180 or 190F (82 or 88C). Thus, a simple thermostatic cutoff and a gradual cooling-down period are effective. Electric medium pasteurizers come in various sizes, up to 2 cubic yards (765 l) of capacity. Fill loosely with slightly moistened growing medium, put the lid on tightly, and begin.

Soilless mixes may require sanitation if they have become contaminated by contact with unsterile growing media. Such contact often occurs when mix is placed on top of soil outdoors, when it comes into contact with growing media residue in the building or bin, or when you have used dirty equipment to mix it. Of course, a previously pasteurized or fumigated mix can likewise become recontaminated! Be careful how you handle and store "clean" growing media.

Whatever method you use to initially cleanse the planting media can be in vain if you fail to prevent recontamination. If planting medium is used as soon as it is sanitized, you will run very little risk of recontamination. This is why many pot plant growers prefer to sanitize planting media in small batches just prior to use. If you do have to sanitize larger quantities of planting media at any one time, it is important to devise a system where you do not have to move the media about after sanitization. Each time a batch is moved, it stands a chance of being recontaminated.

Many growers spend good money and time in sanitizing planting media but then proceed to put the crop into dirty, reused pots! Pots, walkways, benches, hoses, and water lines must be sanitized occasionally to make sure they are free of fungal root-rotting pathogens (fig. 3.17).

Disinfectants. There are many disinfectants on the market today. Falling into several chemical groups, products that have been traditionally used for plant pathogen elimination include chlorine bleach, formaldehyde, 70-percent alcohol, phenolics, and quaternary ammonium chloride salts. All these products work differently and have different properties.

Fig. 3.17. Sanitize trays and pot spacers in a disinfectant before using them again.

- Chlorine bleach. Chlorine is an effective disinfectant. However, it rapidly evaporates when mixed in water. The half-life (time required for 50 percent reduction in strength) of a chlorine solution is only two hours. Thus, after two hours, only half as much chlorine is present as was present at first! After four hours, only one fourth is there, and so on. To ensure the effectiveness of a chlorine solution, you should prepare it fresh just before each use. Objects require 30 minutes of chlorine soaking to become sanitized.

   The concentration normally used is one part of household bleach (5.25 percent sodium hypochlorite) to nine parts of water, giving a final strength of 0.5 percent. Chlorine is corrosive, so repeated use of chorine solutions may be harmful to plastics or metals. No rinsing with water is needed, however.

- Formaldehyde. Formaldehyde disinfectants are made by adding one part of Formalin to 18 parts of water. Formalin solutions are relatively stable. *However, the product is harmful to users and gives off a noxious tear gas.* Furthermore, exposure to formaldehyde may have long-term health consequences. For these reasons, formaldehyde is not widely used as a disinfectant. If you wish to use it, do so with gloves in a well-ventilated area, and soak items for 10 minutes. Rinse well with water after soaking.

- 70 percent alcohol. This is a very effective sanitizer that acts almost immediately upon contact. Do not use any alcohol stronger than 70 percent, as it will not work as well. Alcohol is not practical as a soaking material because of its high cost and extreme volatility. It is used as a dip or swipe treatment on knives and other cutting tools. No rinsing with water is needed.

- Phenolics. Several phenolic compounds were widely used for plant pathogen elimination some years ago, but they were never labeled for greenhouse use. It is rare to see them in use now. They required 30 minutes of soaking and thorough rinsing with water.

- Quaternary ammonium chloride salts. Q-salt products currently available for greenhouse use include GreenShield, Physan 20, Consan 20, Prevent, and Triathlon. Q-salts are becoming the most widely used sanitizing products in U.S. greenhouses.

    Q-salts are quite stable and work well when used according to labeled instructions. Objects to be sanitized should be soaked for 10 minutes. Some of the products can be used as sprays on certain plants, but they are not plant protectants! They may eradicate certain pathogens but will have little if any residual activity.

    Q-salts last much longer than chlorine, making them much cheaper to use. Contact with any type of organic matter will inactivate Q-salts. Thus, it is wise to clean objects to remove dislodgeable organic matter prior to application. Because it is difficult to tell when Q-salts become inactive, prepare fresh solutions every day. The products tend to foam a bit when they are active. Thus, when foaming stops, it is a sign they are no longer effective. No rinsing with water is needed for treated objects.

Pathogen-free water. Pathogens that cause root rot diseases often gain entry into a greenhouse by contaminated watering ponds, pipes, and other irrigation devices. If you have trouble with the constant appearance of root rot pathogens in an otherwise sanitary greenhouse, you might investigate your water contamination levels. The tests are tricky and must be done by clinics. Water treatments can be easy, but they would not be prescribed generally unless a water analysis indicated that they were necessary.

Clean stock. Using clean stock is another important aspect to rid greenhouses of root rot disease. Although most crown and root rots are not systemic in the upper portion of the plant, they can be present there if splashed up in muddy water droplets or moved up through careless handling. Such surface contamination of cuttings often leads to root and crown rots. Identify plants that you intend to use as stock early in the production cycle. Treat these plants carefully and give them extra fungicidal sprays to make sure the cuttings derived from them will be clean of root-rotting pathogens (fig. 3.18).

Fig. 3.18. Limit access to the area where stock plants are growing.

Keep growing areas clean. During actual crop production, growers can take many sanitation steps to help prevent and control root rot diseases. Basically, all of these activities involve keeping growing areas clean and tidy. Discard problem plants as soon as you notice them (fig. 3.19). They may not actually be infected with

Fig. 3.19. The diseased plant shown here must be removed as soon as possible.

root rot yet, but they can lead to root rot in the crop because they are weak and easily infected. Keep walkways clean and free of plant debris. Keep your feet off the benches. Avoid splashing when watering the crops. Keep the hoses off the ground so that they do not pick up contaminated muddy water from under the benches or near the walkways. Clean up benches between crops, carefully removing all plant debris. Clean out automatic "spaghetti tube" watering devices with disinfectant to free them of fungal pathogens between crops.

Environmental modification

Environmental modification will sometimes vary according to the specific disease and pathogen involved in a root rot problem. One common denominator, however, is to avoid plant stress. Stress will lead to a weakened plant, which then can be easily infected by any number of root-rotting organisms.

Specific conditions to avoid include high salts (which may lead to *Pythium* or *Fusarium* root rot infection); wetness and poor planting media aeration (which may lead to *Pythium* and *Phytophthora*); dryness, especially between waterings (which may lead to *Rhizoctonia* or *Fusarium*); and cool temperatures (which favor some *Pythium* and *Fusarium* root rots). Compacted planting media, hit-and-miss fertilization programs, and intermittent and uneven watering can all lead to root rot if not corrected. Stress management means setting up a good growing environment and maintaining the stability of that environment.

It has long been recognized that one of the most responsible jobs in flower and foliage crops production is watering correctly! This is because a crop that is over- or underwatered or watered irregularly can succumb to stress and then to infectious disease very quickly.

Fertilization techniques also demand that good, thorough irrigation be done with each watering to avoid excessive salt buildup. The pH and mineral makeup of the irrigation water also can relate to stress. The high-calcium, alkaline groundwater that is very common in many parts of the country can lead to stress and root health problems. Finally, growing medium moisture problems may stem from other things going on in the greenhouse. For instance, energy-efficient greenhouses may have water condensation and drip problems. Such a drip may produce an area of wet, waterlogged media, which will then stress a portion of the crop. If pathogens gain a foothold in any such stress site, they may rapidly proliferate, spread, and infect the rest of the crop.

Another important stress management tactic in controlling root rot diseases of greenhouse crops is to employ planting media with a proper degree of aeration and drainage. Planting media that hold about 40 percent water (by weight) when irrigated, but with about 20 percent air-filled pore space (by volume) after irrigation and initial drainage, are generally root health promoting. There are simple measurement tests you can carry out to determine if your planting media fulfill these aeration and drainage guidelines.

Resistant plants

The host corner of the disease triangle is also a point worth investigating when trying to control root rot diseases of floral and foliage crops. Some hosts are particularly prone to certain types of root rot diseases. For instance, some poinsettia cultivars are quite susceptible to *Rhizoctonia*. Some seedling geranium cultivars are prone to *Pythium* black leg. African violets and peperomia are often seen with *Phytophthora* crown rot. There is not a great deal of published information on which hosts will be more or less resistant to which crown rot diseases. However, many growers have made a series of good observations over the years and have altered their plant lists accordingly.

Biological root rot management

"Soilless" media are usually teeming with beneficial microbes, some of which chemically inhibit or parasitize the pathogens. In addition, there is not much natural pathogen content of these growing media. In other words, soilless media are of low inoculum potential. The growing media that contain composted hardwood bark or light-colored peat are especially rich in these inhibitory microbes. As long as the activity of these microbes can be kept high, biological root rot control will result. There are also some growing medium additives that consist of living microbes designed to inhibit many crown- and root-rotting pathogens. These are to be added to growing media just like fungicide drenches. The formulations must be fresh, stored properly, and applied exactly according to labeled directions.

Whether naturally occurring or added, biological control components of growing media seem to be quite active for several weeks after the plants are potted, then their activity wears off. They can be reapplied, or the grower can switch to conventional fungicides.

Fungicides

There are many good fungicides on the market for the control of root and crown rots of greenhouse crops. Sometimes we have to use a combination of products because we have many fungi involved in such diseases. This is especially important when dealing with a water mold along with *Rhizoctonia, Thielaviopsis, Cylindrocladium,* or *Fusarium. Disease complex* is the term sometimes used to describe simultaneous interactions of multiple pathogens on a single host.

More will be said about root rot and crown rot managing fungicides in chapter 19. More information on the disease groups of floral and foliage crops will be provided in the following several chapters.

Fungicide application for root and crown rots. Growing medium drench fungicides are widely used for the prevention and control of many root rot diseases. Think of drench fungicides as a fourth line of defense, coming into play after consideration of resistant varieties, stress management, and sanitation measures. To use medium drench fungicides effectively, we must first prepare a proper dilution of the fungicide and then water it or drench it through the growing medium thoroughly.

Preventive programs usually involve monthly treatments, the fungicide acting as a protective barrier on the entire developing root system. Soil fungicides may also act as effective curatives or eradicants, if there are spots of infected roots within the root mass here or there. If root masses are inspected frequently, curative programs may serve you along with your general preventive program.

Recently, many root rot-managing fungicides have become available as granulars, which generally work best when mixed into the planting media prior to potting. Personnel potting up plants in treated growing media will have to be trained as handlers and wear the prescribed personal protective equipment (PPE) or wait until the Restricted Entry Interval (REI) is over before working with the growing media. Soil surface applications also work, especially when followed by thorough irrigations. Granular products are best used as preventives.

Summary

Prevention and control of infectious pathogens involves truly integrated programs in the growing of floral and foliage crops. Many of the things you will do to manage pathogens are coincident with things that a good grower would do normally to produce a high quality crop ready for sale in the shortest amount of time. Keep in mind the general management strategies we have outlined above, and you will not have to be too concerned about specific infectious disease problems on this or that plant or crop. In the next chapter, however, we will outline more specific disease management strategies for common diseases of floral and foliage crops.

Determining air-filled pore space (aeration) of growing medium

Growing media that contain peat and composted tree bark will slowly age and decompose, becoming compacted. Eventually, the compaction reaches the point that there are no longer enough large pores, or spaces, in the growing media to hold air, especially right after a thorough watering. Roots in these poorly aerated, waterlogged growing media will rot and become sickly. The plants will decline and eventually die.

Much of the black peat (muck peat) growing media packaged and sold is in fact poorly aerated, being too compacted from the start. One test you can do yourself is determining the air-filled pore space of the growing media. If your crops routinely become prone to waterlogging, you should conduct this test to see if compacted growing media are at fault.

Air-filled pore space is the medium volume that is still filled with air after a thorough wetting followed by a day of normal drainage. This is figured as a percentage of the growing medium and root volume in the container. Roots need to take up oxygen and give off carbon dioxide if they are to function healthily. Air-filled pore space is an important measure of how well the exchange of gases between the root and the atmosphere will occur. Insufficient air-filled pore space increases the stress on roots and the probability of root disease. Precise recommendations for good air-filled pore space of potted plants have not yet been established for greenhouse crops. Good root health has been observed, however, with plants growing in media containing 10 to 20 percent air-filled pores, when tested according to the following procedures.

The four quantities you will have to measure to determine the percentage of air-filled pore space are as follows:

W1 = water-flooded weight of the potted plant, when all of the growing media pores are filled with water

W2 = weight of the potted plant after being allowed to drain for 24 hours

W3 = weight of the container, emptied of growing media and roots and filled to the original growing media line with water

W4 = weight of the empty container

Procedure

1. Flood the potted plant with water by slowly immersing it into a container of water until the water appears at the growing medium surface. Immersing slowly avoids trapping air in medium pores. Be careful not to let any water enter from the top of the container, or this may also trap air and give an erroneous reading.

2. Remove the potted plant and quickly transfer it to a bucket, being sure to catch any water that drains out. Record W1, the weight of the potted plant, water, and bucket (fig. 3.20).

3. Remove the potted plant from the bucket and allow it to drain for 24 hours.

4. Reweigh the drained potted plant and bucket (W2).

5. Mark the growing medium line on the inside of the container and remove the plant from the container. Place a watertight plastic bag into the container, fill it with water to the medium mark, and weigh the water and the container (W3).

Fig. 3.20. Determining the air-filled pore space of a growing media involves flooding the pot first.

6. Empty the water from the container and record the weight of the empty container and plastic bag (W4).

7. Solve the following equation:

$$\frac{W1-W2}{W3-W4} \times 100 = \text{Percentage air-filled pore space}$$

Chapter 4

Powdery Mildews

The powdery mildews belong to a distinct group of pathogenic fungi that attack a wide variety of plants. They are characterized by a nearly colorless and superficial growth habit on the host, by the ability to survive on hosts under desert conditions, by possessing airborne, single-celled conidia (spores), and by having a short life cycle. Many of them form a tiny, black survival structure, a cleistothecium, that contains ascospores. (Ascospores are spores that are derived from a genetic "mating" of mildew strains. They can infect plants.) Cleistothecia readily persist on plant debris between crops.

Powdery mildew fungi are obligate parasites, meaning they cannot develop on host plant tissue that is not alive. They make up for this by having the ability to develop on many vigorous host plants not under a great deal of stress. This means that holistic plant health management practices aimed at increasing the host's vigor are usually not the first line of defense against powdery mildews.

While infection by powdery mildew fungi seldom causes the death of affected plants, it almost always reduces their aesthetic appeal and value. Serious economic losses are common unless control measures are employed in a timely and effective manner.

Symptoms

Powdery mildews are recognized primarily by the white, powdery appearance of the infected portions of the host. This is because powdery mildew fungi produce abundant superficial hyphae (fungal threads) bearing great numbers of colorless conidia (spores). The pathogens usually attack young foliage, stems, flowers, or fruit. However, the older leaves of some hosts may be more susceptible than the young foliage.

Infection and development is frequently confined to the upper leaf surface, but some powdery mildews attack only the lower leaf surface or both leaf surfaces. Sometimes the surface that is more commonly attacked depends on the host variety rather than the powdery mildew species. Powdery mildew on roses is a good example of this (fig. 4.1). Other powdery mildews show little preference for specific host tissues. They can infect flower or stem tissue, as well as leaf tissue. Severe infection may result in yellowing and curling of

Fig. 4.1. Powdery mildew on the lower surface of a rose leaf.

leaves, general stunting of growth, distortion of flowers or fruits, and death of tissue.

The physiological debilitation caused by the infections results in various stress symptoms, such as premature defoliation, witches'-brooms, drying and withering of plant parts, leaf roll, leaf shot hole, twig dieback, fruit russet, and viruslike symptoms. The pathogens do not directly attack belowground parts of the plant, but they may indirectly affect the root physiology. Severely infected plants frequently recover slowly even after the disease has been arrested. They may be more susceptible to cold weather, insect attack, air pollution, and root rot.

Disease cycle

Powdery mildew fungi undergo a rather simple life cycle on most ornamental plants. Simple, single-celled *conidia* (spores) are formed on stalks of fungal growth called *conidiophores*. Conidiophores begin as swelling of the *hyphae* (the fungal threads growing on the host tissue) immediately above a cell nucleus in the hypha. The conidiophore develops a generative cell at its upper end.

The generative cell continues to divide and produce conidia until environmental conditions become unfavorable or the vigor of the infection deteriorates. In most cases, one conidium is produced each day on each conidiophore, on a somewhat diurnal or daily cycle. This daily cycle makes powdery mildews especially troublesome on greenhouse crops.

Conidia usually mature on the second day of their "lives" and are released from the conidiophore in the middle of this second day. Factors that contribute to the release of spores into the air include a rapid drop in relative humidity, moving air, moderate temperatures, and the heating and drying effects of solar radiation on the leaf tissue and the fungal lesion. All of these factors serve to "snap" the mature conidium from its conidiophore and send it into the air.

Long-distance dispersal of conidia has been reported but is difficult to verify. Few powdery mildews seem capable of it. Most, due to the more fragile nature of their conidia, are more limited in spore dispersal.

A conidium normally germinates by developing germ tubes from its "corners" rather than from the middle or the end (fig. 4.2). More than one germ tube can emerge from a single conidium! In most compatible host reactions, the initial germ tube is quickly followed by the development of additional germ tubes from each of the remaining corners of the spore. Various physical

Fig. 4.2. A powdery mildew spore has germinated and started a new lesion only two hours ago.

and chemical leaf components reportedly affect the spore germination process. If conditions are favorable, germination can be completed in an hour or so.

Following spore germination, the fungus penetrates the host epidermis and forms *haustoria* (nutrient-gathering pegs or sacs) inside the epidermal cells. Host penetration by powdery mildew fungi was believed by early plant pathologists to be strictly a mechanical process. More recent work has verified the role of chemical processes at work during penetration.

Host cuticle and cell wall thickness are also reported to influence the penetration process of many powdery mildew fungi. Environmental factors—light, temperature, relative humidity—may significantly alter cuticle thickness. In some host genera, cuticle thickness may vary considerably from plant to plant within a species or from leaf to leaf on the same plant, thus altering susceptibility of the plants and leaves to infection and disease development.

After initial host penetration, the developing hyphae (fungal threads) gather nutrients and energy and soon branch and spread over the host tissue (fig. 4.3). Within 24 to 48 hours after inoculation, secondary branching of the

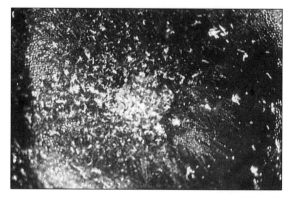

Fig. 4.3. Note the fungal strands growing outward from this powdery mildew lesion.

hyphae occurs, and conidiophore initials may form within 60 hours. Mature conidia can be present in as little as 72 hours in highly compatible host-pathogen situations when optimum environmental conditions prevail. The time from inoculation to secondary sporulation is more frequently five to seven days or longer, however.

Some kinds of powdery mildew undergo genetic recombinations in the fall of the year. This results in the formation of tiny, black, thick-walled structures called *cleistothecia*. Cleistothecia contain ascospores, which are freed to the air the following growing season. Most of the powdery mildews on tropical or greenhouse plants do not undergo this stage, but commonly persist through inhospitable climatic periods as "dormant" mycelia in buds.

Epidemiology

The occurrence, distribution, and severity of powdery mildews are affected primarily by temperature, relative humidity (RH), vapor pressure deficit, light, leaf wetness, and wind or drafts. Because their effects are often interrelated, it is important that all factors be considered holistically while examining the effects of any single factor.

Wind. Drafts have long been recognized by growers of nursery and greenhouse crops as a factor contributing to the occurrence and spread of powdery mildews. Infection frequently begins near doors or other openings and gradually spreads to other parts of the growing area. Similar effects also are observed in the field when powdery mildew appears on a plant and spreads in the direction of prevailing winds.

Temperature. Response to temperature appears to be conditioned somewhat by the climate in which the powdery mildew species has become adapted. For instance, *Erysiphe cichoracearum* has an optimum temperature of about 82F (28C) on cantaloupe isolates from the hot Imperial Valley in California. Isolates of *E. cichoracearum* collected from squash in California's coolest agricultural region had an optimum temperature of only 59F (15C). It has been suggested that most hosts can tolerate more heat than can the powdery mildews that infect them. In the

Midwest, powdery mildew diseases on nursery and greenhouse plants commonly develop in the spring and fall. During the hot summer, many plants recover from these diseases to some extent.

Few powdery mildew conidia germinate (nor do hyphae grow well) at temperatures above 86F (30C). A moisture-saturated atmosphere is essential for high-temperature germination in order to prevent spore desiccation. Because temperature and RH are so interdependent for spore germination and growth of powdery mildews, the individual assessment and management of one of these factors without attention to the other is of little value. This is why many computerized mildew management programs incorporating vapor pressure deficit values are workable and are becoming popular.

Relative humidity. Although most powdery mildew spores germinate best in a saturated or nearly saturated atmosphere, some germination occurs over the entire relative humidity range, if conditions are such that some water is available to the spore. The powdery mildews have been divided into three groups according to their spore-germinating dampness responses:

1. those that germinate only under damp conditions (*Sphaerotheca pannosa*)

2. those that germinate optimally under damp conditions, with a small percentage of conidia capable of germinating under dry conditions (*Erisyphe cichoracearum*, *E. graminis*, *Leveillula taurica*, and *S. macularis*)

3. those that germinate well throughout a range of dampnesses from relative humidities slightly below saturation to very dry conditions (*E. polygoni* and *Uncinula necator*)

Vapor pressure deficit (VPD) has been used as a more precise indicator than relative humidity to predict the germinability of powdery mildew conidia. Vapor pressure deficit is calculated by the formula VPD = (1 − RH)E, where E is the vapor pressure of water at saturation at a given temperature and RH is the relative humidity. Thus, VPD does take into account the temperature of the leaf environment. VPD is a measure of the tendency of water to remain as such on a surface versus its tendency to evaporate from that surface. Measuring VPD is therefore a practical way in which the greenhouse grower can predict how water will behave on the crop leaves.

Leaf wetness. Recent observations on greenhouse roses have linked leaf wetness episodes to powdery mildew disease development. It has been shown that partial contact with small water droplets or films of water are beneficial to powdery mildew spore germination. Such conditions may also favor development of mycelia and production of conidia.

The relative humidity and temperature effects already discussed may actually affect pathogen development through their influence on the occurrence of leaf wetness. Minute films of moisture on rose leaves have been observed frequently. They often occur diurnally (on a daily cycle). They can persist for extended periods of time, up to several hours.

Factors such as leaf to air temperature gradients, moving air, RH, incoming solar radiation, outgoing radiant energy loss, and leaf transpiration undoubtedly govern the occurrence and persistence of leaf wetness. Since it is difficult if not impossible to measure these surface phenomena, leaf wetness meters have sometimes been useful to detect a period favorable to infection, during and after the fact (fig. 4.4). Vapor pressure deficit has been tried to predict leaf wetness.

Leaf wetness can also be harmful to powdery mildew pathogens, which has long been recognized. Soapy water has been used to control peach powdery mildew, and rose growers have historically sprayed plants with water in the middle of the day to reduce infection. Apparently, the

Fig. 4.4. Some growers use leaf wetness meters to determine when infection periods have occurred.

physical relationship of the spore to the water greatly influences the response. Continuous water films that totally immerse the spores reduce germination. However, partial contact with minute films of water or flotation of spores on the water surface may be beneficial to some powdery mildews.

Light. Because both host and pathogen are profoundly affected by light, it is difficult to determine the direct effect of light on powdery mildews. The diurnal cycle of spore maturation for these fungi is commonly believed to be a result of light variations. Conflicting research reports cast considerable doubt on any effect of light quality and quantity on the infection process of powdery mildews.

High-light conditions are frequently accompanied by high temperatures, resulting from incoming radiant energy. The pathogen growth may be more influenced by temperature response than as a direct light effect. Plant parts directly exposed to the sun frequently develop temperatures in excess of the optimum for growth or even survival of these fungi. Many powdery mildew infections primarily occur and thrive on shaded foliage or on leaves deep within the canopy. In landscape plantings, shaded sections of plant beds are often noted to be more heavily diseased.

Host nutrition and pH. It is generally believed that vigorous plants are more susceptible to infection by powdery mildew than are plants under various nutritional stresses. Cucumber plants grown with slight or moderate nutrient stresses, however, have been shown to have larger *Erysiphe cichoracearum* colonies and more conidiophores than non-stressed plants. While lowered plant vigor may enhance susceptibility on cucumber, there are many exceptions that would invalidate such a generalization pertaining to all other plants, fruits, vegetables, and ornamentals. Likewise, soil pH may affect the availability of nutrients to the host, which may indirectly affect powdery mildew growth. No correlation between the pH of host plant tissues and powdery mildew development has been demonstrated, though.

Recently, there have been studies demonstrating the effects of increased silicon in the fertilizer on the reduction of powdery mildews and some other diseases. This effect is seen in plant-growing systems where silicon is lacking, such as hydroponic culture of roses. In soil or organic growing media systems, silicon would not normally be limiting to the plant. Thus, no beneficial effect of supplemental silicon would be predicted.

On the basis of available evidence, it would appear that with the exception of nitrogen and silicon (in special cases), soil amendments or alteration of soil pH are not practical means of reducing infection by powdery mildews. For many ornamental plants, it may be advisable, from a cultural point of view, to avoid excessive nitrogen use. High nitrogen tends to result in soft, leggy plant growth. Tissue resulting from this growth may be economically unacceptable as well as susceptible to other fungal and bacterial diseases.

Management

Since Robertson first controlled powdery mildew by applying a sulfur and soap solution to peach trees in 1824, chemical control has played the major role in reducing losses caused by powdery mildew fungi. This has been especially true when dealing with powdery mildew on greenhouse crops. Other control measures that form the basis of a holistic or integrated management strategy are sometimes equally important, however. Eradication (removal or reduction of inoculum by various horticultural practices), exclusion (plant quarantines and other measures to prevent introduction of the pathogen into areas where it is not known to exist), host resistance, cultural control, and biocontrol all offer needed disease management tools.

Protection or eradication with chemicals

Sulfur has been in continuous use for powdery mildew control since its efficacy was documented more than 100 years ago. Applied under optimum conditions, sulfur is a very effective mildicide for plants that are tolerant of it. Fungicides have been developed to reduce the phytotoxicity of the sulfur and improve effectiveness.

Sulfur and sulfur-containing fungicides have been applied to plants primarily as sprays, but they have also been widely used as dusts. In European greenhouses of the nineteenth century, sulfur was first used in the vapor form. It was noted to be particularly effective for controlling grape powdery mildew when sprinkled on moistened hot-water heating pipes in the greenhouse. Sulfur fumes can provide protection for a wide variety of greenhouse-grown ornamental plants, and this technique is used by many greenhouse growers today (fig. 4.5).

The major complaint against sulfur in both the greenhouse and in the field is its tendency to oxidize, especially at high temperatures. If sulfur as a vapor comes into contact with a flame of any sort, it will oxidize to sulfur dioxide, one of the most damaging air pollutants, destroying leaf tissue in a matter of minutes. Sulfur is also highly flammable and somewhat dangerous to use in a greenhouse.

Fig. 4.5. Sulfur fumigators are arranged in a group behind a fan.

The vapor-phase activity of sulfur against powdery mildews is not unique. Many fungicides—such as drazoxolon, oxythioquinox, binacapryl, dinitro-octyl phenyl crotonates, propaconizole, fenarimol, triadimefon, triforine, and others—have been demonstrated to have vapor action. Studies have also shown that the volatile activity of certain fungicides can be enhanced by heating. Greenhouse disease control by heat volatilization of a variety of fungicides is feasible but not currently permitted on product labeling.

The dinitrophenol fungicides came into prominence in the 1940s. Dinocap (Karathane) began to replace sulfur, particularly on sulfur-sensitive plants and in the cooler growing areas of the world, where sulfur was frequently unsatisfactory. Dinocap provides good control for many powdery mildews on widely divergent hosts. Although dinocap is not completely safe, it is less phytotoxic on most plants than sulfur and is more effective at lower temperatures. Dinocap is still occasionally used on nursery crops in the United States. It generally cannot be used on crops with exposed flower tissue, as tissue burn would likely result.

Quinomethionate (Morestan), introduced in 1962, is for many powdery mildews more effective than dinocap. Phytotoxicity has been reported on certain ornamentals. An organic hydrocarbon, it is used in repeated spray programs as a preventive fungicide.

Piperalin (Pipron), introduced in 1965, is an organic foliar fungicide with eradicant properties. It has been used widely to control powdery mildews on greenhouse-grown ornamental plants, especially roses. The label has recently been expanded to include many more hosts of common powdery mildews. Piperalin is one of the few fungicides that will eradicate powdery mildew without harming plant foliage. It is very specific for powdery mildews but of no value for controlling other infectious diseases.

The benzimidazole fungicides comprise one of the most important groups of systemic chemicals for disease control on ornamental plants. Benomyl (Benlate) has probably been used more extensively than any other ornamental fungicide because it controls a broad range of plant diseases. Since benomyl was taken off the U.S. ornamental market in the early 1990s, thiophanate-methyl (Cleary's 3336, Domain, Fungo, Systec 1998) has taken its place as another benzimidazole fungicide. Thiophanate-methyl is more stable in acidic environments and breaks down quite differently than benomyl. All benzimidazoles convert to carbendazim in and on plants and appear to be translocated in that form. Carbendazim is the part of the thiophanate-methyl molecule that is active against fungi. Carbendazim is available as a formulated fungicide in some areas of the world, but is not sold as such in the United States. Fungi resistance to benzimidazole fungicides has caused widespread concern. For this reason, plant producers should not rely solely on them for continued powdery mildew management.

Pyridine and pyrimidine carbinol fungicides, under development since the mid-1960s, are very effective against powdery mildews. Parinol (Parnon) was registered for use on roses and zinnias and for nonbearing apple trees and grape vines. Although this fungicide is not currently available for commercial application on ornamental plants, it may play an important role in future control of powdery mildew diseases.

Triforine is a highly effective systemic fungicide for control of powdery mildews. In addition, it provides control of rose black spot, rose rust, apple scab, and several other diseases of ornamental plants. Like many contemporary systemic fungicides, triforine is a demethylation-inhibiting fungicide that affects spore germination and mycelial development. It is often used in combination with thiophanate-methyl.

Dodemorph (Meltatox), belonging to the morpholine group of fungicides, has shown good activity against powdery mildews and certain other ornamental crop diseases. It provides both protectant and eradicant effects but has little residual activity on plant surfaces. It is no longer available in the United States, however. Tridemorph is a closely related compound that has been used in Europe and other parts of the world but not in the United States.

Triadimefon (Bayleton), propiconazole (Banner), triflumazole (Terraguard), myclobutanol (Systhane), and fenarimol (Rubigan) are other demethylation-inhibiting fungicides now being used extensively on ornamental plants for powdery mildew management. They have good activity against powdery mildews. Repeated applications may cause stunting in some plant species, due to their growth-regulating inhibition of gibberellic acid. More of these sorts of fungicides are expected to be registered soon for powdery mildew control on ornamental crops in U.S. nurseries. The growth-regulator effects of the newer of these products seem to be less severe than those of the earlier ones.

Demethylation-inhibiting fungicides can be quite volatile, dissipating into the air too quickly when used or in the greenhouse in hot weather or outside in windy conditions. On the other hand, when applied under over-cast conditions or in the winter, the lowered volatility may influence per-formance because the effective dose is higher on the plant being sprayed. This can result in longer residual or increased growth-regulator effects. Microencapsulated formulations of this type of fungicide are being researched and may well result in improved volatility predictability.

Imazalil (Fungaflor), a relatively new systemic fungicide, comes from the N-substituted imidazole group. It has a broad spectrum of activ-ity against fungal pathogens, including powdery mildews, and appears to be particularly active against benzimidazole-resistant strains of plant-pathogenic fungi. The vapor phase distributes readily in confined areas, making it a good candidate as a fumigant for control of diseases in the greenhouse and confined plant storage areas. It is not yet available for use in the United States.

A chelated copper fungicide, Phyton-27, is now labeled for the con-trol of many powdery mildews on greenhouse crops. Whereas coppers have not traditionally been used for management of these diseases, this product seems to offer fair eradicative and protective properties. It is par-ticularly useful because it is reasonably safe on plants in flower.

Currently under development are products containing oils, soaps, and bicarbonate salts, alone or in combination. These have been used for years as home remedies for powdery mildew by many organic gardeners. It is hoped that the refinement of the products by commercial companies will make the products of sufficient efficacy and low enough cost to fill growers' needs. Apparently, these sorts of products work by physically disrupting the physiology of the mildew pathogen growing on the surface of the host tissue.

A good approach when combating a powdery mildew problem with routine sprays is to combine an eradicant with a protectant, if the label does not warn against this practice. Also, if you are using a DMI, change to another after three or four applications. There has been reported resistance to DMIs after repeated use. This is less of a problem with the newer products.

Proper application of chemicals

Because powdery mildews are characterized by largely superficial growth on host plant tissue, application methods that wet plant and fungal surfaces well have traditionally been the most effective way to control powdery mildews with chemicals. Such application methods are usually classed as high-volume sprays. High-pressure aerosol applicators with targeting nozzles have recently been developed for applying fungicides onto plants in greenhouses. These "coldfoggers" do not overwet the foliage, yet they provide good tissue coverage.

High-volume sprays or targeted aerosols can be adjusted to optimize their effectiveness at controlling powdery mildews. All potentially infectible plant surfaces must be covered. Leaf undersurfaces, bud tissue, and flower parts can sometimes be particularly difficult to spray properly. Adjusting the pressure and the nozzle size to keep the spray particle small is a primary concern. Using an appropriate spreader-sticker will help. Adjusting nozzle directioning or movement patterns may be needed with hand-held nozzles to increase the effectiveness of the chemical application.

The selected interval between sprayings can have a great influence on the effectiveness of either a preventive or an eradicative powdery mildew spray program. If systemics are not being used, rapidly growing crops usually need to be sprayed more frequently. Weather patterns will influence the need for follow-up sprays. If some of the newer fungicides with growth-regulator side effects are being used, care must be taken not to apply them too frequently or under improper weather conditions.

Many growers have used low-volume, nontargeted chemical application methods to successfully manage powdery mildew diseases. The advantages of these methods are that they are fast, can be done in a timely manner after a disease outbreak is first noticed, and do not excessively expose the crop or handler to large amounts of pesticide. The main disadvantage is that it can cause localized overdoses here or there on a crop. Furthermore, fungal structures are not directly wetted, possibly leading to lack of fungitoxic action in an eradicative program.

Eradication

The sole means of overwintering of many powdery mildews appears to be by dormant mycelium in infected ornamental buds. The pruning and destruction of infected ornamental buds reduce the overwintering inoculum and can aid in disease management where appropriate. Of course, such a strategy is not particularly useful for greenhouse or nursery flower crop producers who deal in continuous, year-long production.

For mildews with broader host ranges, such as *E. cichoracearum*, the removal of weed hosts from the vicinity of the cultured plants can afford a measure of control. As was mentioned earlier, most powdery mildew conidia are dispersed only over relatively short distances from the infected plants. Keeping greenhouse doors closed to eliminate incoming air has often been effective as a control procedure. Also, drafts and winds blowing over infested plants from one part of the greenhouse to another should be avoided whenever possible.

Exclusion

Because they already occur on most ornamentals, little effort is made to exclude mildew-infected plants from international trade. In many cases, it is almost impossible to confirm disease freedom on batches of plants or cuttings. Detection of dormant mycelia in the buds is difficult without an extended quarantine period. However, unrestricted plant movement has resulted in widespread occurrence and losses from powdery mildew-infested crops in recent years. In addition, the possibility of introducing more damaging races or isolates of the pathogen into previously uninfested nurseries or areas of the world is a serious concern for the future.

Host resistance

Most ornamental plants are selected because they have certain desirable horticultural characteristics. Their susceptibility to powdery mildew is often not a major selection criterion. When it is considered, the plants are usually only subjected to local races of fungi during the selection process. Although they may at first appear resistant, they may succumb to disease when grown in different geographic areas.

Host structure and varying plant constituents do play a role in susceptibility to powdery mildews. The frequency of plant hairs and high osmotic pressure of the cell sap has been correlated with susceptibility. Cuticle thickness can affect host penetration by powdery mildews. Various host-cell nutrients or other chemical constituents have been suggested as inhibitory to fungal infection. Although the mechanism of host resistance to powdery mildews is not well understood for many ornamental crop plants, it should remain the goal of plant breeders to select cultivars that are most resistant.

Biological agents

Management of powdery mildews by biologic agents is an intriguing possibility. It has not been pursued seriously because chemical fungicides currently provide adequate disease control and have been readily available. In addition, most biocontrol agents have special environmental requirements not easily controlled under field conditions. Their use in nurseries or greenhouses, however, where the environment could be more readily controlled, appears to have been largely overlooked.

Predation upon powdery mildew fungi by mycophagous beetles, larvae, snails, and thrips is known. However, it is considered of no practical value for control. More recently, mycoparasitism by various leaf surface-dwelling fungi has been suggested as a control strategy. Two such products

(AQ-10 and Sporodex) are labeled for powdery mildew management on vegetable crops in other parts of the world. Most of these mycoparasites presumably secrete fungistatic compounds. The intimate relationship between the host powdery mildew and its mycoparasite has not been intensively studied for most of the fungi known to antagonize powdery mildew pathogens.

Environmental modifications

The discussion of the epidemiology of powdery mildews outlined the factors necessary for their spread and development. The converse viewpoint of creating or enhancing conditions that will impede the spread and development of the pathogens is the basis of environmental control strategies. Many strategies can be successfully employed, depending on cropping conditions and economic constraints.

The avoidance of wind drafts was mentioned as an eradication measure. This tactic can be very successful with nursery and greenhouse crops. The converse—promotion of wind drafts or air movement—can also be an important aspect of environmental control. Air movement over host plant surfaces is an effective way to prevent localized areas of high RH and to prevent leaf wetness episodes. In greenhouses this is accomplished by effective ventilation and fan systems, proper spacing of plants on benches and beds, and appropriate greenhouse design. Outdoors, increasing the drying air movement can often be accomplished by increasing plant spacing and clearing away surrounding buildings and vegetation that block the movement of air over the crops.

High relative greenhouse humidity is commonly managed by venting outward the trapped indoor air, bringing in and heating outdoor air as the air cools at the end of the day. If done thoroughly and in a timely fashion at the end of the day, such a technique effectively reduces relative humidity as well as prevents condensation of water on plant surfaces.

The widespread use of computers to constantly monitor and control greenhouse environments has made such a practice even more practical. Computerized venting and heating can be programmed more effectively than merely to open vents and run heat at the end of the day. Important considerations are that the venting and heating begin early enough in the day to prevent moisture condensation in the greenhouse rather than to try to dry off crop surfaces after they have become damp. VPD or RH sensors can indicate when this process should begin from one day to another.

In addition, air exchanges that are pulsed or intermittently applied to the greenhouse just after a bit of heat is added to the air will very efficiently move moisture-laden air outward. A constant venting and heating procedure at moderate temperatures often does not change atmospheric conditions quickly enough. This pulse dehumidification method has the effect of dropping the greenhouse temperature more gradually at the end of the day. Keeping low-velocity horizontal air moving over the leaves during this period will offer additional leaf-drying potential. Many growers are using this method to effectively manage powdery mildews.

Night curtains, high-intensity lighting of plants, and radiant heat pipes above a crop have all been shown to effectively reduce the development of powdery mildew diseases. Apparently, such practices add to or preserve the radiant heat energy of the plant tissue. This prevents cooling of plant surfaces below the temperature of the surrounding air. The end result is the prevention of water condensation on the susceptible surfaces. Again, such practices must be employed properly, as soon as crops cease to be irradiated (sun-heated) or as soon as the greenhouse air begins to cool.

Note how the outlined practices constantly depend on the interrelationships of several environmental factors, primarily temperature and air moisture. Although most powdery mildews develop more readily under moderate temperatures (below 86F, 30C), high temperature has not been used as a disease management strategy by nursery growers except when it occurs naturally. The quality of most crops falls off rapidly under cultural temperatures above 86F (30C), so the economics of heating a greenhouse to these temperatures is not favorable. Of course, such a program might be practical if it were carried out for only a short period of time, corresponding to the diurnal cycling of the pathogen. Determination of such effective times would depend on which of the pathogen structures were most affected by high temperature. Such information is not presently available. Elevated temperatures might also be useful to rid plants of dormant mycelia, but no research has been carried out on this point, either.

Nutrition

The lack of sufficient research also prevents growers from using nutritional methods to enhance crop resistance to impede the development of the powdery mildew pathogens. An ornamental crop's worth is intimately related to precise, highly controlled nutritional programming. Variation of the programming as a cultural disease management strategy has to be done cautiously. Some greenhouse growers who are growing roses in rock wool or coconut fiber are adding 100 ppm of silicon dioxide to the nutrient solution in an attempt to enhance the plants' resistance to powdery mildew.

Rust Diseases

The plant rusts are so named because some of the spore stages of these fungi are yellow-brown to dark brown. Produced in large numbers, released spores give the affected areas a rusty appearance. There are many plant rusts throughout the world, some of them economically important. In general, those affecting ornamentals are not too damaging, although on occasion they may be serious enough to severely limit good growth, cause extensive defoliation, or even kill plants or parts of plants. Many of the rusts tend to have rather limited host ranges and infect only one or several species in a genus.

Disease and pathogen cycles

The rust pathogens make up an interesting and sometimes complicated group of fungi, partly because many of them have two separate, distinct hosts involved in their yearly life cycles. Such *heteroecious* rusts may have one stage on an herbaceous plant and the other on a woody plant. The herbaceous host may be annual or perennial grasses, flowering plants, or ferns. The woody plants may be conifer or deciduous broad-leaved plants. In contrast to the heteroecious rusts are *autoecious* rusts, with which all of the spore stages are found on one type of plant.

Some rust fungi may produce as many as five distinct types of spores as they complete the yearly cycle. The kinds of spores produced in a yearly life cycle varies greatly from one rust to another. A rust with all five spore types is called a *macrocyclic* rust. In contrast are the *microcyclic* rusts, which produce from four to one spore stage. Macrocyclic rusts can be heteroecious or autoecious. Microcyclic rusts are almost always autoecious, having only one host. Most of the rusts affecting greenhouse crops are microcyclic.

Each of the spore stages serves a specific function and has a specific name. People working with the rust fungi use Roman numerals as a shorthand way of noting which of the spore stages occurs on which host. In the following paragraphs, general descriptions are given of each of the spore stages. The appearance of the spore stage, the associated symptoms, the stage name, functions, and the number used to designate it are outlined. If you encounter a rust on a particular ornamental and know which spore stages occur on the plant of concern, you will be able to devise an effective management program more quickly. For instance, if you see the uredospores, chances are that the pathogen is in a period of rapid spread. On the other hand, if you are detecting teliospore, this usually means that the rust is going into dormancy for a time.

Pycnospores (pycniospores or spermatia)

These very small spores do not infect plants but instead act as a sexual stage to provide for genetic recombination. The pycnospores (spermatia) are borne in small structures called pycnia or spermagonia. Usually formed on the upper leaf surfaces, they are very small and may be conspicuous as small black dots in brightly colored yellow or orange circular areas. The spore number for this stage is 0 (granted, not a Roman numeral).

Aeciospores

These very light-colored (pale yellow to orange) spores are borne in specialized structures, usually on the undersides of leaves on herbaceous plants. The structures bearing the spores, aecia, are often cuplike. Tissues associated with aecia may be discolored and swollen. On some plants aecia appear as ruptures or cracks in stems and branches. In heteroecious rusts this spore infects the other host. The aecia frequently are associated with the pycnia, either surrounding them or being formed on the leaf surface opposite the pycnia. Aecia generally are the largest of the rust structures on herbaceous plants. Because of their distinctive appearance, they aid in diagnosis of the rusts. The aecial stage is numbered I.

Uredospores

The uredospore (also called urediospore) is the spore stage that is most common on economically important rust diseases of ornamentals. The production and release of these spores often gives the infected plant parts a rusty appearance (fig. 5.1). The uredospores are capable of immediate germination and infection. This spore stage generally acts as a repeating stage or secondary cycling stage on the host where it is formed. This results in the rapid increase in the rust lesions on a plant. In some of the microcyclic rusts, this may be the only spore formed. They are usually formed on the undersides of leaves. Leaf tissue near the uredia (spore-bearing lesions) and sometimes surrounding them are discolored and may be pale green, yellow, or tan to brown. This yellowing can be seen from the top surface of the leaf. The spore stage number is II.

Fig. 5.1. Rust lesions on the undersurface of a geranium leaf give affected areas a rusty appearance.

Teliospores

The teliospores (teleutospores) are the resting spores. They may be formed in the same areas as the uredospores or in areas around the uredospores. They are usually produced in abundance as the plants begin to mature and senesce. The teliospores are darker than the uredospores and frequently black. In many rusts, the teliospores germinate only after a winter rest period. Thus, this spore stage is often responsible for the survival of the pathogen between crops in the greenhouse. The teliospores do not usually infect plant tissues. Each teliospore produces four very small spores, called basidiospores. The tissues in which the teliospores are produced are called telia, which are usually raised, darkened areas. Teliospores are given the number III.

Basidiospores

Basidiospores are windborne spores formed from teliospores. In the autoecious rusts, these spores infect the same host on which the teliospores were produced. In the heteroecious rusts, they infect the other host in the cycle. This spore stage is given the number IV.

Diagnosis

Rust fungi do not grow on dead organic materials. This makes them obligate parasites. On most plants, rust fungi infect the leaves, although some also may infect stems or flowers. Usually, the lower leaves are infected first. The typical symptom is the abundant number of orange to brown spores formed at the site of infection (fig. 5.2). Generally described as rust colored, this symptom provides the name of the diseases these pathogens cause.

Rust infections sometimes may be so severe that an entire leaf or a number of leaves may be killed. Rarely is an entire infected plant killed, although sometimes infected seedlings die. On some plants, such as geraniums, severely infected leaves will drop from the plant, which can lead to serious plant weakening and other troubles.

Fig. 5.2. A geranium with rust lesions visible on the undersurfaces of the lower leaves.

Rust cankers from stem infections can result in stem death, especially if the canker is active for more than one year. This is commonly seen on roses with rust.

Epidemiology

The rust fungi, as is typical of most leaf-infecting fungi, need condensed moisture for the spores to germinate and infection to take place. Infection can take place in as short a time as $4^1/_2$ hours. These fungi can thus be important in areas where nightly dew formation may be of long enough duration to allow infection to occur. Warm days and cool nights result in such dew-forming situations. Moreover, cool temperatures (50 to 75F, 10 to 24C) favor spore-bearing lesion production for most of the rust diseases. In areas of the country where summer temperatures get well above 75F (24C), rust diseases are not readily expressed all season long. They seem to come and go on the plants and are generally more evident in the spring and the fall.

Many rusts of greenhouse crops seem to go through a prolonged incubation period between host infection and development of host symptoms, so they can be moved long distances on infected material. Rust diseases express themselves first by producing spores, often on leaf undersurfaces. Leaf yellowing is often seen on upper leaf surfaces in spots associated with these spore-bearing lesions. Spray programs begun at the first sign of disease may not bring immediate results, since most fungicides are good infection preventers but will not eradicate existing infections.

Management of rust diseases

Sanitation

Control of rust fungi is not easy. Plant debris that may harbor teliospores, the resting stage (III), should be buried deeply or taken away. In the early stages of rust development, removal of infected leaves can be effective. In areas where susceptible herbaceous plants will grow all year, set aside a period when the plant is not grown to break the rust cycle. For example, snapdragons will grow all year in mild climates. Because rust is a problem, they should not be grown continuously but should be removed each year and not replanted for several months. When irrigating, avoid getting the foliage wet, especially in the evening, for this fosters rust fungi. Also, avoid splashing water from leaf to leaf.

Many rust diseases are spread by infected or contaminated plant material. Infection can occur on semidormant material, on seedlings, in buds, or on tiny leaves. Many days or weeks can pass before spore-bearing rust lesions can be seen. If a rust disease appears to suddenly break out on a crop, it could be that infection occurred prior to the plant material entering the greenhouse. In such a case, notify the plant supplier as soon as possible.

Environmental

To avoid water condensation forming as dew on the leaves or water dripping onto the leaves, vent and heat the greenhouse in the late afternoon. This will reduce the relative humidity and prevent dew as the air cools for the night. Keep air circulating during this operation. Continue circulating air until the night temperature has been reached. Keep plants sufficiently spaced on the bench or in the growing bed to allow air to circulate freely about them.

Chemical

Chemical sprays can be effective if applied correctly. Many fungicides act only as protectants, meaning that they need to be applied in advance of infection to give control. Because infected plants will continue to grow, good protectant control will involve spraying at regular intervals. Furthermore, since most germinating spores infect on the lower leaf surfaces, fungicide must be directed beneath the leaf to cover this surface with protectant. Fungicides that give protection against rust infection include mancozeb (Protect T/O, Dithane T/O, FORE) and chlorothalonil (Daconil 2787).

Some fungicides move systemically in the plant and may both protect it and kill any established fungi. Oxycarboxin (Plantvax) is a systemic that is quite specific for rust disease control. Some of the newer systemics named for powdery mildews are also effective and labeled for rust diseases. Triforine, propiconazole (Banner), and triadimefon (Bayleton) are particularly effective and well labeled.

Resistance

Varieties of some plants show variations in resistance to rust fungi. For example, many varieties of chrysanthemums are susceptible, whereas others are resistant. Bearded irises vary considerably in their susceptibility to rust.

Some rusts of greenhouse crops

Ageratum

Puccinia conoclini. Pycnia, bearing pycnospores (0), are mainly on the upper leaf surfaces. Aecia, bearing aeciospores (I), are on both surfaces and are in small groups. Uredia, bearing uredospores (II), are borne on the upper leaf surfaces and are cinnamon brown. Telia, bearing teliospores (III), are chocolate brown and are found mainly on the undersides of the leaves.

Alcea (hollyhock)

Puccinia malvacearum. Pycnia, bearing pycnospores (0), aecia, bearing aeciospores (I), and uredia, bearing uredospores (II), are not found. Telia, bearing teliospores (III), are small, raised, yellow to chestnut brown mounds formed on the undersides of the leaves, on the petioles, and on the main stems. The teliospores sometimes germinate in place and give the telia an ashen gray appearance. This is found commonly on *Alcea rosea L.* wherever it is grown. Young plants may die when infections are severe.

Anemone (windflower)

Puccinia anemones-virginiana. Pycnia, bearing pycnospores (0), are unknown. Aecia, bearing aeciospores (I), and uredia, bearing uredospores

(II), are not found. Telia, bearing teliospores (III), are compact, blackish brown structures on the undersides of the leaves. They may become ashen gray as a result of teliospore germination.

Antirrhinum (snapdragon)

Puccinia antirrhini. Pycnia, bearing pycnospores (0), and aecia, bearing aeciospores (I), are not found. Uredia, bearing uredospores (II), are found on the undersides of the older leaves, although when severe, all leaves may be infected. Stems and calyxes also may be infected. The rust pustules frequently are in circles or concentric rings. The uredospores are chestnut brown. Telia, bearing teliospores (III), mainly are found on the lower leaf surfaces and are blackish brown. This important disease of snapdragon is general wherever *Antirrhinum majus L.* is grown.

Aster

Coleosporium asterum. Uredia, bearing uredospores (II), are round, orange-yellow and are found on the lower surfaces of leaves. Telia, bearing teliospores (III), are reddish orange and are also found on the lower leaf surfaces. This rust is found throughout the United States and southern Canada but is more prevalent throughout the northern and western United States. Many *Aster* species are infected. Pycnia, bearing pycnospores (0), and aecia, bearing aeciospores (I), are found on members of the Pinaceae (pines).

Centaurea (cornflower, bachelor's button)

Puccinia cyani. Pycnia, bearing pycnospores (0), are scattered on both leaf surfaces. Aecia, bearing aeciospores (I), are found in pustules on both surfaces and contain dark cinnamon brown spores. Uredia, bearing uredospores (II), are not formed. Telia, bearing teliospores (III), are found on both leaf surfaces and are chestnut brown. The fungus may move systemically through the plant, and the leaves may be covered with the spores of the fungus.

Dendranthema (florist's chrysanthemum)

Puccinia horiana. Pycnia, bearing pycnospores (0), aecia, bearing aeciospores (I), and uredia, bearing uredospores (II), are not found. Telia, bearing teliospores (III), are mainly on the leaf undersides, though they may occur on the upper leaf surfaces and on the stems. The telia are pink at first, but as they mature, they become white. Because of this, the disease is called white rust. Teliospores may germinate in place to produce basidiospores (IV) that are the means of spreading the fungus.

    Puccinia chrysanthemi. Pycnia, bearing pycnospores (0), and aecia, bearing aeciospores (I), are unknown. Uredia, bearing uredospores (II), are found on the undersides of the leaves. Uredospores are chestnut brown and frequently found in rings. Yellow spots appear on upper leaf surfaces above infected areas. Telia, bearing teliospores (III), are not found in the United States. They are found on *Dendranthema* × *grandiflora* Ramat throughout the United States and Canada wherever the plant is grown.

Dianthus (carnation, pinks, sweet William)

Uromyces dianthi. Uredia, bearing uredospores (II), are on both leaf surfaces, frequently in rings. They are dark cinnamon brown. Telia, bearing teliospores (III), are chestnut brown and are also found on both surfaces. Pycnia, bearing pycnospores (0), and aecia, bearing aeciospores (I), occur on *Euphorbia* species but not in North America.

Epilobium (fireweed, willow herb)

Pucciniastrum pustulatum. Uredia, bearing uredospores (II), are scattered or in small groups on discolored areas. They open by a central pore to release orange-yellow spores. The telia, bearing teliospores (III), are small and develop into extended crusts, which are reddish brown and turn blackish brown as they mature.

Fuchsia

Pucciniastrum pustulatum. See *Epilobium*. They are found on *Fuchsia hybrida* Voss in Alaska, Washington, Oregon, and California. Telia, bearing teliospores (III), are not reported on *Fuchsia* sp.

Heuchera (coral bells)

Puccinia heucherae. Pycnia, bearing pycnospores (0), are not found. Aecia, bearing aeciospores (I), and uredia, bearing uredospores (II), are not produced. Telia, bearing teliospores (III), are formed mainly on the undersides of the leaves. They are chestnut or chocolate brown, often becoming ashen gray due to germination of the teliospores.

Impatiens

Puccinia argentea. Uredospores (II) are cinnamon brown and are found on both leaf surfaces. Telia, bearing teliospores (III), are dark chestnut brown and are also found on both leaf surfaces. Pycnia, bearing pycnospores (0), and aecia, bearing aeciospores (I), are found on *Adoxa moschatellina L.* (Adoxaceae).

Iris

Puccinia iridis. Uredospores (II) are found on both sides of the leaves and are cinnamon brown, frequently occurring in rings. Telia, bearing teliospores (III), are also found on both leaf surfaces and are chestnut brown.

Pelargonium (geranium)

Puccinia pelargonii-zonalis. Pycnia, bearing pycnospores (0), and aecia, bearing aeciospores (I), are not known. Uredospores (II) are found on the lower leaf surfaces. They are scattered and frequently form irregular to regular concentric circles. They are cinnamon brown and are surrounded by the torn host epidermis. Teliospores (III) are pale brown and are mixed with the uredospores. They are found on *Pelargonium hortorum* Bailey throughout the United States.

Rosa (rose)

Phragmidium americanum. Pycnia, bearing pycnospores (0), are not abundant and are inconspicuous. They are found on the upper leaf surfaces. The aecia, bearing aeciospores (I), are orange-yellow and are found on the leaf undersides and on the petioles. Uredospores (II) are small and scattered on the lower leaf surfaces or on stem cankers. The telia, bearing teliospores (III), are on the undersides of the leaves.

Salvia (sage)

Puccinia farinacea. Pycnia, bearing pycnospores (0), are found on the upper leaf surfaces. Aecia, bearing aeciospores (I), are cup-shaped and are found mainly on the lower leaf surfaces. Uredospores (II) are cinnamon brown and found on the undersides of the leaves. Teliospores (III) are chocolate brown and are also found on the undersides of the leaves.

Vinca major

Puccinia vincae. Pycnia, bearing pycnospores (0), are scattered among the aecia, bearing aeciospores (I), on the undersides of the leaves. Aecia are cinnamon brown. Uredospores (II) are dark cinnamon brown, scattered, and on the leaf undersides. Teliospores (III) are chestnut brown and are mainly on the lower leaf surfaces.

Viola

Puccinia violae. Pycnia, bearing pycnospores (0), are found in groups on both leaf surfaces. Aecia, bearing aeciospores (I), are cup-shaped and are found mainly on the undersides of the leaves. Uredospores (II) are cinnamon brown and are found on the undersides of the leaves. Teliospores (III) are chocolate brown and found on both leaf surfaces.

Botrytis Blights

T he most commonly encountered diseases of herbaceous ornamentals include those caused by the *Botrytis* fungi, especially those *Botrytis* forms grouped together as *B. cinerea*. *Botrytis* species occur in cool temperate zones and in the higher elevations of subtropical areas.

Botrytis fungi attack a vast range of hosts, including almost every herbaceous ornamental. In addition to ornamentals (both herbaceous and woody), *Botrytis* attacks glasshouse and field vegetables, small fruits, bulb- and corm-producing plants, and forest tree seedlings. *Botrytis* species are also important as spoilage organisms, causing considerable losses in storage and transit of flowers, fruits, cuttings, and greenery.

Diagnosis

Blights of any plant part; leaf spots; stem cankers; rots of corms, rhizomes, roots, tubers, and seeds; and damping-off of young seedlings are all symptoms of *Botrytis* diseases (fig. 6.1). The name of the disease on a certain host may describe a characteristic symptom particular to the disease of that host. In general, all the diseases may also be called *Botrytis* blight. Both crown rot of cyclamen and stem canker of exacum, for example, may be known as *Botrytis* blight. In each case, the causal agent is *B. cinerea*.

Fig. 6.1. *Botrytis* blight on geraniums.

Prolific, brown sporulation on blighted tissue is observed in most *Botrytis* diseases. The presence of this sporulation is the most distinctive diagnostic tool the grower can use to verify the presence of a *Botrytis* blight. The name *gray mold*, referring to a grayish fungal growth, is also used to describe some diseases caused by *Botrytis* species. Certain species cause diseases with more specific names, such as tulip fire, caused by *B. tulipae*, and narcissus smoulder, caused by *B. narcissicola*.

Pathogen cycle

Infection may be by germinating conidia, with penetration through undamaged tissue, stomata, or wounds. Infection may also occur from hyphae growing from either dead plant parts or from extraneous organic matter in contact with host tissue. *Botrytis* species, especially *B. cinerea*, are often reported as wound pathogens. Wound inoculations nearly always result in infection, but direct penetration of germ tubes into undamaged tissue has been observed in some host-parasite relationships. Tulip leaves are infected by *B. tulipae* through the stomata. Gladiolus leaves are infected by *B. gladiolorum* through stomata under conditions of low humidity, but direct penetration through the cuticle can occur under high humidity. Penetration into a host through stomata seems to be the exception rather than the rule in *Botrytis* species.

Infections by hyphae are typically observed when infected flowers or leaves that act as "food bases" have fallen onto healthy tissue (fig. 6.2). Geranium petals that are readily colonized by *B. cinerea* provide such a food base when appressed to wet plant surfaces. Conidia often seem less important than such saprophytically based mycelial inoculum in establishing infections in diseases caused by the *B. cinerea*, which is not host-specific.

Fig. 6.2. The *Botrytis* fungus has invaded this dead petal tissue before moving into the leaf tissue.

With many plants, there can be latent or dormant infections that go undetected, sometimes for several weeks. In a latent or dormant infection, the actual infection takes place as described above. Initial development in the host is not yet macroscopically visible. Further growth of the hyphae is delayed, usually for several days or weeks. When environmental conditions change, the infections resume development to a symptomatic stage. *Botrytis cinerea* can produce latent infections in flowers, such as cut roses. When infected flowers are initially packed, they appear healthy. After unpacking, they have large *Botrytis* spots!

Conidia of most *Botrytis* species are dry and dispersed in air currents in very large numbers. The spores are easily dislodged from a heavily sporulating lesion by shaking or blowing on it. The dislodged spores look like a cloud of brown "dust."

Sometimes spores are dispersed in or on water droplets. Conidia in a film of water with dissolved nutrients for a minimum period (depending on temperature and other factors) is the basic requirement for infection. Conidia can also be dispersed by insects, such as bees and aphids.

To some extent, the mycelial inoculum is more independent of persistent water films containing nutrients. Water does improve the adherence of diseased plant parts, such as blossoms, to healthy tissue. Mycelial inoculum may be minute to very large and are usually not as susceptible to environmental conditions as conidia. Pieces of wind-blown and rain-splashed plant debris containing mycelia are important dispersal propagules. Petals and whole senescent flowers, easily infected by *B. cinerea*, may drop onto healthy tissue or be wind- and rain-dispersed.

Epidemiology

Botrytis diseases are often called "diseases of bad management." In the controllable environment of the greenhouse, this often is true. An epidemic of *Botrytis* depends on a complex sequence and interaction of biological events, such as the production and dispersal of inoculum, infection, development of the pathogen, and pathogen survival. Each event is predisposed by different sets of environmental and agricultural factors, such as temperature, rainfall, humidity, chemical crop protection, nutrition, and stage of the host's growth (flowering or with aging flowers, for example).

Epidemics caused by *Botrytis* species can happen very fast in comparison with those of most other diseases. The disease cycle can be very short. A conidium can be formed on a new lesion within eight hours after infection. Many factors predispose crops to *Botrytis* diseases (see table 6.1), but many factors also enable plants to escape infection. Epidemics can be controlled, but only by integrating a wide variety of crop management practices.

Generally, *Botrytis* epidemics occur in cool, wet, and humid weather—conditions that favor sporulation, infection, and also predispose the host to susceptibility. Surface wetness and temperature operate together in determining the success of initial infection from spores and the transition of latent infections to developing lesions.

The stage of host development is an important factor in epidemiological studies. Typically, *Botrytis* diseases affect older and especially senescent tissues. In some crops, young tissues, such as bedding plant

Table 6.1 Factors predisposing plants to *Botrytis* epidemics

Predisposing factor	Susceptible host
Moribund tissue	Any rapidly drying floral part or any aging vegetative tissue
Frost	All frost-damaged tissue
Low temperature	Gladiolus corms
Wounds (caused by any agent), windblown sand, sun, hail, fungal lesions, rapid water intake	Most crops, especially grapes
Deficiencies and excesses of crop fertilizers N, P, K, Mg, Ca	Many crops, such as strawberries and chrysanthemums
Atmospheric pollutants, such as ozone	Geranium, poinsettia
Ethylene	Cut flowers, especially carnations
Pesticides and growth regulators	Tomato, grapes
Insecticides	Snapdragon
Chloropropham	Tulip
Microorganisms, epiphytic organisms, parasitic microorganisms, such as *Puccinia antirrhini*	Snapdragon
Corynebacterium zonale, a bacterium	Geranium
Mites, thrips	African violet

seedlings, are very susceptible. Between these two extremes, there is normally a period of relative resistance, when epidemics are rare.

Many factors may predispose plants to *Botrytis* diseases. Overirrigation of geranium cuttings, poor drainage of bulb crops, crop shading and shelter from the drying effects of wind and sun in landscape plant beds, spacing of plug seedlings, high humidity in the greenhouse, and dense growth of geranium stock plants are only some examples of predisposing factors.

Disease management

Even though *Botrytis* diseases can be controlled in many ways, they remain among the most economically destructive diseases, both in the greenhouse or field, as well as in stored products. Control of these fungi is difficult because they can attack crops at almost any stage in their growth and they can infect all plant parts. *Botrytis cinerea* occurs on a wide range of living cultivated and wild host species, as well as persisting on dead plant material. Thus, it presents a constant threat of infection.

Botrytis species other than *B. cinerea* are more specialized pathogens, with restricted host ranges. Control is often possible by a single method, such as seed treatments or crop rotation practices.

Chemical management

Fungicides are usually valuable, but mainly as protectants. Since conidial infection can be rapid, infection may have occurred almost by the time the grower discovers environmental conditions unfavorable to the fungi. Some fungicides combat the production of spores, one eradicative mode of action. Outdoors, fungicide applications often cannot be made when conditions are favorable for infection. This means that *Botrytis* can get a start and must be eradicated.

In the early 1960s, chemical control was greatly enhanced by the introduction of such systemic fungicides as benomyl (Benlate, now banned), thiophanate-methyl (Cleary's 3336, Domain, Systec 1998, Fungo), and carbendazim. These chemicals, extremely toxic to *Botrytis* species, were superior to the standard protectant fungicides used at that time, such as captan and dichlofluanid. The level of disease control was significant, but the development of tolerance by *Botrytis* species to benzimidazole fungicides was a serious setback.

Following the emergence of resistance to benzimidazoles, dicarboximide fungicides (iprodione, procymidone, vinclozolin) have been used widely for control of *Botrytis* diseases on many crops. Recently, though, dicarboximide-insensitive isolates of *B. cinerea* have been found in many greenhouses.

The contact fungicides mancozeb (Protect T/O, Dithane T/O, FORE) and chlorothalonil (Daconil 2787) are widely used today to counter *Botrytis'* resistance to the other compounds. Most growers favor preventive, regular spray programs.

The combination products Zyban and Benefit are also labeled for *Botrytis* control. Only certain plant types are listed. Follow labeled directions. The possibility for *Botrytis* fungicide resistance is greater with Benefit than it is with Zyban.

Environmental control

Crop-handling techniques are of prime importance in controlling *Botrytis* storage diseases. Postharvest rots caused by *Botrytis* species can be controlled by careful storage and shipping techniques, such as controlled-temperature or controlled-atmosphere storage, pasteurization, irradiation, fumigation, treatment with vapor-phase fungicides, and protectant fungicide dips.

The greenhouse environment can be manipulated to promote conditions unfavorable for infection. The humidity can be reduced by increasing the temperature and venting at the end of the day. The techniques are similar to those discussed for powdery mildews.

Air circulation over and through the crop with low-velocity horizontal airflow is also very helpful (fig. 6.3). The greenhouse is the place where a large number of the ornamentals attacked by *Botrytis* species are generally found. The humid conditions often created there are excellent for *Botrytis* diseases. Since this environment can be manipulated to be unfavorable for disease development, this is one of the most effective means of control.

In the greenhouse and the field, cultivar selection; crop fertilization planned to avoid lush

Fig. 6.3. Low-velocity horizontal airflow helps circulate air over and through the crop.

growth during damp weather; cultural practices including watering methods, spacing, and sanitation (including removal of weed hosts, as well as debris) are all measures that can contribute to control by reducing the inoculum and creating environmental conditions less suitable for plant infection.

The following measures can be generally applied to producing all ornamental crops and form the basis for an integrated *Botrytis* management program.

1. Before initiating crop production, remove and destroy all diseased plants or parts and all plant debris and weeds. Continue sanitation practices throughout production.

2. Use disease-free seeds, plants, stock plants, and such propagating stock as bulbs, corms, tubers, and rhizomes.

3. Handle all plants carefully during transplanting to avoid damaging any tissue.

4. Water plants without wetting the foliage. Overhead watering is not satisfactory. Not only does it wet the leaves, but it also jars the plants. This has been shown with geranium crops to release a great number of spores into the air.

5. Space plants with leaves not touching so that air circulation over all plant surfaces is possible.

6. Keep humidity as low as practical. Evacuate warm, moist air in the evening and replace it with cool, dry air. This cool, dry air should be heated, reducing the relative humidity and thus the tendency for condensation of water on plant parts.

7. Apply protective fungicides thoroughly, before the concurrence of developing inoculum and susceptible plant growth in the greenhouse. Continue on an appropriate schedule as long as the weather remains cool and damp. With some crops it may be possible to apply fungicides after blossoms open.

Control in the field is not as easily manipulated as it is in the greenhouse, but a combination of cultural methods and chemical controls applicable to specific crops is effective.

Chapter 7

Fungal Leaf Spots, Blights, and Cankers

In the previous chapters, we have discussed the most important kinds of pathogens that attack the above ground parts of floral and foliage crops in greenhouses and outdoors. A host of other fungal microbes can, on occasion, cause serious diseases. This chapter discusses these "miscellaneous" pathogens.

Diagnosis

All of the diseases discussed here are caused by fungi. The various fungi are, however, rather diverse, and the disease symptoms are somewhat varied (see table 7.1). Blights or spots may appear on leaves, stems, or flowers, depending on which disease is present. Many of the microbes in this group can attack all three of these plant parts, but few occur on below-ground portions.

Table 7.1   Fungal diseases of stems, leaves, and flowers

Pathogen and disease	Important hosts	Comments
Ascochyta blight	Chrysanthemum, fern, hydrangea	Can cause a serious flower blight on mums. Also causes a cutting rot and leaf spots.
Alternaria blight	Geranium, carnation, pansy, zinnia, statice, schefflera, others	Causes a targeted leaf spotting, black spotting, black or dark brown. Can also cause a stem canker.
Black spot (*Diplocarpon*)	Rose	Begins on lower leaves; leaves turn yellow and drop. Very common on outdoor roses.
Leptosphaeria (*Coniothyrium*) canker	Rose	Causes a cankering on canes. Cankers are slow to develop but can eventually kill the cane.
Downy mildews	Rose, snapdragon, cineraria, grape ivy, strawflower, others	A different pathogen on each host. Usually sporulates abundantly on lower leaf surfaces. Spores rarely seen on roses, where the disease causes severe defoliation.
Septoria leaf spot	Chrysanthemum, phlox, carnation, others	Can be serious in warm, wet weather.
Sclerotinia flower blight	Camellia	Needs rain and warmth. Common in the South.
Conynespora leaf spot	Aphelandra	Causes a large lesion; a wound invader.
Exobasidium leaf gall	Azalea	Causes thickened, red swellings on leaves. These later become covered with white spores.
Ovulinia flower blight	Azalea	A common galling and blighting disease of azaleas in the South.
Phytophthora blights	Petunia, vinca, pansy, others	Begins on lower portions of the plant. Can be severe in warm, wet weather.
Rhizopus rot	Poinsettia, others	A general rotting of closely spaced plant material in hot weather.
Nectria (*Fusarium*) canker or basal rot	Poinsettia, carnation	A stress pathogen. Rarely serious, but difficult to control once it appears.
Anthracnose leaf spots	Dieffenbachia, ficus, English ivy, cyclamen, statice, pansy, others	Black spore-producing structures or pink to cream colored spore masses readily seen in lesions.

Table 7.1 continued

Pathogen and disease	Important hosts	Comments
Brown leaf spot (*Leptosphaeria*)	Dieffenbachia	Circular spots, with an orange halo or border.
Fusarium leaf spot	Dracaena	Reddish leaf spots. Can be severe in warm climates.
Cercospora	Ficus, peperomia, statice	Usually causes a small, raised spot on leaf undersides. Often mistaken for oedema.
Phyllosticta leaf spot	English ivy, dracaena, snapdragon	Brown, with rings.
Myrothecium leaf spot	Peperomia, gloxinia dieffenbachia, others	Fruiting bodies easily seen, cottony white to coal black. Can also cause a crown rot.
Ramularia leaf spot	Primula	Common on outdoor-grown plants with overhead irrigation.
Fairy ring spot (*Cladosporium*)	Carnation, cissus	A dark, powdery spotting of leaves, often ringed or targeted. Can be severe on carnations.
Brown leaf spot (*Coniothyrium*)	Yucca	Small, target-ringed spotting, more severe on lower leaves.
Leaf spot (*Drechslera* and *Exerohilum*)	Palm	Small, brown spots.
Stem canker (*Phomopsis*)	Ficus	Occurs on weakened trees.
Curvularia leaf spot	Gladiolus, others	A warm-weather disease.

Generally, the leaf blights and spots are first noted on lower foliage or foliage within the canopy (fig. 7.1). Plants in the center of a bench or bed may become infected more readily.

Most of these diseases are caused by fungi that produce abundant conidia (spores). Therefore, their specific diagnosis usually depends upon finding the conidial-forming structures. Sometimes they are produced in great number, giving a fuzzy appearance to infected tissue. Downy mildew of snapdragon would be a good example.

Sometimes spores are produced in tiny saclike structures (pycnidia) or on pads of thickened fungal tissue (acervuli) at or just under the plant tissue surface. In these cases, you do not usually see the spores but see only the sacs or pads of fungus tissue, which are often very dark and may occur in rings. Some of these pathogens do not produce visible fungal structures or spores on infected plants. Naturally, this makes it harder to diagnose them. In such cases, you will find that prior knowledge of the disease or the help of a plant clinic will be useful.

Many of the pathogens produce rather characteristic spots or lesions. *Alternaria*, for instance, commonly produces a targeted, or bull's-eye, spot of concentric rings of light tan color. *Cercospora* produces spots with a red border on many hosts. Some of these pathogens cause a characteristic host reaction, such as the rapid defoliation that occurs on roses shortly after a downy mildew epidemic or black spot infestation begins.

Fig. 7.1. *Alternaria* blight is starting on the lower leaves of these zinnia plants.

Epidemiology

There are specifically unique means of spread and conditions for development for many of these diseases, and there are also important general epidemiological considerations. As with so many diseases of ornamentals, the most common long-distance way these fungal pathogens spread is with diseased (but often symptomless) plant material or on crop debris. Debris associated with poorly cleaned lots of seed can often contain spores, many of which have thickened, tough cell walls that adapt them to transfer with dried, dormant seed.

There are many means of local pathogen spread. Splashing water from plant to plant is the most common local spreading mechanism. Sometimes spores can be spread in the air or on the bodies of insects. Handling of diseased plants can also spread the pathogens about. Tiny bits of infected plant tissue can be carried on hands or tools to nearby plants.

Water on the surface of plant tissue is necessary for spores of these pathogens to germinate and for the fungal strands to infect. Usually, the water must be present for several hours. Temperature requirements for the different pathogens vary. Most are warm-weather pathogens, preferring damp night temperatures higher than 75F (24C) and correspondingly hot and humid daytime weather.

Wounds are often necessary for infection of many of the pathogens in this group. Nutrients, primarily carbohydrates, are formed in the plant sap associated with these wounds. The pathogens respond to these nutrients. Many different kinds of wounds can serve as "infection courts." Tiny leaf wounds made as plants are handled or as they are sprayed or watered, pruning wounds, and insect-feeding and egg-laying wounds are all possible infection courts. Sometimes, though, the pathogens are limited to aging flower or leaf tissue. As such, they are noticeable but rarely become serious.

Management

Most of these diseases respond well to integrated control procedures carried out routinely or when the diseases are first noticed. In many cases, it is not necessary to use fungicides. The control procedures are similar to those discussed in other chapters.

Sanitation

At the end of a cropping cycle, clean up as much crop debris as you can (fig. 7.2). Sanitize benches and walkways with a quaternary ammonium chloride sanitizer to destroy pathogen spores or tissue in tiny bits of crop debris. For bed-grown plants, till the remaining residue into the bed so that it can degrade. This will destroy most of the spores of these pathogens. Steaming or fumigating the bed prior to reuse will kill the pathogens as well.

Inspect incoming plant material carefully. Discard plants or plant portions that show any signs of these diseases. The importance of this procedure must be emphasized, for it is often

Fig. 7.2. Crop debris must be cleaned up after each crop.

skipped in the rush to get a new crop potted or bedded out. Remember, incoming material is the most common way these diseases gain entry to your production area.

Space plants adequately so that air can freely move over flowers and foliage. This is the most effective way to keep plant surfaces dry or to quickly dry them out after a dew period, overhead watering, or rain. If possible, do not overhead-irrigate crops. This is especially important if disease has been noted in the crop or if there is a history of disease in that location. If you must water by wetting the plant leaves and flowers, do so early in the day. If plants are wet in the evening, they will almost certainly remain wet all night. Watch out for and eliminate drips onto plants under cover. Condensation drips from the inside surface of double-layered plastic coverings can be especially conducive to the development of many of these diseases.

Chemical management

Although sometimes serious, most of these diseases are not considered common. Thus, it is difficult to find fungicides specifically registered for their control (table 7.2 lists some available choices). Thiophanate-methyl and mancozeb products are the most useful because of their rather extensive labeling.

Begin thorough-coverage sprays at the first sign of disease to protect the plant from new infections. The sprays will not eradicate old lesions but may greatly decrease sporulation within them. Use high-volume, wet-down sprays or targeted coldfogger sprays. With wettable powders or dry flowable formulations, add a spreader-sticker to increase the protective ability of the fungicides.

Several fungicide applications, at intervals suggested on the label, are needed in most cases. Sometimes interval ranges (such as seven to 14 days) are given. These are intended to guide you when crops are outdoors or subjected to watering that will wash off the protective fungicide residue. Obviously, where a lot of weathering has taken place or when plants are growing rapidly, use the shorter end of the interval range. Keep an eye on the visible residue. Watch that it does not become objectionable as far as plant sales are concerned.

Table 7.2   Some fungicides registered for control of miscellaneous fungal pathogens of ornamentals in the United States

Common name and (brand name)	Pathogen	Host
Thiophanate-methyl (Cleary's 3336, Domain, Systec 1998)	*Ovulinia*	Azalea, rhododendron
	Sclerotinia	Azalea, rhododendron
	Anthracnose	Ornamentals
	Cercospora	Ornamentals
	Entomosporium	Ornamentals
	Ramularia	Ornamentals
	Septoria	Ornamentals
	Phomopsis	Ornamentals
	Ascochyta	Ornamentals
	Didymellina	Iris
	Diplocarpon	Rose
	Others	
Mancozeb (Protect T/O, Dithane T/O, FORE)	*Alternaria*	See labels. Protect T/O labeled on more than 100 host plants.
	Anthracnose	
	Cercospora	
	Diplocarpon	
	Sclerotinia	
	Ascochyta	
	Leptosphaeria	
	Fusarium	
	Curvularia	
	Didymellina	
	Mystrosporium	
	Dactylaria	
	Sphaceloma	
	Cephalosporium	
	Phytophthora	
	Downy mildews	
	Many others	
Chlorothalonil (Daconil 2787, Thalonil)	*Ovulinia*	Azalea
	Alternaria	Carnation, statice
	Ascochyta	Chrysanthemum, leatherleaf fern
	Septoria	Chrysanthemum, hydrangea
	Curvularia	Gladiolus

Table 7.2   continued

Common name and (brand name)	Pathogen	Host
	Cercospora	Hydrangea, statice, leatherleaf fern
	Didymellina	Iris
	Diplocarpon	Rose
	Anthracnose	Statice
	Fusarium	Dracaena
	Cylindrocladium	Leatherleaf fern
	Bipolaris	Parlor palm
	Helmintho-sporium	Maranta
	Cephalosporium	Syngonium
	Dactylaria	Philodendron
Cupric hychloride (Kocide 101, 77WP)	*Alternaria*	Aralia, carnation
	Cercospora	Aralia, azalea, yucca
	Anthracnose	Begonia
	Septoria	Chrysanthemum, yucca
	Diplocarpon	Rose
Iprodione (Chipco 26019, 50 WP)	*Alternaria*	Eighty-seven plant types listed on the label for this pathogen.
	Fusarium	(See above)
	Helmintho-sporium	(See above)
	Drechslera	Iris
	Ascochyta	Chrysanthemum
Quintozene (Terraclor 75WP)	*Ovulinia*	Azalea
	Sclerotinia	Camellia
Vinclozolin (Ornalin 50WP, 4F)	*Ciborinia*	Camellia
	Ovulinia	Azalea
	Sclerotinia	Camellia, snapdragon, zinnia, hyacinth, narcissus, scilla
	Etromatinia	Gladiolus
Triadimefon (Strike 25TOF)	*Cercospora*	Ageratum, marigold, phlox, rhododendron, zinnia
	Didymellina	Iris
	Cephalosporium	Nephthytis

Note: This list is not complete because the pathogens involved are so numerous. See chapter 19 for more information.

Bacterial Diseases

*A*grobacterium, *Corynebacterium, Erwinia, Pseudomonas,* and *Xanthomonas* are the most common kinds of bacteria that cause diseases of greenhouse crops. Some of these bacteria can live for several months or even years in soil or water. They can live on or in roots, leaves, stems, and flowers of host as well as nonhost plants. They become pathogenic when environmental factors are favorable for infection and disease development.

Types of bacterial diseases and diagnoses

Some plant-pathogenic bacteria attack only one or a few plant species, while others attack numerous kinds of plants, often in different families. The specific bacterium involved in a given disease cannot usually be determined solely on the basis of symptoms. Similar symptoms can be caused by more than one type of bacterium. Conversely, some bacteria can cause many different types of symptoms. The environment plays an important role in the symptoms caused by most bacteria.

Erwinia chrysanthemi, the single most destructive bacterium affecting tropical foliage plants, is a potentially destructive pathogen of many floriculture crops, including chrysanthemum, carnation, poinsettia, begonia, and African violet. It causes many kinds of symptoms, including soft rots, root rots, leaf spots, blights, and wilts.

Erwinia carotovora causes soft rot symptoms similar to those caused by *E. chrysanthemi*. In fact, many plant pathologists consider *E. chrysanthemi* a strain of *E. carotovora*. Beginning symptoms appear as areas of water-soaked plant tissue that later develop into a mushy rot. Humid and warm, but not hot, conditions favor the disease. *E. carotovora* causes soft rots of stems and basal crown tissue on many crops, including poinsettia, dahlia, cyclamen, calla lily, and many foliage plants. These rots are usually characterized by foul odors.

Pseudomonas solanacearum, the cause of southern bacterial wilt, can also cause serious problems on plants in more than 61 different families. Symptoms generally include wilting of lower leaves, followed by yellowing and, later, death of affected leaves. The leaf yellowing progresses up the plant as the infection develops. Often the affected leaves will be only on one side of the plant. Internal symptoms of infected plants usually include a brown discoloration of the vascular system.

Pseudomonas cichorii causes brownish black lesions on the leaves of pothos, philodendron, and several other foliage plants. It also causes a leaf spot and blight on chrysanthemum and geranium. Additional species of Pseudomonads that infect herbaceous ornamentals do not normally have broad host ranges, sometimes attacking only one species. The symptoms they cause range from leaf spots to blights, but leaf spots are the most common.

Several variants of *Xanthomonas campestris* cause leaf spots on many important flower and foliage crops, including begonia, geranium, poinsettia, zinnia, dieffenbachia, philodendron, and aglaonema. Symptoms range from small, well-defined spots to leaf death when infections are numerous. Yellowing of the leaf margins is often seen on some plant species. Symptoms can vary, depending on the age of the leaf tissue infected.

In addition to causing leaf spots, some strains of *Xanthomonas campestris* can cause stem rots, such as those attacking geranium, anthurium, and begonia. Symptoms include the wilting and eventual death of infected leaves. Infected stems later turn dark green and collapse, killing the plants. Such systemic Xanthomonads can go undetected in plants and cuttings during periods of cool temperatures. Propagation and movement of these infected cuttings can result in tremendous losses under the warm, wet conditions that occur later on in the season. Xanthomonads cause some of the most feared plant diseases in the greenhouse industry.

Fig. 8.1. Crown gall on roses.

Agrobacterium tumefaciens is the cause of crown gall of several floricultural crops, including chrysanthemum, dahlia, and rose (fig. 8.1). This pathogen also affects numerous woody and herbaceous perennials. Tumors or galls of varying sizes occur on roots and shoots of infected plants. Plants exhibiting these symptoms are unsalable. In addition, they usually decline in vigor as they grow older.

Only a few species of *Corynebacterium* are pathogenic on herbaceous ornamentals. *Corynebacterium fascians* causes a fasciation (shoot proliferation) from the crown or lower stem of geranium, and *C. poinsettiae* causes a canker or blight on poinsettia. Symptoms on poinsettia include spots or blotches on leaves and longitudinal, water-soaked streaks on stems. Both of these diseases are rare but can cause serious losses.

General pathogen cycles

Bacteria are single-celled organisms. They can reproduce by simple cell division every 20 minutes, depending on the temperature and the availability of water and nutrients. The two daughter cells are identical. Bacterial populations on, in, or near plants can reach very high numbers within a short time, which is what causes the damage to host plants.

Environmental factors influence the reproduction and death of bacterial populations. As the temperature, food supply, moisture availability, pH, gas supplies, and the presence of toxic materials and antagonistic organisms change, many bacterial cells die. Those individuals that survive sometimes become adapted to the new environment (through mutation) or were already better adapted and are thus selected out. In either case, new types proliferate even in changing environments, if the changes are not too extreme. This makes the management of bacterial diseases very difficult.

Under extremely adverse conditions, surviving cells often enter a state of reduced metabolism or dormancy until conditions once again become favorable for growth and reproduction. In such states they are undetectable on or in plants, pots, growing media, or water. Bacterial cells undetected within plants create serious problems with long-distance spread in ornamentals.

Local spread of bacterial pathogens is through splashing water, on hands or cutting tools, or in crop debris. Plant infection generally comes through tiny wounds. It may be weeks before an infected plant shows symptoms.

Epidemiology

Survival

Plant-pathogenic bacteria do not have the capability of producing spores or other overwintering structures, as do fungi. Pathogenic bacteria are considered to be poor competitors with other organisms, especially in the soil.

Surviving bacterial cells are likely very different in both morphological and physiological characteristics from actively metabolizing cells. Cells that survive often do so in a state of reduced metabolism. They are generally more resistant to antagonistic factors. Cells gradually enter this state due to adverse environmental conditions, the lack of available nutrients, or the lack of a susceptible host. They survive best when they are in aggregates and when in a semidehydrated state in association with moist plant debris.

Bacteria can stick to plant parts, especially leaves, and are not easily removed, even by repeated washings with water. However, most bacteria on exposed plant surfaces die, probably due to desiccation, exposure to sunlight, lack of sufficient nutrients, production of antagonistic substances by other organisms, and competition from other organisms.

Bacteria are found within leaves as well as on the leaf surface. Surviving bacteria are most likely found in aggregates in protected positions, such as deep depressions between epidermal cells on the undersides of leaves as there is less exposure to sunlight there. Trichomes (leaf hairs) can be survival sites for bacteria. Hydathodes and other natural openings may also serve as protective positions.

In greenhouse production areas, with their controlled environmental conditions, survival pressures for plant-pathogenic bacteria are not normally as severe as in the natural environment. Many pathogenic bacteria can survive in plant debris for extended periods in the warm, humid environment. Such natural environmental stresses as drying and extreme temperatures reduce populations of many bacterial species outdoors.

Some plant-pathogenic bacteria can survive as saprophytes by growing on the leaves of host as well as nonhost plants as harmless, surface-dwelling microbes. Later, when environmental conditions permit, they will rapidly multiply, infest the host plant, and cause disease.

Several *Pseudomonas*, *Xanthomonas*, and *Erwinia* species are able to survive in association with nonhost plants for long periods of time. As environmental conditions permit bacterial growth, the surviving bacteria can resume metabolic activities. Rapid increases of bacterial inoculum on nonhost leaf surfaces may occur during this time, but that has not been demonstrated yet. The leaves themselves might be acting as sources of inoculum, since bacteria spread from leaf to leaf and plant to plant by splashing water, on hands and tools, and probably by insects.

It is not uncommon for bacterial pathogens to survive in association with seeds, either within the seed or as surface contaminants. Drying causes the death of many bacteria residing on the external parts of seeds. Infested seed moved around the world is an excellent source of pathogen dispersal, so many seed crops are grown in areas where rainfall is minimal during harvest, helping ensure freedom from bacteria contamination.

Spread

It is easy to see how a previously noninfested greenhouse site could be contaminated with symptomless plants harboring populations of pathogenic bacteria either in the plants, on the plants, or in the potting media. For this reason, cuttings and plants subject to serious bacterial diseases should be obtained only from greenhouses where strict disease management strategies are practiced. Potting media should never contain crop debris unless it has been thoroughly sanitized.

Humans are perhaps the most important agents in the dispersal of plant-pathogenic bacteria. Simply touching an infested plant, then touching a noninfested plant, may result in the transmission of a pathogen. Bacteria often are transmitted from plant to plant on a knife during propagation (fig. 8.2) and pruning procedures. Bacteria surviving in plant debris and in the soil are often carried from one area to another on shoes and machinery.

Water is an excellent dispersal agent of bacteria. Many producers use overhead irrigation to water plants. In addition, pesticide application may serve as an excellent source of dispersal. Dipping cuttings or plant divisions in fungicide or rooting hormone is a good way to spread

Fig. 8.2. Taking cuttings can spread diseases if the stock plant is infected with a systemic pathogen.

bacteria. When bacteria are present on a cutting, they can be released into the dip, where they can later be introduced onto other plants.

Insects may also play an important role in dispersal and survival of pathogenic bacteria. This is probably of minor importance in properly maintained production areas. Greenhouse whiteflies have been shown, however, to carry the geranium wilt pathogen to healthy plants.

Infection and development

A film of moisture is usually required for plant-pathogenic bacterial infection. Moisture also acts as an important vehicle for moving bacteria from a survival position to a natural opening or a wounded area. Moisture can have infection-promoting effects on the pathogen, the host, or both. When moisture is available, plant tissues may be more succulent, thus providing a more conducive environment for bacterial multiplication after they have obtained entrance into the intercellular spaces of the plant. It is therefore essential that producers of ornamentals prevent moisture from remaining on leaf surfaces for extended periods.

In general, low temperatures do not foster bacterial disease development. As temperatures increase, the bacteria increase their metabolic activities and cause disease if other factors are favorable. Disease development is usually most rapid as the temperature increases, especially as it rises to levels that are stressful to the host. There is an upper limit for bacterial disease development, in many cases. For instance, *Erwinia carotovora* is usually most severe up to 70F (21C), becoming less severe when temperatures go higher.

Nitrogen can influence bacterial disease development of ornamentals, but in different manners, depending on the disease. Several foliage plants are more tolerant of bacterial pathogens when fertilized with excess amounts of nitrogen. However, in some situations, more disease develops on plants fertilized with more nitrogen.

When all conditions are favorable, both saprophytic and pathogenic bacteria can invade the intercellular spaces of a plant. Entrance occurs either through wounds or natural openings. Once inside the plant, the pathogenic bacteria generally multiply intercellularly. However, in some vascular diseases, they can multiply in the xylem. Bacteria release biologically active substances that kill and disorganize tissues as they move throughout the plant tissue. As a result, cell substances are released into the intercellular spaces. Bacteria use these nutrients for growth and reproduction processes.

The different effects that bacteria have upon plants are brought on by the substances released from the host cells. In many cases, very limited bacterial reproduction occurs within the plants. Systemic spread of the bacteria can still take place, however, resulting in the symptomless but infected situation we spoke of earlier.

Management

Control of bacterial diseases of ornamentals involves cultural and chemical prevention. Good sanitation practices, such as destroying diseased plants and keeping production areas clean, are essential since many bacterial pathogens can survive on both host and nonhost plants near production areas. Pathogens also may survive in potting media and soil and be introduced from other areas on shoes, shovels, hands, etc.

Cultural practices

Good cultural practices include proper fertilization, spacing plants to provide good air movement and to prevent water splash, and watering to avoid wetting foliage. Plants stressed from improper fertilization, poor watering practices, or inadequate lighting are usually more susceptible to disease. Good watering practices are essential in order to reduce the severity and spread of bacterial diseases. Avoid plant wounding, as wounds enhance, and are often required for initiation of, disease development.

Pathogen-free propagative materials are essential, as several bacterial pathogens can be introduced to a crop or a greenhouse on seeds and cuttings. Seeds produced in dry climates without overhead irrigation are more likely to be free of bacterial pathogens. Bacterial pathogens may sometimes be eliminated from seeds by soaking them in hot water at 122F (50C), sodium hypochlorite, or hydrochloric acid. The importance of obtaining pathogen-free seed or cuttings cannot be overemphasized as a bacterial disease management tool.

Chemicals

Streptomycin, oxytetracycline, and copper sprays have been used to control or reduce the severity of numerous ornamental bacterial diseases. Exercise caution, as these sprays may cause phytotoxicity on various plants under certain environmental conditions. Mancozeb mixed with fixed coppers is more effective in controlling certain bacterial diseases than fixed coppers alone. The mancozeb-copper combinations are most effective when mixed 90 minutes prior to application.

A newer, chelated copper fungicide-bactericide (Phyton-27) has recently become popular for use in the greenhouse. Labeled for a number of fungal and bacterial diseases, it is reasonably safe on plants in flower. It is labeled for use in low-volume applicators.

Numerous other studies on bactericides have been made, but, unfortunately, growers still do not have the effective chemical control of bacterial diseases as they have with many fungal diseases.

What is a cultured cutting?

Many bacterial, viral, and fungal wilt pathogens are transported into crops by infested cuttings. A cutting may look normal and healthy but contain tiny amounts of pathogen. Later on, the pathogen develops, and disease spreads throughout the crop.

One of the best ways a grower can reduce the likelihood of getting infested cutting material is to purchase *cultured*, or *culture-indexed*, cuttings. Cultured cuttings are the end point in an elaborate program to develop and produce pathogen-free vegetative propagative material. These programs, begun in the late 1940s, have preserved the quality and healthiness of many of our most important flower and foliage crops.

Here's how the programs work. Two or three years before final sale of cuttings of a particular culture-indexed cultivar, a plant is selected that is believed to be pathogen-free. The plant may have come from a stem tip or meristem taken from a heat-treated parent plant.

Cuttings taken from this plant are brought directly to a laboratory. In the lab, the basal end of the cutting is removed and subjected to various culturing tests for bacteria and fungi and to various indexing tests for viruses. This is where the term *culture-indexing* comes from.

The top portion of each cutting is carefully rooted and potted in an isolation greenhouse. If all the tests come out negative, the cutting is grown on to form a *nucleus block* to yield more cuttings. These, too, may be run through the culture-indexing procedure to check for misses the first time around. Sometimes a third round of culture-indexing is done.

Cuttings that survive all this become the *mother block* of the mother block system of plant increase. Mother block plants are grown under strict sanitary conditions, usually in screened greenhouses with limited access.

Cuttings taken from these mother block plants go into *increase blocks*. Increase blocks are kept as disease-free as possible, given the increased area required for production. Clean white coats may be put on before anyone goes into these greenhouses.

From increase blocks, large *production blocks* are formed. Sanitation is an important element of the culture of these blocks, but it must be kept in balance with practical growing methods. For instance, shoe soles and hands are usually disinfected before entering such greenhouses, although many workers with unsterilized shoes may enter these facilities from time to time. If knives are used for harvesting cuttings, alcohol is used to treat them between each use or between plants.

A grower who purchases "cultured" material gets plants from these production blocks. Notice that production block cuttings are not directly cultured. They are at least four generations from culturing. Also, production blocks may be in different greenhouses—even in different countries—from the original nucleus material. The material may have been pathogen-free to start with, but it could become infested again by the time you get it.

You can never assume that such plant material has any special resistance to infections. If the material is placed into a disease-ridden greenhouse, the plants will get infected as easily as any others.

Also note that indexing programs are not aimed at ridding the plants of all disease pathogens. They are useful for systemic pathogens that can be in a plant but not be detectible, such as bacteria, viruses and vascular fungal pathogens. Root rots, *Botrytis*, rusts, powdery mildews, or other leaf spots would not be effectively eliminated from plants by the indexing program directly. The sanitary growing conditions of production blocks would, however, tend to keep these diseases in check.

There is nothing really wrong with the culture-indexing system. It is a proven, successful system to rid plants of systemic pathogens. As long as growers buy cultured material from the company who administers the original steps in the program (or from a licensed propagator), there is a great likelihood of pathogen-free material. These companies have their reputations to uphold. They take great care to protect material properly while it is being increased for eventual sale from production blocks.

Wilt Diseases

Wilts are recognized easily in most plants. Common symptoms of wilt diseases include drooping or wilting of a portion of leaf, an entire leaf, a portion of a plant, or an entire plant. The wilt is often accompanied by leaf vein clearing, general yellowing, vascular browning, and stunting of the plant. Wilt symptoms may occur suddenly or develop over a period of time.

Losses due to wilt diseases vary greatly. Slight wilting of one or several leaves on mature plants close to sale or harvest may not result in extensive losses. Severe wilting of young plants, however, often results in plant death.

Noninfectious wilt diseases

Wilting may be due to noninfectious, environmental causes. Soil or a potting mix may dry to the point where roots are temporarily or permanently damaged. If soil moisture stress is not too great, plants will recover from wilting when moisture is again provided. After a period of such intermittent moisture stress, however, the plant may not recover.

Prolonged soil saturation or waterlogging may result in an oxygen shortage in roots, and plants will wilt. Recovery occurs when soil drains and is aerated, if the low-oxygen stress has not been present for too long. If soil is waterlogged for a very prolonged period, roots may die. Also, infectious root rotting may occur after waterlogging. In either case, plants will be permanently damaged. Infectious root rot diseases can thus be a cause of wilting. They are not normally thought of as wilt disease pathogens, however, because they do not invade a plant's upper vascular system.

Plants also may wilt in response to physical root injuries. Chewing insects, burrowing animals, and nematodes may feed on roots, reducing root volume or root function and causing wilting. Physical evidence of root damage by these pests is usually evident upon laboratory examination.

High soluble salts in soil or potting media can damage roots and result in wilting. This type of wilting will be seen under high light and high temperature situations, when plant transpiration rates are high.

Infectious wilt diseases

Bacterial and fungal wilt pathogens are so designated because the infection symptoms result from a pathogen's presence and activities in the xylem, or water-conducting tissues, of the plant. Vascular wilt diseases may be caused by several species of fungi and bacteria.

The fungi known to cause vascular wilts of ornamentals include *Ceratocystis* spp., *Fusarium oxysporum*, *Verticillium albo-atrum*, *V. dahliae*, and *Phialophora cinerescens*. Different host plants are attacked by special forms, or races, of *F. oxysporum*. *F. oxysporum f. sp. chrysanthemi* attacks chrysanthemums, and *F. oxysporum f. sp. dianthi* attacks carnations.

V. albo-atrum and *V. dahliae* can attack a wide range of ornamental plants, while *Phialophora cinerescens* is primarily a problem on carnations. *Ceratocystis* spp. cause vascular wilts of shade trees, notably elm (Dutch elm disease) and oak (oak wilt).

The bacteria causing vascular wilts in ornamentals include *Erwinia chrysanthemi*, *E. caratovora subsp. caratovora*, *Pseudomonas caryophylli*, *Pseudomonas solanacearum*, and various pathovars of *Xanthomonas campestris*.

Aside from *Ceratocystis*, fungal wilt pathogens are soilborne. They primarily attack through plant roots. Chemical substances exuded from root hairs, root tips, or root wounds serve as initial nutrients for potential pathogens. *Ceratocystis* spp. are transported from tree to tree by root grafts or on insects' bodies.

Bacterial pathogens require a wound or natural opening to invade plant organs. Bacterial wilt pathogens usually invade leaf tissues. Both bacterial and fungal wilt pathogens may be carried in stem tissues of cuttings used for propagation. They may often be present in such cuttings without showing symptoms.

Diagnosis

Generally, wilt symptoms are the result of invasion of the xylem of the host plants by pathogenic organisms. In the process of this invasion, the fungi or bacteria interfere with the translocation of water and nutrients by clogging water-conducting vessels. Fungi that cause wilts remain almost entirely in the vascular tissues until plant death. Bacteria that cause wilts often spread into other leaf or stem tissues, causing a general leaf blighting or stem rotting and cankering before the plants die. Xylem vessels may be blocked by the physical presence of the pathogen, by gummy exudate of the pathogens, or as a result of pathogens rupturing plant cells. Toxins secreted by some wilt-inducing fungi, particularly *Fusarium* spp., also may be involved in symptom development.

Basically, vascular wilt path-ogens cause wilting, a nonspecific symptom that does not help us determine which pathogen is involved (fig. 9.1). Indeed, it does not even show that an infectious disease is present. The specific plant parts affected and the pattern of wilt progression may point to the specific pathogen present. The host plant involved, due to known susceptiblility, may also indicate the presence of one pathogen over another.

Fig. 9.1. Nonspecific wilting caused by *Fusarium* wilt of cyclamen.

Initial symptoms of a wilt disease are a yellowing of a leaf portion or perhaps several leaves on one side of a plant. The yellowing can occur on older or younger leaves, depending on the pathogen involved. Leaf margins may wilt a few days before entire leaves. Eventually, branches and entire plants will yellow and wilt in severe cases.

In *Verticillium* wilt and *Fusarium* wilt, the early wilting may involve only half a leaf or one side of a plant. For most wilts caused by these fungi, the symptoms begin first on older leaves and progress up the stem. Defoliation and dieback of branches and branch tips may also occur in wilts caused by these fungi. Infected plants can be severely stunted.

Examining vascular tissue can help further diagnose the problem. A brown or reddish brown discoloration of the water-conducting vascular tissues is often evident in plants attacked by *Verticillium* or *Fusarium* (fig. 9.2). This discoloration is the most reliable, specific field symptom of a wilt pathogen infection. When a woody stem or branch is examined in cross section, an incomplete to complete brown ring can be seen at times.

In the case of bacterial blight and wilt caused by pathovars of

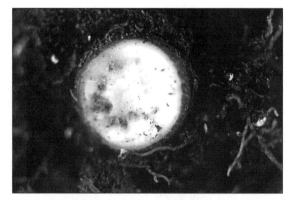

Fig. 9.2. The darkened vascular elements of this cyclamen corm are infected by *Fusarium* fungus.

Xanthomonas campestris, symptoms usually begin on individual leaves. Leaf margins wilt (fig. 9.3). Entire leaves yellow and wilt as the infection spreads to leaf petioles. When bacteria invade the water-conducting tissues of the stems, stem tissue will turn brown to black. Externally, stems appear gray and dull, eventually rotting in cankered areas. Roots can be blackened by bacterial blight but not decayed. Symptoms of bacterial blight may proceed up or down a stem, depending on where the initial infection occurred. Infection by the southern bacterial wilt organism, *P. solanacearum*, normally occurs through roots. Roots and then stems decay, turning from brown to black. In the case of *Erwinia* slow wilt of carnation, wilting symptoms develop over several months before a plant is killed. Symptom development in other *Erwinia* wilts may be much more rapid.

Fig. 9.3. Geranium with bacterial wilt.

Cuttings may be infected by a wilt pathogen but usually fail to express any recognizable symptoms during propagation. However, this is not always true. Infected cuttings may sometimes fail to root and may decay from the base upward. Cuttings may root slowly or poorly and develop typical wilt symptoms prior to transplanting.

Pathogen survival and spread

Most vascular wilt pathogens can readily survive in soil or potting mixes. Generally, the bacterial pathogens survive shorter periods (one to six months) than do *Fusarium* and *Verticillium* spp., which can survive several years. *Ceratocystis* spp. survive as mycelia in dead wood for varying periods of time, depending on the host and disease.

In most cases, the pathogens, especially the bacteria, survive in plant debris. The length of survival is dependent on the amount of the pathogen present in the tissue and the rate of decay of the plant material. *Fusarium* and *Verticillium* spp. survive in soil or plant debris as resting structures called chlamydospores (*Fusarium*) or microsclerotia (*Verticillium*). They have thickened outer cell walls and are resistant to weathering and to attack by other soil-dwelling organisms. The resting structures usually form in plant tissue shortly after the host tissue dies and begins to dry up.

The primary dispersal of fungal wilt pathogens occurs when mycelia, spores, and so on are carried by water movement through soil, splashing of soil; by physical movement of soil in pots, in flats, or on equipment; in dust; and in or on cuttings. As mentioned earlier, *Ceratocystis* is spread by root grafts or by contaminated insects.

Water movement, specifically splashing water from one plant to another during irrigation, is of prime importance in the spread of bacterial wilt pathogens. Bacteria may be spread by physical contact between leaves upon which a water film is present. In the case of bacterial blight of geraniums, the pathogen can also be spread by insects, especially whiteflies.

Infested cutting knives are also an extremely important way of spreading wilt pathogens. Although an infected stock plant may be symptomless, a cut made through an infected stem is sufficient to leave particles of wilt fungi or bacteria on the blade surface. If the knife blade is not disinfected between cuts, an entire batch of cuttings may be contaminated. The importance of infected cuttings in the spread of wilt pathogens cannot be overemphasized. Wilt diseases can be spread throughout the world in this manner.

Infected cuttings can lead to cutting bed contamination. If infected cuttings are not removed before they yellow and die, the cutting bed media may become infested with the wilt pathogens, and serious wilt epidemics may result. This can lead to the spread of pathogens into batches of healthy cuttings put into the beds later on.

Factors favoring wilt disease development

Generally, plants growing under optimum cultural conditions will be less susceptible to vascular wilt pathogens. Plants may be predisposed to wilt disease by stressful environments, such as high or low air or soil temperatures, lack of water, improper mineral nutrition or pH, and physical injury.

Generally, high air and soil temperatures and high relative humidity promote the development of bacterial wilt diseases. Symptom development of bacterial blight on geranium is generally enhanced between 70 and 86F (21 and 30C) but is largely suppressed at 50 to 60F (10 to 15C) or at 89 to 100F (32 to 38C). Symptom development for bacterial blight of chrysanthemum can be slowed or arrested by temperatures lower than 80F (27C) with less than 80 percent relative humidity. Southern bacterial wilt derives its name from the prevalence of high soil temperatures and high soil moisture in the southern United States, both of which favor development of *Pseudomonas solanacearum*.

Development of *Fusarium* wilt diseases is also affected by temperature. This may relate to host stress more than pathogen response. Development of *Fusarium* wilt of carnation is fostered by soil and air temperatures greater than 70F (21C). The optimum temperature for *Fusarium* wilt of chrysanthemum is somewhat higher (80 to 90F, 27 to 32C). Chrysanthemums prefer warmer temperatures than carnations; thus, their heat stress thresholds are higher. Although wilting symptoms fail to develop at lower temperatures, infected plants may still be stunted.

Mineral nutrition can affect the rate of wilt disease development. Nutrition below or above the optimum for plant growth will usually enhance disease development. Under conditions of high nitrogen, symptoms of bacterial blight of geranium develop more rapidly than under low nitrogen.

The type of nitrogen fertilizer may also be important. Symptoms of *Fusarium* wilt of chrysanthemum are less severe with nitrate nitrogen fertilization than with half-ammonium, half-nitrate nitrogen fertilization. The disease's symptom severity also decreases with increased soil pH.

Management of wilt diseases

Sanitation

The most important management strategy for vascular wilt diseases of ornamentals is the use of pathogen-free seeds or cuttings. Seed certified as disease-free will minimize the introduction of a wilt-causing organism into a seed bed or field. Since a stock plant may be infected but symptomless at the time cuttings are taken, propagation stock should be from culture-indexed material.

Strict sanitation procedures in the greenhouse will further reduce the possibility of wilt diseases infesting a crop. For instance, avoid dipping cuttings in liquid hormone or fungicide suspensions since this could spread wilt pathogens among the cuttings. Destroy any old and unhealthy plants. Wash benches, pots, and equipment to remove contaminated soil and then rinse them with a Q-salt disinfectant. Regularly wash and sanitize cultivation equipment and other tools. Keep ends of water hoses off the floor.

When cuttings are made, break them out or make cuttings with a knife blade sterilized by dipping in 70 percent ethyl alcohol prior to each cut. Sterilize the blade between each stock plant if it is not practical to dip the blade between each cut.

Soil treatment

Soil and potting media can be treated with steam (fig. 9.4) or chemicals to eradicate wilt pathogens that might be infesting the media. Steam treatment, the best method, should be applied so that the coolest portion of the treated batch reaches a temperature of 180F (82C) for at least 30 minutes. The media should be moist but not wet for best results while steaming.

Fig. 9.4. Steam pasteurizing a planting bed can eradicate wilt pathogens infesting the media.

Pasteurization with mixtures of steam and air has been successfully used to sanitize growing media for many years. With this method, steam is mixed with just enough air to lower its temperature to 140F (60C). This temperature eradicates soil-borne pathogens but permits the survival of beneficial microorganisms. The resulting growing medium will better support plant growth and development.

If steam treatment is not possible, chemicals such as methyl bromide-chloropicrin may be used where still permitted. Unfortunately, methyl bromide use is being curtailed in the United States. Other available soil fumigants are not as effective at removing soilborne pathogens. With any fumigation method, allow sufficient time for soil to air out prior to use. The effectiveness of any sort of chemical disinfestation is questionable for eradicating *Verticillium* spp.

Cultural practices

Follow good horticultural practices to keep crop plants vigorous. Following proper fertilization schedules will ensure good plant growth. Maintain proper soil or growing media pH with potted plants. Irrigation should provide an even supply of sufficient water. Splashing during watering should be avoided to prevent dispersal of possible pathogens among plants.

Chemical management

Management of vascular wilts with pesticides has generally not been effective. Vascular wilts of some container-grown crops induced by some fungi can be partially managed with drenches of systemic fungicides, such as thiophanate-methyl (Cleary's 3336, Domain, Systec 1998, Fungo) or iprodione (Chipco 26019). These fungicides are taken into a plant and can act on the pathogen in the vascular system to suppress symptom development. Recent research with chelated, systemic copper bactericides (Phyton-27) has shown some promise in managing bacterial wilt pathogens. However, copper-containing products are better used as protectants.

Chapter 10

Root- and Crown-Rotting Diseases

Root and crown rots are a constant threat to the profitability of a flower or foliage plant production operation. This is true for many reasons. There are many different fungi that can cause root and crown rots. Each of these pathogens has its own set of environmental needs. Thus, one or another can appear at any time during a crop's production cycle.

Root and crown rots can kill plants in the greenhouse or drastically shorten their usable life after sale. In this way, they directly contribute to the amount of harvested crop. Most importantly, however, root and crown rots debilitate a crop. They can destroy a crop's uniformity and nutritional balance. They can subvert a grower's attempt to schedule a crop for sale on a certain date.

Root rot is a general term to describe a general or localized rotted condition of roots, whether the cause is infectious, noninfectious, or the result of natural aging. Root rot begins when cortical cells become non-functional or are killed. As cell death proceeds, the root takes on a rotten appearance (brown to black discoloration), and the outer cells readily slough off the vascular cylinder. Root proliferation is greatly reduced because no new roots are generated from dead root tips. In some cases, the root-rotting pathogens will continue to invade crown and stem tissues, causing crown rots.

Root rot that occurs on young plants with relatively few roots will usually kill the plants. Many of these sorts of diseases are called damp-ing-off (fig. 10.1). When root rot occurs on more mature plants with many roots, the extent to which the pathogens affect the root system will determine how severe the symptoms will be on the above ground parts of the plant (that is, stunting, discol-oration, wilt, death). A significant amount of root rot can sometimes occur on a plant without obvious symptoms on the above ground

Fig. 10.1. Damping-off disease.

portion. When sudden environmental stress occurs on such a plant, how-ever, it may quickly die from the "latent" disease.

Root rot may be caused by noninfectious factors, such as flooding, drought, or freezing; excesses of heat, fertilizer, or salts; or by other toxic chemicals in the soil. In most, if not all, of these cases, secondary microorganisms colonize the damaged tissue. These microorganisms then can lead to a pathogenic root rot syndrome. These organisms are pathogens but are incapable of infecting plant tissue unless it has been severely disturbed. Management of these organisms centers on correcting the stress that led to the initial damage.

Causes of infectious root and crown rots

Root rot diseases, for the most part, are caused by soilborne fungal pathogens. The fungal genera most frequently involved in root and crown rot diseases of floral and foliage ornamentals are *Pythium, Rhizoctonia, Phytophthora, Thielaviopsis, Fusarium, Cylindrocladium, Phymatotrichum, Macrophomina, Ramularia, Sclerotium, Sclerotinia,* and *Myrothecium.* Some soilborne bacteria are causal agents of root rots but are known primarily as causal agents of other types of disease.

Diagnosis of infectious root and crown rots

Field diagnosis of root rots rests largely on correctly interpreting nonspecific symptoms. A plant will exhibit nutrient deficiency symptoms, reduced growth, wilt, or death as a result of the number of roots that are rotted. A plant with 10 percent of its roots rotted can probably maintain a healthy appearance. If conditions are favorable for continued pathogen development, the plant will soon have 20 to 30 percent or more of its roots rotted and will begin to exhibit above ground symptoms. Such plants respond to reduced root capacity by wilting during periods of peak transpirational loss, beginning to grow more slowly, developing foliar discoloration typical of nutrient deficiencies, defoliating, or dying. If the infection has progressed to the plant's crown, plant death quickly follows.

When root rot fungi injure or destroy roots, they alter total root function, not just water or nutrient uptake. Root infection affects plant growth and development by interfering with the plant's natural growth regulators, such as cytokinins and gibberellins. Cytokinins, produced in the root apex and moving through the xylem to the shoot, promote cell division, leaf expansion, stolon or shoot initiation, translocation of assimilates and inorganic phosphorus, and transpiration. They inhibit leaf senescence (lower leaf yellowing). Produced in root apices and translocated in the xylem, gibberellins promote stem elongation, flowering in some long-day plants, leaf expansion, abscission, and fruit growth.

When the root cortex is invaded and killed by root pathogens, the cells become brown, much as leaf or stem tissues brown in response to injury or infection. In some cases, fungal toxins may be responsible for the killing and discoloration of cortical cells. In other cases, it is simply the growth of the pathogen into the tissue that kills it. Fungal sporulation may occur in these lesions. Later on, lesions can coalesce to involve major portions of roots. The root cortex may become so completely rotted that it can readily be slipped off the

Fig. 10.2. *Pythium* root rot. Note how the outer root tissue has rotted away from the inner core tissue.

vascular cylinder, which remains as a stiff, threadlike core (fig. 10.2).

Unlike with some foliar pathogens, direct signs of the presence of root pathogens cannot readily be seen by the field diagnostician. It usually takes a microscope to view the resting spores, fruiting structures, or strands of mycelia in or on the infected root tissue. Sometimes strands of mycelia can be noted near the crown of seedlings damped off from *Pythium* or *Rhizoctonia*.

In most cases, a particular root-rotting pathogen will have to be confirmed in the laboratory, where microscopic examination or culturing of the symptomatic tissue will be done. Culturing, which takes seven to 10 days, involves placing a tiny piece of the tissue on a surface of a gelatinlike growth medium. If the suspected pathogen is present, it will usually grow out onto the surface of the growth medium, where it can be seen and identified.

Epidemiology

Because of the diversity of plant species and cultural situations, as well as pathogens, that may be involved, a single set of conditions that consistently affects all root rot disease is difficult to describe. However, there are some common denominators as to the source of the organisms in production systems, how they function in their parasitic or saprophytic phases, and how most of them survive.

Survival and spread

All the fungal root rot pathogens can exist in the growing medium either as mycelia or spores in or on the infected host tissue, or as resting structures (chlamydospores, oospores, resistant hyphal fragments, sclerotia) in the host debris or free in the soil. Most of these organisms are confined to the soil and are thus able to parasitize only roots or the lower crown of plants. Some can colonize the upper portions of plants. In such cases, mycelia or spores may grow or be blown, splashed, or otherwise carried to other areas or plants.

Most root rot pathogens exist in the soil, other growth media, containers, or propagative material in an inactive state. When they come into contact with a susceptible host plant, they become active (resting structures may "germinate") and infect the root. Eliminating the inoculum source or preventing this inoculum activity is the key to the control of most root rot diseases.

Most occurrences of root disease result from plants that are growing in infested soil. The fungus is already in position to contact host roots. The infested soil may have been used directly, mixed with some other noninfested growing media components, or come into contact with the growing media surface through some means of transfer (fig. 10.3).

Infested soil or potting mix may be dispersed by workers on tools, hands, or shoes, on containers, by wind (as dust), by moving water (rain or irrigation), or by animals. Tiny amounts of microscopic soil particles that contain propagules of root rot pathogens may be sufficient to initiate root infections. It is difficult to prevent the introduction of small particles of infested soil into growing areas. Soil can be dispersed by a watering hose contaminated by being

Fig. 10.3. Plants thrown onto this pile of growing media will contaminate it with pathogens, even if disease is not apparent in the discarded plants.

dropped onto infested soil on walkways or by containers that previously contained infected plants and weren't thoroughly disinfected.

Water is an effective carrier of root rot pathogens. Contaminated growing media in water can be splashed by rain or irrigation to nearby plants or containers. Puddles of standing water on a bench or plant bed can be a source of root-rotting pathogens. In many production areas, irrigation water comes from storage ponds that have collected runoff water from irrigation and precipitation. Runoff water can carry root rot pathogens. Storage ponds may harbor these fungi, especially in areas of the country where winters are mild.

The water mold pathogens (*Pythium* and *Phytophthora*) produce spores (zoospores) that can swim for short distances in water. These organisms are especially troublesome because they may be carried so readily in surface water or capillary water films on mats or in growing media. Water mold zoospores can pass out the drain holes of a container holding an infected plant, travel or be washed some distance on bed or bench surfaces, and be drawn up by capillarity into another container. They probably cannot survive a journey to a holding pond and back, though.

The plant material itself can harbor root rot pathogens and become a means of their dissemination. Seed transmission of root pathogens is possible but rare. Flowers or seed pods may touch the soil or become contaminated by dust or soil particles during harvesting.

Cuttings taken from stock plants may carry root pathogens as surface contaminants in growing media splashed up from below. This is especially true of cuttings taken from the lower portions of plants. Occasionally, cuttings may touch the soil or may be placed into contaminated containers for transport to the propagation beds. Placing cutting containers on bench surfaces or onto the ground or walkway is a common method of contaminating the cuttings. Inoculum on contaminated cuttings can be washed down onto new roots as they form in the rooting medium.

In cases where pathogens are able to cause stem or foliar infections as well as root infections, cuttings taken from infected stock plants could be infected already with the leaf or stem phase of the disease. When the infected leaf abscises, it becomes a substrate for the production of inoculum, which can wash down into the medium and infect newly formed roots.

Bulbs or corms may also carry root rot pathogens, especially if they were field-grown in infested soil. Lily bulbs, for example, are harvested from fields by machines that sever the roots below the bulb. Such injured roots may have been or may become infected with *Pythium, Fusarium,* or *Rhizoctonia,* and that infection may carry over with the bulb as it is potted up for greenhouse forcing. Some of those organisms are also capable of colonizing the surfaces of bulb scales, and are thus in position to initiate infections on roots as they form.

Infection and development

In the presence of susceptible host roots, propagules of the pathogen (either resting structures or spores) are stimulated to germinate. The germination process is a response to host root exudates that provide food for the pathogen.

Root rot pathogens invade the cortical root cells and cause dysfunction and death of each cell they enter. The invasion of cortical cells often progresses from the root surface via runner hyphae that grow along the roots' outer edges. The pathogens usually produce spores in or on the infected tissue shortly after infection. Spores produced on the root surface may be carried readily by moving water to other uninfected roots. This process may take hours, days, or weeks, depending on the environmental conditions, the pathogen, and the host's relative susceptibility.

Environmental factors that promote root diseases

Root rot diseases may often remain restricted, more or less, to the original infection site. As a result, there may be a low enough proportion of the root system involved that no top symptoms are visible. The host may be able to generate new roots at a rate comparable to the rate of root killing by the pathogen. If the new roots are capable of sustaining the plant, no top symptoms would be expressed. If environmental conditions remain generally favorable for the host, it may survive for an indefinite period.

If an infected plant has a change in environment, possibly as a result of sale or transplanting, pathogen development may be favored or host susceptibility may be increased. The result can be a badly diseased plant in a short time. Stress predisposition to root diseases is extremely difficult to document precisely. It is common to encounter situations in which disease rather suddenly appeared after some change in cultural practices or after plants were shipped to another geographical location. When root disease incidence suddenly increases, the environmental factors more frequently involved are changes in light levels, fertilizer levels, watering practices, and soil pH; increased salt levels; application of a pesticide or growth regulator; repotting to a different sized container; an air pollution episode; and insect infestation.

Each root rot pathogen has different temperature, pH, and moisture optima and ranges for disease development. Some trends that may be useful as generalizations include: low soil temperature usually reduces *Rhizoctonia* root rot; low soil moisture usually inhibits *Pythium* and *Phytophthora*; maintenance of soil pH below 5.5 generally reduces *Thielaviopsis* and *Pythium* root rots.

Such information is very useful for root rot control because the disease-suppressing conditions are usually consistent with those needed for good plant growth. This is, again, an example of holistic plant health management. Usually, healthy plants will be less susceptible to root rot infection than poorly nourished plants in a state of low vigor from a variety of stresses. (Some specific conditions relating to the development of many root rots of ornamentals are given in table 10.1.)

Management of root and crown rots

Susceptibility of a host is always a reflection of its vigor and its genetic characteristics. Many food and fiber crops have been developed for genetic resistance to root rots. However, this is generally not true for ornamental plants. Thus, holistic health management principles become even more important.

Sanitation

The best approach to controlling root and crown rot diseases is prevention. You must constantly be aware of the potential of the pathogens to get into soil or potting mixes, to contaminate planting stock and containers, and to be carried in by water. Although it is difficult to devote time and resources to prevent root rot diseases, it is still a good investment. Special

Table 10.1   Environmental stress-promoting conditions that predispose ornamentals to root and crown rot diseases

Pathogen	Stress-promoting condition
Fusarium	Wounds caused by insects or handling
	High ammonium
Pythium ultimum	Cool temperatures (<20C)
	Overwatering or poor drainage of media
	High soluble salts
Phytophthora parasitica	High temperatures (>25C)
	Overwatering and poor drainage
	Wounds at the crown of the plant
Pythium irregulare	High soluble salts
	Overwatering
Rhizoctonia	Alternating extremes of wetting and drying
	High temperatures
	Wounds at the crown of the plant
	High soluble salts
Thielaviopsis	High pH
	Temperature out of range for the crop (too high or too low)
	High ammonium

cultural practices, if followed routinely, will exclude most of the root rot pathogens from the production system. If those practices fail, then you must face the problem of dealing with an established pathogen.

Many, if not most, natural soils contain fungal pathogens capable of causing root rot. Because soils may contain root pathogens, and partly because of shipping costs and availability, most growers shifted to soil-less potting mixes some years ago. Growers sometimes assumed that the components in soilless mixes have been treated so they are pathogen-free. This would be true for components that are produced by a heat process, but it is not true for other natural ingredients, such as peat or noncomposted bark. It may be advisable to sanitize even soilless mixes prior to use.

Treating soil or potting mixes to control root rot pathogens can be done by heat, chemical fumigation, or drench. The method you chose will depend on economics, availability of steam, and the nature and location of the soil or mix to be treated. Outside ground beds generally are not easy to steam-treat, but they could be treated chemically.

With any method of growing medium treatment, if root pathogens such as *Pythium* and *Rhizoctonia* are not completely eliminated by the treatment, they may flourish in the relative biological void created and cause worse disease than if treatment had not been applied at all. Another hazard of the complete or overkill approach with either heat or chemicals is the ease with which subsequently introduced pathogens can become established. It makes good sense to eliminate the root pathogens but leave some organisms with potential buffering or antagonism to introduced pathogens.

Some of the composted bark mixes available today are specially pre-pared to retain beneficial organisms. For this reason most growers will not treat prepared potting mixes to rid them of root-rotting pathogens (fig. 10.4). Another reason that prepared potting mixes are not commonly treated is that they generally have aeration and mois-ture-holding properties that man-age plant stress well. Roots grow-ing vigorously in a good potting mix that is properly watered will rarely succumb to root rot, even if some contamination is present.

Fig. 10.4. Carelessly stored bags of potting mix can easily become contaminated with root-rotting pathogens.

Treatment of irrigation water known to carry, or suspected of carrying, root pathogens is possible and advisable if pond water from field runoff or return water is being used, especially in areas of the country with mild winters. Small volumes can be filtered or heated to remove pathogens; larger volumes can be treated by injection of chlorine gas into the irrigation line, by filtering through sand, by reverse osmosis, or by some other treatment.

If using chlorine, the chlorine must be in contact with the water for 30 minutes prior to its use. Also, you must determine the amount of chlorine to add by calculating the residual chlorine left in the water after the 30 minutes. Residual chlorine levels should be around 2.5 ppm.

Treatment of used containers is almost always necessary in order to exclude root pathogens from production areas (fig. 10.5). The small size of infective fungal propagules makes it apparent that containers cannot be cleaned thoroughly enough to remove residual soil or potting mix that may still harbor root pathogens.

There are many good disinfectants available for this task, most belonging to the tetra-ammonium chloride salt group (known as Q-salts or quad salts). Remember, many chemical disinfectants are readily inactivated by soil, either

Fig. 10.5. Once-used trays and pot spacers must be disinfected before being used again.

chemically or physically. Thus, dirty containers are difficult to sanitize effectively. Wet heat or steam treatment will ensure that the containers are pathogen-free, even if they had a good deal of residual soil on them.

Extend the principles and practices of sanitation to other details in production, such as tools, hoses, walks, and boots. Failure to remember the ways that pathogens can invade pathogen-free production systems could cancel out all of your earlier efforts to create pathogen-free production.

Exclusion of root pathogens from production areas also involves the planting stock. Seeds, cuttings, or bulbs may carry root pathogens if they have been in contact with soil or if they have been contaminated by water-splashed soil or dust-containing pathogens. Signs of infection or contamination of such plant material are not usually apparent.

If you know or suspect that propagules carry root pathogens, then decontamination measures are suggested. Fungicide seed treatments or fungicide dips for cuttings or bulbs can be done. The effectiveness of these treatments depends on whether the pathogen is on the surface or in the tissues. In addition, you must be careful not to inadvertently spread a bacterial pathogen by dipping a plant propagule in a fungicide. The fungicide, of course, would have no effect on the bacteria! For this reason, cutting dips are generally not recommended as a root rot management tool.

Heat treatment may be useful, provided the pathogen is less sensitive to heat than the plant propagule. Chemical or heat disinfestation may be essential to the initial establishment of pathogen-free propagules in a strict sanitary program involving stock plants. Once stock plants are pathogen-free, you may establish protected propagation areas from which future propagules will be taken.

Once production systems become infested with root pathogens to the extent that their exclusion or eradication is not feasible, a grower can only hope to manage the system in such a way as to suppress the disease incidence or severity. Generally, this is accomplished by manipulating cultural practices, by application of chemical pesticides, or by developing or encouraging biological control systems.

Cultural practices

Cultural management or control of root pathogens depends on some knowledge of the biology of the pathogens involved. A study of table 10.1 will indicate effective practices. For instance, *Pythium* or *Phytophthora* are water mold fungi that are promoted by excess soil water. Naturally, those conditions should be avoided by careful watering or by growing the crop in a well-drained and aerated medium.

Knowing that certain pathogens are encouraged or discouraged by various nutritional, soil pH, or temperature conditions should prompt the grower to chart a management course to avoid disease. For example, high ammonium can increase the incidence of *Fusarium* root rots. Therefore, you could reduce *Fusarium* disease incidence or severity by limiting the use of ammonium sources of nitrogen. *Thielaviopsis* readily attacks poinsettias or pansies if the pH is allowed to get too high. Actually, this is a matter of stress on the host more than an effect on the pathegen's development.

Chemical management

Fungicides are commonly used to suppress root pathogens. Certain fungicides have a broad disease spectrum, while others are very specific. Some are eradicative, but most act as protectants. If root rot problems are consistently present, a regular preventive fungicide program may be economically justifiable.

Fungicides can be applied as dusts, dips, or drenches at the time of propagation, perhaps also at regular intervals thereafter. It is important to know something of the phytotoxicity potential of the chemical being applied as well as the mode of action. Most "fungicides" are really fungistats; that is, they help to keep the fungus in check but don't kill all of its propagules. Thus, you should not expect a material to eradicate a soilborne fungus when the medium is drenched. Furthermore, even with the so-called systemic materials, you should not hope to eradicate internal infections that occurred prior to treatment.

Etridiazole (Truban, Terrazole) fungicide continues to be widely used for water mold-incited diseases. Many believe that etridiazole is more effective for *Pythium* than it is for *Phytophthora*. Recently, manufacturers have developed several formulations of etridiazole to better fit into greenhouse production methods. The product comes as a granular, wettable powder or flowable. Etridiazole can cause plant stunting or leaf burn if used at too high a rate, however. The problem is more prevalent with highly organic growing media or with the flowable formulation. Always use the lower of the dosage ranges given on the label unless situations warrant more extreme treatments.

Etridiazole is also one of the active ingredients in Banrot fungicide. Banrot is a broad-spectrum product that can be used for other crown and root rots in addition to the water mold diseases. This is because it contains two active ingredients, etridiazole and thiophanate-methyl. (More will be said about Banrot and thiophanate-methyl in a few paragraphs.)

Metalaxyl (Subdue) is a fungicide with good effectiveness at quite a low cost. Many crops are listed on the label. Recently, a 25 percent WP and a 2 percent granular formulation were released, in addition to the 24 percent EC also available. One can mix the 2 percent G formulation into potting media or a plant bed prior to use. Metalaxyl is highly active, especially against the *Phytophthora*-incited diseases. Only very small dosages, such as one-half ounce per 100 gallons, are needed, in many cases. Metalaxyl has been associated with plant stunting on rare occasions. The problem will be worse in hot weather or when plants get excessively dry between waterings. Metalaxyl has also been suspect regarding control of all *Pythium* genera or strains present in and on greenhouse crops. It is not known whether this is due to acquired resistance or to a narrow spectrum of activity against the many species of *Pythium* found rotting the roots of floral and foliage crops.

Propamocarb (Banol) is a recently introduced product that is quite effective for water mold suppression. It is currently labeled at relatively high rates, which means high cost. Propamocarb is quite safe on plant material, even producing a growth regulator type of growth stimulation in many cases.

Fosetyl-Al (Aliette) is a new systemic for many flower and foliage crops. It can be sprayed on plants, where it will move to the roots and prevent these water mold root rot diseases! Dosages are quite high when it is used as a spray, which results in a heavy spray residue. Fosetyl-Al has been widely used on hardy mums as a root rot-managing spray. Recent research has demonstrated that a combination of fosetyl-Al plus mancozeb (Protect T/O) applied as a heavy spray will result in good management of *Phytophthora* crown rots.

Thiophanate-methyl (Cleary's 3336, Domain, or Systec 1998) is labeled for *Rhizoctonia* control on all ornamentals in greenhouses or nurseries. The product comes as a flowable or wettable powder. Cleary's 3336 WP is available in water-soluble bags for less pesticide exposure and ease of mixing. It also has a chemigation label. A granular formulation of 3336 is also available. The 3336 flowable has improved stability over the other thiophanate-methyl flowables. This should correct the temporary soluble salt damage to roots sometimes seen when drenching flowable products of any sort into potting media.

Quintozene (Defend, PCNB, or Terraclor) fungicide is an older product. However, it remains very effective against *Rhizoctonia*. Quintozene is labeled as a pot drench, as a soil mix, and as a banded treatment for field-grown flower and foliage crops.

Iprodione (Chipco 26019) and triflumazole (Terraguard) give us some new chemistry against *Rhizoctonia*. Although they are effective, the crop list is limited on these products, and their use is a bit tricky. Growers should adhere to labeled instructions and not use iprodione on plants not listed on the label. Iprodione has been combined with thiophanate-methyl in a new product called Benefit. As such, it is labeled as a drench for *Rhizoctonia* control.

Banrot, as mentioned earlier, contains two active ingredients. Etridiazole fights water molds, and thiophanate-methyl targets *Rhizoctonia* and other root rots. This combination gives us a broader spectrum of activity against soilborne pathogens. The crop list is good. The company making Banrot produces an 8 percent granular formulation, which can be premixed into potting media, as well as a wettable powder that is to be used as a watering-in drench.

Black root rot, caused by *Thielaviopsis (Charala) basicola*, has become prevalent in recent years. Pansies, vincas, and petunias have been hard hit. Triflumazole (Terraguard) and thiophanate-methyl (Cleary's 3336, Domain, and Banrot) are labeled for management of this pathogen. Follow labeled directions closely for crops and timing of applications.

Cultural practices and fungicides generally suppress or mask root diseases. These practices may effectively reduce the incidence or severity of root disease symptoms as long as suppressive conditions are maintained. If conditions change, diseases may no longer be suppressed and they may develop rapidly. Naturally, thorough disease prevention by eliminating pathogens greatly reduces this risk of sudden disease development as a crop matures or after it is sold.

Biological management

Root pathogens in natural soils live in a balanced state with a myriad of other organisms, each being limited by the rest. That limitation produces a balance that naturally controls severe root disease. Man's disturbance of the balance, especially in ornamental plant production, reduces the limitation beneficial microbes place on root pathogens.

Thus, in soilless growing media systems, such as those used to produce flower and foliage crops, there is great need to restore the balance and reestablish biological suppression of root pathogens. To establish beneficial microorganisms in or on the roots of herbaceous ornamentals early in the production cycle is a worthy goal. Evidence to date suggests these organisms show tremendous potential in helping plants grow and repelling root pathogens.

Three products recently registered in the United States contain beneficial organisms for the suppression of root-rotting microbes. Mycostop, a strain of *Streptomyces*, is labeled for a broad range of microbes. Soil Guard, a strain of *Gleosporiun*, and Root Shield, a strain of Trichoderma, also available as potting mix additives. Since these products involve living organisms, exercise care in their storage and use.

Future research will provide the technology to introduce beneficial inoculum into treated soils and reconstitute natural biological buffers that can effectively block root pathogen invasion. Also, some potting mixes containing composted bark are becoming available that are supposed to be suppressive to root rot pathogens, due to chemical and biological factors in the bark that inhibit normal pathogen behavior. For certain crops, such mixes may have potential for root rot control.

Chapter 11

Diseases Caused by Nematodes

Most plant-pathogenic nematodes feed on roots with a needlelike mouth part called a stylet. This feeding usually causes dead areas in root tissues. In addition, root knot nematodes cause abnormal growth in root cells. In all cases, the host plant root functions are greatly decreased. This results in a variety of nonspecific symptoms, such as stunting and slow growth, and various symptoms of mineral imbalances and water shortages.

There are other types of plant-pathogenic nematodes. Foliar nematodes invade leaf tissue and cause general blighting. Stem nematodes are pathogens of stems and shoots of many ornamental plants.

Plant-pathogenic nematodes also interact with other pathogenic microorganisms, causing further disease damage. Pathogenic bacteria may use foliar nematodes as a way of getting into plants. Some viral pathogens have nematode vectors. Nematode interactions with soilborne fungi are common. These fungi invade nematode wounded roots and cause root rotting or vascular wilting.

Many kinds of plant-parasitic nematodes cause damage on ornamentals (see table 11.1). However, the most significant damage to herbaceous ornamentals is caused by relatively few genera, and *Meloidogyne*, *Pratylenchus*, *Paratylenchus*, and *Aphelenchoides* are the most important.

Aphelenchoides (foliar nematode)

These nematodes have rapid reproduction rates. They are extremely active, capable of moving rapidly up stems and across leaves in thin films of water. They are quite resistant to fluctuations in temperature and humidity.

Symptoms

Aphelenchoides can enter leaves through stomata or wounds. They cause a range of symptoms, including brown, dead lesions and overdevelopment of red or purple leaf pigments (fig. 11.1). Some of these symptoms may mimic symptoms caused by sunscald, pesticide damage, or high-temperature injury.

When these nematodes feed in buds, rosetting and growth deformations result. Young foliage of infected plants becomes hardened and stiff to the touch. Some plants have a high degree of tolerance to foliar nematodes, harboring substantial populations with few visible symptoms.

Fig. 11.1. A bird's nest fern with foliar nematodes. Nematodes kill leaf cells by feeding on them.

Table 11.1 Plant-parasitic nematodes found on ornamentals

Genus name	Common name
Aphelenchoides	Foliar nematode
Belonolaimus	Sting nematode
Crionemoides	Ring nematode
Ditylenchus	Stem nematode
Heterodera	Cyst nematode
Hoplolaimus	Lance nematode
Longidorus	Needle nematode
Meloidogyne	Root knot nematode
Paratylenchus	Pin nematode
Pratylenchus	Lesion nematode
Radopholus	Burrowing nematode
Rotylenchus	Uniform nematode
Scutellonema	Spiral nematode
Trichodorus	Stubby-root nematode
Tylenchorhynchus	Stunt nematode
Tylenchulus	Citrus nematode
Xiphinema	Dagger nematode

Management

Under moist conditions, large aggregations of *Aphelenchoides* form on lower leaf surfaces of infected plants. These masses of nematodes are easily moved by splashing water or on tools or hands. Careful watering and humidity control are important controls for *Aphelenchoides*.

Foliar nematodes survive for extended periods in dried infested plant debris, particularly when this material is not subjected to alternating wetting and drying. Plant material adhering to benches, pots, and production equipment can serve as sources of inoculum for susceptible crops. Removing individual infested leaves is effective for management because most crops are not infected systemically by *Aphelenchoides*.

Nematode-free propagating stock is basic to complete control of foliar nematodes. Hot water treatments have been used to eradicate foliar nematodes from foundation stock plants, but this technique is impractical on a large scale. Furthermore, high temperatures frequently disfigure or destroy treated plants. The practice is not useful unless plants are being grown for stock use, or shoot tips only are to be taken from them. Hot water treatments can also be an excellent means of disseminating fungal and bacterial plant pathogens, since these pathogens are not destroyed by the lower temperatures used for nematode eradication.

Systemic nematicides have been used to control *Aphelenchoides* on many ornamentals. Oxamyl applied either as a soil drench, granules mixed with soil, or as a foliar spray has been extremely effective in controlling these nematodes for about three weeks.

Tissue culture techniques producing clean planting stock also provides control of *Aphelenchoides.* If foliar nematodes are accidentally introduced into the callus tissue cultures, they can cause considerable damage. However, they are readily recognized in the cultures, thus preventing symptomless infestation and dissemination in the callus or plantlets.

Meloidogyne (root knot nematode)

Almost all ornamentals are potential hosts of this nematode, which is often a serious problem. Because the nematodes are within host tissue, they are transported easily in rooted cuttings or on symptomless plants. Movement also occurs by dirty machinery, hands, shoes, and irrigation water. Once established, these nematodes maintain themselves on a wide range of crop plants and weeds and can become an endemic problem.

Symptoms

Infected roots are knotted as a result of the feeding activities of *Meloidogyne* developing within the roots (fig. 11.2). The type and amount of root knotting depends on the species present, the behavior of the nematode, root characteristics, and population of the nematodes. Warm-temperature species of *Meloidogyne* cause extremely large galls, resulting in roots with a tuberous look. Cool-weather

Fig. 11.2. Some nematodes cause knots or galls to form on infected roots.

species usually develop small, discrete galls. Infected plants may react by developing numerous lateral roots above the developing gall. Fine-rooted grasses may become infected but may not produce readily visible galls at all. Fleshy-rooted plants may produce extremely large galls, even with low populations of nematodes.

Aboveground, root knot nematodes produce the sort of nonspecific symptoms mentioned earlier: signs of nutrient or water deficiency, stunting and slow growth, patchy growth patterns of affected plants in the bed or bench, and increased sensitivity to herbicides.

Management

The primary root knot nematode control is soil treatment, since the pathogens are soilborne. A wide range of soil fumigants have been available for effective control of soilborne nematodes since the 1940s. Highly refined dichloropropane-dichloropropene mixes, methyl-isothiocyanate, metam-sodium, ethylene dibromide, and various combinations of these materials are all effective in controlling *Meloidogyne* in field soils. Fumigants such as methyl bromide with chloropicrin have been used for many years as effective soil sanitizers for potting mixes and greenhouse or nursery bed soils. Unfortunately, many of these are no longer available for use in the United States.

Steam disinfestation of soil or potting mix is extremely effective in controlling root knot nematodes. Fumigants do not completely sterilize the soil. Low nematode numbers remaining after the treatments can increase to damaging levels in two or three years, especially if nematodes are reintroduced with transplants. Many of the newer contact/systemic nematicides are useful as bareroot dips of transplant materials. Hot water dips can also be used for this same purpose.

Paratylenchus (pin nematode)

Symptoms

For the most part, pin nematodes feed from the outside, either on root hairs or on the epidermal cells, but sometimes they penetrate the roots and feed on the tissues from within. Thus, they produce symptoms similar to those of the lesion nematodes. They have been found by different investigators in many parts of the world, usually in small numbers, and they feed on the roots of many different kinds of plants. Investigators may have underestimated the abundance and importance of these parasites. Because of their small size, they may pass through the sieves used to separate them from soil in diagnostic laboratories. As many as 10,000 per pound of soil have been found. Poor growth of many ornamentals has been correlated with high numbers of the nematode on bed-grown ornamentals outdoors as well as in the greenhouse.

Management

Control of pin nematode is the same as for the lesion nematode. In fact, the two nematodes are often found together in one crop.

Pratylenchus (lesion nematode)

Symptoms

Brown and dead flecks or lesions result from primary root feeding by larvae or adults of this nematode (fig. 11.3). The nonspecific symptoms on aboveground parts of plants infested by *Pratylenchus* are the same as those caused by any factor that damages roots or restricts root development.

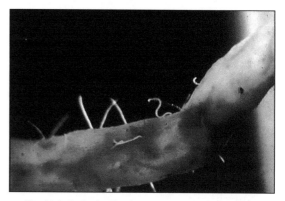

Tissue damaged by lesion nematodes is susceptible to infection by soil fungi. These fungi then cause progressive rotting of the roots. The lesions not only serve as infection sites but also greatly stress the host and increase its susceptibility to a variety of root rot fungi.

Fig. 11.3. Stylet feeding by nematodes causes areas of dead cells on roots.

Pest and Disease Diagnosis Guide

Y ou will recall that chapter 2 on diagnosis stressed the importance of compiling enough information about a problem to be sure you are diagnosing it correctly. If you do not carefully work through a diagnosis, trouble can arise from a number of directions. Diagnostic carelessness may cause you to react improperly to a nonspecific symptom. For instance, you might conclude that yellowed leaves were caused by lack of fertilizer, and you would fertilize the crop. If the cause was actually Pythium root rot, though, you would have made a costly mistake indeed, for the fertilizer would greatly worsen the root stress.

Another problem arising from incomplete diagnosis is not understanding specifically what pests or pathogens are present, how they got there, and what is favoring their development. Many pests are transported great distances on cuttings or small plants. Close inspection of newly arrived plant material is a basic part of your plant protection program. You need to know where to look and what to look for. For instance, sometimes the "typical" adult of various insect pests may not be present. Feeding scars or eggs may be all that you will find.

The following pages illustrate some views of diseases and pests to help you increase your diagnostic skills. This is not a complete guide. Do not attempt to find all the pests and diseases of floral and foliage crops neatly illustrated for you to simply match your material to. That is not diagnostics, and that is not the way to become good at diagnostics. Use this guide to stimulate your thinking and help you find solutions when problems occur with your plants.

1
Dodder is a parasite that will overgrow and strangle many ornamentals such as this impatiens. Dodder produces flowers and seeds as it matures.
←

2
Powdery mildew infections can occur on ↑ the flower tissue of many plants, such as this gerbera. Notice how easily the superficial fungal growth can be seen when the light is angled onto the object you are viewing.

3
Here you can see the powdery ↑ mildew fungus growing thickly on the stems of chrysanthemums. Stems are more severely affected on some plants than on others.

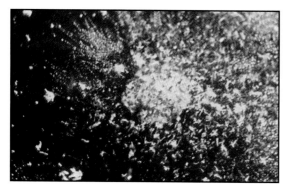

4
In this magnified view of a powdery mildew lesion on a begonia, taken through a 30x field microscope, you can see the strands of fungal growth radiating outward from the older part of the lesion. The accumulated material in the center is the mass of spores.
←

5
Under the right conditions, powdery mildew can spread rapidly. When this happens, the plants are beyond saving. Even though the fungus on this poinsettia can be killed, the spots will remain.

←

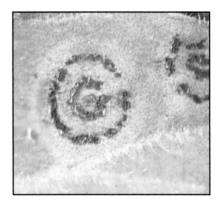

6 ↑
The geranium rust fungus pushes outward from within this leaf as the fungus produces more and more spores. The spores are what you are seeing. This happens more readily on the undersurface of the leaves, and it occurs on many plants.

7 ↑
These blisters on chrysanthemum leaves are caused by white rust. This difficult-to-control disease is presently found only in our West Coast states and in other parts of the world.

8
Botrytis readily produces mold growth bearing brown spores. The growth can be seen here over the infected crown tissue of a petunia. →

9
Botrytis fungus is blighting this geranium flower. To confirm the diagnosis, look for the brown spores discussed and pictured in the previous photo. You may need to use a hand lens magnifier for this.

11
Botrytis often causes stem cankers, as on this marigold. Take plants like this and put them in a plastic bag with a damp paper towel for two or three days. The fungus will start producing spores if *Botrytis* is truly the cause.

10
Botrytis blight of cuttings often results in a soft rot that becomes covered with a gray mold. The moldy growth will engulf all the plant tissue eventually, then spread to neighboring poinsettia cuttings.

12
Botrytis stem canker on fuchsia: this disease can be seen on many hanging basket plants. Notice the brown spores on the edge of the canker.

13
The fungi causing damping-off of seedlings occasionally grows up onto the leaves and stems of fallen plants. This can help you determine if damping-off is the problem. It cannot help you decide which fungus is involved, however, because many damping-off pathogens can do this. Send this sort of material into a plant clinic for a complete analysis.
←

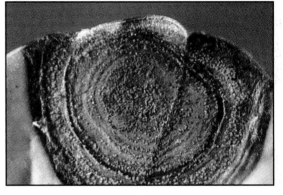

14 ↑
This brown, blighted area of a peperomia leaf can be diagnosed as a fungal infection by noting the concentric rings of discolored tissue and the raised structures near the center that bear the fungal spores.

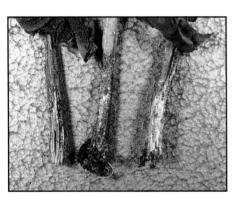

15 ↑
Rhizoctonia cutting rot typically results in a dry, stringy rot, such as seen on these chrysanthemum cuttings. If you look closely at the rotted tissue, you will often see strands of brown fungus.

16
Rhizoctonia can rapidly attack a recently transplanted cutting, especially if it is placed too deeply in the pot. As poinsettias and other plants mature, they become resistant to *Rhizoctonia* infection. →

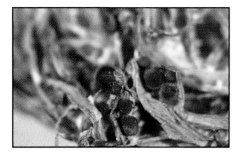

17
This creeping phlox is being attacked by the *Sclerotinia* crown rot fungus. White tufts of fungus will mature in two or three days into brown structures that look like seeds. These structures can be transported many miles and survive for years.

←

18
These fern fronds have been infected with the anthracnose fungus as they grew up through older, previously infected leaves in the bed.

→

19
The *Xanthomonas* bacterium causing this blight of begonia infects the leaf through the leaf's edge. By noting the progression of symptoms, you can visualize how the pathogen is moving down the veins of the leaf toward the petiole. It will continue into the stem, becoming systemic in the plant. The plant will die.

←

20
The *Xanthomonas* that causes bacterial wilt disease is rapidly spreading through these geraniums in splashing water. It helps when deciding how to manage diseases to remember that it is the pathogen that spreads, not the disease that results from infection.

→

21
These *Pseudomonas* bacterial spots on impatiens are localized and not systemic. Note that they have a definite border and are scattered through the leaves.

←

22
Calla lily rhizomes often get a smelly, soft rot caused by *Erwinia* bacteria. The only effective management is to discard infected plant parts when replanting.

23
Symptoms of a problem on this cyclamen are evident on only a part of the plant. You are correct to conclude that a localized injury or infection has occurred.

24
This is a crosscut through the corm from the plant in the previous photo. Note how the veins in the corm area of the yellowed leaves are brown and diseased. Laboratory cultures of this tissue will indicate that *Fusarium* is present.

25
These gladiolus corms have various storage rots. There are many fungi that can cause such superficial rotting.

26
This pansy plant is affected by yet another kind of root rot. After washing the root system, you can see definite blackened areas throughout the roots. These symptoms are typical of black root rot disease caused by *Thielaviopsis* (*Charala*).

27
Thielaviopsis (*Charala*) black root rot resting spores are shown here inside a pansy root.
←

28
Pythium, which is causing these brown, rotted poinsettia roots, often begins at the bottom of the container.
→

29
Phytophthora root and crown rot attacks the underground plant parts rapidly and indiscriminately. The result on this African violet is total plant collapse.
←

30
Root rot is the cause of this poor quality crop.
→

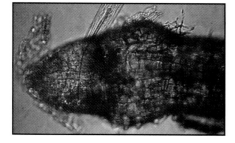

31
Plant pathogenic nematodes damage root cells by piercing the cells with styletlike mouths. Here you can see a nematode piercing a root tip from the top.
←

32
This impatiens is systemically infected with tobacco mosaic virus causing the plant to become stunted and malformed. Any cuttings taken from the plant will be like this plant.

←

33
The yellow spots seen on this geranium are caused by tomato ringspot virus, a virus that has a wide host range. Tomato ringspot symptoms normally go away as the weather warms and brightens.

→

34
Impatiens necrotic spot virus can cause a severe symptom in many ornamentals, such as gloxinia. Note how the plant's growing point has become infected. This plant will die.

←

35
The stem cankering on this begonia may be a result of impatiens necrotic spot virus. Be careful, however. Other factors can cause similar symptoms.

→

36
By viewing this begonia leaf as the light shines through it, you can see the various symptoms of impatiens necrotic spot virus.

←

37
Aphids on plant stem. Aphids can be found on leaves, flowers and stems (even roots). Mature aphids may or may not have wings. Mature aphids are 1 to 2.5 mm long and variable in color.

←

38
Melon/cotton aphids in chrysanthemum flower. Individuals in this species range from light green to nearly black in color. Both wingless and winged aphids are shown in this photo. →

39
Aphids and aphid skins on leaves. The cast-off skins (and sticky honeydew) are indications of an aphid infestation.

←

40
Orange larvae of the predatory aphid midge (*Aphidoletes aphidimyza*) feeding on melon/cotton aphids. Aphid midges can be purchased from commercial insectaries. →

41
Adult and immature silverleaf whiteflies, *Bemisia argentifolii*. Adults are generally smaller than greenhouse whiteflies and hold their wings at a more vertical angle. (Courtesy Lance Osborne, University of Florida)

←

42
Adult greenhouse whitefly. Note the slight difference in how wings are held, compared with silverleaf whiteflies.

←

43
Adult and immature silverleaf whiteflies on poinsettia leaf. This insect can develop well on poinsettias.

→

44
Parasitoid *Encarsia formosa* on immature silverleaf whitefly. Although *Encarsia* will parasitize silverleaf whiteflies, control often is not satisfactory.

←

45
Two adult thrips on a plant leaf. Note the narrow wings held over the back. Feeding injury (light colored areas) and dark spots of fecal matter deposited by the thrips are also shown.

→

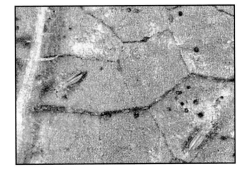

46
Adult thrips on rose bud. Thrips often enter the bud area before any color is showing and lay eggs. When flowers open, the thrips infestation is already well-established.

←

47
A predatory mite, *Neoseiulus* sp., attacking an immature thrips. These mites have been used for thrips control on some greenhouse vegetable crops, but results on ornamentals have generally not been satisfactory. (Courtesy Marilyn Steiner, Alberta Environmental Centre)
←

48
Western flower thrips injury to petunia leaves. Certain petunia cultivars are very useful as indicator plants for thrips and virus presence.
→

49
Mealybug on poinsettia. Although exposed on this photo, mealybugs often are located deep within developing leaves and stems, making control very difficult.
←

50
The mealybug destroyer, *Cryptolaemus montrouzieri* (center), among its mealybug prey. These predators are sometimes used for mealybug control in greenhouses and interior plantscapes.
→

51
Adult fungus gnat on yellow sticky trap. Note the relatively small head, long legs, and antennae.
←

52
Adult shore fly on yellow sticky trap. Note the resemblance to fruit fly and leafminer adults. Also note the white spots on the wings.
←

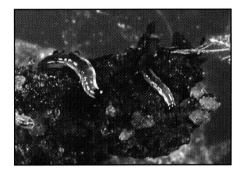

54
Fungus gnat larvae. Note the black heads. Fungus gnat larvae can help spread plant pathogens as well as stunt or kill plants by feeding on developing roots.
→

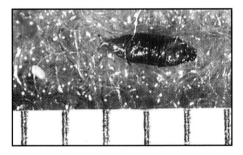

53
Shore fly pupa and egg (*lower left*) on irrigation matting. These insects feed on species of blue-green algae. The marks at the bottom of the photo are each 1 mm.
←

55
Adult leafminer, *Liriomyza trifolii*. This is one of the most common leafminers found on ornamental crops. Adults are about 3 mm long. (Courtesy Michael Parrella, University of California, Davis)
→

56
Adult leafminer, *Liriomyza huidobrensis*. The approved U.S. common name is the pea leafminer, but it also is a problem on numerous ornamental crops worldwide. This species is slightly larger than *L. trifolii* and has more black than yellow. (Courtesy Michael Parrella, University of California, Davis)
←

57
Beet armyworm larva on chrysanthemum leaf. This species can injure numerous ornamental crops, especially in southern and western states. (Courtesy James Price, University of Florida)
←

58
Cabbage looper larva. These and other Lepidoptera can sometimes become problems on greenhouse ornamentals.
→

59
Soft scale on cyclamen leaf. Soft scales are 1 to 4 mm long, and can be found on all plant areas. Soft scales, like aphids, whiteflies and mealybugs, produce large amounts of sticky honeydew.
←

60
Circular armored scale on palm leaf. Circular scales are 1 to 3 mm in diameter and variable in color. Armored scales do not produce honeydew.
→

61
Heavy armored scale infestation on greenhouse rose stem. These infestations are difficult to detect initially and develop over many months. Generally when infestations are this heavy, plant removal is the best control option.
←

62
Two-spotted spider mite adult female and egg. Spider mites are among the most common pests of ornamental plants. Adult females are about 0.5 mm long.

←

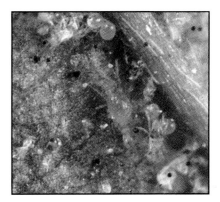

64   ↑
A predatory mite, *Phytoseiulus persimilis*. This beneficial mite is used to control two-spotted spider mites on many greenhouse vegetable and some ornamental plants. The reddish-orange adult females are more rounded and slightly larger than two-spotted mites.

63   ↑
Spider mite infestation on marigold, resulting in dead plants and much webbing.

65
Another spider mite, *Eotetranychus lewisi*, the Lewis spider mite. This mite has been found infesting poinsettias in several areas of the U.S. Adults are slightly smaller than two-spotted spider mites.

→

66
Lewis spider mite injury to poinsettia leaves. Leaf injury resembles that caused by two-spotted spider mites.

67
Moth fly (Family Psychodidae). These flies have been observed more frequently recently. They are often found in areas harboring shore flies. Note the "fuzzy" wings, from which these small flies get their name.

68
Moth fly larva. Occasionally, these larvae are seen damaging roots in hydroponic plant production systems.

69
Four-lined plant bug. These and other plant bugs (e.g., tarnished plant bug) injure plants by injecting a toxic saliva. Typical four-lined plant bug injury can be seen in the background.

Management

Pratylenchus is easily moved by anything that moves soil: shoes and hands of workers, machinery, surface water, wind. The nematodes are moved frequently in host plants themselves. Many kinds of ornamentals and weeds can support lesion nematodes. As a result, these nematodes are likely to become a long-term problem once introduced into areas of intensive ornamental production. Using only *Pratylenchus*-free planting stock is one of the first steps in successful control of this nematode. Effective crop rotation to control lesion nematodes is difficult since common species have wide host ranges. Weed control is necessary in crop rotation schemes.

Preplant soil fumigation is a major control method for lesion nematodes. The nematodes are successfully controlled by the same materials as mentioned for root knot nematode. Postplant applications of the contact/systemic nematicides are successful in controlling *Pratylenchus* in plants in containers or closed-bottomed beds. The most severe problem in chemical control is the fact that present product labels for ornamental crops are not widespread.

Virus Diseases

Viruses have been causing increasingly serious problems on greenhouse crops in recent years. This is probably due to the increased movement of plant material throughout the world. Like many plant pathogens, viruses can move within an apparently healthy cutting or seed. Growers must all be on the lookout for unwanted plant viruses!

A virus is an infectious parasite that carries its own set of genes but needs the ribosomes and other components of its host cell for multiplication. Viruses are extremely small organisms, visible only through the electron microscope and when they form crystals or other types of "inclusion bodies" in the host cells (fig. 12.1). Plant viruses have traditionally been named after the disease symptoms they cause in the host in which they were originally described. For example, the virus that causes light and dark green areas on dieffenbachia leaves is named dasheen mosaic virus because it was first described on dasheen, a southern weed, and the light and dark areas are angular and fit together like a Roman mosaic.

Many viruses share one or more characteristics that are often not revealed by the name. Plant viruses are thus grouped according to their physical and chemical structures, including shape and size, immunological properties, natural methods of transmission, and host reactions. Currently, plant viruses are divided into 23 groups (see table 12.1). Sixteen virus groups are known to include viruses infecting floral and foliage plants. Five of these groups have elongated particles, and eight groups have particles with an isometric or almost spherical shape.

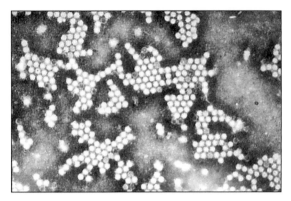

Fig. 12.1. Plant pathogenic viruses in an infected plant cell.

Disease cycles

The disease process begins with a tiny cell wound that allows entry of the virus particle but does not kill the cell. Wounds may result from physical scraping of the leaf surface with some outside object. In table 12.1, this is referred to as "mechanical" transmission. More commonly, the tiny wounds result from insect feeding. Insects may carry virus particles from diseased plant to healthy plant as they feed.

Once the virus has entered the cell, it begins multiplying. Virus multiplication results in virus spread from the originally infected cell to neighboring cells. The host may react in several ways. In a local infection, affected host cells die after a very limited amount of cell-to-cell virus spread, a brown, dead spot is all that remains of the virus infection itself. Usually, with important ornamental viruses, though, the entire plant eventually becomes invaded and symptomatic. Such a situation is called a systemic infection. Viruses generally survive by means of systemic infections. As systemic pathogens, they can be picked up by an insect or disseminated by an infected cutting or seed or on workers' hands or tools.

Table 12.1 Plant viruses infecting ornamental plants

Virus group	Virus name	Host plants
Carlavirus—Rod-shaped, aphid transmitted	Cactus virus 2	*Cactus* spp.
	Carnation latent	*Dianthus caryophyllus*
	Chrysanthemum B	*Dendranthema*
	Helenium virus S	*Helenium*
	Hippeastrum latent	*Hippeastrum hybridum*
	Honeysuckle latent	*Lonicera japonica, L. periclymenum*
	Lily symptomless	*Lilium*
	Narcissus latent	*Narcissus*
	Nasturtium mosaic	*Nasturtium*
	Nerine latent	*Nerine bowdenii, N. sarniensis*
	Passiflora latent	*Passiflora caerulea, P. suberosa*
Caulimovirus—Spherical, DNA-containing, aphid-transmitted	Carnation etched ring	*Dianthus caryophyllus*
	Dahlia mosaic	*Dahlia* spp.
	Tobacco necrosis	*Tulipa* spp., *Primula* spp.
	Alfalfa mosaic	*Lupinus* spp., *Daphne* spp., *Viburnum opulus*
Closterovirus—Long rods, aphid transmitted	Carnation necrotic fleck	*Dianthus caryophyllus*
	Carnation yellow fleck	*Dianthus caryophyllus*
Cucumovirus—Spherical, seed- and aphid-transmitted	Chrysanthemum aspermy (tomato aspermy)	*Dendranthema grandiflora*
	Cucumber mosaic	*Begonia tuberhybrida, Celosia argentea, Canna generalis, Dahlia* spp., *Dieffenbachia picta, Gladiolus* spp., *Hydrangea macrophylla, Iris* spp., *Lilium* spp., *Lupinus augustifolius, Narcissus tazetta, Pelargonium zonale, Peperomia magnolifolis, Salvia spendens.* many others
Geminivirus—Spheres, in joined pairs, DNA-containing, transmitted by leafhoppers and whiteflies	Abutilon mosaic	*Abutilon*
	Euphorbia mosaic	*Euphorbia pulcherrima*
	Ageratum yellow vein	*Ageratum*
	Balsam leaf curl	*Impatiens*
	Hollyhock yellow mosaic	*Alcea*
	Hibiscus leaf curl	*Hibiscus*
	Zinnia leaf curl	*Zinnia*
Ilarvirus—Spherical with several component particles, mechanical pollen transmission	Apple mosaic	*Rosa* spp.
	Prunus necrotic ringspot	*Rosa* spp.
	Tobacco streak	*Dahlia* spp., *Rosa* spp.

Table 12.1   continued

Virus group	Virus name	Host plants
Nepovirus—Spherical, transmitted mechanically, by seed, and by aphids	Tobacco ringspot	*Pelargonium hortorum*
	Tomato ringspot	*Pelargonium hortorum, Hydrangea macrophylla*
	Arabis mosaic	*Narcissus* spp.
	Raspberry ringspot	*Narcissus* spp.
Potexvirus—Rod-shaped, mechanically transmitted	Cactus X	*Cactus* spp.
	Cymbidium mosaic	*Cattleya, Cymbidium*
	Hydrangea ringspot	*Hydrangea macrophylla*
	Nandina mosaic	*Nandina domestica*
	Narcissus mosaic	*Narcissus*
	Nerine virus X	*Nerine sariensis, N. manselli, Agapanthus praecox* subsp. *orientalis*
	Viola mottle	*Viola adorata*
	Zygocactus virus X	*Zygocactus*
Potyvirus—Flexuous rods, aphid and seed transmitted	Bean yellow mosaic	*Gladiolus, Iris hollandica, Lupinus luteus, Freesia*
	Bearded iris mosaic	*Iris susiana*
	Carnation vein mottle	*Dianthus caryophyllus*
	Dasheen mosaic	*Dieffenbachia* spp., *Aglaonema* spp., *Caladium hortulanum, Colocasia* spp., *Xanthosoma* spp., *Zantedeschia* spp.
	Hippeastrum mosaic	*Hippeastrum equestre, Hippeastrum hybridum*
	Helenium virus Y	*Helenium*
	Iris mild mosaic	*Iris hollandica, Iris xiphioides*
	Freesia mosaic	*Freesia* spp.
	Narcissus yellow stripe	*Narcissus* spp., *Nerine bowdenii*
	Statice virus Y	*Limonium sinuatum*
	Tulip breaking	*Tulipa* spp., *Lilium*
	Turnip mosaic	*Zinnia elegans, Tropaeloum officinale, Petunia hybrida, Anemone coronaria, Matthiola bicornis, Limonium perezii*
Rhabdovirus—bullet-shaped, with lipid envelope, transmitted by mites, leafhoppers, and aphids	Several ornamentals contain rhabdovirus-like particles; they have not been named	*Dendranthema* spp., *Dendrobium* hybrid, *Dendrobium phalaenopsis, Gerbera* spp., *Iris germanica, Dianthus caryophyllus*
	Orchid fleck	*Cymbidium, Dendrobium, Odontoglossum*

Table 12.1   continued

Virus group	Virus name	Host plants
Tobamovirus—Short rods, mechanically transmitted	Tobacco mosaic Odontoglossum ringspot (orchid tobacco mosaic)	*Hippeastrum, Petunia, Gerbera* *Cattleya, Cymbidium, Phalaenopsis, Vanda*
Tobravirus—Short rods, mechanically transmitted	Tobacco rattle	*Hyacinth, Tulipa, Narcissus, Lilium, Crocus, Aster, Gladiolus*
Tombusvirus—Spherical, transmitted mechanically and "through soil" (probably by fungi)	Carnation mottle Carnation ringspot Cymbidium ringspot Pelargonium leaf curl Petunia asteroid mosaic	*Dianthus caryophyllus* *Dianthus caryophyllus* *Tolmiea mengiessi, Tulipa fosteriana, Pelargonium zonale* *Pelargonium peltatum* *Petunia* spp.
Tospoviruses—Spherical with lipid envelope, transmitted by thrips and seed, weakly mechanically transmitted	Tomato spotted wilt virus and impatiens necrotic spot virus; others	*Impatiens* spp., *Begonia* spp., *Petunia* spp., *Verbena* spp., *Dahlia variabilis, Gladiolus* spp., *Ageratum houstonianum, Lupinus* spp., *Calendula officinalis, Zinnia elegans, Gerbera* spp., many others
Tymovirus—Spherical, transmitted mechanically and by beetles	Scrophularia mottle Poinsettia mosaic	*Scrophylaria modosa* *Euphorbia pulcherrima*
Viroids—No protein coat	Chrysanthemum stunt Chrysanthemum chlorotic mottle	*Dendranthema grandiflora* *Dendranthema grandiflora*

Diagnosis of virus diseases

A localized infection may develop at the site of infection. It may be a yellow, brown, or red spot. The tissue may be dried out as well as discolored. These infections may begin as small spots of affected tissue that gradually increase in size as the virus moves slowly from cell to cell. Tissue in the lesions or spots may die. Further spread of the infection is prevented in these cases. In other cases, symptoms from local infections simply precede systemic spread and further symptoms.

Most plant viruses of economic importance infect the host and spread from the site of infection to the vascular tissues, where they move throughout the plant. The first symptom of such a virus infection may be associated with the vascular system. Symptoms associated with the vascular tissue may include vein yellowing, vein mosaic, or vein banding. The latter is a clearing or yellowing of leaf cells along the veins, giving a widening effect called banding. Vein death may appear in sensitive species, sometimes resulting in death of a section of the stem or death of the entire plant.

Symptoms do not always increase in severity in the virus-infected plant. During the initial infection process, severe symptoms develop, and the host may die. This is a shock phase or acute phase of disease. If the host survives, a chronic phase ensues, in which some of the affected parts show recovery. New growth may be seen with less severe symptoms. Eventually, the plant may develop without symptoms at all. This is called a latent phase or latent infection.

In any plant, symptom visibility may be related to how long the plant has been infected, the age of the plant at the time of infection, the strain of virus, and the environment in which the infected plant is grown. For instance, virus infection may occur without any visible symptoms, even initially after infection. Such latent infections are a problem in controlling the spread of viruses. Many weeds can be infected by viruses without symptoms.

The importance of virus infection in reducing the quality of ornamental plants has been repeatedly demonstrated with many crops. Stunting is a general symptom of many virus-infected plants. Affected plants may have smaller leaves, reduced internode length, and smaller flowers. Stunting is an important symptom leading to the reduction of the quality of a floral or foliage plant.

Yellowing is a symptom that may be uniform in the virus-infected plant or may be confined to only a portion of a leaf or leaf vein. Yellowing may be found primarily along the edge of the leaf. Yellowing symptoms usually appear in the newly expanding leaves. It is difficult to know whether this sort of yellowing is due to virus infection or to cultural and environmental situations.

Mosaic symptoms are produced by patches of normally colored, uninfected cells intermingled with abnormally colored, infected cells. The patches are usually delineated by small veins. The mosaic appears as elongated patches or streaks in leaves that have parallel veins, such as lilies (fig. 12.2), iris, or narcissus.

Fig. 12.2. An Easter lily with fleck virus.

Mottling is when the abnormal coloration in the leaf does not follow the veins. Patches are not sharply bordered, developing across vein boundaries. The sizes and shapes of the discolored areas vary. Often, such a symptom is referred to as a speckling, stippling, spotting, or blotching.

Virus-induced tissue death can range from severe browning of large areas of leaves, shoot tips, or stems to mild browning or etching of the leaves. Browning from viruses can appear as rings, spots, or darkening of the veins on leaves or stems. In very susceptible plants, dead growing points may appear as viruses move systemically toward the top part of the plant. An example of this would be the reaction of gloxinia to impatiens necrotic spot virus (fig. 12.3). Mild systemic dead spots are more common. This appears as brown spots or fleck symptoms on leaves, such as the common fleck virus in Easter lilies.

Several viruses infecting ornamentals produce color breaking or color variegation. The most classical virus symptom on flowers is color breaking. Viruses can cause either light streaks and areas or dark streaks and flecks. Some viruses cause a spotting of dark or light color in flowers.

Fig. 12.3. Gloxinia infected with impatiens necrotic spot virus.

Flower greening is a modification of flower color that is frequently associated with myco plasma-like organisms. Flower death or brown spotting is also produced by some viruses.

Complete diagnosis of virus diseases is usually not based on visual symptoms alone. Bioassay, serology, nuclelic acid analysis, DNA probing, and electron microscopy are procedures used in laboratory identification.

Many of the viruses infecting ornamentals can be mechanically transmitted, a fact used in laboratory investigations. Sap from the suspect plant is rubbed onto the leaves of the indicator or assay host. The characteristics of the resulting infection help identify the virus.

Serological tests are usually used to confirm visual diagnosis or results from mechanical transmission tests. Recently, the use of serology in routine indexing has expanded with the use of the enzyme-linked immunosorbent assay (ELISA) procedure.

By electron microscopy, virus particles can be observed in crude sap extracts from infected plants. The virus can be recognized and tentatively identified on the basis of its size and shape. Finally, a new technique based on isolating and identifying portions of the nucleic acids present in symptomatic tissue can be used to determine which virus is present.

Epidemiology

Viruses must initially penetrate and enter the plant through a wounded cell. However, depending on the virus, efficient transmission can occur through seed or by vegetative propagation of plant parts after the initial infection is established.

Seed transmission can introduce into a crop a plant virus that then serves as a source of infection for transmission by mechanical means, insects, or nematodes. This is the way papaya ringspot virus has gotten into portulacas throughout the United States.

The percentage of seed infected by a virus may vary from a few hundredths of a percent to 100 percent. Viruses may persist in seed for long periods, permitting transport over great distances. The proportion of seed infected depends on several factors, including the virus strain, host plant, time at which the plant is infected, location of seed on the plant, age of seed, and temperature. Groups of viruses in which transmission is known to occur in or on seed include the tospoviruses, tobraviruses, tobamoviruses, potyviruses, nepoviruses, cucumoviruses, and ilarviruses.

Certain nematodes can pick up viruses as they feed on infected plant roots. Nepoviruses and tobraviruses can be acquired in 15 minutes to one hour by feeding nematodes and are inoculated in a similar time period. Both groups of viruses are retained in the nematodes for many weeks and can be transmitted by both larvae and adults. Virus-carrying nematodes are not common in greenhouse soils or potting mixes. They do cause problems in field-grown woody perennials, especially in the South and the West.

Plant viruses can be transmitted by aphids, leafhoppers, mites, thrips, mealybugs, and beetles. Aphids are important vectors of viruses of herbaceous ornamentals. Viruses in the carlavirus, potyvirus, closterovirus, cucumovirus, and caulimovirus groups are aphid-transmitted.

Viruses that are aphid-transmitted can be separated into groups by the length of time the virus persists in the aphids. Nonpersistent viruses, which usually cause mosaic symptoms, can be acquired in as short a time as 10 to 30 seconds. Inoculation occurs just as quickly. With many nonpersistent viruses, aphids become noninfective very rapidly. Semipersistent viruses persist for longer times in the vector than nonpersistent viruses. The probability of virus transmission with these viruses increases with feeding periods on affected plants up to four hours. Semipersistent viruses are efficiently transmitted by fewer species of aphids. Persistent, or circulative viruses, have minimum aphid acquisition and inoculation feeding periods of 10 to 60 minutes. They often have a latent period of 12 hours or more, during which an aphid that acquires a virus will be unable to transmit it. Persistent viruses are retained in the aphid, and the insect remains infective after the molt. No viruses of ornamentals have been shown to be transmitted in this way, however.

Western flower thrips (*Frankliniella occidentalis*) and several other species of thrips transmit tospoviruses. Impatiens necrotic spot virus (INSV) has been particularly serious on greenhouse crops in recent years. The virus is widely distributed in the United States and has a wide host range. The virus strain found most commonly in greenhouses is vectored in a persistent manner by the thrips, which acquire the virus as larvae and transmit it throughout their adult lives (up to 45 days). They apparently do not pass the virus through their eggs to their offspring.

The sweet-potato whitefly (*Bemisia tabaci*) has been known for many years to be a vector of economically important plant viruses in tropical and subtropical areas of the world. Some 70 or more diseases have been reported to be induced by the feeding of these infectious whiteflies. Recently, two species of *Trialeurodes*, another kind of whitefly, have been implicated in the vectoring of some plant viruses. The range of the sweet-potato whitefly has been increasing in the last few years into greenhouses thoughout all areas of the world. In fact, a new species and common name have been proposed for the *Bemesia* whitefly attacking greenhouse crops in North America. This is *Bemisia argentifolia*, the silverleaf whitefly. It is known to transmit many geminiviruses in a persistent manner, closteroviruses in a semipersistent way, and carlaviruses nonpersistently. Other as yet undescribed viruses are also transmitted by these insects. Their threat as virus vectors of economically important viruses of greenhouse crops remains to be seen.

Intensive cultivation of greenhouse crops, with plants closely spaced and often touching each other, leads to mechanical transmission of many viruses. Of even greater concern, however, is the spread of viruses on cutting tools, hands, pots, and potting surfaces. Without disinfection of knives used to make cuttings, harvest flowers, or divide plants, many viruses rapidly spread from plant to plant.

A virus residing in a weed is often not obvious because most weed infections occur without symptoms (fig. 12.4). Thus, a virus present in weeds may become a source of disease when a susceptible ornamental crop is introduced to a nearby area. Also, insect vectors move freely from the weeds to the crop.

A similar situation may also occur when a virus that is not causing severe economic damage

Fig. 12.4. Weeds near greenhouse can harbor viruses and the insects that spread them.

in one type of plant in the greenhouse or nursery is transmitted to a newly introduced crop with greater sensitivity. For instance, impatiens or gloxinias introduced into greenhouses carrying INSV-infected thrips can become infected quickly. These plants, although healthy and virus-free when they entered the greenhouse, can quickly sicken and die.

The relative efficiency of local spread of viruses depends on the distance that the vectors can be transported. For example, the numbers of thrips entering or moving in a crop may vary from year to year and month to month. Weather conditions in the winter will have a major influence on thrip survival and multiplication. Nematode vectors in soil generally move slowly, and the viruses they transmit may spread only limited distances.

Management of virus diseases

Virus diseases are managed by prevention. This involves growing crops from virus-free seeds or stocks, stopping the viruses from entering the crop, and stopping them from spreading if infection is noted. Virus spread can be minimized by utilizing resistant varieties or by reducing vector populations with insecticides.

In the ornamentals industry of today, intensive efforts are often made to produce plants for propagation that are free of known pathogens—fungi and bacteria as well as viruses. The indexing approach to clean stock production depends on detection methods that are rapid and specific. Indexing also depends on developing methods to eliminate viruses known to be in proposed stock plants. Heat treatment of nuclear stock plants and meristem culturing permit the establishment of virus-free plants that can be used as stock plants. The very damaging viruses of chrysanthemums and carnations have been removed from commercial varieties by such procedures and are rarely seen today. Rose viruses can also be eliminated, if propagators will take on the added expense such procedures require.

Virus indexing is the testing process used to determine if a virus is present in a plant and to identify it. The choice of the indexing method will depend on the crop and the stage of growth when a test is performed. Indexing has a high unit cost, so tests are usually applied to a limited

number of nuclear stock plants, which are then used for large-scale propagation. (See the discussion of culture indexing presented in chapter 8.)

If no plant material free of viruses is available to start a clean stock
program, there are still several techniques that will eliminate viruses from
propagated plants: (1) exploiting erratic distribution of viruses within the
plant, (2) heat treatment, and (3) shoot-tip or meristem culture.
Propagation of small tissue pieces, usually shoot tips, from some vegetative branches may yield virus-free plants. Heat treatment, or thermother-
apy, has been successfully used in combination with the removal of small
tip cuttings or shoot-tip culture to obtain healthy plants. The most common method of producing virus-free explants is to heat-treat the virus-
infected source plants before tissue is excised. The infected plant is
exposed to 95 to 105F (35 to 40C) for varying periods of time, depending
on the virus and plant species or cultivar. Treatment normally involves
exposure of actively growing plants to hot air for three to 12 weeks and
occasionally longer.

One of the most effective ways to limit the spread of virus, thus somewhat controlling the disease, is to eliminate the insect vector from the
cropping area. Installing insect-proof screens over fan intake vents or pas-
sive ventilation devices keeps
insects away from susceptible
crops (fig. 12.5). Such screens
have to be installed carefully to
prevent tiny insects like thrips
from getting in, while still permitting sufficient airflow to cool the
greenhouse. In spite of difficulties, screens have proven to be a
cost-effective alternative to the
intensive insecticide spraying
programs needed once a vector
like thrips is found on the susceptible crop.

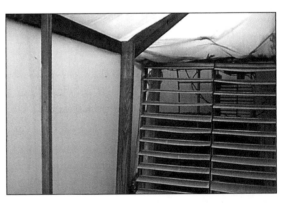

Fig. 12.5. Screening on a greenhouse helps keep out insects that
spread viruses.

When a virus that is spread in a persistent manner by an insect is
detected in a crop, the vector population must be reduced to extremely

low levels, if not eliminated entirely. Complete elimination of some greenhouse virus vectors, such as thrips, is not practical. Thus, if tospoviruses are found in a greenhouse, management depends on several integrated practices:

1. Scouting for symptomatic plants, then testing such plants with field tospovirus-detection kits or by sending them to a laboratory.

2. Discarding any plants known to be virus carriers.

3. Developing better methods for controlling access to suspect areas by workers.

4. Handling all plants and harvesting cuttings with tighter phytosanitary procedures.

5. Using disinfectants weekly on benches, work areas, and floors.

6. Screening greenhouses, at least where stock will be kept.

7. Intensifying vector management practices, usually with increased spraying of organic pecticides.

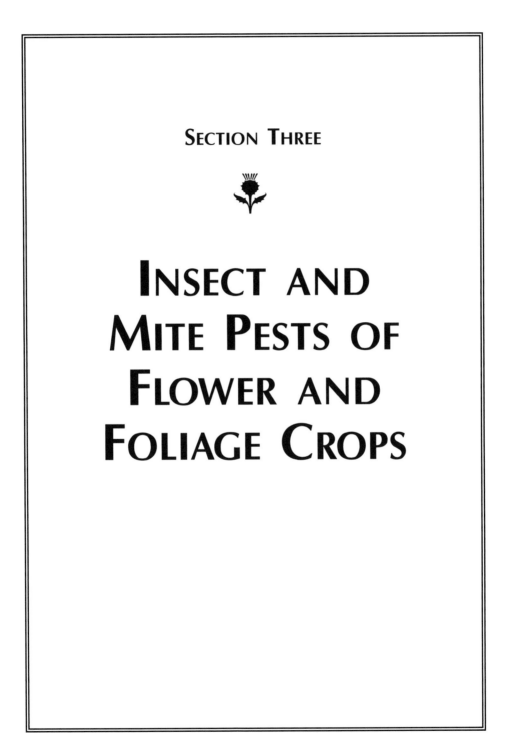

SECTION THREE

INSECT AND MITE PESTS OF FLOWER AND FOLIAGE CROPS

Chapter 13

Classification and Management of Insect and Mite Pests

Classification of living organisms

All plants and animals are classified in an organized way. Most people are at least somewhat familiar with the basics of this classification system. Organisms are classified from broader to narrower groups as follows: phylum, class, order, family, genus, and species. This system is important because it gives every plant or animal a single scientific designation, so

173

people all over the world can speak a common language when researching and discussing particular organisms.

Insects and mites (plus many related animals) are members of the animal phylum Arthropoda. Arthropods are everywhere. In addition to the insects (class Insecta) and mites (class Arachnida), other well-known arthropods include crayfish, lobsters, shrimp, and sowbugs (class Malacostraca); scorpions, spiders, and ticks (class Arachnida); millipedes (class Diplopoda); and symphylans (class Symphyla).

Scientific and common names

The final two names in most classifications are the genus and species. Most people are not familiar with these names, especially because most seem very long and difficult to pronounce! This is because Latin is used. Latin—a "dead" language, not spoken commonly—is universally used by scientists because it will not change as other languages do.

Fortunately for most, nearly all economically important plants and animals also have common names to go with their scientific names. For example, the thrips in the genus *Frankliniella* with the species name *occidentalis* has the common name in North America of "western flower thrips." The whitefly *Bemisia tabaci,* (or *B. argentifolii*) is called either the sweet potato whitefly, the tobacco whitefly, the cotton whitefly, or the silverleaf whitefly. There may or may not be two or more different whitefly species involved in these common names.

Common names can thus be locally handy but confusing in ways. In many parts of the world, the western flower thrips is known as the California thrips and perhaps other local names. *Bemisia* whiteflies have numerous common names. It is easy to see that common names will work fine for general discussion in specific geographic areas, but not in others. This is why we must place some emphasis on using scientific names as well as common names in most of the chapters of this book (sometimes even the scientific names are not certain). Floriculture is a global business, and it is necessary that we discuss these topics in more global terms.

Insects

Insects are arthropods in the class Insecta that have bodies with three distinct parts: the head, thorax, and abdomen. There are three pairs of legs (although some insects do not have legs), one pair on each segment of the thorax. The main groups of insects are divided into 27 different orders.

The insects are by far the most numerous of the arthropod groups and in fact are the largest animal group on earth. Most insects are not problems for humans, and many are beneficial or even extremely valuable to humans. The pollination of crops by bees makes the production of many crops possible. Other insects are considered beneficial because they prey on, or parasitize, insect pests, helping to regulate their populations.

Insects are food for other animals, including humans in many societies. They help clean up various kinds of debris, including dead animals and plants, from the landscape. The small fruit flies in the genus *Drosophila* have been invaluable in genetic research.

A relatively few insects are very harmful to humans, either by feeding on structures (such as termites), cultivated crops, or stored products. Many insects can carry and help spread pathogens that can cause diseases of animals and plants. As most growers know, insects (and associated animals) can be very serious problems on floricultural crops.

The life cycles of insects range from the somewhat simple to the very complex. Many insects pass through significant changes as they mature. In other cases, the young insects resemble smaller adults. All of these changes are called *metamorphosis*. The types of metamorphosis of the different pest and beneficial insects are very important in proper detection and management. Metamorphosis may be simple, intermediate, or complete. It may seem unnecessary to worry about knowing the different developmental stages of pests, but pest management depends to a large extent on this knowledge.

Insects, mites, and flower and foliage crops

Flower and foliage crop production for domestic and export markets is a significant component of agricultural income in many countries. Crops are produced in heated and unheated greenhouses, plastic-covered tunnels, outdoors under shade screening, or in open fields. Because of the similarity of crops being produced, there is a fairly consistent group of insect, mite, and related pests attacking these flower and foliage crops, mostly from six hexapod orders and one mite order. These include Homoptera (aphids, whiteflies, mealybugs, and scales), Hemiptera (plant bugs), Diptera (leafminers, midges, shoreflies, and fungus gnats), Thysanoptera (thrips), Lepidoptera (caterpillars), Coleoptera (beetles, grubs), and Acari (mites). Other arthropod pests include springtails (Collembola), millipedes (Diplopoda), sowbugs (Isopoda), and symphylans (class Symphyla). Slugs and snails (phylum Mollusca), nonarthropod pests, are included in this discussion for convenience because they can be plant pests.

Occasionally, one or more pest species cause severe problems and may even limit production of certain crops. Some recent examples include western flower thrips (*Frankliniella occidentalis*), melon or cotton aphids (*Aphis gossypii*), green peach aphids (*Myzus persicae*), silverleaf whiteflies (*Bemisia tabaci*—B strain, or *B. argentifolii*), two-spotted spider mites (*Tetranychus urticae*), Lewis spider mites (*Eotetranychus lewisi*), and beet armyworms (*Spodoptera exigua*).

These pests, along with continued problems with other insect and mite species—including leafminers, (*Liriomyza trifolii* and *L. huidobrensis*), greenhouse whiteflies (*Trialeurodes vaporariorum*), and fungus gnats (*Bradysia* spp.)—have provided serious challenges to growers, researchers, and pest control advisors in the development of pest management programs. None of these pest groups is particularly new. Extension and research bulletins written between 1900 and 1930 mention problems with most of the pest groups causing problems today. The individual species names are sometimes different because of changes in classification, pest movement, or pesticide resistance.

Insect and mite pests become problems because of one or more of the following interrelated factors:

Adaptation. They may be well adapted to the greenhouse or outdoor floricultural environment and are able to survive on numerous host plants.

The most serious insect and mite pests of floricultural crops can survive on numerous host plants, are quite small, have high fecundity (reproductive capacity), and have rapid life cycles. Most can be serious problems inside and outside greenhouses. Most are also pests of other horticultural or agronomic crops. There are exceptions. The chrysanthemum aphid (*Macrosiphoniella sanborni*) and rose aphid (*Macrosiphum rosae*) primarily infest the plants in their common names.

Identification. People can fail to properly identify pests and have inadequate biological knowledge. It is important to know the species because, although in many ways similar, different species within a pest group will have different life cycles and pesticide resistance characteristics. This is a problem for growers, researchers, and crop advisors. In the "good old days" of broad-spectrum, long-residual pesticides (like DDT), it was only necessary to know that a pest was a whitefly, an aphid, or a mite. Perhaps it was not even necessary to know that much—the broad spectrum insecticides could be applied on some kind of schedule, without concern for proper identification of any pest group. Identification was required only when something survived the pesticide applications. Now this identification is necessary to help know what pest management tactics will be effective against particular species.

Pesticide resistance. This probably is the most important problem in insect and mite management today. Among the major insect and mite pest groups discussed in the next chapter, resistance to one or more pesticides has been documented in at least one species within each group. Pesticide resistance is not a new phenomenon, nor is it unique to floriculture. However, there are some aspects of floriculture crop production that virtually ensure the development of pesticide resistance.

Many flower and foliage crops are produced by specialty propagators who carry on intensive pesticide programs to ensure that pest-free plant material is shipped to producers. After all, the problem of pests arriving on plant material is something no grower wishes to receive. This intensive program can select for pesticide-resistant pests. If pesticide-resistant pests are selected for at the propagation site, they will soon appear wherever the plants are shipped. Selection for resistance continues at the destination, because these growers also must try to produce crops as pest-free as possible to avoid problems with their customers. Pesticide resistance in greenhouses may be greater than in the same pest species on field crops.

Plant pest quarantines may or may not be imposed for biological reasons. Sometimes quarantines are political, and they may not always be necessary. However, quarantines are a fact of life and certainly can contribute to excessive pesticide use. If there is a serious pest problem in any area where flower and foliage crops are produced, the plant distribution system provides opportunities for that pest to be distributed widely. Many of the most important pests of flower and foliage crops are very difficult to see on plants. When the allowable pest level in a quarantine is zero, this places a heavy burden on the producer.

In such cases, pesticide use could be extremely heavy, which will eventually lead to pesticide resistance, ensuring the spread of already-resistant pests. We do not have an answer for this problem, except to suggest that propagators and growers use as many nonchemical pest management tactics as possible to delay resistance. The politics of quarantines will not be easily changed, because there are too many convenient targets to blame for problems.

Integrated pest management

Integrated pest management (IPM), *integrated crop production*, and *holistic plant health management* have similar meanings. We are taking a systematic approach to managing plant diseases, insects, and mites in this book. With such an approach, a variety of pest and disease management tactics must be used. The rest of the chapter briefly covers the major components of an insect and mite pest management system.

Pesticides are still the primary means of pest management on flower and foliage crops. Both conventional and biorational pesticides are used, with biorational pesticides becoming more numerous. Where pesticides, especially conventional pesticides, are used, the development of pesticide resistance is inevitable. One of the major potential benefits of using integrated crop production tactics is in slowing the onset of pesticide resistance development. Pests may become resistant to biorational pesticides as well, but this development generally takes longer than with conventional products. Do not overuse any pesticide. The only question regarding resistance development is the time it will take to appear. Therefore, a grower must take management of pesticide resistance into account whether using conventional or biorational pesticides.

Use as many nonchemical control tactics as possible. In greenhouses these tactics include sanitation, steaming ground beds between crops, microscreening for exclusion, a plant-free period, crop rotation, biorational products, and beneficial insects or mites. Most of these tactics will be discussed below and mentioned further in connection with individual pest groups.

Sanitation

Weed removal within and around the crop production area is very important in reducing pest numbers in the area (fig. 13.1). Otherwise, many insect and mite pests can survive on these plants and eventually move onto the crops. Destroy harvested cutflower crop residues quickly. Throw away unsold potted plants. Avoid the temptation to keep "pet" plants in the vicinity of the crop. Also, the greenhouse should be completely cleaned between crops (fig. 13.2).

Fig. 13.1. Whiteflies on discarded plants outside the greenhouse.

Fig. 13.2. Between crops, the greenhouse needs to be completely cleaned.

Steaming and fumigation

Steam the soil between crops that have been infested with insects such as leafminers and thrips. Both of these pest groups spend part of their development cycles in or on the soil. Allowing these stages to survive between crops will lead to problems later. Steaming will also help reduce problems with symphylans and springtails. Methyl bromide, a commonly used soil fumigant, is very effective if used properly. There are plans to eventually phase out the use of methyl bromide in the United States, however.

Microscreening

Installation of screening is a relatively old idea that is now being implemented quite widely on greenhouses. Even the Saran screening covering some outdoor plantings will help exclude some pests (such as Lepidoptera). Greenhouse screening does help to exclude some flying insect pests, including whiteflies, leafminers, aphids, and thrips. Metal, polyethylene, and polyester screening are available. Metal screening is used to protect valuable stock plants, metal being the most durable screen, but it is also the most expensive. The other screening types are less expensive but less durable.

Microscreening will help in pest management, but screens will not exclude all insect pests. Because of the fine mesh size required to restrict insect movement, especially with tiny pests such as thrips (the most difficult pests to exclude), air circulation can be restricted, causing temperature and moisture problems. Increasing the surface area of air inlets or increasing fan capacity will be necessary to counteract these problems, or the screens will need removing in warm weather. Screens also need to be cleaned regularly, depending on the amount of dust and other debris in the area.

Screening should be combined with positive air pressure to prevent pest entry when greenhouse doors are opened. Small vestibules or entryways can be constructed for this. Some greenhouses install screening only on the sides facing the prevailing wind direction. Others have screened over all the openings in the greenhouse structure, including walkways between separate greenhouses.

Information on screening installation on new and existing greenhouses is available from suppliers and extension specialists. There is a computer program available from North Carolina State University that will help the grower considering screening determine what will be required in specific situations.

Scouting and spot treatments

Use plant pest scouting, indicator plants (fig. 13.3), and sticky traps or blacklight traps, and apply pesticides to so-called hot spots, rather than make applications to the entire crop. This may not be practical for some pests, such as the western flower thrips, but can be very effective for aphids, spider mites, and whiteflies. (These tactics were discussed in greater detail in chapter 2, "Diagnosing Problems.")

Fig. 13.3. Petunias are useful indicator plants for thrips detection; yellow sticky traps are used to help attract thrips adults.

Pesticide rotation

Use common sense with pesticides. Rotate pesticide families and application methods. In addition to conventional pesticides, use biorational products such as soaps and oils, insect growth regulators, microbials, and botanicals in a rotation program. Rotation does not necessarily mean strict alternation, although there are some researchers who have recommended using the same pesticide only once per crop, changing pesticide families after each application.

In the longer rotation programs, the same pesticide or pesticide combination is used for the equivalent of one pest generation. Depending on the pest and environmental conditions, this may be 10 days to one month or more. There are some suggestions that the pesticide rotation should be about two months for the greatest success in delaying resistance. There is no overwhelming evidence to support any particular rotation program. A major difficulty in some cases is finding enough pesticides to rotate for any particular pest.

Beneficial insects and mites

As anyone who has followed pest management trends knows, there is tremendous interest in using beneficial insects, mites, and nematodes (we will simply call them *beneficials*). There are numerous insectaries that raise, package, and sell beneficials to commercial producers and home gardeners worldwide. Nearly everyone is familiar with ladybird beetles and lacewings (fig. 13.4), and how they feed on harmful pests. However, there are many other beneficials, including tiny wasps that lay eggs inside insects such as aphids, whiteflies, mealybugs, and leafminers; mites that prey on other mites, thrips, and fungus gnat larvae; and nematodes that invade the bodies of beetle larvae and fungus gnat larvae. (Many of these beneficials are discussed in chapters 14 and 15.)

Fig. 13.4. Predator (beneficial insect) used for biological control.

At the present time, most commercial use of beneficials is on greenhouse vegetable crops. There have been some successes on flower and foliage crops, usually on crops that have only one or two main pests attacking them. (Specific beneficials will be discussed in connection with each pest group in the next two chapters. A table showing the most widely available beneficials is in chapter 18.) Widespread use of biological control on flower and foliage crops using only beneficials is still in the future—perhaps very far in the future. The best approach will probably be to integrate beneficials with other management tactics, including "soft" pesticides.

Postharvest treatments

Treating plants or cut flowers after harvest has normally been based on quarantine inspections at ports of entry. However, there is considerable research on postharvest pest-elimination treatment as a part of a total pest management program. There are many types of treatments being attempted, including aerosols, fogs, vapor heat, controlled atmospheres, fumigants, and irradiation. Most of these treatments are at least partially successful in pest control, but disadvantages include time for treatment (up to one week) and possible plant injury. The most successful postharvest treatments have been with methyl bromide (alone or combined with dichlorvos) and controlled atmospheres (low oxygen combined with high carbon dioxide). Unfortunately, both methyl bromide and dichlorvos may be unavailable in the near future. At a minimum, there will be severe restriction on their use.

Each plant-pest combination requires different treatments. The key to postharvest treatment success is related to preharvest treatment success. There must be a total pest management program.

Chapter 14

Major Insect and Mite Pests

In this chapter the general biology, economic importance, and suggestions for management of many pests of flower and foliage crops are discussed. This chapter and the next should be considered starting points in locating detailed information about any insect or mite pest. A few specific pesticide suggestions and biological control programs are given here, but consult your state extension service or consultant for specific suggestions for your business. Beneficial insect suppliers and technical representatives of greenhouse supply companies and chemical companies are often excellent sources of current information, as well. Keep in mind that the person from whom you seek help may need to send insects or mites to a specialist to be certain of identification. This need not stop you from trying to implement a general pest management program, however, while waiting for identification. Also see chapter 18 for information on currently registered insecticides and miticides, plus available beneficial insects and mites, in the United States. The Internet (e.g., the World Wide Web) has some excellent information sources. Some of these are listed in the reference section at the end of the book.

Remember that pests and diseases usually do not appear individually. It is very likely that there will be more than one insect or mite pest to contend with when producing any crop. Also, most growers produce more than one crop in the greenhouse or field, further complicating pest management. Although it is convenient for organizational purposes to consider pests individually, reality is rarely so organized.

Thrips (Thysanoptera–Thripidae)

There are more than 6,000 species of thrips (fig. 14.1), with several hundred species attacking cultivated plants. Only a few species cause problems on floricultural crops, but those problems can be severe. Major pests of flower and foliage crops include the onion or tobacco thrips, *Thrips tabaci*, greenhouse thrips, *Heliothrips haemorrhoidalis*, eastern flower thrips, *Frankliniella tritici*, gladi-

Fig. 14.1. Thrips adult and larva.

olus thrips, *Thrips simplex*, palm thrips or melon thrips, *Thrips palmi*, and the western flower thrips, *F. occidentalis*. (The word *thrips*, by the way, is singular, as well as plural.)

The western flower thrips is an excellent example of a previously secondary pest that has become extremely difficult to manage. It has spread well outside of its native area due to the factors mentioned in chapter 13. At this time the western flower thrips is the most important and serious insect pest in greenhouses in much of the world. In the United States more than 240 plant species in more than 60 plant families have been recorded as hosts for this insect.

Biology

Most of the following discussion is based on the western flower thrips. Thrips are very small, narrow insects, less than 1 mm wide and 1 to 1.5 mm long. Adults have long, fringed wings, but are not strong fliers. However, their small size allows them to move long distances on wind currents.

Both male and female western flower thrips occur. Female thrips can lay eggs without mating, but these offspring will all be male. Offspring from mated females are mostly females. The western flower thrips female places her eggs individually within leaf or flower tissue. The eggs cannot be seen by simply looking at plants. The number of eggs deposited is variable but may be as high as 300. If there is pollen present as a food source, females produce more eggs.

Depending on temperatures, eggs hatch in two to seven days into small, translucent larvae. There are four larval development stages. After one to two days, the first-instar larvae molt into second-instar larvae, which generally become yellow as they feed. These first larval instars are usually found protected within developing leaves or flowers.

After two to four days, the second-instar larvae generally move off the plant and burrow into the soil or growing medium and undergo two transformation stages, called pseudopupae. These transformations can also occur within flowers. The first transformation stage is called the prepupa, and the second is the pupa. Thrips do not feed or move much during this time, which can range from two to five days or longer. Adults then emerge. At normal greenhouse temperatures, the egg-to-adult cycle can be completed in eight to 20 days (fig. 14.2).

Thrips do best in hot, dry conditions. However, high humidity does not seem to reduce their numbers; only relatively constant moisture on the leaves and flowers will do so. The amount of moisture required, however, probably makes leaf wetting impractical as a pest management tactic. Female western flower thrips can live from 10 to 45 or more days. The shortest life spans occur at the higher temperatures. The rapid life cycle and high reproductive capacity, plus the fact that the larvae are concealed within plant parts much of the time, lead to great difficulties in detection and management.

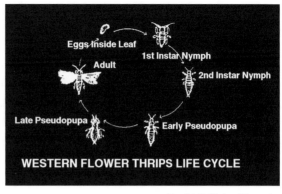

Fig. 14.2. Thrips life cycle.

Economic impact

The western flower thrips has a very wide host plant range, which includes many ornamental crops. All plant-feeding thrips damage plants directly by inserting their mouthparts into plant tissue. Thrips are not true piercing-sucking insects, such as aphids and whiteflies, but feed by inserting their modified left mandible into plant tissue and removing plant fluids with a needlelike stylet.

Leaves, stems, and flowers can be damaged. Much of the injury caused by larval feeding occurs within developing leaves and flowers and is not seen until the affected parts expand (fig. 14.3). These areas are often distorted, and affected flowers may not open normally. Because the injury occurred earlier, however, thrips may not be present when the damage is seen.

Fig. 14.3. Thrips injury to flower.

Thrips also feed on expanded leaves (upper or lower surface) and flowers. This feeding damage appears as silvery areas on leaves, due to removal of the cell contents. Usually, feeding injury is accompanied by numerous dark spots of fecal material. Feeding on flowers results in petal scarring and distortion. Depending upon petal color, the injury may result in light or dark areas. Thrips also feed on pollen and nectar of plants such as African violets, causing premature senescence of the flower. Pollen feeding is a significant factor in thrips reproduction.

A very serious additional problem with some thrips species is the transmission of tospoviruses, including tomato spotted wilt virus (TSWV) and impatiens necrotic spot virus (INSV). TSWV normally affects vegetable crops, whereas INSV is found mostly on ornamental crops (fig. 14.4). Several thrips species are vectors, including the onion thrips, palm thrips, and western flower thrips. These viruses occur almost everywhere. About 300 plant species in more than 45 families can be virus reservoirs. Thrips acquire the virus as larvae, in as little as 30 minutes feeding on infected plants, and can become infective after three to 10 days. Usually, adult thrips trans-

Fig. 14.4. Thrips-transmitted virus symptoms on dahlia.

mit the virus and remain infective throughout their lives. There apparently are geographical differences in the ability of the same thrips species to transmit these viruses, which is a subject of considerable interest.

There is no cure for virus infection, so management of these pathogens depends on management of thrips or changing crop production practices. In some cases, it may be necessary to stop production of certain crops during some seasons.

Detection

A monitoring system is required for a successful thrips management program. Many growers and pest management advisors suggest setting out sticky traps for monitoring adult thrips numbers. Although several trap colors can be used, many advisors suggest blue or white traps, which some studies have shown to be more effective than yellow. However, since yellow traps are useful for other insect species, these may be best to use in a general monitoring program. It is important that the thrips species be identified. Consult chapter 2 and the suggested reading list for more information.

Thrips are usually seen on traps before becoming visible on plants. The basic rule of using traps for thrips monitoring is this: If thrips are seen on traps, chances are excellent that they are also on plants. However, if no thrips are seen on traps, there may still be thrips on plants. The lesson is not to rely on traps alone to tell the story.

In greenhouses place traps near doors and vents, as well as just above crops known to be attractive to thrips or very susceptible to virus. Traps may also be placed outdoors, which can provide something of an early warning of a thrips invasion of the greenhouse. The number of traps will vary, but one trap per 10,000 square feet (1,000 m^2) should provide a reasonable estimate of population trends. More traps will be better. Check the traps at least weekly. Learn to recognize these very small insects as they appear on traps. Keep records of numbers caught and try to relate these numbers to visible plant damage as part of an effort to develop an injury, or action, threshold.

Thrips will have definite population cycles in each greenhouse or outdoors. Over time, sticky traps will help show these cycles. The time between peak adult numbers will vary, depending on temperature, but for the western flower thrips, it will normally be between 14 and 28 days. Knowing cycles is useful in designing a pesticide application program. Evidence now exists that properly timed insecticide applications help reduce peak thrips numbers and reduce the number of applications required to do so.

Some growers use indicator plants, or IPs, to help detect thrips or viruses. IPs are used where feeding injury is more easily seen than on the main crop, where the IPs are more attractive to the pest (i.e., the pests appear on the IPs before the main crop), or virus symptoms are readily seen. The petunia cultivars Summer Madness and Calypso, as well as the fava bean cultivar Toto, have been useful. The plants are placed around the greenhouse much as sticky traps. Flowers are removed so that the thrips are forced to feed on the leaves. On these IPs, thrips feeding injury is easy to see, and the virus symptoms appear before those on most crops. It is important to quickly remove from the crop area indicator plants showing virus symptoms, as these infected plants can be virus sources.

Inspect plants of the thrips-susceptible crop weekly. Pay special attention to plants on the perimeter of the planting, near doors and side vents. Look for thrips injury on leaves or flowers. Shake some flowers over a piece of white paper to see if thrips are present. Blowing gently into a flower will usually activate thrips.

Control

Cultural/physical control. Because of their flight habits and wide host plant range, it is difficult to remove enough vegetation from around the production area to lower thrips populations. Conventional wisdom would say that no flowering plants should be permitted to grow in areas immediately adjacent to the production area. However, with more research, it might be possible to grow certain flowering plant species around the perimeter of the greenhouse or outdoor planting. These plants may act as attractants for thrips and beneficial insects or mites, reducing overall numbers moving into the crop.

Several attempts have been made to use screens or barriers as a method to protect valuable stock plants and other plants very susceptible to INSV or TSWV. This has been quite successful in restricting thrips movement, but screening will not keep all of the thrips from moving into the greenhouse. (See chapter 13 for more discussion of microscreening.)

Reflective tapes and screens placed around greenhouse vents may help to reduce thrips movement into greenhouses. Aluminum shade cloth or reflective aluminized tapes have significantly reduced the numbers of western flower thrips moving into commercial greenhouses from adjacent fields.

Crop rotation may be necessary to disrupt thrips populations. Changing to less susceptible crops, immediate destruction of crop residues, and harvesting an entire planting area at one time will help reduce thrips numbers. For crops produced in ground beds, steaming/fumigation should be done after harvest. Do not produce a virus-susceptible crop adjacent to a crop that is likely to harbor a thrips population (fig. 14.5).

One of the worst situations is a crop production system in a large greenhouse that always contains plants of different ages. Thrips simply move from one area to another—usually to those plants in flower. Because of the

Fig. 14.5. Gloxinia crop adjacent to African violets.

rapid thrips life cycle, crop residues remaining in the greenhouse or field are excellent reservoirs for increasing thrips populations. Crops extremely susceptible to thrips or spotted wilt virus should be produced in separate areas.

Pesticides. Insecticide control of thrips, especially the western flower thrips, is difficult. Pesticide-resistant thrips exist in most production areas. Many thrips species can survive on a wide range of host plants, both cultivated and wild, which can provide sources of infestation and reinfestation.

The most susceptible larval stages are only present for about one-third of the egg-to-adult cycle. Contacting thrips deep inside plant growing points or flower buds is very difficult. Current control strategies are thus based on frequent (e.g., at least two applications at three- to five-day intervals) applications of nonsystemic insecticides. In some southern areas, applications have been made every second day. Use high- and low-volume sprays, aerosols, and fogs to protect developing flowers and foliage. Targeting adult thrips may be more practical than trying to control larvae. Adults are more active and are normally on the upper surfaces of leaves and flowers, making them easier to contact with insecticide applications.

Apply high volume sprays as late in the day as possible, keeping plants wet longer and increasing the chances of the thrips contacting the spray deposit. Foliage wetness may cause more problems with plant pathogens, but if the thrips infestation is heavy enough, it may be necessary to risk a disease to obtain more effective thrips control. In such situations, some of the low-volume sprays will be useful because the leaves are not wet. (See chapter 17 for more details.)

Combining a pyrethroid insecticide with an organophosphate or carbamate insecticide has been successful in some management programs. The pyrethroid insecticide causes the thrips to become more active, increasing their chances of contacting an amount of pesticide sufficient to cause death. Using white or brown sugar with an insecticide has also increased control in some cases. The sugar acts as a bait. When the sugar plus insecticide has been used, best results were obtained when only about 25 to 50 percent of the normal spray volume was applied (not a wet spray).

Systemic insecticides may act more slowly against thrips, compared with other insects that feed on phloem (such as aphids and whiteflies). Systemics generally do not reach flowers in sufficient concentration to kill insects in these areas. However, there are indications that combinations of systemic insecticides (such as acephate or imidacloprid) applied to the potting mix preceded by sprays of insect growth regulators (such as azadirachtin or fenoxycarb) are very effective at western flower thrips control in flowers of some plants.

Postharvest fumigation of flowers may offer the best hope for producing essentially thrips-free plants and flowers. Most of the experimental work has been on fresh cut flowers for export. Treating harvested flowers with methyl bromide, gamma radiation, and modified atmospheres (low O_2 or high CO_2) have all been attempted as possible ways of eliminating thrips (and other pests).

Although none of these methods has been completely successful, there will probably be situations in which they can be used. One of the major problems to date is the time required to achieve control. The hours (or days) spent in postharvest treatment will reduce the total shelf life of the product. It's possible that several postharvest operations can be combined to reduce the time required.

Biological control. Biological control of western flower thrips using introduced beneficial insects or mites has not been very successful on flower and foliage plants. However, there have been some encouraging developments, especially on vegetable crops. In recent years there has been a great deal of research on biological control of western flower thrips, because controlling this species is the key element in implementing a total IPM/biological control program on flower and foliage crops.

Some programs involve introducing predatory phytoseiid mites, including *Neoseiulus* (= *Amblyseius*) *cucumeris* and *N. barkeri* (= *A. mckenziei*). One or both of these mite species are being reared and distributed by commercial insectaries and research institutions. To date, successful control of the onion thrips has been reported on greenhouse peppers in the Netherlands. Results against the western flower thrips have been variable. Much of the problem is that the predators are effective against thrips on foliage but do not move into flowers. A recent experiment in California indicated that using both of the above predators might be more effective than either species alone.

Predatory insects in the family Anthocoridae, such as *Orius insidiosus* and *O. tristicolor* (minute pirate bugs), have been very effective predators on the onion thrips and western flower thrips. *Orius* will move into crops if no pesticides, or if pesticides without adverse effects, are being used, but only after thrips populations have reached high levels.

Some entomopathogenic fungi (fungi that attack insects) attack thrips. *Beauveria bassiana* (Naturalis-O) contains a patented fungus strain registered as a commercial product for thrips control in the United States. Preliminary results in commercial greenhouses have been quite good against the western flower thrips. In experimental trials, fungi including *B. bassiana* or *Paecilomyces fumosoroseus* combined with azadirachtin-based products have provided excellent western flower thrips control.

Whiteflies (Homoptera–Aleyrodidae)

Whiteflies are primarily tropical insects, but some species (of the approximately 1,100 species in the family) have become pests wherever flower and foliage crops are produced. The two most important whitefly pests in floriculture are the greenhouse whitefly, *Trialeurodes vaporariorum*;

and the *Bemisia* whitefly (fig. 14.6), *Bemisia tabaci*—B Strain/*B. argentifolii*, also called the silverleaf whitefly because it causes a silvering condition on squash plants. At the time of this writing, there is some question whether there are two or only one whitefly species involved as the silverleaf whitefly (also not an approved common name). Nevertheless, we will refer to this whitefly as the

Fig. 14.6. Adult and immature *Bemisia* whiteflies.

silverleaf whitefly. The banded-winged whitefly, *T. abutilonea*, may also occasionally infest crops such as poinsettia, but to date has not been a problem. This species is seen mostly on sticky traps, where its banded wing patterns make it easily recognizable.

The greenhouse whitefly has caused problems on numerous crops for more than 100 years—and from all indications will continue on its present course. The greenhouse whitefly has been recorded from about 250 plant genera in 84 families. The silverleaf whitefly is widespread, as well, and is now established as a pest of ornamental and vegetable crops in North America and in other areas of the world. It has been collected from more than 500 plant species in 74 families. It is the most important virus vector species among whiteflies. Most of the viruses affect vegetable crops at this time, but there may be virus problems on ornamentals in the future.

Biology

The basic biology of the major whitefly pests is similar. Adults and immature stages have piercing-sucking mouthparts, which are inserted into phloem tissue and remove plant fluids. Both males and females occur. Females may live up to two months and produce 30 to 500 or more eggs, but most probably live about one month and produce 60 to 80 eggs. Egg production in these insects sometimes increases with increasing adult whitefly density. Females usually begin producing eggs within a few days after emergence. The eggs generally hatch in seven to 10 days.

The newly hatched immatures, or "crawlers" (properly called either nymphs or larvae), move for a short distance before settling down to feed. Following this, the nymphs do not change location until adult emergence. After three molts a "pupal" stage is formed, from which adults emerge in about six days. Whiteflies complete their egg-to-adult cycle in 21 to 36 days, depending on temperatures (fig. 14.7). Newly emerged adults are pale green to yellow at first but soon become covered by a powdery white wax. Adults have four wings.

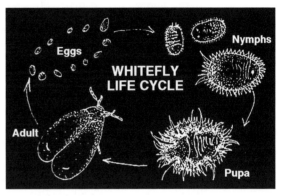

Greenhouse whiteflies do best at moderate temperatures, while silverleaf whiteflies (and banded-winged whiteflies) do best at higher temperatures. All developmental stages are found on leaf undersides. Adults usually prefer the undersides of upper leaves for feeding and egg-laying.

Fig. 14.7. Whitefly life cycle.

Economic impact

Much of the economic impact of whiteflies is due to their wide host plant range. The mere presence of the small flying adults can result in consumer complaints. High populations weaken plants, and reduced plant vigor may eventually result in plant death. Moderate to heavy silverleaf whitefly infestations on poinsettia can cause stunting, bract deformity, and a condition called "white stem."

Whiteflies (and other piercing-sucking insects, such as aphids, mealybugs, and soft scales) also produce a sticky substance called honeydew, a digestive by-product rich in sugars. Often enough honeydew is produced to act as a substrate for a black sooty fungus. If this fungus becomes well established, leaves or even entire plants can be killed because of reduced photosynthesis and respiration. Of course, the black fungus also makes plants unsightly.

Another increasingly important impact of whiteflies is as virus vectors. Most virus problems are associated with silverleaf whiteflies, rather than greenhouse whiteflies, and are on crops such as tomatoes, lettuce, melons, and soybeans. However, there are several whitefly-transmitted virus diseases of ornamental plants. These include diseases on geranium, hibiscus, rose, salvia, zinnia, and anthurium. If silverleaf whiteflies continue to spread and cause problems, the incidence of these virus-caused plant diseases may also increase.

Detection

On whitefly-susceptible crops, inspect plants weekly. Make a map or diagram of the production area so that infested areas can be noted and recorded. Be especially alert when receiving shipments of known whitefly host plants. Initially, whiteflies do not occur uniformly throughout the crop, and there will be definite areas of high numbers as well as areas without any insects. Pay special attention to plants near open side ventilators and entry areas, but do not neglect plants in the center of the production area.

Shake plants, turn leaves over, or use a mirror to observe the undersides of leaves. You will need a 10 to 15× hand lens to see eggs and small larval stages. Sequential whitefly sampling plans have been developed for poinsettia crops that will provide accurate information at a preselected level of precision. In other words, the person doing the sampling can decide on a number of whitefly nymphs per plant to tolerate and a level of sampling accuracy before beginning plant inspections. Published tables (see reading list) help establish these numbers and determine if the cumulative (running total) number of sampled whitefly larval stages are above or below the preestablished levels.

A minimum number of plants must be sampled before determining whether whitefly numbers are within the tolerable range. Theoretically, only one plant will need to be sampled if the whitefly count is high. If the number of whitefly larvae is below the established threshold, no treatment will be needed at that time, but sampling must be done each week.

Yellow sticky traps placed throughout the crop will help detect adults. Trap spacing can vary but should be about one trap per 1,000 square feet (100 m²). Sticky traps will not replace plant inspection as a method of detecting low numbers of whiteflies. Large numbers of whiteflies on sticky traps will mean that there probably are large numbers on plants. The opposite situation is not always true.

Once whiteflies are found, it is important to determine the species. Adult silverleaf white-flies are usually smaller, more yellow, and more active than greenhouse whiteflies (fig. 14.8). The wings of silverleaf white-flies are normally held more ver-tically, while greenhouse white-flies hold wings nearly horizon-tally. Banded-winged whiteflies, as the name implies, have rather indistinct dark bands on the wings.

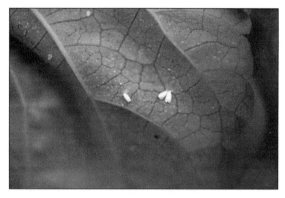

Fig. 14.8. Adult greenhouse (*right*) and *Bemisia* (*left*) whiteflies.

The immature stages of greenhouse and silverleaf whiteflies are also different, especially in the pupal stage. However, species separation can only be made in the pupal stage, because the shape of earlier immature stages will vary with the plant on which they develop. Silverleaf whitefly pupae are convex or flat-tened, without spines or fringes. On some host plants (such as poinsettia), silverleaf whitefly pupae are yellow and have a "lemon drop" shape. Greenhouse whitefly pupae, on the other hand, have vertical sides, with obvious spines and fringes of setae around the top perimeter (fig. 14.9).

Fig. 14.9. Empty pupal cases of greenhouse (*right*) and *Bemisia* (*left*) whiteflies.

Control

Cultural/physical control. Weed removal inside and outside of the crop production area is very important. If possible, separate stock plant production areas from other production. Install microscreening or insect barriers for this purpose. Screening can also reduce the movement of whiteflies into greenhouses from outdoors. On some outdoor crops, mulching with aluminum or yellow polyethylene sheets has reduced virus transmission by silverleaf whiteflies. The mechanism of how the two colors work may be different. The theory behind using yellow mulch is that the adults are attracted to the mulch's color and are killed after a short time by exposure to the mulch's high temperatures. Aluminum mulches work by reflecting UV light, repelling whitefly adults. Mulches basically delay infestations and resulting virus infection. When the mulch becomes covered by the crop canopy, though, its effectiveness is eliminated. In greenhouses, large numbers of yellow sticky traps may be used to suppress populations, but only if the mass-trapping program is begun before large numbers appear.

Removal of lower leaves from plants containing large numbers of whitefly eggs and nymphs will help reduce future population increases. This is labor-intensive, but so is the task of many pesticide applications. The systemic insecticide imidacloprid, when applied as granules or drenches, will move to the growing point, largely bypassing infested lower leaves. Coverage of these leaves with spray applications of other pesticides is extremely difficult. Removing leaves and reducing the potential for whitefly increase will also improve the chances of success with biological control.

Pesticides. Whitefly populations from different geographic areas have been reported to be resistant to one or more organophosphate, carbamate, and pyrethroid insecticides. At this time, there is an effective systemic insecticide (imidacloprid), representing a different chemical class (chloronicotinyls), that is providing whitefly control for eight to 10 weeks with a single application as drenches or granules. However, for those who remember aldicarb, another systemic insecticide-miticide-nematicide, long-term control was also initially obtained with that product. Resistance will develop sooner or later to most any substance.

Systemic insecticide applications are usually made on a preventive basis, because they are slow-acting and should be applied while plants are actively growing and before significant numbers of whiteflies appear. Other pesticide control programs are with short-residual, nonsystemic conventional and biorational products. Usually, you will need to use the systemic and nonsystemic products during a crop production cycle, because no systemic product will persist for the entire crop.

Pesticide application technique is very important in whitefly control programs and must relate to the pesticide's mode of action. For contact insecticides, direct the sprays toward the lower leaf surfaces. Generally, smaller spray drops or higher spray pressures are most effective. With some pesticides, spray volume is also very important. Plant spacing may need adjusting to allow better spray coverage. Whenever possible, combine spray applications with aerosol, fog, or smoke generator applications. (See chapter 17 for more details on pesticide application methods.)

To check the success of chemical (or biological) control, mark or tag in some way plants known to be infested with whiteflies. Check the marked plants following the application(s) to determine the control effort's success. These plants are sometimes called *sentinel plants.*

Biological control. The primary natural enemy used against the greenhouse whitefly is the parasitic wasp *Encarsia formosa* (fig. 14.10). This parasite is commonly used on protected tomato and cucumber crops in the United States, Europe, and Canada, but there have been relatively few successes with *Encarsia* use on flower and foliage crops, especially if plants are infested with silverleaf whiteflies.

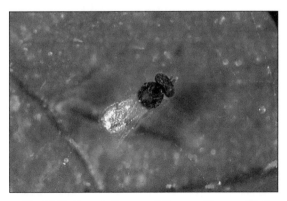

Because *E. formosa* generally is less effective against silverleaf whiteflies compared with greenhouse whiteflies, research is being conducted to locate and evaluate other parasites. Other species that are being evaluated and show some promise as silverleaf whitefly

Fig. 14.10. *Encarsia formosa* adult, a parasitic wasp effective against the greenhouse whitefly.

controls are *E. luteola* and *Eretmocerous* spp. There is currently conflicting information on the effectiveness of the other parasites. For example, there is some evidence that *Eretmocerous* is very effective on plants with smooth leaves, such as hibiscus, but not on plants with hairy leaves, such as poinsettia and tomato. However, there are other studies that show *Eretmocerous* is quite effective on poinsettias. Further studies will no doubt clarify all of this. If *Eretmocerous* parasites are shown to be effective controls of silverleaf whiteflies, it should be good news. This species will also work against greenhouse whiteflies. *Eretmocerous* is also relatively more resistant to pesticides than *Encarsia*.

A predatory coccinelid beetle, *Delphastus pusillus*, has been very effective in reducing high populations of silverleaf whiteflies. This predator is available from some commercial insectaries.

Other promising biological controls are naturally occurring entomopathogenic fungi. The fungi are applied as normal insecticides with conventional and low-volume spray equipment. They are generally compatible with other biorational and conventional insecticides and miticides, but not fungicides (i.e., they cannot be tank-mixed), and are cost-competitive.

The fungi evaluated the most against pests of flower and foliage crops in North America are *Beauveria bassiana* and *Paecilomyces fumosoroseus*. *B. bassiana* is registered in the United States for greenhouse and outdoor crops. Both of these fungi are used against pests other than whiteflies, including thrips and spider mites, but whiteflies are among the prime target pests. Experimental and commercial results with *B. bassiana* have been conflicting, but some results have been promising. *P. fumosoroseus* has also been very effective against silverleaf whiteflies and other pests in experimental greenhouse and large commercial trials. Another fungus product, *Verticillium lecanii*, is effective in controlling whiteflies and other pests. *V. lecanii* is registered in some European countries, but not in North America.

Aphids (Homoptera–Aphididae)

There are more than 4,000 species of aphids (fig. 14.11), but only about 250 species are problems on crop plants. Many aphid species are found on only one, or at most a few, host plants, but some have very large host plant ranges. The species with the ability to survive on numerous crops are, as one might expect, the species most likely to be the most important economically. On flower and foliage crops, several aphid species are considered pests, with the most common ones the green peach aphid, *Myzus persicae*; melon/cotton aphid, *Aphis gossypii*; chrysan-themum aphid, *Macrosiphoniella*

Fig. 14.11. Aphid adult and nymph.

sanborni; rose aphid, *Macrosiphum rosae*; potato aphid, *M. euphorbiae*; foxglove aphid, *Acyrthosiphon solani*; and leaf-curling plum aphid, *Brachycaudus helichrysi*.

Biology

Aphids are soft-bodied, generally sluggish insects that have piercing-sucking mouthparts, which are inserted into the phloem tissue of plants to remove fluids (fig. 14.12). They range in length from 0.06 to 0.14 inches (1.5 to 3.5 mm). Aphids are the only insects that have tubes, called siphunculi or cornicles, on the abdomen. These tubes some-times make aphids appear as if they were jet-propelled. Special-ists often use the length, shape, and color of the tubes to identify different species. Although often green, aphids can be many colors, including black, brown, pink, red, or white. Color and body size often vary within individual species.

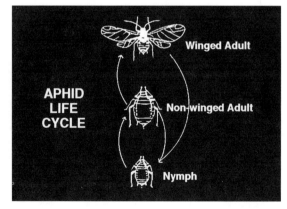

Fig. 14.12. Aphid life cycle.

Adult aphids may be winged or wingless. Winged aphids appear if the environment changes (day length, temperature), when aphids become overcrowded on their food plants, or the plants begin to deteriorate. These winged individuals are able to disperse within the crop and are often the first to arrive in a new location from outside the immediate area, such as from field crops or overwintering sites (fig. 14.13).

In greenhouses and tropical areas, all aphids are usually females that produce live young (nymphs) without mating (parthenogenesis). On outdoor plants in temperate zones and under some greenhouse conditions, the life cycle includes the appearance of males, subsequent mating, and the production of eggs. Each female can produce about 50 to 250 nymphs during her life span,

Fig. 14.13. Winged adult aphid.

and these nymphs can begin reproducing in four to 10 days. Adult aphids can live for about one month. Aphid reproduction depends to a large extent on temperature, host plant quality, and nutrition.

Economic impact

Usually, the presence of aphids is only a nuisance, because large numbers are required to actually affect plant growth on most plant species (fig. 14.14). However, aphids can stunt and deform plant growth if not controlled. The insects, or their white, cast-off skins (exoskeletons), detract from a plant's value. Aphids produce sugar-rich honeydew, which can cover leaves and flowers with a

Fig. 14.14. Aphid colony on flower bud.

sticky deposit. If humidity conditions are right, a black fungus called sooty mold grows on the honeydew. The sooty fungus reduces photosynthesis because of reduced light reaching the plant surfaces. The sticky, sweet honeydew can also attract ants and flies.

Aphids are important as vectors of plant viruses that affect many crops. *M. persicae* is mentioned most often because of its worldwide distribution and very wide host plant range (more than 400 host plants). This aphid can transmit more than 150 viruses or virus strains. *A. gossypii* transmits more than 50 viruses.

Detection

Winged aphids are attracted to yellow sticky traps, so these can be used as monitoring tools for aphids flying into or within the crops. However, most aphids do not have wings, so plant inspection is the most important way to detect aphids. Pay special attention to terminal shoots, and to flower buds *before* flowers open. Aphids can be found on all areas of the plant, so do not neglect some lower leaves. Lifting a few potted plants and looking from below is a good way to detect aphids. Another good way is to look for white exoskeletons left on plants by aphids during molting (fig. 14.15).

Fig. 14.15. Aphid skins on lily leaves.

Frequent plant inspection, especially of new plant shipments or after windy thunderstorms, will also help detect aphids (fig. 14.16). The presence of ants or

Fig. 14.16. Aphids on leaf undersides.

flies can be another clue to an aphid infestation. Some ant species "tend" aphids for their honeydew. In return, the ants protect aphids from predators and parasites. The larvae of syrphid flies (sometimes called hover flies or bee flies) are aphid predators, and seeing adult syrphid flies around the crop means that aphids are present.

Control

Cultural and physical control. Cultural controls include removal of weeds from around the plant production area. Weed host plants often serve as reservoirs for reinfestation. Fertilizer management also is very important. High nitrogen levels promote higher aphid populations.

Physical control methods include screens or other barriers. Screens are especially important in stock plant production areas to reduce the threat of virus transmission. Workers should not wear yellow clothing, because aphids attracted to the color may be carried into previously non-infested areas on this clothing.

Pesticides. Aphids can be difficult to control with pesticides for several reasons. They have high reproductive capacities and often occur on lower leaf surfaces deep within plant canopies or in flowers. Pesticide resistance, especially among green peach aphid and cotton/melon aphid populations, is quite widespread. Individual aphid populations, as well as species, vary widely in susceptibility to certain pesticides. Many organophosphate and carbamate insecticides are no longer effective. Pyrethroid insecticides may even stimulate aphid reproduction.

Outdoors, the use of some pesticides will destroy beneficial insects that help keep aphid numbers low. This may also happen in greenhouses if these beneficials have been introduced or have moved in from outside. Using pesticides that kill beneficials and do not control aphids will result in very high aphid populations.

The registration of the systemic insecticide imidacloprid has helped control aphids on flower and foliage crops. A single application can control aphids for up to 10 weeks. Systemic insecticides will usually not control aphids on or in flowers, however.

There are several biorational pesticides now registered for aphid management. The key to using these products is to take a proactive rather than reactive approach. They should be a part of a total management program (as mentioned earlier in chapter 13).

The good news, as far as control is concerned, is that there usually are no dormant growth stages (as with eggs or pupae) to contend with, and all development stages occur on plants. Thus, if pesticide resistance is not a problem, control with pesticides should be straightforward. Decisions relate mostly to pesticide selection, application method, and application interval.

Biological control. Most biological control programs involving parasites, predators, and fungi are now applied to protected vegetable crops, but there is increasing interest in using biological controls on ornamental plants as well. Predators, such as larvae of the predatory midge *Aphidoletes aphidimyza* (fig. 14.17) and lacewings (*Chrysopa* species), have been successfully used. Both are available from commercial insectaries. Parasites in the genus *Aphidius* often occur naturally when pesticide use is minimal, but they are usually too late to achieve control before high aphid populations develop. Parasitized aphids appear as light brown "mummies" on leaves (fig. 14.18). *Aphidius* parasites are available from commercial insectaries and can be introduced into infested crops.

Fig. 14.17. Aphid midge predator and aphid.

Fig. 14.18. Parasitized aphids.

Some greenhouses use the so-called *banker plant method* with aphid parasites. This method involves producing an aphid species, usually on a grain crop in pots or flats, that does not infest the main crop in the greenhouse. The aphids on the banker plants are exposed to parasites, and the banker plants containing parasitized aphids are placed in the greenhouse. Parasites emerging from the aphids on the banker plants will then disperse and find aphids on the crop to be protected. This, in effect, is placing small parasite-rearing units within the crop to supply a steady number of beneficial insects.

Several species and strains of naturally occurring entomopathogenic fungi have been used against aphids (fig. 14.19). The fungus *Beauveria bassiana* is registered for control of aphids on flower and foliage crops in the United States. *Paecilomyces fumosoroseus* is another fungus being evaluated. *Verticillium lecanii* is a fungus registered in Europe. Generally, aphid control with fungi has not been as successful as whitefly control. Control has been improved by tank-mixing fungi with other biorational pesticides, including soaps and oils. It may be possible to integrate fungal applications with beneficial insect introductions for aphid control.

Fig. 14.19. Fungus-infected aphid (*left*).

Scale insects (Homoptera–Diaspidae, Coccidae, and Pseudococcidae)

The scale insects are a very large and diverse insect group. The three main families of scale insects are represented by the armored scales, the soft scales, and mealybugs. There are significant differences among the three in terms of biology and development. Worldwide there are about 6,000 species, with 1,000 species occurring in North America. All scale insects have piercing-sucking mouthparts and do share many similarities in their life histories. In all scale insect families, females and males differ radically. Males of mealybugs usually resemble typical insects, with well-developed legs, eyes, antennae, and usually wings. The scalelike mealybugs are females.

Scale insects are known mostly as pests of foliage plants, but sometimes flowering potted plants (such as poinsettia) are infested by mealybugs, and long-term cut flowers (e.g., rose) by armored scale insects.

Biology

Members of the Family Diaspidiae are the so-called armored scales (fig. 14.20). This group gets its name from the hard, waxy cover the adults produce over their bodies. This covering, a mixture of wax and cast skins, comes in many shapes. It helps protect the insect from the weather, parasites, and some insecticides, as well as helps protect the eggs produced by most species. Coverings of males and females of the same species may vary in size and shape. The covering can be separated from the scale's body. Over time, extremely high populations can develop on plants (fig. 14.21). Armored scales do not produce honeydew.

As mentioned, most armored scales produce eggs, which hatch beneath the covering into crawlers. The crawlers move to new plant growth, where they settle and feed. At this time the females lose their legs and remain sessile for the rest of their lives. Females pass through three

Fig. 14.20. Armored scales on palm.

Fig. 14.21. Heavy armored scale infestation on rose stem.

instars, and the males five, before reaching adulthood (fig. 14.22). There may be as many as four generations per year.

The soft scales are in the Family Coccidae (fig. 14.23). They are so named because only when they are mature do the skins form a scale similar to that of the armored scales. Unlike with the armored scales, the covering of soft scales cannot be separated from the body. Soft scales are generally larger than armored scales, sometimes reaching a length of 0.12 to 0.16 inches (3 to 4 mm). Soft scales produce large amounts of honeydew.

The reproductive potential of these insects is tremendous. Soft scales may reproduce with or without mating, and females may lay eggs or produce live young. Females pass through three instars, and males five (fig. 14.24). In warm climates and in greenhouses, there may be five or six generations per year.

Mealybugs belong to the Family Pseudococcidae and are the least scalelike of the group (fig. 14.25). They are soft-bodied insects that produce a waxy powder over their bodies. Most mealybugs also produce waxy projections around their bodies, and many

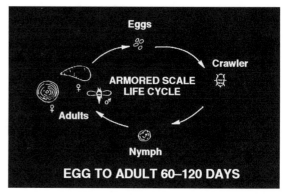

Fig. 14.22. Armored scales life cycle.

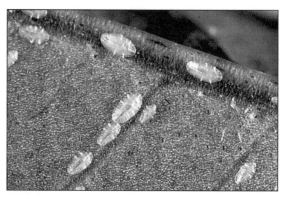

Fig. 14.23. Soft scales on leaf.

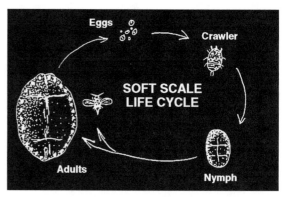

Fig. 14.24. Soft scale life cycle.

have long, filamentous "tails" consisting of waxy projections.

Mealybug infestations sometimes appear as small pieces of cotton on the plant. This is especially true when females produce masses of waxy threads in which the eggs are laid (called the ovisac). Preferred feeding sites are nodes and crotches of host plants. Mealybugs often form large colonies around nodes and

Fig. 14.25. Mealybugs and egg sacs.

where stems branch. Females pass through four instars, and males five. As with soft scales, mealybugs produce large amounts of honeydew.

After egg hatch or live birth, crawlers move about until they locate a suitable feeding site. Unlike other scale insects, mealybugs retain their legs throughout their development (fig. 14.26) and move around (as well as among) plants. However, once they locate a suitable feeding site, there is minimal movement. There may be as many as six generations per year in greenhouses and tropical areas.

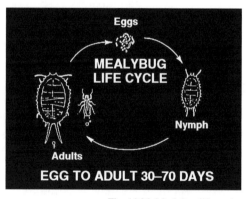

Fig. 14.26. Mealybug life cycle.

Economic importance

This insect group has a very wide host plant range. Populations develop over relatively long periods of time and are often not discovered until numbers are very high. These high populations will weaken and can kill plants directly, or indirectly, by making them susceptible to other stresses. Chlorosis and leaf drop will occur with lower populations. Honeydew deposition from soft scales and mealybugs covers leaves with a sticky coating, and if humidity is high enough, a black sooty fungus grows on the honeydew.

The cost of a control program can be high because it may take months to accomplish, perhaps involving numerous pesticide applications. Sometimes replacing or destroying plants is less expensive.

Detection

Early detection is the most important aspect of a management program for these insects. Plant inspection is the only effective detection method. Scale insects can be found on nearly all plant parts. Pay particular attention to new plant shipments, because infestations often begin on only a few plants and build up to large numbers over time. If infested plants are located, separate them from other plants to reduce spread.

Because soft scales and mealybugs produce honeydew, look for the presence of sooty fungus on leaves. As with aphids, the presence of ants, wasps, bees, and predatory insects on plants are signs that a scale insect infestation may be present. The ants may help move scale insects throughout the production area.

Control

Pesticides. Many pesticides will be effective only against crawlers. If the infestation is already well established, all stages will be present, most of which are not affected by the pesticides. Applications of nonsystemic pesticides should be made at 14- to 21-day intervals. As many as six to eight applications may be required.

Because these are piercing-sucking insects, systemic insecticides would seem like the best kind to apply. However, infestations often occur on older, slower growing, woody plants, and systemic insecticides are usually less effective on these plants. One way to determine a control program's success or failure is to observe new plant growth to see whether the infestation is spreading. Dried up and flaky insects are other signs of successful control.

Biological control. Both predators and parasites have been used for biological control of soft and armored scale insects. At least two species of ladybird beetle predators are commercially available for pest management programs. *Lindorus lophanthae* is sometimes introduced for control of soft scales. For citrus mealy-bugs, the Australian ladybird beetle, *Cryptolaemus montrouzieri*, has been successful on numerous occasions. The larvae of the latter predator resemble mealybugs, thus being a type of wolf in sheep's clothing (fig. 14.27).

Metaphycus helvolus, a parasite, is sold for management of several species of soft scales. Another parasite, *Aphytis meli-*

Fig. 14.27. Mealybug destroyer, the Australian ladybird beetle.

nus, is used against some armored scales. For citrus mealybugs, a tiny wasp, *Leptomastix dactylopii*, has supplemented control obtained with predators.

Leafminers (Diptera–Agromyzidae)

Of the 150 or so species of agromyzid leafminers known to feed on cultivated plants, only about a dozen have a wide enough host plant range to cause problems on greenhouse and outdoor crops. Some of the best known species include *Liriomyza sativae, L. trifolii, L. bryoniae, L. huidobrensis,* and *Chromatomyia (= Phytomyza) syngenesiae.*

In the late 1970s, *L. trifolii* caused serious problems on North American greenhouse and outdoor crops, mainly on chrysanthemum, gypsophila, gerbera, and bedding plants. Shortly afterward, infestations were reported on these same crops in other areas of the world. Subsequently, in addition to *L. trifolii*, heavy infestations of *L. huidobrensis* were found on chrysanthemum, petunia, and many vegetable crops (potatoes, onions, snow peas) in Central and South America. Infestations of *L. huidobrensis* on greenhouse ornamental crops have also occurred in several northern European countries. leafminers are still causing problems for some growers, particularly those producing chrysanthemum and gerbera, in North and South America.

Biology

Although the specifics of biology vary with each species, general aspects relating to pest management are similar (fig. 14.28). leafminer adults are small, black and yellow flies about the size of fruit flies. Females make small feeding and egg-laying punctures in leaves with the ovipositor, the egg-laying apparatus. Both males and females feed on fluids that ooze from the leaves. Each female can produce several hundred eggs, depending on the host plant and its nutritional condition.

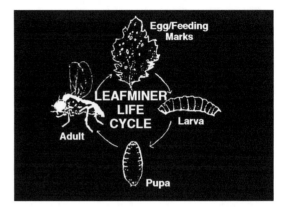

Fig. 14.28. Leafminer life cycle.

The eggs hatch in four or five days into small larvae. The larvae feed within the leaves, forming characteristic narrow trails, or mines (fig. 14.29). *L. trifolii* larvae become yellow when about half grown. *L. huidobrensis* larvae are lighter, almost cream colored. The leaf mines made by *L. trifolii* are easily seen on upper leaf surfaces, but *L. huidobrensis* mines are sometimes (but not always) on leaf undersides (as on chrysanthemum) and are not easily seen from above.

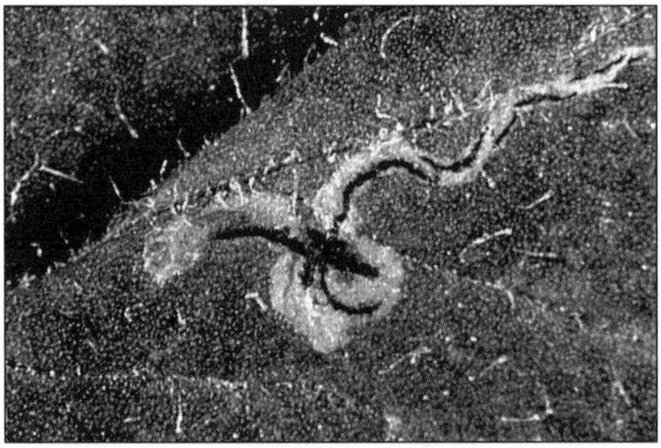

Larvae pass through three larval instars in four to seven days, then emerge from the leaves, dropping off the plants to pupate. Pupation may occur quite deep within the soil or potting mix. The pupal stage lasts about nine days, after which adults emerge. As with other insect and mite pests, the length of the developmental cycle depends greatly on temperature and host plant.

Fig. 14.29. Leafminer larva in leaf mine.

Economic impact

leafminers cause mainly aesthetic injury to plant foliage. They are especially serious problems on gerbera, chrysanthemum (both potted plants and cut flowers), and many bedding plants. The adults' feeding and egg-laying punctures as well as the larval mines can reduce plant value. Feeding injury is difficult to measure unless the crop is completely destroyed. However, in California *L. trifolii* was estimated to have caused a 23 to 27 percent loss to the chrysanthemum crop from 1982 to 1986. In addition to direct injury, growers spent more than $15 million on control programs. *L. huidobrensis* is also a very serious pest problem in some areas.

Detection

Inspect plants weekly for the presence of leaf punctures or leaf mines. Pay special attention to new plant shipments (such as cuttings). Monitoring of adult populations with yellow sticky traps is useful to detect infestations and to observe the success of management tactics. For monitoring, space traps approximately 45 to 50 feet (15 m) apart. Place traps at or slightly above crop height, concentrating them near susceptible cultivars and main entry points into the crop production area. It is not necessary to count all of the leafminers caught on the traps. Counting them on a 1-inch (2.5-cm) vertical strip will provide enough information.

Control

Cultural/physical control. For greenhouses, screens or other barriers can be effective in preventing leafminer invasion or movement among crops (see the discussion of microscreening in chapter 13). Some growers in Central and South America have used hand-held vacuum suction devices to remove leafminer adults in an attempt to reduce future larval injury. The vacuums will capture large numbers of adults, but there are few data available to indicate their effectiveness. It seems safe to say that removing adult insects will not be harmful to the crop.

Treating rooted chrysanthemum cuttings with a combination of cold storage (33.5 to 35.5F, 1 to 2C) and methyl bromide fumigation has been effective against *L. trifolii* eggs and larvae but less effective against pupae. Plant nutrition is also important. More leafminers may occur on plants receiving higher amounts of nitrogen.

Removing weed host plants near the producing crop will help a great deal. This is accomplished more easily in greenhouses than around outdoor crops. Grouping cultivars or host plants known to be susceptible to leafminers will help in chemical or biological control. Destroy residues of cut flower crops promptly after harvest. Steam or fumigate beds before planting another crop.

Pesticides. Whenever leafminers reach severe pest status, there is pesticide resistance or poor pesticide management. Many, if not most, leafminer outbreaks are the direct result of using insecticides that destroy natural controls and select resistant populations. These insects obviously have a great ability to develop pesticide resistance. In Florida most insecticides used for *L. trifolii* control had an effective life of about two to three years before resistance reached the point where the products could no longer be used. The rapid appearance of pyrethroid resistance among leafminer populations may have been due to widespread previous use of DDT and other insecticides.

The time of day that pesticides are applied is important. Research has shown that early morning is the best time to apply pesticides. This is the time when most of the larvae are emerging from their leaf mines and dropping onto the substrate to pupate. In addition, most adults emerge from pupation in early morning. This is also the time when the females are laying most of their eggs. Pesticide applications should therefore place residues on the leaves over which the emerging larvae must move. Applications at these times may also disrupt female egg-laying.

Biological control. Biological control of leafminers (mostly *L. trifolii*) is possible on many flower and foliage crops, including chrysanthemum, gerbera, marigold, and others. Most biological control programs for leafminers involve releasing one or more hymenopterous parasites in the genera *Dacnusa* (Braconidae) (fig. 14.30) and *Diglyphus* (Eulophidae). Both are available from commercial insectaries.

A computer model program has been developed in California to help growers determine how to release *Diglyphus begini* for leafminer control. To use the model, four things must be known: (1) average number of leaf mines per leaf, (2) average number of adult leafminers per sticky trap, (3) average number of parasites per sticky trap, and (4) the date when parasite releases

Fig. 14.30. Parasitic wasp laying egg in leafminer larva.

began. Results show that parasites need to be released within 14 days of planting for satisfactory control. In theory, a single parasite release, properly timed, will work, but it seems better to make several introductions 14 days apart. In reality, biological control of leafminers is not used much at this time because of problems with the western flower thrips. Many pesticides used to control thrips are harmful to the leafminer parasites.

Caterpillars (Lepidoptera–Noctuidae, Pyralidae, and Tortricidae)

Many Lepidoptera species attack flower and foliage crops (fig. 14.31). Most of these species are in the Family Noctuidae, including cabbage loopers (*Trichoplusia ni*), beet armyworms (*Spodoptera exigua*), Egyptian cotton leaf worm (*S. littoralis*), and cutworms, such as the variegated cutworm (*Peridroma saucia*). Other pests are in the families Pyralidae, which includes European corn borers (*Ostrinia nubilalis*), and Tortricidae, including the omnivorous leafroller (*Platynota stultana*).

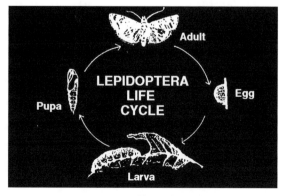

Fig. 14.31. Lepidoptera life cycle.

Most of these insects are rather general pests of a wide variety of agricultural and horticultural crops, inside and outside of greenhouses.

Biology

The only common aspect of the above species is that the adults are rather dull-colored moths that generally are most active at night or on dark days. In many cases, moths may be attracted into the crops by lights used in plant production. Sometimes moths move onto flower and foliage crops because of the harvest or decline of field crops (fig. 14.32).

Fig. 14.32. Beet armyworm adult moth.

Cabbage looper (*Trichoplusia ni*). These caterpillars are commonly found on chrysanthemum foliage and flowers, particularly late in the summer in northern areas of the United States. The larvae, slightly longer than 1¼ inches (3 cm) when mature, are pale green, with white stripes on each side and along the back. These insects are called loopers because of the way in which the larvae form loop shapes while moving across the plants.

Adult females lay eggs singly on the foliage. After seven to 10 days, the eggs hatch, and the tiny larvae begin to feed. Damage by young larvae causes a windowpane appearance on leaves; that is, the leaves are not completely eaten through, and a thin, transparent cell layer remains. Larvae develop for two to three weeks, consuming progressively more plant tissue as they grow. Entire leaves and flowers may be eaten. Pupation usually occurs on leaf undersides, and the adults emerge in 10 to 14 days.

European corn borer (*Ostrinia nubilalis*). These insects have occasionally caused problems on chrysanthemums, particularly in production areas near cornfields. Eggs are laid in scalelike masses of 15 to 35 on undersides of leaves. The eggs hatch in about seven days, and the emerged larvae feed on foliage for a short time before boring into stems. Sometimes the only sign of a corn borer infestation is a small hole in the stem surrounded by powdery frass (fig. 14.33). Larval development takes about 30 days.

Fig. 14.33. European corn borer entrance into stem.

Beet armyworm (*Spodoptera exigua*). These are among the major pests of chrysanthemums and other plants, particularly in southern and western parts of the United States. Occasionally, moths may move north by flying or on infested plants, so that plants in many areas are subject to attack by this insect. Eggs are laid in groups of about 100 on undersides of leaves. The eggs hatch in two to nine days.

Young larvae often are found feeding near growing points, often webbing young leaves together. Sometimes feeding by small larvae will cause plants to become pinched, causing excessive branching. Older larvae will consume entire leaves and flowers and may bore into stems and flower buds (fig. 14.34). The larvae are indistinctly striped, green to almost black caterpillars that are about 1¼ inches (3 cm) long when fully developed. There usually is a prominent dark spot just behind the head area on an older larva. Larval development occurs in

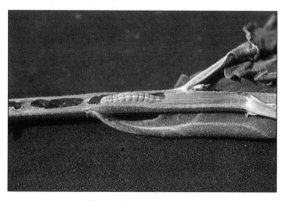

Fig. 14.34. Beet armyworm larva inside stem.

seven to 16 days, depending upon temperatures. Adults emerge from pupae in four to 11 days.

Leafrollers (e.g., *Platynota stultana*). The larvae of this family of Lepidoptera sometimes become problems on numerous flower and foliage crops. They can be major pests of roses and also have caused problems on poinsettia and geranium. Adults are small moths that lay eggs in greenish clusters on host plant leaves.

After eggs hatch in seven to nine days, the young larvae begin to feed on leaves. Initially, leaves are skeletonized or simply "gouged," but later the larvae web or tie and roll leaves together (fig. 14.35). This injury significantly affects plant appearance. The larval period lasts from 30 to 50 days, and pupation occurs on the plants. Adults emerge in about 10 days.

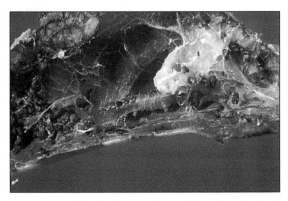

Fig. 14.35. Leafroller inside "nest" in rolled leaf.

Cutworms. Cutworms are caterpillars that spend daylight hours beneath pots or growing media, feeding on plants at night. Therefore, damage may not be accompanied by a visible insect. Cutworm feeding may cut plants off at the base of the stem. Leaves, buds, and flowers may be damaged by so-called climbing cutworms.

One of the most common cutworms affecting ornamentals is the variegated cutworm (*Peridroma saucia*), a climbing species (fig. 14.36). Adult variegated cutworm females generally lay several hundred eggs, which hatch in four to five days. Larval development takes 20 to 35 days. When fully developed, the larvae may be 2 inches (5 cm) long. The larvae are usually variable in color, but generally are gray to black. There may be yellow or white stripes and spots. Cutworm infestations are frequently localized within a crop.

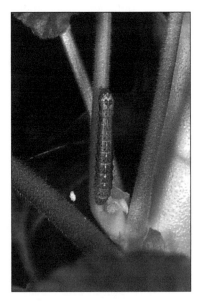

Fig. 14.36. Variegated cutworm larva.

Economic impact

Lepidoptera larvae can be very destructive by direct feeding damage. Early instar larvae of some species (such as beet armyworm) often feed on terminals, causing stems to branch. Larvae of other species consume leaves and flowers and can bore into stems. Any significant visible feeding injury will reduce the crop value, perhaps destroying it entirely (fig. 14.37).

Fig. 14.37. Beet armyworm and plant injury. (Courtesy James Price, University of Florida)

Detection

Adults are generally attracted to blacklight traps, but placing traps inside of a greenhouse may actually attract egg-laying adults. Pheromones (chemical sex attractants) are available for most economically important Lepidoptera, but these traps are not very successful inside of a greenhouse. They are effective, however, in outdoor production areas.

Knowing when adults are present in an area is a great help in timing insecticide applications inside and outside of greenhouses. Many states operate networks of blacklight or pheromone traps for economically important species. This information is published, usually via printed newsletter and on the Internet. It is also available through your state extension service.

Thorough plant scouting for plant injury or the presence of larvae is one of the major detection methods. Larvae all have chewing mouthparts and can cause conspicuous damage by consuming leaves and flowers, by tying or rolling leaves, boring into stems and buds, or cutting plants off at the bases. Young larvae often do not feed completely through leaves, resulting in "windows." Fecal pellets on the foliage are another sign of an infestation (fig. 14.38).

Control

Pesticides. Pesticide applications are almost always directed at larval control. Fumigants or aerosols used in greenhouses will help control adults. Several species, notably the beet armyworm and the cabbage looper, have developed resistance to one or more insecticides. A number of pesticides, representing nearly all pesticide classes, are used to manage these pests. An important group of biorational pesticides are the microbial products developed from *Bacillus thuringiensis*, or simply *B.t.* There are a number of *B.t.* strains available under several brand names and formulations.

Fig. 14.38. Caterpillar fecal pellets on leaf.

One of the most important aspects in managing Lepidoptera (and other pest groups) is detecting the infestation and making pesticide applications before larvae become large. Smaller larvae are much easier to control. Systemic insecticides are generally not very effective against larvae, so thorough coverage with contact/residual insecticides is required.

Biological control. Other controls, not yet used commercially on flower and foliage crops, include different viruses that attack individual species. The fungi mentioned in connection with whiteflies, aphids, and thrips (*Beauveria bassiana* and *Paecilomyces fumosoroseus*) have potential for controlling at least some species of pest Lepidoptera.

Fungus gnats (Diptera–Sciaridae)

Fungus gnats can be found nearly everywhere plants are grown or maintained. The most common species in North America are the many dark-winged fungus gnats in the genus *Bradysia*; more than one-third of identified species are in this genus. The two most common species in North American greenhouses are *B. coprophila* and *B. impatiens*.

Fungus gnat adults are often seen running across the growing media surface or flying around plants (fig. 14.39). They are considered weak fliers but, in the proper circumstances, can fly considerable distances away from plants. The adults are often nuisances in homes, office buildings, hotels, and retail flower shops.

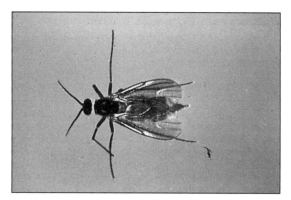

Fig. 14.39. Adult fungus gnat.

Biology

The life cycle consists of egg, larva, pupa, and adult (fig. 14.40). Adults are dusky gray flies with long antennae, mosquito- or midgelike in shape, about one-fourth inch (6 mm) long. Adults do not feed on plants. Females lay eggs in cracks and depressions in the soil surface. The eggs are white and often can be seen with a hand lens. Each female may lay more than 100 eggs. Offspring

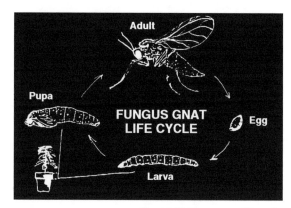

Fig. 14.40. Fungus gnat life cycle.

from an individual female will be either all male or all female.

In five or six days, the eggs hatch into white, translucent larvae with shiny black heads. The larvae pass through four instars and are about one-fourth inch (6 mm) long when fully developed. Fungus gnat larvae are easily seen on growing media surfaces at this point. Most larvae occur in the top inch (2.5 cm) or so of the growing media. Larvae feed on fungi, decaying organic matter, and healthy plant tissue. Feeding on healthy plant tissue apparently occurs if no fungal food source is available.

After 10 to 14 days, the larvae pupate within silky chambers in the growing media. Several days later adults emerge. The egg-to-adult cycle takes two to four weeks. Larvae from the same female have different development times, even when exposed to the same environmental conditions.

Economic importance

The adults do no direct damage to plants but are nuisances in many interior situations. Adults also are associated with several plant pathogens and, as with houseflies and humans, have the potential to carry pathogens from diseased to healthy plants. This pathogen spread has been demonstrated in numerous experiments. It is not known how important a role adults play in spreading pathogens in commercial crop production.

Larvae can cause direct injury to plant roots and stems. Seedlings and transplants can be stunted, even killed. Recent research on poinsettias in and just following propagation showed a direct relationship between the number of fungus gnat larvae and overall plant health. Sometimes even mature plants are injured by larvae feeding within the stem. This relationship has been demonstrated on other greenhouse and outdoor crops, as well. Generally, however, once the root system is well established, direct feeding injury is unlikely. Most fungus gnat feeding injury occurs when temperatures are moderate (77F, 25C), compared with low (62F, 17C) or high (90F, 32C).

Fungus gnat larvae have also been associated with a number of plant pathogens. They can ingest pathogen spores, which survive in the gut through digestion. The larvae may then help transmit pathogens through excretion. Fungus gnat larvae also can ingest pathogens and transmit them by feeding on healthy plant tissue.

Detection

Fungus gnat adults can be seen flying or walking near growing media surfaces. They also are attracted to yellow sticky traps. Traps for fungus gnat monitoring can be placed horizontally on growing media surfaces (fig. 14.41). Traps can also be placed under benches, but in these areas vertical traps may be more efficient. The adults caught on sticky traps will provide information on the general population trends in the area, but adult numbers on traps caught over a one-week period may not be related to larval numbers in individual flats or pots at a particular time. Blacklight traps are also attractive to adults and can be used in monitoring or control.

Larvae can be sampled by placing potato slices or wedges on, or slightly in, growing media surfaces. If the potato pieces are left in place for 72 hours or more and then examined, a picture of the larval population in individual

Fig. 14.41. Horizontal sticky trap for fungus gnat adults.

containers can be seen. This method works well with plants such as poinsettia but has not been successful with potted lily plants.

Control

Cultural/physical. Fungus gnat numbers will be higher in certain kinds of growing media (for example, media containing hardwood bark or manure). Highest numbers are produced during the first five to six weeks. Avoiding the use of media with the above components will not eliminate fungus gnats but may reduce the numbers and make other control methods more efficient. Covering media surfaces with a layer of sand will discourage egg-laying by adults.

Pesticides. Most pesticide applications are directed at the larvae. Applications are made as drenches or coarse sprays (sprenches) to the surface. Products registered for larval control include conventional and biorational pesticides. Applications should be repeated in three to four weeks. Probably only two applications will be needed. Aerosols, fogs, and smoke generators (space treatments) are effective against adults. These need to be repeated frequently (every four to five days). Some growers also treat areas under benches with hydrated lime or copper sulfate.

Biological control. At this time, the greatest success with biological controls against pests of flower and foliage crops is against fungus gnats.

Biological control, directed against larvae, involves applications of entomopathogenic nematodes (nematodes that invade insects) or predatory
mites. Isolates of the nematode
Steinernema feltiae have been the
most successful. There are several
commercial products containing
these nematodes. Predatory mites
in the genus *Hypoaspis* have also
controlled fungus gnat larvae (fig.
14.42). These mites persist in
growing media because they can
survive on a variety of prey,
including thrips.

Fig. 14.42. *Hypoaspis* predator near fungus gnat larva.

Shore flies (Diptera–Ephydridae)

There are more than 1,000 species of shore flies, but the one species most
commonly associated with flower and foliage crops worldwide is *Scatella
stagnalis*. Shore flies are usually found in the same situations as fungus
gnats and are often confused with them. The two groups are distinctly different, however. Adult shore flies are nearly all black and have reddish

eyes, white spots on the wings,
and short antennae (fig. 14.43).
They resemble fruit flies and
leafminer adults in shape and
size. Adults sometimes gather in
large numbers on surfaces of pots,
flats, and irrigation matting,
wherever algae are found. The
larvae are maggotlike and light
tan in color (fig. 14.44). Larvae
have two breathing tubes at the
rear to enable them to survive in
their very wet environment.

Fig. 14.43. Adult shore fly.

Biology

Shore flies pass through the same developmental stages as fungus gnats (complete metamorphosis). Shore fly adults are semiaquatic, and the larvae are totally aquatic (living in water). Both adults and the brown larvae feed on algae. *S. stagnalis* can survive very well on several species of yellow-green and blue-green algae. Eggs are

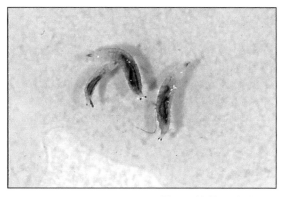

Fig. 14.44. Shore fly larvae.

deposited in wet areas containing algae. Larval development and pupation take place in these areas, as well. The time for larval development and pupal formation to adult emergence is 12 to 15 days.

Shore flies and fungus gnats may coexist in the same areas, but they generally do not occur in the exact same places. Fungus gnats usually are the first to appear in a crop, followed by shore flies as algae appear.

Economic importance

Direct injury to plants is rare, although larvae have been reported to injure roots of plants grown in media such as rock wool. Large numbers of adults create a nuisance and also leave fly specks on leaves. The presence of shore flies on plants received by customers usually creates problems. There are also studies that indicate a link between shore flies and some plant pathogens.

Detection

Adults are attracted to yellow traps, so traps used for detection of other insects (such as fungus gnats and whiteflies) will be useful for shore fly detection as well. Adults leave easily seen spots of fecal material on leaves and edges of flats and pots. Place some sticky traps under benches because shore flies will be active in these areas.

Control

Cultural/physical. Eliminating areas of algae on benches, walls, and floors with either physical methods (such as irrigation mat covers, fig. 14.45) or chemical methods (e.g., bromine or quaternary ammonium salts) will help reduce shore fly numbers. Areas that are always wet and nutrient-rich (like near a dripping hose containing liquid fertilizer) are excellent sources of shore flies.

Fig. 14.45. Covering over irrigation matting helps eliminate algae.

Pesticides. There are several pesticides now registered for controlling shore fly larvae. All are classified as insect growth regulators, disrupting larval development. Because the registered pesticides will not provide total control, eliminating as much algae as possible will help. The pesticides should be applied to individual pots or flats as well as other infested areas, including underneath benches.

Biological control. There currently are no commercially available biological controls for shore flies.

Spider mites (Acari–Tetranychidae)

Spider mites are so named because they produce webbing similar to spiders. There are many spider mite pests of agricultural and horticultural crops, but the most important mite species affecting flower and foliage crops worldwide is *Tetranychus urticae*, the two-spotted spider mite (fig. 14.46). Another *Tetranychus* species, *T. cinnabarinus*, the carmine spider mite, also can cause problems on several crops. *Eotetranychus lewisi*, the Lewis spider mite, has recently been found infesting and damaging poinsettias. The mites' small size, rapid reproduction, and pesticide resistance all contribute to their pest status.

Biology

Both males and females can be found in two-spotted spider mite colonies, but females usually predominate. Females can produce eggs without mating. Mites hatching from these eggs will all be males. Adult female two-spotted spider mites are about 0.02 inches (0.5 mm) long and range in color from light yellow or green to dark green, straw brown, and black.

Fig. 14.46. Adult two-spotted spider mite female next to greenhouse whitefly pupal case.

The carmine spider mite is, naturally, reddish in color and is commonly found on some plants such as carnation. Males are smaller and have more pointed abdomens. Normally, two dark spots are visible on either side of the abdomen.

Female *T. urticae* lay between 50 and 200 eggs, depending on the host plant. Development from egg to adult is very dependent upon temperature, host plant, age of plant tissue, and plant nutritional status, but the following will serve as a general guide (fig. 14.47). All development usually occurs on undersides of leaves. Eggs hatch in four to seven days into six-legged larvae. The remaining stages are protonymph, deutonymph, and adult. The total development time for the immature stages is seven to 14 days. Spider mites develop extremely high populations during hot, dry conditions. Webbing is usually visible during moderate to heavy infestations.

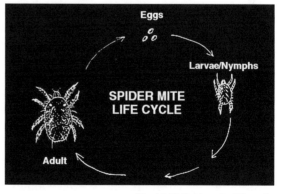

Fig. 14.47. Spider mite life cycle.

In latitudes where there are significant seasonal differences in day length and temperature, some spider mites will diapause (hibernate, or go into a resting stage) during the winter months. This diapause even occurs in greenhouses. In the latitude of northern Ohio (41N), for example, mites begin to diapause in November and emerge from diapause in mid-February. Diapausing spider mites are reddish, so they are sometimes confused with predators or carmine spider mites. Diapausing mites do not feed and are less susceptible to pesticides. Not all spider mites within a greenhouse will diapause. Some will remain active as long as there are host plants available.

As mentioned, spider mite biology will vary considerably with the host plant and cultivar within the host plant species. Table 14.1 shows some of these differences on rose and chrysanthemum.

Table 14.1   Spider mite biology and behavior on different host plants

Rose	Chrysanthemum
Dense colonies	Distribution uniform
Heavy webbing	Little webbing
> 100 eggs	< 20 eggs
Long life (15 days)	Short life (5 days)

Economic impact

Heavy mite infestations can kill plants or cause severe defoliation. The mites penetrate leaf surfaces with styletlike mouthparts and remove cell contents. Injured areas of leaf tissue have no chloroplasts, giving the leaves a chlorotic, stippled look. Plant species vary widely in the amount of visible injury from a given number of spider mites (table 14.1). In addition to direct feeding injury, spider mites may inject toxins or growth-regulating chemicals, which can result in leaf desiccation and defoliation. Spider mites produce large amounts of webbing (fig. 14.48). The webbing can cover foliage and flowers, making plants worthless.

Detection

Monitoring generally involves frequent inspections of plants, looking for feeding injury or webbing. Because mites are found on leaf undersides, this inspection will require some effort. A hand lens of 10 or 15× will be very useful in detecting spider mites.

Fig. 14.48. Spider mite damage on marigold.

Be especially alert during hot, dry periods and as mite-susceptible crops mature. Carefully inspect new plant shipments before moving the plants into the main production areas. Indicator plants (plants more attractive to spider mites than the main crop), such as beans, are used in some areas to help detect spider mites.

Control

Cultural/physical control. Spider mites often develop higher populations on moisture-stressed plants. Plants do not have to be showing obvious signs of wilting for this to happen. Irrigating thoroughly at the proper times will avoid moisture stress and can help keep these high populations from developing.

High nitrogen is associated with severe mite outbreaks. Ensuring that no weeds are growing within the production area, or immediately around it, is another pest management tool. Keep workers from moving through known spider mite-infested areas, because mites often disperse by clinging to clothing. Visit known mite-infested areas last on rounds.

Pesticides. Frequent pesticide applications are often necessary to maintain low levels of spider mites throughout a cropping cycle. On continuous crops (such as rose), applications might be made an average of two to three weeks apart (up to 25 times per year or more). Despite this application schedule, high mite populations often develop. This may be related to application interval. With most pesticides, it is best to make at least two or three applications to known mite-infested areas about five to seven days apart, rather than regular applications, in a rotation, to the entire planting at 14-day intervals. An exception to this is with the recently registered insecticide-miticide pyridaben. Residual activity following applications of this material will last 21 or more days under normal conditions. Only one or two applications of pyridaben will probably be required.

Be sure to use proper application techniques, because most mites will be found on undersides of leaves. Be careful with pesticide selection. Certain pyrethroid insecticides can stimulate spider mite reproduction and dispersal.

Biological control. There are numerous beneficial mites that prey on spider mites. *Phytoseiulus persimilis* is the most well known and widely used beneficial mite (fig. 14.49), but other species—such as *Mesoseiulus longipes, Neoseiulus californicus,* and *Galendromis occidentalis*—are also spider mite predators available from commercial insectaries. Mixtures of predator species are being suggested and used, because the different species are each effective only under certain environmental conditions.

Fig. 14.49. *Phytoseiulus persimilis*, a spider mite predator.

Predatory mites for spider mite management are used mostly on food crops because the heavy pesticide regime normally followed on flower and foliage crops for other pests usually prevents the use of predators.

However, biological control of spider mites is being used on several flower and foliage crops where mites are the major pests. Most of these crops are in the foliage plant category. On crops such as roses, chrysanthemum, and gerbera, there are possibilities for using predatory mites, but the number of other pests that must also be controlled has, up to now, prevented the widespread use of biological control. Spider mite predators with some pesticide resistance are available, but this resistance does not extend to pyrethroid insecticides.

One of the major problems with the *P. persimilis* predator in recent years has been a decline in predator vigor and quality. This has occurred with mites from several commercial sources. The major problem is not with predator survival in shipment, but with the number of eggs produced per female following release into the crop. To date these problems have not occurred with other predator species.

Chapter 15

Other Insect, Mite, and Associated Pests

Plant bugs (Hemiptera–Miridae)

Plant bugs represent the true bugs, and several species can cause problems on flower and foliage crops. The tarnished plant bug, *Lygus lineolaris* (fig. 15.1), and four-lined plant bug, *Poecilocapsus lineatus*, are among the most common species. The tarnished plant bug is a light brown insect with lighter markings, about one-fourth inch (0.6 cm) long. Four-lined plant bugs, yellow with four black stripes on the wing covers, are slightly larger than tarnished plant bugs. Several related species can also occur.

Plant bugs have piercing-sucking mouthparts. Females insert eggs into plant tissue individually or in small clusters. The eggs hatch into nymphs, which are very active and do considerable feeding. After four or five nymphal instars, the adults appear. Adult plant bugs are winged. A generation can be completed in about 30 days or less, depending upon temperatures.

Fig. 15.1. Tarnished plant bug adult.

Plant bugs feed on numerous host plants. In the southern United States, they are often serious pests of outdoor crops. Plant bugs can also invade greenhouses and injure plants. Plant bugs inject toxic saliva during feeding, resulting in dark spots on leaves of host plants (fig. 15.2). By feeding in growing points, the tarnished plant bug causes plants to branch excessively. Feeding on buds causes flowers to abort. Often the damage caused by these insects appears before the pests are detected. In areas prone to plant bug injury, thorough scouting of crops, particularly when close to flowering, is very important.

Fig. 15.2. Four-lined plant bug injury.

Beetles (Coleoptera–Scarabaeidae and Curculionidae)

The beetles are very common insects ranging in size from almost microscopic to very large. This order contains nearly 40 percent of the known insect species.

Coleoptera adults have the front pair of wings hardened, forming a protective "shell" (elytra) over the rear pair. This insect group has chewing mouthparts. Many adults cause very severe foliage and flower injury through feeding (such as the Japanese beetle, *Popillia japonica*). Beetle larvae are called grubs. The larvae of many species develop in the soil and feed on plant roots. These include the black vine weevil (*Otiorhynchus sulcatus*) and the species group collectively called "white grubs," including Japanese beetle larvae (fig. 15.3).

Detection is usually by seeing the adults feeding on leaves and flowers, noticing the damage from their feeding, or observing plant growth symptoms associated with root injury. Some adult species are detected by light traps. Pheromone or food lure traps, which chemically attract adult beetles, help determine when adult activity is occurring in a particular area. Also, traps are used to determine the proper time for pesticide application.

Fig. 15.3. White grub (Coleoptera larva).

Adults are killed with foliar sprays of several insecticides, but the most effective control is usually directed at the larvae. Soil drenches or applications of granular insecticides to the soil are required. There have been some successful uses of the microbial pesticide known as milky disease spores (*Bacillus popillae*). A new *Bacillus thuringiensis* isolate has shown promising control results. Entomopathogenic nematodes have been used, but with mixed success. Fungal pathogens effectively control some larvae. One of the most important factors in management is to properly identify the species causing the plant damage. This insect group is so large and diverse that generalizations are very difficult.

Grasshoppers (Orthoptera–Acrididae)

Grasshoppers are general feeders that cause locally severe injury to ornamental plants in many areas of North America. Usually, they are most numerous and damaging in areas with average yearly precipitation from

10 to 30 inches (25 to 75 cm). High populations in an area generally develop over a period of three or four favorable years, and individuals move into greenhouses from adjacent field crops.

Grasshoppers have chewing mouthparts and can consume entire plants or specific plant parts. Several insecticides control these insects, but often only after considerable feeding injury has occurred. Screens placed on vents and fan intakes are very effective in keeping these large insects out of a greenhouse. Outdoors, row covers may help keep grasshoppers off nursery crops temporarily.

Springtails (Class Collembola)

Springtails are now considered by many authorities not to be insects (fig. 15.4). However, they are very closely related. They are quite common creatures but are not often seen because of their small size, 0.2 to 0.25 inches (5 to 6 mm) long. Generally they are found in concealed situations. On potted plants, for example, springtails are noticed when large numbers emerge from the growing media after irrigation. Chances are good that plants with these springtails have been around a long time.

Most springtails have a forked structure, the furcula, that is folded forward under the abdomen and held in place by a clasping structure, the tenaculum (fig. 15.5). These insects jump when the tenaculum releases the furcula against the substrate.

Springtails in Greenhouses

Fig. 15.4. Outline of springtails in greenhouses.

Fig. 15.5. Springtail with jumping apparatus extended.

Some species can jump 6 inches (15 cm). This jumping ability distinguishes springtails from symphylans.

Springtails have styletlike mouthparts and feed on decaying plant material, algae, pollen, fungi, bacteria, and young roots. Most species do not cause economic injury. However, serious root damage can occur on cut flower crops produced on ground beds. Although rarely needed, insecticides applied to the soil control Collembola.

Tarsonemid mites (Acari–Tarsonemidae)

The two best-known members of this group are the cyclamen mite, *Stenotarsonemus pallidus*, and the broad mite, *Polyphagotarsonemus latus* (fig. 15.6). The life cycles of both species are similar. In contrast to spider mites, tarsonemid mites do best in cooler, more moist conditions. The tiny adults, less than 0.01 inches (0.3 mm) long, are colorless or tinted brown. Female cyclamen mites lay eggs on upper leaf surfaces, whereas broad mites lay eggs on undersides of leaves or dark, moist places on plants. After two to 11 days, the eggs hatch into

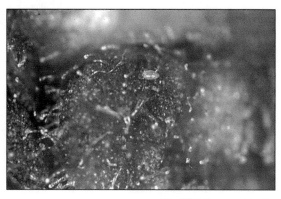

Fig. 15.6. Tarsonemid mite.

whitish larvae, which develop for three to seven days, then pass through a quiescent stage, molting into adults. The general time from egg to adult for cyclamen mites is 18 days, and for broad mites 10 days. Favorite host plants of cyclamen mites include African violet, ivy, snapdragon, geranium, cyclamen, azalea, and fuchsia. Broad mite hosts include ivy, impatiens, and peperomia. Injury symptoms include leaf distortion, stunting, bronzing, and plant death.

Noticing injury caused by these tiny mites is the best way to recognize an infestation. The symptoms resemble pesticide injury or nutritional problems, but generally they are localized, rather than occurring everywhere in the crop. If only a few plants are affected, the best solution is to remove those plants. Larger affected areas should be sprayed with a pesticide. Several applications at weekly intervals will be required.

Bulb mites (Acari–Acaridae)

These mites, *Rhizoglyphus* species, infest bulbs of many plant species (for example, onion, narcissus, hyacinth, tulip, and lily). The lily bulb mite, *R. robini*, is one of the most frequently encountered bulb mite species, simply because of the popularity of lilies. Lily bulb mites, found infesting field-grown bulbs in the western United States, are sometimes inadvertently shipped on the harvested bulbs to other areas of the country. This species is a secondary pest and prefers to feed on plant tissue previously weakened by other factors. However, the mites can invade healthy tissue and sometimes reach very high numbers on bulbs during the greenhouse production season.

The generalized life cycle of bulb mites is as follows: eggs are laid individually or in groups near injured and decaying tissue on bulb surfaces, as well as between bulb scales. Each female can produce about 100 eggs. The egg-to-adult cycle is completed in about 10 days at 80F (26.7C). Adult bulb mites are about 0.03 inches (0.8 mm) long, which makes them quite large as mites go. They have a pearly white body and move slowly on short, reddish legs.

The economic injury caused by bulb mites is variable. The exact relationship between bulb mite populations and plant injury through feeding damage or secondary invasion of plant pathogens (such as *Pythium, Rhizoctonia, Fusarium*) at the feeding sites is not known. However, there is certainly some kind of relationship, and damage can occur (fig. 15.7). Treatment for bulb mites on a preventive or "insurance" basis may be necessary. Keeping bulb mite numbers low may improve root-rot pathogen control with fungicide drenches.

Fig. 15.7. Injured lily bulb, from bulb mite feeding.
(Courtesy Marle Ascerno, University of Minnesota)

Symphylans (Class Symphyla)

Symphylans are not insects but are classified somewhere between centipedes and insects. Adults are about 0.3 inches (8 mm) long, with 12 legs and 14 body segments, and are less than 0.04 inches (1 mm) wide (fig. 15.8). Symphylans have rather long antennae with about 60 segments. Symphylans have no eyes, and the antennae serve as sensory organs. The adults move very rapidly and attempt to escape from light.

Fig. 15.8. Symphylan.
(Courtesy Oregon State University Extension Service)

Eggs, 0.02 inches (0.5 mm) in diameter, are laid about 12 inches (30 cm) deep in the soil. They hatch in one to three weeks into tiny 0.06-inch (1.5-mm) larvae. The larvae are very sluggish and have six antennal segments. They are sometimes confused with Collembola. The larvae become very active after the second molt. Symphylans reach sexual maturity in 40 to 60 days and may live more than two years.

Symphylans do best in cool, moist conditions, with the optimal temperature about 62F (17C). As the temperatures increase, they move to the subsoil, sometimes going down 24 to 35 inches (60 to 90 cm). Because they are not able to create their own burrows in the soil, symphylans use trails made by other animals.

Symphylans injure plants by eating off root hairs, chewing cavities in larger roots and stems, and hollowing out seeds. In addition to cutting off the plant's food supply, the feeding injury provides a place for pathogens to enter the plant. Most symphylan injury occurs along paths and walkways not disturbed by cultivation or not pasteurized.

Detection is usually made by eliminating other possibilities for poor plant growth. Wilting plants during sunny afternoons indicate possible root problems. One of these problems with plants produced in ground beds in soil could be symphylans. Another detection method is to place soil samples in a container and slowly add water to force the symphylans to the top of the soil.

Control is based on prevention (avoiding contaminated soil, using soilless media, or producing plants on raised benches), cultural practices (deep cultivation), or preplant soil treatments (fumigation or insecticides).

Slugs (Class Gastropoda)

Slugs feed on a wide range of plants inside and outside of greenhouses (fig. 15.9). Several species can occur, and they have caused problems on ornamental plants for many years. Slugs are classified as molluscs, which also includes snails, clams, and squids. Slugs range in length from less than 0.4 inch (1 cm) to more than 10 inches (25 cm). Most species that affect ornamentals are about 1 to 1.6 inches (2.5 to 4 cm) long. Generally active at night, slugs are found beneath flats, pots, and dense foliage.

Fig. 15.9. Slugs.

Slugs are essentially snails without shells. Eggs are laid in groups of 15 to 50, usually in cracks in soil or in loose soil. If soil moisture and temperature conditions are favorable, the eggs hatch. If not, eggs await those conditions. Slugs mature and begin to reproduce in three to five months. There may be several generations a year. Cool, wet conditions are best for slug survival and development. They are most active at night or on cool, cloudy days.

Slugs can feed and survive on nearly any kind of plant material, but they have definite preferences if presented with a choice. Damage is through direct feeding injury (fig. 15.10). Characteristic injury consists of irregular holes eaten in foliage. Sometimes, entire plants are stripped of leaves. Usually, a shiny, slimy trail of a mucouslike substance is present.

The slugs use this slime to help them move across plants and soil.

A good way to detect slugs is to recognize slug feeding injury and the ever-present shiny slime trail. Place boards or other flat objects on the soil surface in the evening and look under them the following day to detect slugs seeking moist, dark daytime sites. A shallow dish of beer placed in the soil so that the top of the dish is flush with the soil surface also traps slugs.

Fig. 15.10. Slug injury to lupine.

To control slugs, use specialized baits containing metaldehyde. Eliminating slug habitat through better sanitation, raising flats or pots off the ground, and reducing excessive moisture will also help a great deal.

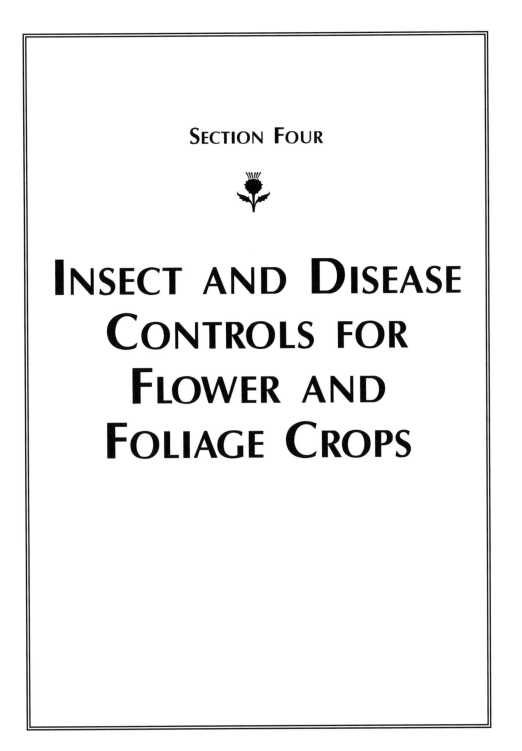

SECTION FOUR

INSECT AND DISEASE CONTROLS FOR FLOWER AND FOLIAGE CROPS

Chapter 16

Understanding Pesticide Safety

Pesticide safety and pesticide toxicity are not the same thing. The general subject of pesticide safety can be separated into three areas: acute toxicity, chronic toxicity, and hazards. Each of these areas has more or less importance to people working in greenhouses. Let's see what these different categories of pesticide safety mean and how they relate to us as users of pesticides.

Acute toxicity

As the term implies, acute toxicity is the ability of a pesticide to cause an acute toxic reaction immediately or shortly after exposure. Such reactions include shortness of breath; tunnel vision; skin itching; or eye, ear, nose, or throat irritation.

Acute toxicity reactions are often confused with allergenic reactions, which may occur in some people after an initial sensitization exposure. Allergies would also tend to be independent of exposure dosage and might occur after even minute exposure!

Acute toxicity is usually measured by a figure that's called the *lethal dose (LD) 50.* LD 50, a population toxicity measurement, is the level of dosage of a particular toxin that will kill 50 percent of a test population of animals. The lower the LD 50, the more acutely toxic the pesticide is. It is measured by different kinds of exposure paths, such as dermal exposure, inhalation exposure, or ingestion exposure.

LD 50 is a useful measure for a chemical company because it tells the company in general how toxic its chemical will be. That is important because the chemical is sold to a "population" of users. If one chemical is generally more toxic than another, a company will label and package it more carefully. For instance, if the word "WARNING" and a skull and crossbones are on the label, it means the pesticide is a Category 1 with a relatively low LD 50.

LD 50 is measured in terms of a dosage in relation to the weight of the test animal. It is usually expressed as milligrams per kilogram of body weight. In other words, it takes more of a particular toxin to kill a larger organism, or a bigger human being, than it does a smaller one. This is because of the body's ability to dilute the toxin as it enters the body's biochemical pathways. Dilution makes a dose less harmful.

Many chemicals that we come in contact with in our lives can be acutely toxic if used carelessly or stored improperly. In many cases, the level of this toxicity exceeds that of pesticides we may be using. (Table 16.1 lists some of these common chemicals.) The table does not infer that pesticides are safe! It does serve to illustrate that pesticides can be no more or less toxic to you than other chemicals in our world.

In table 16.1, remember that it takes more of the products with larger numbers to hurt us than it does for the products with lower numbers.

Table 16.1   Acute toxicity levels of common chemicals

Material	Oral LD 50
Systox	6
Nicotine	1/0
Kerosene	50
Lesan fungicide	64
MetaSystox	65
Rotenone	75
Diazinon	108
Gasoline	150
Caffeine	200
Sevin	850
Kelthane	1,100
Aspirin	1,200
Malathion	1,375
Pyrethrin	1,500
Table salt	3,320
Maneb	6,750
80-proof liquor	13,300
Captan	15,000

We might be inclined to think of lower numbers as meaning less danger, but they mean less substance creates danger.

Acute toxicity information is important. Generally speaking, chemicals with lower LD 50s are more dangerous. However, this has little meaning to us on an individual basis, simply because we don't know whether we will be test animal number 1 or 1,000 in the test population! In other words, we could be quite susceptible to the toxic property of a pesticide even though it has a rather high LD 50! For this reason, LD 50s are not placed on the pesticide packages that we buy. And for this reason, you should be careful with any pesticide!

Chronic toxicity

The second area of pesticide safety concerns chronic toxicity, which is the sort of thing that has long-term effects. It largely results from long-term exposure. Such exposure may be in minute dosages, but if they accumulate in an organism over a lifetime, they can result in chronic toxicity problems. Chronic toxicity can cause such things as cancer, reduced fertility levels, or an offspring's birth defects.

There are two inherent problems of chronic toxicity that make it difficult for scientists to reach firm conclusions as to how it relates to you or me as pesticide users. In the first place, proving that a substance does *not* cause a chronic toxicity problem becomes a very difficult exercise in proving a negative. Actually, it is impossible for the scientific method to really ever prove a negative. All that can be done, as masses of data become large enough, is make most people accept the "fact" that such a happening does not occur. For example, have we actually *proven* that spontaneous generation does *not* occur or that Santa Claus is *not* real?

The other problem with chronic health effects and how it relates to you as a pesticide user centers on dosage. Many compounds are tested for chronic toxicity problems at the highest tolerable dose of the test population. This dosage is much, much higher than any dosage that anyone would ever be exposed to in use patterns once the materials are registered, labeled, and released into the marketplace. If a problem occurs at the massive dose, then we must guess about what the result would be at a very minute dose. Many people believe that at even a minute dose, a small but noticeable effect occurs in the general population. Others believe that as the dosage goes down, we do truly reach a zero effect, or threshold level.

The point is, it is practically impossible to define these sorts of guesses, because we have no means of gathering data on these minute dosages in human populations. It is especially troublesome when we don't really know all the causes for chronic disorders, such as cancers or birth defects. The issue remains largely unresolved in scientific circles.

Deciding whether to use a product implicated in chronic health effects at massive dosages should be made by individuals with proper understanding of the problems. Generally, the chances of contracting chronic problems in even the test animal populations are extremely minute, much smaller than any that we would normally encounter with many things that we do in everyday life. For instance, it has recently been calculated that a person applying 2, 4, 5–T (an herbicide) five days a week with a backpack sprayer, four months a year, for 30 years would have a 0.4 chance per million of developing a tumor. This can be compared with (1) smoking cigarettes: 1,200 chances per million; (2) being in a room with a smoker: 10; (3) drinking one can of beer per day for 30 years: 10; (4) sunbathing: 5,000. One can easily recognize that these sorts of statistics do not necessarily help you with your analysis of personal risk, however. This is where use hazards come into consideration.

Use hazards

The third area of pesticide safety for those of us who use pesticides is use hazards. Use hazard reduction is the most important thing we can do to ensure and improve pesticide safety as it directly affects us!

Use hazards are primarily activities that center around exposure problems. How much pesticide is getting into the body's system as a result of ways in which we are handling, storing, preparing, using, and disposing of pesticide preparations? It is a good general practice to remind ourselves that we should always try to reduce exposure to pesticides. We want to take this point of view regardless of how inherently acutely or chronically toxic a product may be.

There has been a lot of recent research on exposure hazards to pesticides. In most of these research efforts, scientists will monitor people during the normal patterns of product use and measure the pesticide amount that is picked up on hands, face, clothing, and lungs.

Several common denominators have come from most of the studies to give us keys to reducing use hazards. An outer layer of clothing worn over regular clothing when applying pesticides is a primary means of reducing exposure hazards. This outer layer of clothing can be a special spray suit or simply a second pair of pants and a shirt that are removed and laundered after each pesticide exposure.

Many of the use hazard exposure studies around the country have shown that a lot of pesticide exposure occurs during mixing and preparation. It is very easy to get high dosages of pesticides into your system when you are working with concentrates, such as when you are mixing and measuring products as they come from the producer. Hands and forearms are often implicated as heavy exposure sites during mixing and preparation operations. You can see the tremendous value of wearing gloves and long-sleeved shirts when handling pesticides.

Many agricultural industries have adopted closed mixing technologies, where no pesticide comes in contact with you or the air. A simple method may mean water-soluble packets for wettable powders. A more complex system may include automatic can and drum openers that work by remote control and pump hazardous liquid through closed tubing directly into the spray tank. In the future, we will probably see more of these sorts of systems in all areas of agriculture.

There are many other ways to reduce pesticide use hazards that you might consider. For instance, the formulation type can make quite a difference as to how much exposure you are getting. Many companies are now beginning to formulate products as water-dispersible granules. These are not meant to be applied to the crop as granules, but rather to be poured from the bag into the spray tank and dissolved. The fact that they are granules means that there is less dust, less product flying around in the air to get on the hands or into the lungs. Many recent advances have been made in packaging pesticides to reduce exposure hazards. Glass containers are no longer widely used. Childproof openers are often seen on pesticide packages today.

The method that you choose to handle and store your pesticides relates clearly to reduction of use hazards. There are good guidelines available now on how to properly store pesticides. The main thing to remember is to store pesticides in a well-vented area so that toxic fumes do not build up. Also, store the pesticides in a locked room. It is also important to have fire-extinguishing materials and emergency spill-containment items in place nearby.

Finally, pesticide exposure hazards are being reduced by progress made in application methods. Controlled droplet applicators (CDA) are now found in many agricultural systems. These applicators precisely measure and control the size of the droplet, thereby reducing drift and also reducing the splashing and dripping of large globs of pesticides that could occur with older methods. Electrostatic charging of spray particles as they emerge from controlled droplet and other types of applicators is another method of reducing hazards. A positive charge is placed on the particle, which actually bends toward and adheres to charge-accepting material, such as the plant material we are attempting to spray. The result of electric charging is less drift and less exposure to you as a pesticide user. (See chapter 17 for more information.)

Thus, we have separated the topic of pesticide safety into three areas to illustrate how they relate to you as pesticide users. Although acute and chronic toxicity problems are important and need to be considered, there is not much that you can do about them. However, you should constantly be improving your safety skill with pesticides by reducing hazards. If you think about it, you can find many easy methods to reduce exposure.

Worker Protection Standards

The Worker Protection Standard for Agricultural Workers (WPS) contains some key requirements and duties for greenhouse owners who employ workers where pesticides are used or handled. This basic concept was passed by the U.S. Congress to regulate pesticide use in potentially hazardous situations. The specific WPS regulations were formulated by the U.S. Environmental Protection Agency.

WPS is a complicated body of regulations, not all of which are outlined here. Comments made in this chapter may not be correct, because the regulations are changing all of the time. Before adopting any practice given here, check with an official copy of the EPA's *How to Comply* manual before proceeding. There are several "alphabetical" terms that you need to know to properly understand comments regarding WPS. Here are the main ones:

WPS—The Worker Protection Standard for Agricultural Workers. Not a law, it is a set of regulations formulated by the EPA to implement a congressional mandate to more adequately protect agricultural workers from hazards when pesticides are used.

CFR—Code of Federal Regulations. This is a "newspaper" of federal governmental happenings. Labels on pesticides have been rewritten to reflect some of the requirements of the WPS regulations. These new label sections are found in a box that refers to the original reporting CFR publication, such as "The Worker Protection Standard, 40 CFR Part 170."

PPE—personal protective equipment. Pesticide labels have always listed required PPE for product application. Now the labels also give required PPE for workers during REIs.

REI—restricted entry interval. The WPS regulations state that there should be an REI after a pesticide application. Workers should not enter a treated area unless they wear certain PPE, as listed on the label, and receive additional training. REIs can vary from four hours plus ventilation of a greenhouse to 48 or more hours plus ventilation. The most common REIs are 12 and 24 hours after finishing the application and ventilating the greenhouse. The EPA has recently identified 114 relatively low-risk pesticides that can carry a four-hour REI on their labels. These are things like soaps, oils, and biologicals. Companies will have to rewrite labels before you can take advantage of the reduced REIs. Be on the lookout for them.

WPS pesticide label

For some time now, pesticide manufacturers have been packaging their products with the new WPS labels, which refer to REIs and required PPE during entry into an area that is under an REI. Previous EPA regulations said simply that any user of a pesticide must follow all use directions.

The official WPS use guidelines are stated in a box on the label. This box contains three paragraphs. The first outlines the nature of the WPS regulations without going into detail. The second paragraph gives the restricted entry interval (REI) pertaining to treated areas, stating how long to stay out of treated areas without wearing personal protective equipment (PPE). The third paragraph tells you what the PPE is for the product, if you want someone to enter a treated area before the REI has expired. It is important to keep in mind that the REIs and the PPEs for early entry into a treated area will vary, depending on the product.

WPS bulletin board

The rest of the WPS regulations generally have to do with the definition of a treated area; the training required for greenhouse workers, early entry workers, and pesticide handlers; and the duties of employers to provide training, safety equipment, first aid procedures, and notification of pesticide treatments and treated areas. We will try to explain some of the situations that have arisen in our industry regarding these areas.

Information must be posted about pesticide use and how to report accidents on a bulletin board in a prominent location in the greenhouse or nursery. This board must have several items on it, including areas currently under REIs; products used in an area currently under an REI and when the REI will expire; a spray record going back 30 days; the greenhouse person to be contacted in case of an accident or exposure problem; and the location and phone number of the nearest emergency health facility. The *How to Comply* manual provides more details regarding this bulletin board.

What is "the treated area"?

The treated area may seem simple enough to describe, at first look. However, there are some gray areas that may need further definition and resolution by EPA interpretive working groups. It is important that you know something of these definitions. In many cases, your working schedules will receive negative or positive impact by manipulation of application techniques that change the definition of the treated area. Pages 53 to 55 of the *How to Comply* manual outline these definitions.

First of all, if the pesticide is applied as a fog, mist, smoke, or aerosol, the entire enclosed area of the greenhouse must be off limits to workers until the REI is over and ventilation has occurred. Large gutter-connected ranges can be a problem if you are not careful of the timing of applications.

If the pesticide requires that a respirator be worn by the handler (applicator) and a high-pressure, targeted (boom or hand-held) sprayer is being used, the definition of the treated area changes drastically. During the application, the definition situation is just as described above. However, after the application, the treated area that is restricted is only that area specifically wetted by the spray. There is one other important difference. During applications, growers can install or drop plastic barrier walls to limit the "enclosed area." This will allow workers to pass by spraying while it is being done or work in other areas of a gutter-connected range. Of course, you should always practice commonsense approaches regarding drift hazard in case you employ such barriers.

If the pesticide does not require a respirator and you are using a targeted sprayer, you must keep all persons away from the sprayed area plus a buffer area of 25 feet (8 m) in all directions. Again, you can use the plastic barrier walls if you need to reduce the 25 feet in one or more directions from treated areas. After the application, again, the only restricted area is the area actually wetted by the spray.

Finally, if you are applying a "no respirator required" pesticide as a low-pressure drench, 12 inches (30 cm) or less from the planting media, only the benches being treated are restricted for reentry during and after application.

Table 16.2 may help explain these points. Note that the restricted entry areas vary a bit depending on whether you are considering them during or after an application.

Training duties of employers

Workers in areas of the greenhouse where pesticides are being used need training as soon as possible after employment. When you hire new employees, you must provide "brief" or basic training before they enter any area where pesticides are or have been used. The brief or basic training must include informing the workers that pesticides may be on plants,

Table 16.2 Pesticide applications and restricted areas

Method of application	Restricted area during application	Restricted area after application	Comments
Less than 40 psi of pressure, less than 12 in from the growing media, not as a fine spray	The area being treated only	The area that was treated only	Applies to drenches or sprenches
More than 40 psi of pressure, as a fine spray, or more than 12 in from the growing media	The area being treated plus a safety zone 25 ft in all directions from the area	The area that was treated only	The 25-ft zone does not apply if it is on the other side of an enclosure that isolates the treated area
Treatment as above, but when the product requires, a respirator must be worn	The entire enclosed area where the crop to be treated is located	The area that was treated only	Note that you may only be treating part of the crop; still, the entire enclosed area is off limits
Treatment as a smoke, fog, mist, or aerosol	The entire enclosed area	The entire enclosed area	Tight sealing of the treated area is not required
Treatment with a product classed as a fumigant	Treated areas must be sealed off, or adjacent structures not sealed off must be kept free of workers	Sealed-off areas or adjacent structures not sealed off must be kept free of workers until ventilation is accomplished	Look on the label to see if product is classed as a fumigant; follow labeled directions exactly, as WPS regulations are somewhat different for fumigants

on soil, in irrigation water, or drifting from nearby applications. You must also instruct them on how to prevent pesticides from entering their bodies by abiding by these rules:

- Follow directions and signs about keeping out of treated areas.

- Wash your hands before eating, drinking, using chewing gum or tobacco, and using the toilet.

- Wear work clothing that protects you from getting pesticide residues on exposed skin.

- After work, wash or shower with soap and water, shampoo hair, and put on clean clothes.

- Wash work clothes separately from other clothes.

- In cases of direct pesticide exposure, wash immediately in the nearest clean water and shower. Shampoo your hair and change into clean clothes as soon as possible.

All workers must be fully trained within five days of employment. Depending on job requirements, full training is provided in three levels of detail. Levels are: (1) general greenhouse workers; (2) workers entering a restricted area before the REI is over (called "early entry workers"); and (3) workers applying pesticides or assisting in pesticide applications. The EPA calls this last group of persons "pesticide handlers."

The training must be done by persons qualified to teach these subjects. These usually are persons who have pesticide applicator licenses issued by the state in which they work or those who have taken EPA-approved "train the worker" courses.

Most people in our business will find it easiest to use EPA-approved training materials. There are several such video tapes available. The one produced by the Floriculture Greenhouse Industry Alliance (made up of the Society of American Florists; Roses, Inc.; and the Professional Plant Growers Association) is very good. It is available in both English and Spanish. Manuals or booklets are also available to enhance this tape. The official EPA worker protection manual is okay, but it is not very specific for greenhouse situations. Even if you use tapes or manuals for training, be sure to allow for one-on-one questions.

Early entry worker

Our industry has many situations where workers need to be in a treated area before the REI has elapsed.

Early entry workers have to receive a bit more training than regular workers. This is generally because there is more pesticide exposure hazard to early entry workers. Pesticide labels require that certain PPE be worn by early entry workers. The training centers on the wearing of that equipment and the understanding of the pesticide label.

You should be aware of some other work restrictions for early entry workers. These persons are not permitted to stay in an REI area more than one hour in a 24-hour period unless they are conducting work that has been classified as an exception to the REI mandates. Furthermore, no one can enter treated areas until four hours have elapsed and ventilation has taken place.

There are several situations where you might wish to have workers enter treated areas, in the proper PPE, before the REI is over. These are called "early entry situations" and are approved as part of the WPS regulations. First of all, you must know that no early entry is permitted for four hours after any pesticide application in a greenhouse. After this four-hour period, though, here are some options:

1. Any trained, early entry worker can go into a REI-posted area for one hour in any 24-hour period for any reason, but the worker must receive special training and must wear the required PPE.

2. Any trained, early entry worker in a *rose-growing greenhouse* can go into a REI-posted area for three hours in any 24-hour period, as a result of the early entry exemption that Roses, Inc. obtained in 1994. The worker must wear the required PPE. This is a temporary exemption that may only run through June of 1996.

3. Any trained worker can go into a REI-posted area for up to eight hours to carry out activities where there is *no contact with treated surfaces* (plants or soil), such as for irrigation, to make repairs, or to install equipment. No PPE is needed for this sort of entry.

Other work in an REI-area is restricted. Under most situations there is to be no contact with treated plants. PPE must be taken off and left in a specified place for washing or laundry pickup as soon as workers leave the treated area. It cannot be taken home for washing.

How to read a pesticide label

Pesticides, because they are products offered for sale for a certain purpose, have labels that serve various functions. Labels advertise the product, making it seem attractive and beneficial for use. They also teach you how to use the pesticide safely and effectively. This second label function is fairly standard from product to product because it must meet the approval of, and follow the guidelines set up by, our Environmental Protection Agency. The efficiency, safety, and effectiveness with which you use a product depends to a great extend on your familiarity with the label.

Pesticide labels are divided up into several sections. Any one of the following sections may be more or less prominent on the label. There may be many different styles and forms. Also, the order of the sections may not particularly follow the order in which they are listed here.

Trade name and basic product function

Generally the most prominent part of the label will be the trade, or brand, name of the product. This is because the manufacturers want you as a user to become familiar with the products as they are selling them. The trade name may include some sort of an indication as to the manufacturer of the product. The manufacturer's address must also appear somewhere on the label. This is often somewhat removed from the trade name section of the label. Close to the trade name will generally be some statements as to the basic function of the product. For instance, you might see the phrase, "an emulsifiable concentrate insecticide for use on houseplants." You will not precisely know the product function from this initial statement, however.

Ingredients and formulation section

On the front of the package will be an ingredients statement, usually right under or close to the trade name section. The ingredients will be listed, each with its percentage of the package's total weight. The percentage must come to 100 percent, but the companies are only required to list the ingredients that act as a pesticide. All the other ingredients, such as stabilizers and wetters will be listed together as "inert ingredients." The active ingredient will sometimes be listed as a long, rather complicated chemical name or as a shortened name, which we call the common name of the pesticide. Sometimes both names are listed, but not together. Look for asterisks or footnotes on the label that will provide more ingredient information.

The ingredients statement can sometimes be used to advantage because it can tell you how one product may compare with another. Are they, in fact, the same chemical product but under different brand names? Do they differ in strength? Do they contain the same kind of pesticide? Are they combination products with a certain familiar pesticide possibly combined with some that are not familiar to you? You should understand the ingredients statement and be able to sort through it. You will be surprised how much you already know about a seemingly new or unfamiliar product.

Near the ingredient statement will appear the EPA establishment and registration number. These are the official numbers that appear on the government document relating to the product. If there are serious questions about health hazards or plant damage as a result of using the product, you can consult with experts more efficiently by referring to this registration number.

Health and safety information

The front panel and part of the side panels of an insecticide package will contain health and safety information. The statement "Keep out of reach of children" is required to be on all pesticide containers. Other general statements regarding the toxicity hazard category of the chemical will be found. The words "Danger," "Poison," "Warning," or "Caution" may appear. Any special hazards will be prominently displayed in this health and safety information section. For instance, if the product is a restricted-use pesticide available to licensed applicators only, this information will appear quite prominently on the front of the package. If it is a specifically dangerous chemical (that is, it causes eye damage, skin rashes, or breathing difficulties), this sort of information will appear prominently in the health and safety section. Antidotes or treatments in case of accidental exposure will probably be given. Often this health and safety information is boxed in a red- or black-outlined section of the label. (This section is different from the WPS box, which carries general, REI, and PPE information.)

Directions for use

This section of the label can be quite detailed and lengthy. There are several parts of the directions section you should look for. First of all, there are various plant types on the label. Sometimes you can be confused as to exactly what plant types are labeled, when a big category is listed with specific plants in parentheses behind the big category. A statement may read, "foliage plants, such as ficus, schefflera, pothos, etc." Actually, with such listings, it is generally the big category that is registered for product use. Many companies consider this "such as" statement to be a guide only for plant safety information.

The next part of the label's directions section lists the types of pests or diseases that can be managed or controlled with the product. These may be listed specifically by each plant, or they may be set off in a separate section. Sometimes the scientific Latin names are given for individual species or genera of pests. Other times, just a general type (such as "aphids") is listed.

Dosages and dilutions for spray preparations are given somewhere in this section. The dosage and dilution information is generally followed very closely with method-of-application statements. High-volume, spray-to-runoff directions are given most commonly for products used on ornamental plants. Sometimes special low-volume application directions are given as well.

Phytotoxicity or chemical mixing problems

This portion of the label is quite closely related to, and sometimes included in, the use directions section. It is very important that you look for this section because it can tell you about possible problems you might encounter with the particular pesticide. There may be particular kinds of plants that it may warn you not to use the product on. There may be certain cautions about using this particular product with another pesticide in a tank mix. It may give you some guidance as to which products you can more successfully mix.

As you go through some example labels, you will begin to become familiar with the general label layout. You should become aware that knowledge of the label is critical for your effective use of chemicals. In fact, a good review of a label can be very important to you before you have even purchased the product. It may enable you to make some decisions as to exactly how useful this product is going to be in your pesticide program for the particular types of plant material you will be treating.

Understanding material safety data sheets

Material safety data sheets (MSDS) are now a fact of life for individuals and businesses dealing with hazardous chemicals. Chemicals are considered hazardous if they fit into any of several definitions, which can be complicated. Briefly, a material is hazardous if it is: (1) listed specifically in law 29 CFR, Part 1910, Subpart Z, Toxic and Hazardous Substances (the Z list); (2) assigned an exposure threshold limit value (TLV) by the American Conference of Governmental Industrial Hygienists, Inc. (ACGIH); or (3) determined to be cancer-causing, corrosive, toxic, an irritant, a sensitizer, or has damaging effects on specific body organs. For those in the greenhouse business, these sorts of chemicals include pesticides, solvents, oils and lubricants, some paints, and possibly preservatives.

Having to deal with MSDSs may seem unnecessary and trivial. After all, pesticides already have labels on them that alert users to hazards! However, if you take the time to learn about the purpose and makeup of an MSDS, you will realize that it is a good thing to have around.

The objective of the MSDS is to concisely inform you about the hazards of the materials you and your employees work with, so that you can protect yourselves and respond properly to emergency situations. The law states that all of your employees who come into contact with any particular hazardous material must have access to MSDSs and be taught to read and understand them.

It is important for you to study the MSDSs that are now being sent to you by the manufacturer. As you study them, keep in mind several objectives. Imagine how you would respond to emergencies. Think of ways to control day-to-day exposures to materials. Finally, think of how you are going to present this information to your employees. The object, of course, is for everyone to be aware of hazards, not frightened by them!

For pesticides the MSDS is somewhat redundant to the label. It is not identical to the hazard and warning section of the label, however. The following is found on every MSDS:

1. The material's physical properties.

2. Fast-acting (acute) toxicities that make it dangerous to handle.

3. The kind of protective gear you need.

4. The first aid treatment that should be provided.

5. The procedures that must be followed for safely handling spills, fires, and day-to-day operations.

6. How to react to accidents.

The MSDS must be written in English. MSDSs from various suppliers will look different, but they must by law include certain things:

1. The identity of the material: its chemical and common names.

2. All ingredients that are hazardous in the formulation.

2. All cancer-causing ingredients.

3. A list of physical and chemical characteristics that are hazardous, such as the substance's flammability, explosiveness, and corrosiveness.

4. A list of acute and chronic symptoms that might occur.

5. Exposure limits to workers, the primary entry routes into the body, specific organs likely to be affected, and preexisting medical problems that can be made worse by exposure.

6. Precautions and safety equipment needed.

7. Emergency first aid procedures.

8. The name of the manufacturer or of the people who made up the sheet, and the date.

The following descriptions of MSDS sections and comments will let you see how the information required by the Occupational Safety and Health Administration (OSHA) is found and interpreted on a typical, good quality sheet. MSDSs are of varying quality, though, so beware of any sheets with blank spaces or missing information. Return sheets you judge to be of poor quality, and request better sheets. It is your employees' responsibility to read and follow instructions on the MSDS, but if the sheet is not properly done, it is you, as employer, who will also suffer unwanted consequences.

The MSDS heading. The heading tells you three things. First, it gives you the name, address, and telephone number of the company that produced the material. It also gives the MSDSs date of issue (or most recent revision). Third, it gives the name of the material covered.

Section 1. Material identification. This section identifies the material and the supplier. The material name on the MSDS must match the name on the container. If the material has more than one name, each will be listed. The chemical formula may be given. A hazardous-rating fire diamond may appear, giving number ratings for the particular material's degree of flammability, reactivity, and health hazard. More specific fire-related information is found in Section 4 of the MSDS.

Section 2. Ingredients and hazards. The individual hazardous chemicals in the product and their concentration percentage are listed in Section 2. If exposure limits have been established for workers over a period of time, they will be shown for each chemical.

LD 50s will be given, as well. The phrase "Rat, Oral LD 50: 200 mg/kg" means that 200 milligrams of the chemical per each kilogram of body weight is the lethal dose that killed 50 percent of a group of test rats given the chemical orally. This sort of group toxicity data helps establish the degree of hazard to man, but it does not tell you how hazardous the chemical is to any one person.

Another important point to remember when reading this section of the MSDS is that exposure to more than one hazardous substance at a time can be especially harmful. Once in a while, the combined effects of two or more materials can prove to be more damaging than the sum of the effects of the individual materials. This is called "synergy." An example of such a combination would be the use of thiram fungicide followed by the consumption of alcoholic beverages. Maybe there should be MSDSs for beer and wine!

Section 3. Physical data. Physical data include items such as a material's boiling point, solubility in water, melting point, evaporation rate, and appearance and odor. Some of this data will not have much relevance to you. However, some of it will help you predict how the material will act and react during handling and use. This will enable you to select the correct safety, ventilation, and accident-response equipment. This information is particularly hard to understand without some knowledge of chemistry. If you think carefully about the data given, you can see how to use it. For instance, if a material has a low boiling point, high vapor pressure, fast evaporation rate, and a high percentage of volatility, it is likely to be an inhalation hazard, and special ventilation or breathing apparatus may be necessary.

Section 4. Fire and explosion data. Section 4 of the MSDS indicates what equipment should be used by firefighters and what type of extinguishing materials would be best. You may need to be ready with preplanned response procedures and equipment. In the event of a fire, firefighters should have access to this information.

Section 5. Reactivity data. The information found in Section 5 will vary greatly from one MSDS to another because of the many different ways that materials may react with one another. It also gives information on storage hazards as they relate to reactivity. For instance, it will tell you how corrosive the product is on metals. It may tell of its temperature and moisture stability. This section will tell you if the material will polymerize (react with itself), a phenomenon that can cause a rapid buildup of heat and pressure, which can lead to an explosion. Use this information to guide you in your choice of materials for containers, shelving, and personal protection clothing and devices. If the material reacts with natural rubber, you would not want to wear gloves made of natural rubber.

Section 6. Health hazard information. Section 6 of the MSDS must describe all of the ways pertinent to this particular material that the chemical can gain entry into the body. Acute (immediate) and chronic (long-term) health effects must be must be stated. If the material is carcinogenic, that fact must be stated. Medical and first aid treatments for accidental exposure are described in this section as well.

Section 7. Spill, leak, and disposal procedures. This section advises you on how to remedy a spill while safeguarding your health and protecting the environment from further damage. Equally important, the containment and cleanup techniques described will likely reflect compliance with federal, state, and local laws and regulations. This can be particularly important when dealing with pesticides.

Section 8. Special protection information. Methods for reducing your exposure to a particular hazardous material are described. These comments will be similar to those found on pesticide labels, but they will be more general. Many may not even be appropriate for the use in question. The methods may include ventilation requirements, breathing apparatus, and protective clothing. Instructions for the care and disposal of contaminated equipment and clothing are also given.

Section 9. Special precautions and comments. Improper storage and handling of the material can result in the greatest hazard of all to workers. Proper storage and handling methods are described in section 9. The required types of labels or markings for the container are described. Department of Transportation (DOT) policies for handling the material are listed. In addition, section 9 may include other comments regarding the material that do not particularly fit the character of other MSDS sections.

Pesticide record keeping

Every time we see a crop or planting damaged by a pesticide, we are saddened and realize that a bit more attention to detail would probably have prevented the incident. Keeping good records is the best way to prevent mistakes. It is also a good way to improve your chemical control knowledge and skills. Having to write down application techniques, dosages, and materials used serves to emphasize their equal importance. Noting the effects of your actions can help you improve methods or evaluate the need for changes.

Recently, the USDA implemented a set of regulations pertaining to pesticide record keeping. The regulations apply only to restricted-use materials. They are generally the same as those required under the Worker Protection Standards. In addition, most states have record-keeping regulations applying to restricted-use materials. The record must be recorded within 14 days of the application and must be kept for two years. Here are the items that the USDA record must contain:

1. The brand or product name and the EPA registration number.

2. The total amount of product used, in terms of formulated amount, not active ingredient.

3. The size of the area treated.

4. The crop treated.

5. The location of the application. Use a written description (with a map, if you have one) of the exact area where the product was used.

6. The month, day, and year of the application.

7. The certified applicator's name and certification (license) number, if one has been issued by your state. If someone under the supervision of a certified applicator made the application, the certified person must be on the record. It would be a good idea to list both persons.

The following pesticide use report is somewhat basic, but it has the information you will need.

PESTICIDE USE REPORT

Please fill out this report each time a pesticide is applied anywhere!!

DATE OF APPLICATION (M/D/YR): _____

TIME OF APPLICATION: _____

CONDITIONS: LIGHT: _____TEMP: _____WIND: _____

      MISCELLANEOUS: _____

REASON FOR APPLICATION: _____

_____

PESTICIDES USED: _____
(If more than one, list in order of tank mixing)

EPA REGISTRATION NUMBERS FOR THE ABOVE:_____

RECOMMENDED RATES: _____RATE USED: _____

AMOUNT USED FOR THIS TASK: _____GALLONS OF WATER NEEDED:_____

METHODS OF APPLICATION: _____
(mist blower, hyd. sprayer, etc.) _____

AREA APPLIED TO: _____
(field #, house #, bench # / Note any plants not sprayed) _____

SIZE OF AREA (sq. ft. or acres): _____

TOTAL GALLONS (LITERS) APPLIED:____ TOTAL AMOUNT OF PESTICIDE:____

RESULTS OF THIS APPLICATION: _____
(record results several days after application)

DATE: _____OBSERVATION OF PEST CONTROL: _____

_____

OBSERVATION OF ANY DAMAGE: _____

_____

YOUR NAME AS APPLICATOR: _____

NAME OF CERTIFIED APPLICATOR (if different from above): _____

COMMENTS: _____

_____

Please use this area and back of this sheet to do all calculations for this application.

Pesticide Use

Making pesticides work well and avoiding problems with them are two topics of great importance in today's ornamental plant industry. Trying to understand how to do this by trying to remember specific points about this pesticide or that pesticide soon makes one a nervous wreck. We constantly have to try to think in terms of useful, commonsense attitudes regarding pesticides and their use.

Chemistry

Pesticides are complex molecules that are constantly associating themselves with other molecules in various kinds of chemical reactions. These chemical reactions take place as pesticides mix in a spray tank, as they are delivered through the sprayer onto the plant, as they cover the plant surfaces, as they contact the pest, and as they eventually kill or inhibit that pest. The one thing to keep in mind when thinking about pesticide chemistry is that carelessness will mean that this complicated chemistry will work against you rather than for you.

Pesticide formulations

Let's start with the pesticide formulation, which is a pesticide combined with other ingredients in such a way that the product can be used safely to control a pest. There are many kinds of inert ingredients in pesticide formulations, including spreader-stickers, dispersing agents to keep the molecules apart when mixed with water, wetting agents, solubilizers, stabilizers, and substances that simply serve to dilute the active ingredient.

There are many different kinds of formulations. Many pesticides are formulated in more than one way. The kind of formulation used depends on the market in which that product will be used (fruits, vegetables, or ornamentals), the compatibility with application equipment already present in that particular market, and exactly what kinds of crops it's going to be used on. Common pesticide formulations include dusts, wettable powders, flowables, microencapsulated flowables, dispersible granules, soluble powders, emulsifiable concentrates, granulars, and fumigants.

Dusts (D) are pesticides mixed with finely ground talc, clay, powered nut shells, or other material. As the name implies, dusts are to be used dry, never with water. Dusts often coat seeds to prevent seed and seedling diseases. They also can be applied directly to foliage.

Applications of pesticide as a dust tend to be a bit wasteful of product. It is difficult to make sure the dust reaches the target and only the target without drifting into other areas. In fact, the rather random dispersal of dusts makes them potentially hazardous, especially in greenhouses. Of course, on outdoor crops there could be two related problems: (1) drift out of the treated crop into other areas and (2) reduced deposition on the target crop.

Wettable powders (WP) are similar to dusts but contain wetting agents. Furthermore, the particles are not ground quite as finely as in dusts. As the name implies, wettable powders are designed to be mixed with water to form a semistable suspension.

Wettable powders are usually more concentrated than dusts. For instance, Captan is formulated as a 7.5 percent dust, but it also can be purchased as a 50 percent wettable powder. Most of the ingredients included in the wettable powder formulation do not come into play until the formulation is mixed with water. A good wettable powder should mix well with shaking and should not settle out appreciably upon standing for 30 minutes. Of course, all wettable powders will settle out eventually. Agitation of a wettable powder in a spray tank while it's being applied is generally considered necessary to prevent dosage problems resulting from settling.

Many wettable powder products are now being manufactured in water-soluble bags or pouches. This aids measurement if you are using standard quantities of water to make up the spray, but it can make measurement more difficult (or impossible without cutting open the bag) with different water volumes. The exposure hazards from using water-soluble bags are low, as well, but only if you are not breaking the bags open! In fact, breaking bags open to measure smaller pesticide quantities is a violation of label instructions and is therefore illegal.

Wettable powders can be very abrasive to pumps and nozzles and may tend to clog some low-volume application equipment. Wettable powders will leave a visible residue on plant leaf surfaces, particularly when used at 8 ounces or more per 100 gallons (240 ml per 390 l) of spray. This can detract from the salability of many ornamental crops.

Flowable (F) pesticides are very finely ground wettable powders with a wetting agent and water already mixed into the container. They are sold as suspensions, so the user can mix them with water more easily. There are more powerful dispersing and wetting agents in flowable formulations than there are in most wettable powders. For this reason, flowables will not clog nozzles as much as wettable powders. They generally mix with water better than wettable powders, and they are easier to use in low-volume application equipment.

Flowable microencapsulated (FM) pesticides are incorporated into tiny capsules about 15 to 20 microns in diameter. The capsules are then mixed with water, thickeners, and wetting agents into a formulation. Microencapsulated pesticides are sometimes called slow-release pesticides because they release the active ingredient over an extended time period, compared with other formulations. These formulations are usually less phytotoxic than emulsifiable concentrate formulations containing the same active ingredient.

Soluble powders (SP) are powder formulations that dissolve completely and directly in water. Once dissolved, a soluble powder should not require further agitation during delivery. Also, soluble powders are not nearly so troublesome regarding abrasion and clogging of nozzles. Unfortunately, the chemistry of most pesticides prevents them from being formulated as soluble powders. Soluble powder formulations can be particularly hazardous. The pesticide, when dissolved in water, can get into your eyes and nasal passages and be absorbed through your skin more easily.

Emulsifiable concentrates (EC) are oil formulations of a pesticide, with enough emulsifier to enable the pesticide to be mixed with water to form an emulsion. The resulting emulsion is not a solution, but rather a mixture of one liquid dispersed in another. This is why emulsifiable concentrates do not appear clear when mixed with water. They are generally milky white because the tiny droplets of the emulsifiable concentrate are dispersed among fine drops of water.

Many pesticides are not soluble in water but *are* soluble in various oils and organic solvents, such as benzene or naphthalene, so they are formulated into emulsifiable concentrates. Emulsifiable concentrates are not abrasive to spray equipment, but the organic solvents can be somewhat corrosive to washers and other parts of sprayers. The main problem with emulsifiable concentrates is that phytotoxicity (plant damage) from the solvents and emulsifiers can occur. This will be especially hazardous if more than one emulsifiable concentrate is used in any one tank mix.

Granules (G) are pesticides prepared by impregnating or binding an active ingredient on a large particle of some sort. The particles may be calcine clay, walnut shells, corn cobs, or other porous material that has been prepared to a standard size. Many granular pesticides are made to be applied to soil or turf. If applied dry, they don't cling to plants, and this cuts down on phytotoxicity and hazard. They are also safer to apply because of no wind drift and little dust. There is less danger of skin absorption, but sometimes granules collect in shoes and pants cuffs, and around necks and collars of shirts.

Dry flowables (DF) are a popular new type of granular pesticide formulation. They are meant to be mixed with water. Upon mixing, the granules disperse into a sprayable suspension. Their advantage is they are easier and less hazardous to measure and mix into the sprayer tanks. There is less product waste and less dust generated during preparation.

Preparing pesticides for use

Follow the use instructions on the label, and you will be able to take advantage of complicated pesticide chemistry without having to deal with complicated pesticide troubles. For example, always use wettable powders mixed with water as specified on the label—never use them as dusts. There is generally not a great deal of information concerning the chemistry of the product given on a pesticide label; this is found on the material safety data sheet (MSDS) (see chapter 16). However, there may occasionally be a pertinent comment. Reading the label thoroughly and becoming as familiar with the product as possible is a good start to understanding how the product will work.

Be careful when mixing pesticides together in one spray tank mix. This most certainly can be done, and it is generally a fine idea to help save time and increase your effectiveness with pest management. However, give some thought to the mixing process. First of all, make sure that your pesticides are in fact compatible with one another by running a small trial. Mix them together and note whether their physical structure changes in any way. If you do not get a precipitate (that is, some gunk on the bottom of the container), get a change in color, or have a liquid separation problem, then proceed to put this mixture on some plant material to see if you have a biological problem (phytotoxicity).

Write down your experiences so that next time you will know what can and cannot be done. Spray compatibility charts give some guidance as to what can be mixed together. Also, some labels tell you about mixing the products with other pesticides, giving both pro and con information.

When mixing two pesticides together, make sure the concentrated solutions do not come in contact with one another. Each pesticide that you intend to use should be diluted with a small amount of water in a small bucket before being poured into the spray tank. Partly fill the spray tank with water, put the first partially diluted pesticide into the spray tank, mix it well, then add the other partially diluted pesticide. Finally, if an adjuvant or extra spreader-sticker is desired, add this material last, after the spray tank is almost filled with the required amount of water. Agitate the liquid in the spray tank constantly during all these mixing operations.

Thinking about pesticides as complicated, organic chemicals will help you to understand why they may or may not be working. When you deviate from labeled instructions or do things that are not clearly spelled out as successful, you are playing around with a rather serious chemical situation. It is difficult to predict what might happen when labeled instructions are not followed. Pesticide use is an exercise in chemistry that is important to you.

Spray adjuvants

A spray adjuvant is a substance, other than water and without significant pesticidal properties, added to a pesticide that increases its performance. There are three primary reasons to use an adjuvant: (1) to improve the physical composition of a spray mixture (such as to reduce foaming and to improve compatibility); (2) to help improve pesticide efficacy (e.g., to reduce the pesticide dosage or increase the efficacy of the current dosage); and (3) to comply with government regulations (some pesticides have label directions specifying certain adjuvants; certain states require that antidrift adjuvants be used with some pesticides when applied by air). The first two are the primary reasons for adjuvants when applying pesticides to flower and foliage crops.

There are many types of adjuvants used with pesticides:

1. Oils help the pesticide to spread on the plant or target pest surface. Oils also reduce evaporation and help reduce washoff with rain or irrigation.

2. Penetrants help systemic pesticides penetrate plant tissue.

3. Spreaders help pesticides spread over plant surfaces, particularly those with waxy cuticles. In arid areas these spreaders may increase evaporation. However, the organosilicone spreaders help produce an almost instantaneous deposit that is difficult to remove by evaporation or weather.

4. Sticker-extenders help pesticides stay on their targets and resist rainfall or irrigation (stickers), or help increase residual life (extenders).

5. Wetters are already in all formulated pesticides, but usually in low amounts. Similar to spreaders, wetters help increase spray coverage on waxy leaf surfaces.

6. Humectants slow or prevent rapid drying.

Most adjuvants have several modes of action. Spreaders, wetters, humectants, and penetrants can be classified as surfactants (= surface-active agents). Surfactants are either nonionic or ionic; most of the products used on flower and foliage crops are in the nonionic category. Nonionic products help improve pesticide uptake and improve efficacy. They also may have a humectant effect. The ionic adjuvants are more phytotoxic and are used mostly with herbicides.

Several new types of adjuvants are now coming into common use. Two of these are the organosilicone products and the acrylic latex-based products. Their advantage is that they form nearly instant resistance to rainfall or overhead irrigations. They also resist bacterial and ultraviolet light breakdown.

Another type of adjuvant often used when spraying flower and foliage crops is one that will stabilize the pH of the spray solution. This is needed to prevent alkaline hydrolysis of the active ingredient in some pesticide products. In addition, some adjuvants, such as the organosilicone surfactants, work best at a pH of 7, being less effective below or above neutrality.

The key to proper adjuvant selection is to check the label to see if it is sold to be used as you wish to use it and if it is safe for the crops you are growing. Adjuvants can change the chemistry of a pesticide suspension or solution to such a degree that they can contribute to plant damage if used incorrectly. Also, if adjuvants are used at excessive rates, direct plant injury may result. Chemical incompatibilities between adjuvants and pesticides can affect the pesticide's efficacy as well.

There are some general rules that the grower should follow when selecting and using adjuvants to minimize plant damage. First, always check a new spray adjuvant on a small group of plants before spraying an entire crop. Check the adjuvant alone and combined with the pesticides you plan to use on that crop. Do this under conditions in which plants are more susceptible to injury, which is likely to be under warm, sunny conditions. Normally, plants would not be sprayed under these conditions, but this will be a good test to determine if the spray mixture will be safe to use.

To solve the dilemma of how much adjuvant to use, remember one rule: Use the *lowest amount* needed to wet the foliage sufficiently. You will have to determine this amount for yourself when starting to use an adjuvant. Start with very low amounts and increase as needed until the foliage begins to wet well using your water and spray equipment.

For most greenhouse ornamental plants, we suggest starting at 1 to 2 ounces per 100 gallons (30 to 60 ml per 390 l) and adding 1 ounce (30 ml) at a time until the desired result is obtained. Outdoor plants may tolerate higher adjuvant amounts. Probably, 8 ounces per 100 gallons (240 ml per 390 l) is a maximum concentration to use under any circumstances to avoid plant injury. We have applied some organosilicone-based adjuvants that have been extremely phytotoxic when used at the label rate.

Sometimes it may become necessary to spray a crop several times in rapid succession. Perhaps a miticide will be applied one day, followed by an insecticide the second day and a fungicide the third day. Using the same adjuvant in every spray application may produce a buildup and begin to cause plant damage by the time the third spray is applied. In such cases, the adjuvant should not be used in sprays after the initial one. Another solution would be to reduce the amount of adjuvant used in the subsequent sprays. A third possibility is to make only one application using a tank mix of pesticides. Of course, this can lead to other problems!

Certain adjuvants may increase allergenic problems with pesticides. For example, some growers have reported skin reactions among employees when using a particular fungicide with adjuvants. There does not appear to be a consistent pattern here, so no recommendations can be made. However, be aware that this may be a problem.

One final note regarding adjuvants: some pesticide formulations already contain enough spreader-sticker or other adjuvants. Generally, these will be emulsifiable or liquid products, although at least one wettable powder (Talstar) has a label that states not to use any adjuvant. We suggest that adjuvants be used only after reading the label on the pesticide(s) you plan to use. The label will often give guidance concerning the use (or nonuse) of adjuvants.

Water pH and pesticide performance

There has been much interest recently about the possible effects of alkaline (above pH 7) water on pesticide effectiveness. Basically, alkaline water can cause the molecules of some pesticides to break down into inactive parts (= alkaline hydrolysis). This is not a simple matter, and the speed of any reaction depends on the pesticide, pH, buffering capacity, and temperature, but there is no doubt that hydrolysis does occur.

The main question for the commercial grower is: How will this affect me? There is no easy answer to this. Based on the information available to us, it seems that considerable time (hours or days) needs to elapse before significant breakdown of most pesticide products will occur. Therefore, if the pesticide is mixed and used within a few hours and not allowed to stand overnight or at high temperatures, there should not be any adverse effects of spray water pH. If, however, it is suspected that there might be a pH and alkalinity problem with pesticide effectiveness, there are buffering and acidifying products available that will produce the proper pH. Some of the best ones incorporate indicator dyes to help take the guesswork out of the quantity needed.

Pesticide application equipment and techniques

As we have seen, disease, insect, and mite pest management is a system that must utilize many different components. Pesticides (including fungicides, insecticides, and miticides) are important parts of most management programs on ornamental plants. Further, pesticides are likely to remain the most important pest and disease management tools for the foreseeable future.

The primary objective of any pesticide application is delivering the pesticide product to a target in sufficient concentration to control the pest or pathogen involved. Naturally, there are applicator, other worker, environmental, and plant safety factors to consider, as well as economic factors.

The target of the application may be an entire plant, a specific area on the plant, the growing media, or the pest (including pathogen, insect, or mite). Defining the target is an important aspect of proper pesticide application. Are the pests on or in leaf surfaces? Are the pests on upper or lower leaf surfaces? Are the pests on all plant parts or only in certain areas? Are the pests in the growing media or under benches?

It is important to remember that the type of pesticide and its mode of action are crucial to the success of any application. Does the pesticide have vapor or systemic activity? If so, it will redistribute from its point of application or deposition and reach other areas.

Many fungicides are protective, preventing a pathogen from becoming established. Most insecticides are eradicative or curative, eliminating a pest that happens to be present but not preventing future infestations. Systemic insecticides, however, are protective in that they should be applied before pest buildup for best results.

Regardless, pesticide application is a two-step process: (1) deposition and (2) distribution. Deposition is applying the pesticide to the target area, and distribution is getting the material to the correct area in the amounts required to be effective. Spray drop size is important in determining what kind of deposition (if any) and distribution to use with any application method. This is often a neglected aspect of pesticide application. Often the pesticide spray appears as if it is doing an excellent job of covering the target area, when in fact the spray drops are too large (or too small) to deposit on the target in an effective manner or in an effective dose.

Table 17.1 shows the theoretical coverage obtained with spray drops of different sizes produced from 1 liter (1.05 qt). It is easy to see that small drops will *potentially* increase coverage, because there are so many more of them. A number of studies have shown that with certain insecticide and pest combinations, large numbers of small spray drops, if distributed properly, cause higher insect mortality than fewer, larger drops. With other insecticides, however, the smaller drops do not seem to increase efficiency. Such information is not available for plant pathogens but no doubt requires similar consideration.

Table 17.1 Theoretical coverage with different spray drop sizes

Drop diameter (microns)	Drops/cm²
10	19,099
20	2,387
50	153
100	19
200	2.4
400	0.3
1,000	0.02

Note: Overall application rate 1 liter/ha (13.8 oz/acre).

Source: Data from G.A. Matthews, *Pesticide Application Methods* (New York: Longman, 1979).

The relationship between spray drop size and effectiveness against certain targets is shown in the next table. The standard measurement of spray drop size is in microns. One micron is 0.001 millimeters, or 0.00003937 inches. For simplicity, all of the drop sizes are given in the standard micron units without conversion to inches.

According to these data (table 17.2), very small aerosol-sized drops, less than 50 microns in diameter, are generally best at hitting small insects and mites. Midsized drops, from 50 to 100 microns in diameter, are best at foliage deposition. The largest drops, above 200 microns in diameter, are best in sprays directed at the growing medium surface (as "sprenches").

Table 17.2 Best spray drop sizes for different targets

Target	Drop size (microns)
Flying insects	10–50
Insects on foliage	30–50
Foliage	40–100
Soil (+ avoiding spray drift)	250–500

Source: Data from G.A. Matthews, *Pesticide Application Methods* (New York: Longman, 1979).

These data have been developed from outdoor applications. In contrast to this information, our results in greenhouse experiments have shown that very small drops, such as produced by low-volume equipment, also will deposit in sufficient amounts to prevent pathogens from becoming established on foliage or to kill insects and mites on undersides of leaves. Residual deposition was sometimes equal to that obtained with high-volume applications.

Outdoors, spray drops smaller than 100 microns in diameter may drift excessively and cause pesticide to deposit in areas far away from the intended target. In greenhouses and other protected growing areas, spray drift may be an advantage because coverage will be increased. Combined with drop size are target characteristics (such as foliage canopy thickness, plant height, and bed, floor or bench-grown plants) and equipment characteristics (air movement, flow rate).

High-volume sprays

High-volume (HV) sprays are the most traditional ways of applying pesticides in greenhouses and outdoor ornamental crop production, using equipment and methods that have not changed much over the years. HV application equipment includes small, hand-held pump sprayers, larger backpack sprayers, small power sprayers, and large, centrally located power sprayers (fig. 17.1).

HV applications involve mixing a certain quantity of pesticide with a large volume of water and spraying the plants or growing media to some point of wetness. Water is used in two ways: to dilute the pesticide concentrate and as a carrier to deliver the pesticide to the target area.

HV sprays are generally thought to be inefficient in terms of the percentage of pesticide that actually reaches the intended target. Studies on outdoor crops have shown that only about 2 to 6 percent of the pesticide applied actually reaches

Fig. 17.1. HV spray on roses.

its intended target, with the remaining material being lost through evaporation, drift, and runoff.

This apparent inefficiency in HV sprays has been related to spray drop size. Drop size is related to area of foliage covered and potential contact with pests (tables 17.1 and 17.2). Most of the volume in HV sprays consists of large drops (100 to 400 microns), although there is also a significant number of very small drops generated (5 to 10 microns).

Incorrect dosage is another reason for HV spray inefficiency. It seems obvious that the correct amount of pesticide needs to be applied to have the best opportunity for control, but determining that amount may be more complicated than it appears. Labels on pesticides for field crops specify the amount of pesticide to use per unit of area. However, the usual label on pesticides used on flower and foliage crops states that the product should be mixed in water (typically 100 gallons [390 l]) and "sprayed to runoff" to "obtain thorough foliage coverage," or some similar statement. These directions are sometimes given without regard to spray volume per crop area and mean different things to different applicators.

A change in labeling on new and reregistered products sometimes includes specifying a certain amount of active ingredient or spray volume for an area of crop. Determining the correct spray dosage for HV sprays is very important because the HV spray dose is the starting point for calculating reduced and low-volume spray doses.

Despite the potential disadvantages, high-volume "wet" sprays remain excellent general-purpose ways of applying pesticides. The application equipment is widely available and relatively inexpensive. HV sprays remain the only legal ways to apply many pesticides. Many pesticide labels for ornamental plant uses are written to effectively prevent using materials at the higher concentrations required by low-volume sprayers, even though less total pesticide may be applied in low-volume sprays.

The most important aspect of HV sprays is the person handling the spray nozzle. If this person uses proper application techniques (high pressure, getting close to plants, and moving the spray nozzle in an arc), foliage canopy penetration and leaf surface coverage can be quite good and uniform. Therefore, good pesticide deposition and distribution compensates for the time required to make applications.

Low-volume sprays

Many of these sprays utilize specialized equipment, including thermal pulse-jet foggers, mechanical aerosol generators, rotary mist generators, coldfoggers, total-release canisters, smoke generators, and electrostatic sprayers. There are various definitions of low- and reduced-volume sprays, but we will simply call them low-volume, or LV, sprays.

Low-volume sprays are supposed to eliminate many of the disadvantages of conventional HV applications. They take less time, use less (or no) water or oil to dilute and carry the pesticide (no runoff), may use less pesticide, and produce most of the spray volume in small spray drops. As we have seen, small spray drops are potentially more efficient at delivering the pesticide to the target.

Low-volume applications are not new. Various types of specialized equipment have been in use for decades. Smoke generators, total-release aerosols (neither of which use any water), mist blowers, and the equipment mentioned above have been used. All these applicators can be useful and effective in many situations.

Applicators for large areas

Smokes and total-release canisters. These are delivery systems that use no water at all to deliver the pesticides. They are used only in greenhouses. The formulations are ready to use and come in their own applicators. The canisters or smoke generators are spaced over the area to be treated, and applications are made by opening the release valves on the aerosol canisters (fig. 17.2), or by lighting the smoke generators (fig. 17.3). Horizontal airflow in the greenhouse is sometimes recommended to obtain proper distribution. Smoke particles are very small and may not even deposit on

Fig. 17.2. Total release aerosol.

plant surfaces. Drops from total-release canisters are about 25 microns in diameter and will deposit on plant surfaces if the air is stilled following application.

Thermal pulse-jet foggers. Thermal foggers have been in use for more than 35 years. Originally, these devices applied fumigants in enclosed spaces, such as warehouses and greenhouses, as

Fig. 17.3. Smoke generator.

well as outdoors for controlling insects that transmit diseases (e.g., mosquitoes). Research has shown, however, that thermal foggers also can be effective at applying residual pesticides, sometimes depositing as much pesticide as with HV applications. For practical purposes, nearly all thermal fog applications for pest management on flower and foliage crops are made in greenhouses. The greenhouse must be tightly closed during and for several hours following the application.

Most thermal foggers will apply both liquid and wettable powder formulations (fig. 17.4). Where labels permit, conventional and biorational pesticides can be applied. A carrier, or dispersal agent—to be mixed with or used in place of water—may be specified by the fogger manufacturer. Some formulators produce special pesticide fogging formulations that are used as is, without mixing anything additional.

Fig. 17.4. Thermal fogger.

Foggers produce very small drops, usually from 10 to 50 microns in diameter, that are able to move rather long distances from the applicator. With some of the larger units available, the drops travel more than 200 feet (65 m). Liquid flow rates also vary with the unit size. For example, a small thermal fogger model will disperse 10 liters (10.6 qt) in 30 minutes, and a large model will disperse 20 liters (21.1 qt) in 30 minutes.

The area covered with these spray volumes will depend on whether a wettable or liquid formulation is applied. Ten liters will cover about 50,000 square feet (5,000 m²) with a wettable powder and 76,000 square feet (7,600 m²) with a liquid formulation. Obviously, foggers are not used to apply pesticides to small areas in spot treatments. They are designed to treat large areas quickly.

When using foggers to apply residual pesticides, especially wettable powder formulations (which usually produce the highest residual deposits), it is very important to use the proper application technique of aiming the spray over the crop at about a 30-degree angle. If this is not done, there will be heavy deposition in areas immediately in front of the fogger, causing excessive dosage and plant injury.

Some growers who have expanded-metal or other open greenhouse benches have made applications from below the plants, allowing the fog to rise up through the plant canopy. Those who have used this technique report good results, but we have no data to support these observations. Other growers make their greenhouse fog applications from outside by inserting the fogger through specially made openings in the ends of the greenhouses. The basic rule for using thermal foggers is not to remain in one place too long. Move the machine around to help distribute the pesticide.

When applications are made from above the crop and there is no extra air movement, the pesticide distribution within the plant canopy and deposition on undersides of leaves may be poor. In such cases, using thermal foggers with certain pesticide-pest combinations will not be successful. However, using a pesticide that redistributes after application through systemic or vapor action can be very effective. Horizontal airflow fans will help to distribute the pesticide to all greenhouse areas.

Mechanical aerosol generators. There are several models of this sprayer type available (fig. 17.5). They are made for use only in enclosed places, such as greenhouses. All produce aerosol spray drops similar in size to those from thermal foggers (about 15 microns), but by using mechanical energy rather than heat. The water-plus-pesticide spray mixture is placed in a tank, and a timer is set to make the application when no people are present, usually at night. Air pressure, supplied by an air compressor, draws the liquid from the tank and helps to break it up into small drops. A fan in the rear of the applicator helps distribute the spray. Most of the machines sold in the United States have different sizes of nozzles, which can be changed depending on the product.

Fig. 17.5. Mechanical aerosol generator.

Liquid or soluble pesticides work best in these sprayers. Some wettable powder products may plug the spray nozzle, but other wettable powder formulations will work just fine.

Some of the smaller units will treat an area of more than 15,000 square feet (1,500 m^2), using less than 2 gallons (7.6 l) of liquid. Others will treat areas twice (or more) this size; some sprayers will treat up to 60,000 square feet (6,000 m^2). Some machines have adjustable flow rates and fairly sophisticated computer controls. Additional spray distribution is accomplished by the greenhouse air movement system, by horizontal airflow or overhead convection tubes. The greenhouse must remain tightly closed during and following application.

Our results with these applicators, using fluorescent tracer material as well as nonsystemic insecticides, have shown excellent distribution and deposition. Although tracer studies have indicated that deposition on upper leaf surfaces was much greater than on undersides, control of first-instar greenhouse whitefly nymphs on poinsettia with bifenthrin was excellent. Similar results have been obtained against two-spotted spider mites and melon aphids. However, there was little or no control of *Bemisia* whitefly nymphs on poinsettia using an azadirachtin insecticide.

This again points out the importance of the interaction among the pest, the pesticide, and the application equipment. Only a few studies have been conducted using fungicides applied by mechanical aerosol generators, but control of some powdery mildews with certain fungicides has been quite good.

Applicators for large or small areas

Coldfoggers. Coldfoggers are reduced-volume, air-assisted sprayers that produce spray drops in the 30- to 50-micron range. The Pulsfog Colfogger is one sprayer in this category (fig. 17.6). A high-pressure pump breaks up the spray suspension or solution into small spray drops. The flow rate is 1.05 quart (1 l) per minute, and the spray has a range of 10 to 12 feet (3 to 3.6 m). Total spray volume will range from 12 to 45 gallons/acre (112 to 420 l/ha).

Both liquid and wettable powder formulations can be applied. However, when applying microencapsulated formulations, the spray line filters will need to be removed.

Applications are made by walking through the area, aiming the spray ahead and down into the crop. The air assistance will cause many of the leaves to flutter, and this helps distribute the spray on both upper and lower leaf surfaces.

Fig. 17.6. Coldfogger.

Air-assisted rotary mist applicators.

Originally called controlled droplet applicators or rotary atomizers, these machines have been quite useful on many flower and foliage crops (fig. 17.7). They are not widely available for greenhouses in the United States, but are used outdoors for such diverse purposes as mosquito and weed control.

The type of applicators most widely used worldwide is distributed by Micron Sprayers Ltd. in the United Kingdom—the Ulvafan and Turbair Motafan Sprayers. At present they are not commonly available in North

Fig. 17.7. Rotary atomizer.

America, but this probably will change in the near future. Battery-operated or with a two-cycle engine, this hand-held sprayer disperses pesticides by directing the flow onto rapidly rotating notched discs.

Liquid, soluble, or flowable pesticides can be applied, when labels permit. The flow onto the rotating disc causes the liquid to break up into small drops, 10 to 80 microns in diameter. The sprayers have a fan behind the disc that propels the spray toward the target, creating a turbulent airstream.

Depending upon the crop to be treated, the Turbair sprayers will apply from 2.5 to 10 liters of spray per hectare (1.05 to 4.2 qt/acre). The Ulvafans will apply up to 40 liters/hectare (17 qt/acre). As with amount of liquid dispersed, the time to treat a given area will depend upon the crop treated.

These sprayers are aimed ahead about 10 feet (3 m), with a walking speed of one pace/second. The spray must be directed at the crop and moved up and down and from side to side to ensure proper coverage. The maximum "throw" from these sprayers is about 15 feet (5 m). Obviously, bedding plants can be treated more rapidly than roses.

Pesticide deposition and distribution is quite good, but foliage canopy penetration and coverage of leaf undersides can vary significantly, depending upon the crop type—roses, bench-grown potted plants, bedding plants on floor, or other arrangement.

Electrostatic sprayers. Using electrical charging of spray drops to achieve better coverage of leaf undersides, while using less pesticide and reducing spray drift, is an idea that has been around for many years. There have been several prototype sprayers developed and evaluated on greenhouse and outdoor crops over the past few decades, but generally the theory has been better than results in actual practice, until relatively recently. The development and marketing of the air-assisted sprayers have brought theory and results very close together.

Air-assisted sprayers manufactured by the Electrostatic Spraying Systems (ESS) Company are now used in many greenhouse and field operations (fig. 17.8). There are several models available, including greenhouse and field sprayers.

All the sprayer models use the same electrostatic-induction, spray-charging nozzle system, developed at the University of Georgia, to produce the spray drops. All use water-based sprays containing conventional pesticides and formulations. The air assistance provided by these sprayers is very important and may be equal to the electrical charging in achieving good spray

Fig. 17.8. Electrostatic sprayer.

coverage and deposition. However, the combination of electrical charging, low-pressure sprays, and air assistance appears to be very successful.

The ESS sprayers produce drops with a volume median diameter of about 30 microns at a liquid flow rate of 10 fluid ounces (280 ml) per minute. From 4 to 16 gallons/acre (37 to 150 l/ha) are applied, depending on crop size and walking speed.

A very important aspect of electrostatic spray application is the training of the person making the applications. Because the spray nozzles are hand-held and the spray is very concentrated, there can be a "plant position" effect, the spray deposition and subsequent pest or disease control perhaps better on plants nearer the sprayer nozzle (fig. 17.9).

The ESS sprayer, properly used, has been demonstrated to significantly improve total foliage coverage and obtain better control of pests such as aphids—using less pesticide and with less dislodgeable pesticide residues—compared with conventional HV sprays.

Fig. 17.9. Electrostatic spray application.

Future of low-volume application

Technology is still ahead of legality in many cases, but the situation is improving. As mentioned, any application method not prohibited on the label can be employed to apply that pesticide. If the label specifies a specific dilution (for example, 1 lb/100 gal) without any mention of low-volume or concentrate spraying, this effectively prevents low-volume applications. However, many of the newer pesticide labels do mention concentrate or low-volume sprays. Certain labels will simply state to mix and apply the pesticide in sufficient water to obtain adequate coverage. Some labels even list specific sprayer types as examples. Maximum application rates per area are now being included on some labels.

Chapter 18

Major Insecticides, Miticides, and Biological Control Agents

Insecticides and miticides will continue to be the main components of integrated pest management programs on ornamental plants for the foreseeable future. There simply are no other pest management tactics that will totally replace pesticides at this time. However, pesticides are not the only pest management tools and should not be considered as such. Pesticides must always be used as part of a total management program.

During the past decade there has been a significant change in the type of pesticide registered for use on ornamentals. Many recently registered products can be considered to be "green pesticides" or biorational pesticides. These products are generally less toxic (to mammals and beneficial insects and mites) than so-called conventional pesticides and have different modes of action.

Their lower toxicity is a good thing in light of new regulations concerning pesticides (such as the Worker Protection Standards, or WPS; see chapter 16). These regulations established minimum restricted entry intervals (REIs) for pesticides used on greenhouse and outdoor flower and foliage crops (but not interior landscape plants). These intervals specify the hours following application when workers must remain out of the treated area (with some exceptions), extending up to 72 hours or more. REIs are usually shorter for the less toxic pesticides.

Some of the new pesticide products are actually renewals of very old products: insecticidal soaps and horticultural oils. The reincarnation of these pesticides has been a great help to many pest management programs. Pesticide resistance should not be a problem with these materials. That's the good news. The bad news is that many of the newer products are growth stage—specific, affecting only certain immature stages, and are slow acting. These pesticides include insect growth regulators (IGRs), botanicals (such as azadirachtin) and microbials (e.g., fungi). If some of the products are not effective against adults and mortality will not be noticed for one to two weeks following an application, it is imperative that the pest management program include pest scouting by plant inspection and sticky trapping (see chapter 2). These pesticides are not for use in rescue strategies.

Chemical companies have not neglected conventional pesticides during this time, either. Some of the newer pesticides represent entirely new chemical classes, with different modes of action against pests. Two of the newest products and their pesticide families are imidacloprid (Marathon, Merit), a chloronicotinyl, and pyridaben (Sanmite), a pyridazinone. Other products representing still more pesticide families are under development.

The rest of this chapter gives brief descriptions of many of the insecticides and miticides registered on herbaceous ornamental plants in the United States. The pesticides are listed alphabetically within each pesticide family. This list may not be complete, as there may be new products registered and older products removed from the market. Some states have more liberal or restrictive regulations. Remember that the pesticide label is the ultimate authority for pesticide use. The tables that end the chapter are intended to be guides for selecting the proper pesticides for control of different pest groups.

Organophosphates

Acephate (Orthene Tree and Ornamental Spray, Pinpoint 15G, PT 1300 Orthene). Acephate is registered on greenhouse and outdoor ornamentals. An aerosol formulation is registered for use in greenhouses. Acephate is a systemic insecticide effective against a wide range of chewing and sucking pests, including aphids and scale insects. It is an excellent insecticide, but phytotoxicity has occurred on several crops, particularly with the 75 SP and 15 G formulations. At this time the 15 G (Pinpoint) formulation has a very limited label. Be careful when applying this material to any new cultivar, and wait two weeks for symptoms to appear.

Chlorpyrifos (Dursban, PT 1325 DuraGuard). Chlorpyrifos is a broad-spectrum organophosphate insecticide registered on most greenhouse, outdoor, and interior plantscape ornamentals. DuraGuard, a liquid microencapsulated formulation, is registered for use in greenhouses and interior plantscapes for control of many insect pests, including aphids, fungus gnats, thrips, mealybugs, scale insects, leafminers, and whiteflies.

Diazinon (Knox Out GH, Diazinon). Diazinon is a broad-spectrum insecticide, available in several formulations, registered on numerous ornamental plants. Knox Out GH is a microencapsulated formulation of diazinon registered for use in greenhouses, outdoors, and interior plantings. Knox Out GH is registered for control of most of the major insect pests of these crops. PT 1500 R is a directed aerosol spray formulation registered for interior plantings. Diazinon formulations are used mostly on outdoor ornamentals.

Dichlorvos (Vapona, DDVP). Dichlorvos is registered only in greenhouses as thermal fog or smoke generator formulations. Registered crops include ornamentals and some vegetables. Some plants may be injured, particularly if greenhouse temperatures are too high. Dichlorvos is effective at 60 to 65F (15 to 18C). Dichlorvos may be removed from the greenhouse market in the near future, but no final decision has been made as of this writing.

Disulfoton (Di-Syston). Disulfoton is a granular systemic insecticide-miticide used on some outdoor ornamental crops (such as bulb crops) for control of such pests as aphids, mites, thrips, and whiteflies.

Isophenphos (Oftanol). Isophenphos, a granular or liquid pesticide formulation, is used to control a variety of soil-inhabiting insects in outdoor ornamental ground beds. It is widely used to control beetle larvae called white grubs.

Naled (GH-18, Dibrom). This is a formulation for use only in thermal foggers in greenhouses. It is registered for control of mites, mealybugs, aphids, whiteflies, and thrips on several major greenhouse ornamental crops, as well as some vegetables. Dibrom is another well-known pesticide containing naled. It is applied as a vapor treatment off hot plates or heat pipes.

Sulfotepp (Dithio, Plantfume 103). Both formulations are smoke generators registered for use on greenhouse ornamental plants. Listed pests include whiteflies, aphids, and thrips. This product is especially useful for whitefly control on mature crops where sprays would not achieve adequate coverage.

Trichlorfon (Dylox). Dylox is an insecticide used for control of a number of foliage-feeding (both chewing and sucking) and soil pests of ornamental plants. Dylox is registered for use only on interior plantscapes, ornamental gardens, and parks, not on crops in production.

Carbamates

Bendiocarb (Dycarb, Turcam). Bendiocarb is a carbamate insecticide registered for control of several common insect and mite pests on a wide range of greenhouse, outdoor, and interior plantscape ornamentals. Avoid using alkaline water for maximum effectiveness.

Carbaryl (Sevin). Carbaryl formulations have been used for many years to control a broad range of insect pests on numerous ornamental crops. Most carbaryl use is on outdoor ornamentals. Applications are usually made as dilute sprays, but there is a dry bait formulation for control of such pests as grasshoppers, cutworms, and ants.

Methiocarb (Mesurol). Methiocarb is registered for control of aphids, mites, snails, and slugs on greenhouse and outdoor ornamentals. Some growers report that thrips control also is good with this material.

Oxamyl (Oxamyl 10G). Oxamyl 10G is a granular systemic insecticide-nematicide registered on many greenhouse, outdoor nursery, and interior landscape ornamentals. Oxamyl 10G may be incorporated into the potting mix before planting or broadcast on the surface after planting.

Organochlorines

Dicofol (Kelthane). Kelthane Turf and Ornamental Miticide is registered for mite control on greenhouse and outdoor ornamental crops. Kelthane has been registered for use on ornamentals for many years.

Dienochlor (Pentac). Pentac is registered for use on greenhouse and interior landscape ornamental plants for control of spider mites, broad mites, and whitefly eggs. A combination of Pentac and Mavrik (or other pyrethroid) has been effective, as has Pentac and Enstar II.

Endosulfan (Thiodan, Fulex Thiodan Smoke). Thiodan WP and EC are registered for control of several insect and mite pests (cyclamen mite) on greenhouse and outdoor ornamental crops, as well as greenhouse tomatoes. Thiodan EC has injured some chrysanthemum and geranium cultivars. The smoke generator formulation is registered for aphid and whitefly control on greenhouse ornamentals, as well as greenhouse tomatoes and cucumbers.

Pyrethroids

Bifenthrin (PT 1800 Attain, Talstar T&O). Talstar is a pyrethroid insecticide-miticide that is registered for control of most insect and mite pests on greenhouse and outdoor ornamental crops. The PT 1800 formulation is a total-release aerosol product for greenhouses.

Cyfluthrin (Decathlon, Tempo). This broad-spectrum pyrethroid is registered for control of many greenhouse ornamental plant pests (Decathlon) and pests of interior landscape and outdoor plants (Tempo).

Fenpropathrin (Tame). Tame is an insecticide-miticide registered for use on greenhouse, shadehouse, and lathhouse ornamentals. It is often combined in a tank mix with Orthene TT&O 75SP. Growers using this combination spray must pay attention to labeling. Orthene is registered on fewer crops than Tame, and the combination can be legally used only on those crops that appear on the labels of both products. Other pyrethroids combined with Orthene have been as effective as Tame.

Fluvalinate (Mavrik Aquaflow). Mavrik is registered for control of many insect and mite pests on ornamental plants in greenhouse, outdoor, and interior plantings. Mavrik is sometimes combined in a tank mix with Pentac or Enstar II. Mavrik may cause throat irritation if respirators do not fit properly.

Lambda-cyhalothrin (Topcide). Topcide is an advanced-generation pyrethroid insecticide-miticide registered for control of a long list of pests on greenhouse and outdoor ornamental plants. It is not registered for use on interior plantings. Topcide is formulated in water-soluble bags.

Permethrin (Astro). Astro is a permethrin formulation registered for control of several major insect and mite pests on ornamental plants outdoors, in greenhouses, and on interior plantings.

Resmethrin (Resmethrin EC26, PT 1200 Resmethrin, GH-60). The "PT" formulations of resmethrin are either directed-spray or total-release aerosol products for use in greenhouses on ornamental plants.

Resmethrin EC26 is an emulsifiable concentrate formulation registered in greenhouses and interior plantings. GH-60 is a formulation for thermal foggers. This formulation is registered in greenhouses only for control of adult whiteflies. Best results are obtained if greenhouse temperatures are cool (50 to 72F) when applications are made.

Insect growth regulators

Cyromazine (Citation). Citation is a 75WP formulation of an insect growth regulator registered on greenhouse, shadehouse, and lathhouse ornamentals, as well as on interior plantings. It is used for control of leafminers (*Liriomyza* spp.), fungus gnats, and shore flies.

Diflubenzuron (Adept). Adept is a chitin-synthesis inhibitor registered on greenhouse and outdoor ornamentals, plus interior plantings, for control of fungus gnats, shore flies, beet armyworms, and whiteflies. Residual activity is quite long. Label directions state that Adept-treated potting mix should not be reused.

Fenoxycarb (Precision, PT 2100 Preclude). Fenoxycarb is an insect growth regulator classified chemically as a carbamate. Precision 25WP is registered on greenhouse and outdoor ornamentals and interior plantings for control of thrips, whiteflies, soft scales, fungus gnats and shore flies. PT 2100 is a total-release aerosol product only for greenhouse ornamentals.

s-kinoprene (Enstar II). Enstar II is registered for use on greenhouse and interior plantscape ornamentals for control of most groups of sucking pests (except mites), as well as fungus gnats. Enstar II is often used in a tank mix with Mavrik or Pentac.

Botanicals

Azadirachtin (Azatin, Neemazad). These botanical insecticides and insect growth regulator formulations are registered for use against a long list of insect pests on greenhouse ornamentals, vegetables, and interior landscape ornamentals. There is almost no activity against adult insects, only larvae and nymphs.

Nicotine (Plant Products Nicotine, Fulex Nicotine). These are smoke generator formulations registered on greenhouse ornamentals and greenhouse tomatoes, cucumbers, and lettuce for control of aphids and thrips. Growers using these smoke generators report good to excellent aphid control.

Pyrethrum (PT 1600A X-clude, PT 1100 Pyrethrum). PT 1100 is a total-release aerosol formulation of this botanical insecticide registered for use in greenhouses. PT 1600A is a directed aerosol spray registered for use in interior landscapes.

Oils

Horticultural spray oil (Sunspray Ultra-Fine Spray Oil, JMS Stylet Oil, Saf-T-Side). Horticultural oils are registered on greenhouse and outdoor ornamental plants. They are used for control of numerous pests, including mites, aphids, mealybugs and whiteflies. Oils can also be tank mixed with many conventional pesticides at low concentrations to improve control, but check the labels on specific products for any incompatibilities.

Extract of neem oil (Triact). Triact is an insecticide-fungicide, extracted from neem tree seeds, registered for use on greenhouse and outdoor ornamentals. This formulation uses oil extracted from seeds of the neem tree. Other pesticides derived from this tree are listed under azadirachtin in the botanical pesticide category. Pests controlled include aphids, whiteflies, scales and spider mites. Plant pathogens listed include powdery mildew, anthracnose, downy mildew, and *Botrytis*.

Microbial pesticides

***Bacillus thuringiensis* var. *kurstaki* (e.g., Dipel, MVP).** A microbial insecticide, *Bacillus thuringiensis*, is effective against several species of chewing caterpillars on greenhouse and outdoor ornamental and vegetable crops. MVP is a *B.t.* formulation encapsulated in killed *Pseudomonas fluorescens*. The insects must eat this material for it to be effective, so thorough foliage coverage is necessary for best results. Caterpillars stop eating soon after contacting the material but may not die for two to three days. When used as directed, no plant injury has been reported.

***Bacillus thuringiensis* var. *israelensis* (Gnatrol).** This subspecies, *B. thuringiensis* is registered for control of fungus gnat larvae in greenhouses. It is applied as a drench to the potting mix. As with *B. thuringiensis kurstaki*, there have been no phytotoxicity problems. Several applications at three- or four-day intervals may be needed.

***Beauveria bassiana* (Naturalis-O).** This product, containing a strain of a naturally occurring fungus, is registered on greenhouse and outdoor ornamentals and interior plantings for control of many common pests. Label directions say to make several applications at five-day intervals for best results. *B. bassiana* is compatible with conventional insecticides, soaps and oils, but not with fungicides.

Miscellaneous pesticides

Abamectin (Avid). Avid, a macrocyclic lactone, is an insecticide-miticide registered for use on greenhouse ornamentals for control of spider mites and leafminers. The commercial product is derived from soil microorganisms. There is limited movement across leaves from upper to lower surfaces, but this is not a systemic pesticide.

Capsaicin (Hot Pepper Wax). Hot Pepper Wax, containing 3 percent capsaicin, is a hot pepper extract and paraffin wax concentrate used as an insect repellent and insecticide. It can also be combined with conventional or biorational insecticides.

Hexythiazox (Hexygon). Hexythiazox controls spider mites and spider mite eggs. Adult female mites exposed to hexythiazox will produce nonviable eggs. The Hexygon formulation is registered for use only on outdoor ornamentals.

Insecticidal soap (Olympic Insecticidal Soap, M-Pede, Safer's Insecticidal Soap). Insecticidal soaps contain potassium salts of fatty acids, which are effective in controlling several soft-bodied insect and mite pests. Insecticidal soaps are registered for use on greenhouse and outdoor ornamentals and vegetables.

Metaldehyde (Deadline Bullets, Ortho Bug-Geta). Metaldehyde is a soil-applied bait for slug control around greenhouse ornamentals and vegetables. Do not apply to edible plant parts. It is available in dry or liquid formulations.

Imidacloprid (Marathon, Merit). Imidacloprid is a long-residual, slow-acting systemic insecticide in the chloronicotinyl chemical family. This is a new pesticide family for the U.S. Marathon 1% G is a granular formulation registered on greenhouse and nursery ornamentals. Merit 75WSP is a powder formulation registered for use in interior plantings and home landscapes. Although registered for application as a spray, Merit is more effective applied to the potting mix as a drench. Pests controlled include whiteflies and aphids. Mealybugs and thrips are also listed in the label. Growers should be alert for mite infestations, as imidacloprid has no activity against this pest group.

Oxythioquinox (Joust, Morestan). Oxythioquinox is a dithiocarbonate registered only on outdoor ornamental plants for control of whiteflies and spider mites. Mite eggs are also killed.

Pyridaben (Sanmite). Sanmite, a pyridazinone, is an insecticide-miticide registered for use on greenhouse ornamentals. Its primary effect is on spider mites and broad mites, but whiteflies are also listed on the label. Activity against mites is slow, but residual effects last 14 or more days.

Table 18.1   Drenches and "sprenches" registered for controlling fungus gnats and shore flies

Product	Company	Fungus gnat larvae	Shore fly larvae	Use [a]
Adept (diflubenzuron)	Uniroyal	◆	◆	GH, IP
Azatin (azadirachtin)	Biosys	◆		GH, IP, O
Citation (cyromazine)	Ciba	◆	◆	GH, IP, O
Dycarb (bendiocarb)	The Scotts Company	◆		GH, IP, O
Enstar II (kinoprene)	Sandoz	◆		GH, IP
Gnatrol (*Bacillus thuringiensis israelensis*)	Abbott	◆		GH, IP
Knox Out GH (diazinon)	W.A. Cleary	◆		GH, IP
Precision (fenoxycarb)	Ciba	◆	◆	GH, IP
PT 1325 DuraGuard (chlorpyrifos)	Whitmire	◆		GH, IP, O

[a] GH = greenhouse; IP = interior plantscape; O = outdoor

Table 18.2   Granular pesticides registered for control of insects, mites, slugs, and snails

Product	Company	Aphids	Leaf-miners	Mites	White grubs	Mealybugs & scales	Slugs & snails	Thrips	White-flies	Use[a]
Deadline (metaldehyde)	Valent						◆			GH, O
Di-Syston (disulfoton)	Bayer	◆		◆				◆	◆	O
Marathon 1G (imidacloprid)	Olympic	◆				◆			◆	GH, O
Oftanol (isofenphos)	Bayer				◆					O
Oxamyl 10G (oxamyl)	Pratt	◆	◆	◆		◆		◆	◆	GH, IP, O
Pinpoint (acephate)	Valent	◆				◆				GH, O

[a] GH = greenhouse; IP = interior plantscape; O = outdoor

Table 18.3 Smoke generator and fogging formulations registered for control of insects and mites

Product	Company	Aphids	Mealybugs	Spider mites	Scale insects	Thrips	Whiteflies
Fulex DDVP Smoke (dichlorvos)	Fuller	◆		◆			◆
Fulex Dithio Smoke (sulfotepp)	Fuller	◆	◆	◆	◆	◆	◆
Fulex Thiodan Smoke (endosulfan)	Fuller	◆					◆
Fulex Nicotine Smoke (nicotine)	Fuller	◆				◆	
GH-18 (naled)	Aire-mate	◆		◆			◆
GH-19 (dichlorvos)	Aire-mate	◆		◆		◆	◆
GH-60 (resmethrin)	Aire-mate	◆					◆
Plant Products Nicotine Smoke (nicotine)	Plant Products Corp.	◆				◆	
Plantfume 103 Smoke (sulfotepp)	Plant Products Corp.	◆	◆	◆	◆	◆	◆

Note: Greenhouse crops only.

Table 18.4   Spray and aerosol products registered for control of sucking insect pests

Product	Company	Aphids	Mealybugs	Scales	Plant bugs	Thrips	White-flies	Use [a]
Adept (diflubenzuron)	Uniroyal						◆	GH, IP
Astro (permethrin)	FMC	◆					◆	GH, IP, O
Azatin (azadirachtin)	Biosys	◆	◆			◆	◆	GH, IP, O
Decathlon (cyfluthrin)	Olympic	◆	◆	◆	◆	◆	◆	GH, O
Dursban (chlorpyrifos)	DowElanco	◆	◆	◆	◆	◆		GH, O
Dycarb (bendiocarb)	The Scotts Company	◆	◆	◆		◆	◆	GH, IP, O
Dylox (trichlorfon)	Bayer		◆		◆			IP, O
Enstar II (kinoprene)	Sandoz	◆	◆	◆			◆	GH, IP
Hot Pepper Wax (capsaicin)	Wilder	◆	◆	◆		◆	◆	GH, O
JMS Stylet Oil (horticultural oil)	JMS Flower Farms		◆	◆			◆	GH, O

Table 18.4 continued

Product	Company	Aphids	Mealybugs	Scales	Plant bugs	Thrips	White-flies	Use [a]
Knox Out GH (diazinon)	W.A. Cleary	♦	♦	♦		♦		GH, IP, O
M-Pede (insecticidal soap)	Mycogen	♦					♦	GH, IP, O
Mavrik (fluvalinate)	Sandoz	♦	♦		♦	♦	♦	GH, IP, O
Mesurol (methiocarb)	Gowan	♦						GH, O
Naturalis-O (*Beauveria bassiana*)	Troy Bioscience	♦	♦			♦	♦	GH, IP, O
Neemazad (azadirachtin)	Thermo Triligy Corp.	♦				♦	♦	GH, IP, O
Olympic Insecticidal Soap (insecticidal soap)	Olympic	♦					♦	GH, IP, O
Orthene TT&O (acephate)	Valent	♦	♦	♦	♦	♦	♦	GH, O
Precision (fenoxycarb)	Ciba				♦		♦	GH, IP, O

Table 18.4 continued

Product	Company	Aphids	Mealybugs	Scales	Plant bugs	Thrips	White-flies	Use [a]
PT 1100 (pyrethrum)	Whitmire	◆	◆	◆	◆			GH
PT 1200 (resmethrin)	Whitmire	◆	◆	◆	◆	◆	◆	GH
PT 1300 Orthene (acephate)	Whitmire	◆	◆	◆	◆	◆	◆	GH
PT 1325 DuraGuard (chlorpyrifos)	Whitmire	◆	◆	◆	◆	◆		GH, IP, O
Resmethrin EC26 (resmethrin)	Pratt	◆			◆	◆	◆	GH, IP, O
Saf-T-Cide (horticultural oil)	Brandt Consolidated		◆	◆	◆	◆	◆	GH, O
Sevin (carbaryl)	Rhone-Poulenc		◆	◆	◆	◆		O
Sunspray Ultra-Fine (horticultural oil)	Sun Co.	◆			◆	◆	◆	GH, IP, O
Talstar T&O (bifenthrin)	FMC	◆	◆	◆	◆	◆	◆	GH, O

Table 18.4 continued

Product	Company	Aphids	Mealybugs	Scales	Plant bugs	Thrips	White-flies	Use [a]
Tame (fenpropathrin)	Valent	◆	◆	◆	◆	◆	◆	GH, O
Tempo (cyfluthrin)	Bayer	◆	◆	◆	◆	◆	◆	IP, O
Thiodan (endosulfan)	FMC	◆					◆	GH, O
Topcide (lambda-cyhalothrin)	Uniroyal	◆	◆	◆	◆	◆	◆	GH
Triact (neem oil)	Thermo Triligy Corp.	◆	◆	◆			◆	GH, O
Turcam (bendiocarb)	AgrEvo	◆	◆	◆		◆		GH, IP, O

[a] GH = greenhouse; IP = interior plantscape; O = outdoor

Table 18.5   Spray and aerosol products registered for control of mites

Product	Company	Spider mites	Broad mites	Cyclamen mites	Use [a]
Avid (abamectin)	Merck	◆			GH, O
Duraguard (chlorpyrifos)	Whitmire	◆			GH, IP, O
Dycarb (bendiocarb)	The Scotts Company	◆			GH, IP, O
Hexygon (hexythiazox)	Gowan	◆			O
Hot Pepper Wax (capsaicin)	Wilder	◆			GH, IP, O
JMS Stylet Oil (horticultural oil)	JMS Flower Farms	◆			GH, O
Joust (oxythioquinox)	Olympic	◆			O
Kelthane (dicofol)	Rohm & Haas	◆			GH, O
M-Pede (insecticidal soap)	Mycogen	◆			GH, IP, O
Mavrik (fluvalinate)	Sandoz	◆			GH, IP, O
Mesurol (methiocarb)	Gowan	◆			GH, O
Morestan (oxythioquinox)	Bayer	◆			O

Table 18.5 continued

Product	Company	Spider mites	Broad mites	Cyclamen mites	Use [a]
Naturalis-O (*Beauveria bassiana*)	Troy Bioscience	◆			GH, IP, O
Pentac (dienochlor)	Sandoz	◆	◆		GH, IP
PT 1800 Attain (bifenthrin)	Whitmire	◆			GH
Saf-T-Cide (horticultural oil)	Brandt Consolidated	◆			GH, O
Sanmite (pyridaben)	BASF	◆	◆		GH
Sunspray Ultra-Fine (horticultural oil)	Sun Co.	◆			GH, IP, O
Talstar (bifenthrin)	FMC	◆	◆		GH, O
Tame (fenpropathrin)	Valent	◆			GH, O
Thiodan (endosulfan)	FMC			◆	GH, O
Topcide (lambda-cyhalothrin)	Uniroyal	◆	◆		GH
Triact (neem oil)	Thermo Triligy Corp.	◆			GH, O

[a] GH = greenhouse; IP = interior plantscape; O = outdoor

Table 18.6   Insecticides registered for control of other insects and related pests

Product	Company	Fungus gnats (adults)	Leafminers	Coleoptera (beetles)	Lepidoptera (caterpillars)	Sowbugs	Use [a]
Adept (diflubenzuron)	Uniroyal				◆		GH, IP
Astro (permethrin)	FMC	◆	◆		◆		GH, IP, O
Avid (abamectin)	Merck		◆				GH, O
Azatin (azadirachtin)	Olympic		◆		◆		GH, IP, O
Citation (cyromazine)	Ciba		◆				GH, IP, O
Decathlon (cyfluthrin)	Olympic	◆			◆	◆	GH, O
Dipel (*Bacillus thuringiensis*)	Abbott				◆		GH, IP
DuraGuard (chlorpyrifos)	Whitmire		◆	◆	◆		GH, IP, O
Dursban (chlorpyrifos)	Dow Elanco			◆	◆		GH, O
Dycarb (bendiocarb)	The Scotts Company			◆	◆	◆	GH, IP, O

Table 18.6 continued

Product	Company	Fungus gnats (adults)	Leafminers	Coleoptera (beetles)	Lepidoptera (caterpillars)	Sowbugs	Use [a]
JMS Stylet Oil (horticultural oil)	JMS Flower Farm		◆				GH, O
Knox Out GH (diazinon)	W.A. Cleary		◆				GH, IP, O
Mavrik (fluvalinate)	Sandoz				◆	◆	GH, IP,
Naturalis-O (*Beauveria bassiana*)	Troy Bioscience			◆	◆		GH, IP, O
Neemazad (azadirachtin)	Thermo Triligy Corp.		◆		◆		GH, IP, O
Orthene TT&O (acephate)	Valent				◆		GH, O
Precision (fenoxycarb)	Ciba			◆	◆		GH, IP, O
PT 1100 (pyrethrum)	Whitmire	◆			◆		GH
PT 1200 (resmethrin)	Whitmire	◆			◆	◆	GH
PT 1300 Orthene (acephate)	Whitmire				◆		GH

Table 18.6   continued

Product	Company	Fungus gnats (adults)	Leafminers	Coleoptera (beetles)	Lepidoptera (caterpillars)	Sowbugs	Use[a]
Resmethrin EC26 (resmethrin)	Pratt	◆			◆		GH, IP, O
Sevin (carbaryl)	Rhone-Poulenc			◆	◆	◆	O
Sunspray Ultra-Fine (horticultural oil)	Sun Co.	◆					GH, IP, O
Talstar T&O (bifenthrin)	FMC	◆			◆		GH, O
Tame (fenpropathrin)	Valent				◆		GH, O
Tempo (cyfluthrin)	Bayer	◆		◆	◆	◆	IP, O
Topcide (lambda-cyhalothrin)	Uniroyal		◆		◆		GH

[a] GH = greenhouse; IP = interior plantscape; O = outdoor
[b] Lepidoptera leafminers only

Table 18.7   Biological control agents for insect and mite control in greenhouses and interior plantscapes

Insect or mite pest	Biological control agent [a]	Comments
Aphids	*Aphidoletes aphidimyza*	Aphid midge. Widely available. Will become inactive during short days, unless lights are provided.
	Aphidius colemani	Aphid parasite, most effective against green peach, *Myzus persicae*, and melon aphid, *Aphis gossypii*.
	Aphelinus abdomalis	Aphid parasite, most effective against potato aphid, *Macrosiphum euphorbiae*.
	Beauveria bassiana	Fungus-based product. Three to five applications may be needed. Addition of soap or oil may increase efficacy.
	Chrysopa, Chrysoperla	Lacewings. Introduced as eggs or larvae. Will also feed on several other insects and mites.
	Hippodamia convergens	Ladybird beetle.
Fungus gnats (larvae)	*Bacillus thuringiensis israelensis*	Microbial-based insecticide. Apply as drench to potting mix. Three applications at four-day intervals are needed for best results.
	Heterorhabditis bacteriophora	Entomopathogenic nematode. Applied to potting mix in water.
	Hypoaspis miles	Predatory mite. Fair availability. Will persist in potting media. Also some thrips suppression.
	Steinernema feltiae	Entomopathogenic nematode. Applied to potting mix in water.

Table 18.7   continued

Insect or mite pest	Biological control agent [a]	Comments
Leafminers	*Dacnusa sibirica*	Leafminer larval parasite. Larvae usually complete their development, then adult parasites emerge.
	Diglyphus isaea	Leafminer larval parasite. Larvae are killed while still in the leaf mine.
Lepidoptera (caterpillars, worms)	*Beauveria bassiana*	Fungus-based product. Three to five applications may be needed. Addition of soap or oil may increase efficacy.
	Bacillus thuringiensis kurstaki	Microbial-based insecticide. Widely available. Several products based on different strains that are effective against different caterpillar species.
Mealybugs	*Cryptolaemus montrouzieri*	A ladybird beetle called the mealybug destroyer. Widely available. Most effective when mealybug populations are high. Less effective during short days.
	Leptomastix dactylopii	Mealybug parasite. Effective against *Planococcus citri*, the citrus mealybug, only. Does best in warm, sunny conditions.
Mites (broad mite)	*Neoseiulus barkeri*	Predator mite. Also attacks thrips larvae.
Mites (spider mite)	*Beauveria bassiana*	Fungus-based product. Three to five applications may be needed. Addition of soap or oil may increase efficacy.
	Phytoseiulus persimilis	Predator mite. Widely available, and the most commonly used spider mite biological control. Does best at higher humidities.
	Mesoseiulus longipes	Predator mite. Generally more tolerant of warmer and drier conditions than *P. persimilis*. Limited availability.
	Neoseiulus californicus	Predator mite. Able to survive longer in the absence of prey. Also attacks cyclamen mites. Limited availability.

Table 18.7 continued

Insect or mite pest	Biological control agent [a]	Comments
Scales	*Aphytis melinus*	Armored scale parasite. Attacks California red scale, oleander scale, yellow scale. Does best at warm temperatures and higher humidities.
	Lindorus lophanthus	Predatory beetle. Both adults and larvae attack many species of armored and soft scales.
	Metaphycus helvolus	Soft scale parasite. Attacks black scale, brown soft scale, hemispherical scale.
Thrips	*Amblyseius degenerans*	Predator mite. Able to survive on pollen in the absence of prey. More aggressive than other mite predators of thrips.
	Neoseiulus cucumeris = Amblyseius cucumeris	Predator mite. Attacks first-instar immatures. Widely used on greenhouse vegetable crops. Can survive on pollen and spider mites.
	Orius insidiosus	Pirate bug. Both adults and immatures are predators. Can survive on pollen, aphids, spider mites, and whiteflies in absence of thrips.
Whiteflies	*Beauveria bassiana*	Fungus-based product. Three to five applications may be needed. Addition of soap or oil may increase efficacy.
	Delphastus pusillus	A small ladybird beetle. Feeds on eggs and nymphs.
	Encarsia formosa	Parasitic wasp. Widely used on greenhouse vegetable crops. Adults lay eggs in mid-instar whitefly nymphs and feed on early-instar nymphs. Not very effective against *Bemisia* whiteflies.
	Eretmocerous californicus	Parasitic wasp. Use attempted mainly against *Bemisia* whiteflies.

[a] Consult biological control agent supply company for suggested introduction rates for each agent.

Chapter 19

Fungicides and Bactericides

F ungicides and bactericides continue to be fundamental parts of integrated plant health management. The correct approach to fungicides and bactericides is to use them in a holistic framework. Whereas we cannot say that these substances themselves increase the vigor of plants and aid in holistic and environmental health management, we can say that fungicides and bactericides perform best if the plant vigor is maintained at top levels and the environment is kept as inhospitable to the pathogen as possible.

Consider this from the fact that no fungicide or bactericide will protect all of the infection points or inactivate all of the sources of inoculum. If you were to treat plants to prevent *Botrytis* infections, for instance, a good product applied correctly might protect 99 percent of the potential infection sites on a plant and eradicate 70 percent of the existing *Botrytis*. There is no doubt that some of the millions of spores produced by the remaining *Botrytis* will find their way to the unprotected infection sites and initiate new infections. If plant vigor is not kept up, infections will develop into new areas of diseased tissue, giving rise to still more inoculum and disease. The result is a treatment that does not seem to work well!

Fungicides commonly available in the United States

Over the past several years, there has been a dramatic change in the types and numbers of fungicides available for the management of infectious diseases on flower and foliage crops produced in the greenhouse or outdoors. The changes in fungicides have come about because of several stimuli at work in the industry. First of all, we have the universal occurrence of increased governmental actions. In the early 1970s, sweeping new pesticide legislation required that specific crop types, diseases, and sites be listed on product labels in order for the use to be legal. This triggered several years of research to "expand" the labels of products already in use. Long lists of registered crop types began to appear on products intended for greenhouse ornamentals.

New fungicide chemistry is also being developed. Several of our fungicides now benefit from this chemistry and new modes of action.

More are to come in the near future. (The readers should not assume that all ornamental plant fungicides are discussed in this chapter, and no discrimination is intended for omitted products.)

Specific remarks in the following sections are derived from those given on pesticide labels at the time of publication. It is the responsibility of the pesticide user to follow currently labeled instructions. The user should check labels before purchase to be certain labeled uses (rates and application methods) are consistent with planned practices. Also, check whether plants in question are listed on the label. Check whether the product is labeled for use in your state or region of the United States. Finally, check whether the chemical's use is permitted for field-grown material only or for greenhouse-grown material only.

Benzimidazoles

Thiabendazole (Mertect). This systemic fungicide is specifically labeled as a bulb and corm dip for several diseases. Closely follow labeled directions.

Thiophanate-methyl (Cleary's 3336, Systec 1998, Fungo). This systemic fungicide comes in a wettable powder or flowable formulation. It has a broad spectrum of activity, being used as a drench or as a spray. It is labeled for all types of ornamentals. When spraying, a good acid buffering adjuvant is recommended. A spreader-sticker is recommended for hard-to-wet foliage. Mix thiophanate-methyl with other fungicides for a broad-spectrum growing media drenching program.

Dicarboximides

Iprodione (Chipco 26019). Many field and greenhouse ornamentals can be sprayed for *Botrytis* with this 50WP fungicide. There are a few other foliar spray uses on the label, as well. As a growing media drench, iprodione can be used at seeding or transplanting for *Rhizoctonia* control. Be certain to treat only labeled crops.

Vinclozolin (Ornalin, Curalan). This 50WP fungicide is effective for control of *Botrytis* species and *Sclerotinia* species on ornamental herbaceous, woody, and bulb crops grown in greenhouses and outdoors. It is labeled for professional use only as a foliar spray and as a bulb, corm, and fresh cut-flower dip. It is also labeled for use in a thermal fogger.

Demethylation inhibitors

Myclobutanil (Systhane, Eagle). This demethylation-inhibiting fungicide comes in water-soluble pouches for ease of measurement. It is labeled on many crops and carries a direction that allows its use on other plants if you test it first. It is generally labeled for powdery mildews and rusts.

Fenarimol (Rubigan). Fenarimol is a demethylation-inhibiting fungicide specifically labeled for the control of powdery mildews on greenhouse- and field-grown ornamentals. It is locally systemic within the leaf on which it is applied. It works best when sprayed on lightly, to the point of glistening of the foliage. It is a protectant-eradicant with long residual value.

Triadimefon (Strike). This long-lasting systemic fungicide is effective for its labeled uses. Follow label directions closely to avoid stunting plant growth. The fungicide is volatile; thus, in warm weather its effectiveness may be reduced.

Triflumazole (Terraguard). Triflumazole is a new systemic fungicide with very broad-spectrum activity. It has drench and spray uses for root, stem, leaf, and flower diseases. It is a curative as well as preventive product. Triflumazole is generally used at 21- to 28-day intervals, although it is labeled at shorter intervals.

Triforine. This emulsifiable concentrate (EC) fungicide wets foliage well without the need for additional spreader-sticker. Be certain to wear eye protection when using this material.

Propiconazole (Banner). This demethylation-inhibiting fungicide, available as an EC or as a microencapsulated slow-release fungicide, is good for systemic control of powdery mildews, rusts, and several other diseases. It has little if any growth-regulating side effects.

Biorationals

Gleocladium **fungus (SoilGuard).** This biological management tool is now available as a drench for root rot control. It must be stored and used strictly according to labeled directions to prevent its inactivation.

Streptomyces **fungus (Mycostop).** This biological management tool is now available as a drench for root rot control and as a spray for *Botrytis* suppression. It must be stored and used strictly according to labeled directions to prevent its inactivation.

Coppers

Fixed coppers (Kocide 101/404, Bordo-Mix, Phyton 27). Fixed copper fungicides and Bordeaux mixtures have been available for decades. They are safe to users and have a broad spectrum of activity. The general recommendation is approximately 4 pounds (1.8 kg) of a 50 percent copper per 100 gallons (378 l). Because there are so many copper fungicides on the market, be sure to check the label on each fungicide before you use it. Some of the newer ones are more concentrated, so less should be used. Phyton 27 is a newer, systemic copper-based fungicide that can be used as a drench or spray. Phyton 27 is labeled for use in low volume applicators.

EBDCs

Mancozeb (Protect T/O, FORE, Dithane T/O). Use this dithiocarbamate fungicide for leaf spots and blights. It is registered for the control of many otherwise difficult-to-manage leaf spots and blights, such as the *Alternarias, Phytophthora* crown rots, downy mildews, anthracnoses, and rusts. It is especially useful for *Botrytis* control where resistance of the pathogen to other fungicides is suspected. Since it is not systemic, thorough crop coverage is important for control. A good spreader-sticker is recommended for use on hard-to-wet foliage. Recent research has shown that the use of latex- or acrylic-based spreader-stickers work well with contact-protectant products like mancozeb.

Oils and soaps

Soaps (M-Pede). The only soap currently labeled to control diseases of ornamentals is M-Pede. It is only labeled for the control of powdery mildew of roses at this time. Carefully follow labeled directions to avoid plant damage.

Extract of neem oil (Triact 90EC). This oil product is effective for the control of a wide variety of foliar diseases on ornamentals. It is labeled for use on all types of plants but should be used only once in four weeks on roses. It is also labeled as an insecticide and miticide.

Others

Captan (Orthocide). This is a broad-spectrum fungicide with limited registrations for use on woody ornamentals. It can be used as a preplanting growing media treatment for prevention of damping-off and root rot diseases. It is also effective on certain foliar diseases.

Chlorothalonil (Daconil 2787, Thalonil, Exotherm Termil). Daconil 2787, Thalonil, and Exotherm Termil are trade names for this fungicide that is effective in the control of *Botrytis* and other leaf spotting fungi on many crops. Chlorothalonil is the best *Botrytis* eradicant available for use in the greenhouse. Exotherm Termil is a smoke bomb form of chlorothalonil for greenhouses. Fumigate in the evening and close the doors and vents overnight. Do not enter during treatment, and follow labeled or WPS ventilation requirements before reentering in the treated area.

Dinocap (Karathane). This fungicide for powdery mildew control also acts as a miticide. It has good residual activity. Since it may cause damage, the material is usually not used on open flowers.

Etridiazole (Truban, Terrazole). Etridiazole is quite specific for control of water mold pathogens of greenhouse crops, *Pythium* and *Phytophthora*. Thus, it is often combined with other materials in a growing media drench program. Many believe that etridiazole is more effective for *Pythium* than for *Phytophthora*. Recently, the manufacturers have developed several formulations of etridiazole to better fit into greenhouse production methods. The product can be purchased as a granular, wettable powder or a flowable formulation.

Etridiazole can cause plant stunting or leaf burn if used at too high a rate. The problem is more prevalent with highly organic growing media or with the flowable formulation. Always use the lower end of the dosage range given on the label unless situations warrant more extreme treatments. Follow the application with an additional irrigation to improve the penetrability of the material into the planting media and to wash the product off foliage.

Fosetyl-Al (Aliette). Effective for *Phytophthora* and *Pythium* diseases on several crops, fosetyl-Al is a systemic preventive fungicide that may be drenched onto the growing media of existing plants, sprayed on plants where the product will move into the roots, or incorporated into potting media before planting. The rates you use will vary according to the application method. Recent research has demonstrated that a combination of fosetyl-Al plus mancozeb (Protect T/O) applied as a heavy spray will result in good management of *Phytophthora* crown rots.

Metalaxyl (Subdue). This systemic fungicide is effective for *Pythium* or *Phytophthora* disease organisms at extremely low rates. Recently, metalaxyl has been suspect regarding control of all *Pythium* genera or strains present in and on greenhouse crops. It is not known whether this is due to acquired resistance or to a narrow spectrum of activity against the many species of *Pythium* found rotting the roots of floral and foliage crops. Because of possible phytotoxicity problems, use the product at the lower end of the rate ranges given on the label for various crops. Do not apply more frequently than directed on the label. Metalaxyl should be combined with other materials in a preventive growing medium drench program to broaden the spectrum of pathogens controlled. The granular 2G metalaxyl is registered for broadcast application or growing mix incorporation.

Oxycarboxin (Plantvax). This is a systemic fungicide specifically registered for rust control on ornamentals in the field or greenhouse. It is labeled for all ornamentals.

Piperalin (Pipron). Piperalin is an eradicant fungicide registered for the control of powdery mildews on greenhouse crops. Apply it every seven to 14 days, depending on the severity of the disease. It can be mixed with other mildicides and a good spreader-sticker for eradicant and protectant treatment of affected crops.

Propamocarb (Banol). Propamocarb is formulated as an emulsifiable concentrate (EC). It is labeled as a growing medium drench for control of root and crown rots caused by water molds. Specific use directions are given for treatment at seeding (sowing), transplanting of seedlings, planting of rooted cuttings, and planting of bare-root plants. Propamocarb is quite safe on plant material, even producing a growth regulator type of growth stimulation in many cases. It can be mixed with thiophanate-methyl for a broad-spectrum growing mix drench.

Quintozene (Defend, PCNB, Terraclor). Use as a growing medium drench to control some stem- and root-rotting fungi. Quintozene is not effective against water molds but is very effective against *Sclerotinia* and *Rhizoctonia.* It should be combined with other materials in a general growing mix drench. It has a long growing media residual and is generally used only once every three months or so.

Sulfur (Thiolux). If a labeled product can be found, pure sulfur is used by many in electric fumigators to treat crops for powdery mildew. Sulfur sprays or dusts may also be used when properly labeled. Sulfur leaves a residue and may cause plant injury.

Combinations

Banrot. Banrot, a broad-spectrum fungicide made of etridiazole plus thiophanate-methyl, is used for control of root rots caused by *Pythium, Phytophthora, Rhizoctonia, Fusarium,* and *Thielaviopsis.* The material comes as a 40WP for growing medium drenching or as an 8G for growing mix incorporation prior to planting.

Benefit. Benefit is a combination of thiophanate-methyl and iprodione.

Consys. This is a combination product containing chlorothalonil and thiophanate-methyl. (See their earlier individual discussions for uses.)

Zyban, Duosan. Zyban and Duosan are trade names for a broad spectrum, systemic-contact fungicide consisting of a mixture of 15 percent thiophanate-methyl and 60 percent mancozeb. It is labeled for professional use only on many herbaceous and woody ornamentals in greenhouses or fields. A good spreader-sticker is recommended for use on hard-to-wet foliage.

Using fungicides to manage common diseases

The more common greenhouse crop diseases that lend themselves to chemical prevention or management are now discussed with specific reference to the fungicides and bactericides in common use today. The situation is constantly changing, so be sure and keep up to date by reading, working with consultants, and attending meetings.

Water mold root and crown rots

Phytophthora and *Pythium* fungi cause many root and crown diseases of greenhouse crops. These pathogens are called water molds. Etridiazole (Truban, Terrazole) fungicide continues to be widely used for water mold-incited diseases. Many believe that etridiazole is more effective for *Pythium* than it is for *Phytophthora*. Recently, the manufacturers have developed several formulations of etridiazole to better fit into greenhouse production methods. The product can be purchased as a granular, wettable powder or flowable formulation. Etridiazole can cause plant stunting or leaf burn if used at too high a rate. The problem is more prevalent with highly organic growing media or with the flowable formulation. Always use the lower end of the dosage ranges given on the label unless situations warrant more extreme treatments.

Etridiazole is also one of the active ingredients in Banrot fungicide. Banrot is a broad-spectrum product that can be used for other crown and root rots in addition to the water mold diseases. This is because it contains two active ingredients, etridiazole and thiophanate-methyl. (More will be said about Banrot and thiophanate-methyl in the *Rhizoctonia* discussion.)

Metalaxyl (Subdue) is a fungicide with good effectiveness at quite a low cost. Many crops are listed on the label. Recently, a 25 percent WP and a 2 percent granular formulation were released, in addition to the 24 percent EC also available. One can mix the 2 percent G formulation into a potting media or plant bed prior to use. Metalaxyl is highly active, especially against the *Phytophthora*-incited diseases. Only very small dosages, such as one-half ounce (14 g) per 100 gallons (378 l), are needed in many cases. Metalaxyl has been associated with plant stunting on rare occasions. The problem will be worse in hot weather or when plants get excessively dry between waterings. Metalaxyl has also been suspect regarding control of all *Pythium* genera or strains present in and on greenhouse crops. It is not known whether this is due to acquired resistance or to a narrow spectrum of activity against the many species of *Pythium* found rotting the roots of floral and foliage crops.

Propamocarb (Banol) is a recently introduced product that is quite effective. It is currently labeled at relatively high rates, which results in high cost. Propamocarb is quite safe on plant material, even producing a growth regulator type of growth stimulation in many cases.

Fosetyl-Al (Aliette) is a new systemic for many flower and foliage crops. It can be sprayed on plants, where it will move to the roots and prevent these water mold root rot diseases! Dosages are quite high when it is used as a spray, which results in a heavy spray residue. Fosetyl-Al has been widely used on hardy mums as a root rot-managing spray. Recent research has demonstrated that a combination of fosetyl-Al plus mancozeb (Protect T/O) applied as a heavy spray will result in good management of *Phytophthora* crown rots.

Rhizoctonia damping-off, root rots, and stem rots

Thiophanate-methyl (Cleary's 3336, Fungo, or Systec 1998) is labeled for *Rhizoctonia* control on all ornamentals in greenhouses or nurseries. The product comes as a flowable or as a wettable powder. Cleary's 3336 WP is available in water-soluble bags for less pesticide exposure and greater ease of mixing. It also has a chemigation label. A granular formulation of 3336 is also available. The 3336 flowable has improved stability over the other thiophanate-methyl flowables. This eliminates the temporary soluble salt damage to roots sometimes seen when drenching other flowable products into potting media.

Quintozene (Defend, PCNB, or Terraclor) fungicide is an older product. However, it remains very effective against *Rhizoctonia*. Quintozene is labeled as a pot drench, as a soil mix, and as a banded treatment for field-grown flower and foliage crops.

Iprodione (Chipco 26019) and triflumazole (Terraguard) give us some new chemistry against *Rhizoctonia*. Although they are effective, the crop list is limited on these products, and their use is a bit tricky. The grower should adhere to labeled instructions. Do not use iprodione on plants not on the label. Iprodione has been combined with thiophanate-methyl in a new product called Benefit. As such, it is labeled as a drench for *Rhizoctonia* control.

Banrot contains two active ingredients. One is etridiazole, for water molds; the other is thiophanate-methyl, for *Rhizoctonia* and other root rots. This combination gives us a broader spectrum of activity against soilborne pathogens. The crop list is good. The company making Banrot produces an 8 percent granular formulation that can be premixed into potting media, as well as a wettable powder that is to be used as a watering-in drench.

Thielaviopsis black root rot

Black root rot, caused by *Thielaviopsis (Charala) basicola*, has become prevalent in recent years. Pansies, vincas, and petunias have been hard hit. Triflumazole (Terraguard) and thiophanate-methyl (Cleary's 3336, Fungo, and Banrot) are labeled for management of this pathogen. Follow labeled directions closely for crops labeled and application timing.

Powdery mildews

Much new chemistry has recently come to the front in the battle against powdery mildews and rusts. Thiophanate-methyl (Cleary's 3336, Fungo) and piperonyl (Pipron) have been used by many against powdery mildews for years. They are still effective if used properly. Pipron is an eradicant, whereas thiophanate-methyl is primarily a systemic protectant. The label on Pipron is being expanded to include many more crops. Thiophanate-methyl is one of the components of Zyban and Benefit fungicides. Thus, these products are also labeled for powdery mildew management.

The newer products—such as the DMI products triadimefon (Bayleton), fenarimol (Rubigan), triforine, triflumazole (Terraguard), and propiconazole (Banner); and copper pentahydrate (Phyton-27)—have come into widespread use in many ranges. Phyton-27 is moderately effective against powdery mildews, but it is reasonably safe for use on flowering plants in the greenhouse.

Many of these new products, especially the DMIs have long residual and good systemic action. They are extremely effective. Some, unfortunately, have a tendency to inhibit giberellic acid synthesis and can cause plant stunting. Others are quite volatile and will dissipate into the air too quickly when used outdoors or in the greenhouse in hot weather or under windy conditions.

The best bet when combating a powdery mildew problem with routine sprays is to combine an eradicant with a protectant, if the label permits this. Also, if you are using a DMI, rotate to another one after three or four applications. The future of fungicides for powdery mildews will be changing rapidly. Labels are being expanded and new products are becoming available.

Rusts

The rust diseases on leaves and stems of flower and foliage crops are combated with older contact-protectants as well as with some of the newer systemic products. Of the older products, mancozeb (Protect T/O, Dithane T/O or WDG and FORE) and chlorothalonil (Daconil 2787, Thalonil) are useful if sprayed repeatedly and thoroughly. Oxycarboxin (Plantvax) is a systemic that is quite specific for rust disease control. Some of the newer systemics mentioned for powdery mildews are also effective and labeled for rust diseases. Triforine, propiconazole (Banner), and triadimefon (Bayleton) are particularly effective and well labeled.

Botrytis blights

These diseases are the number one reason growers of flower and foliage crops spray plants with fungicides. As a result, there are many fungicides that have been labeled for use against *Botrytis* on such crops. Fifteen fungicides are registered at this time for *Botrytis* diseases on greenhouse crops. Of the older products, the mancozeb and chlorothalonil products (discussed in connection with rusts) are very widely used. Exotherm Termil, a smoke formulation of chlorothalonil, can also be used on many crops.

The most widely labeled products for *Botrytis* diseases are thiophanate-methyl (Cleary's 3336, Fungo, Systec 1998), vinclozolin (Ornalin), and iprodione (Chipco 26029). *Botrytis* resistance can occur with all of these fungicides, although it is most widespread with thiophanate-methyl. Ornalin is labeled as a spray, flower dip, or bulb dip. All of the products are quite effective if used according to labeled directions and if resistance is not present in the greenhouse.

The combination products Zyban and Benefit are also labeled for *Botrytis* control. Only certain plant types are listed. Follow labeled directions. The possibility for *Botrytis* fungicide resistance is greater with Benefit than with Zyban.

Miscellaneous leaf spots and blights

There are many other leaf spots and blights of flower and foliage crops that are occasionally seen by the grower. Although not widely prevailing, they can be devastating! Sixteen fungicides have at least one labeled use against these miscellaneous diseases. The older fungicides do tend to have a broader spectrum of activity against many leaf-spotting fungi.

Unfortunately, few companies are seeking to expand labels on these products. The five most useful products from a "broadly labeled" point of view at this time are chlorothalonil (Daconil 2787), the mancozebs (Protect T/O, Dithane T/O or WDG, and FORE), the coppers (Kocide 101 and Phyton-27), and the combination products Zyban and Benefit. Zyban is particularly interesting because it is a combination of the systemic thiophanate-methyl and the widely used topical fungicide mancozeb.

On the next several pages are drench (table 19.1) and spray (table 19.2) outlines you may find useful. Some products may have been omitted. This has been inadvertent, and no discrimination is intended by such omission.

Table 19.1   Drenches for root and crown rots (damping-off)

Product	Company	Water molds	Rhizoctonia	Fusarium	Thielaviopsis	Sclerotinia
Aliette (Fosetyl-Al)	Rhone-Poulenc	◆				
Banol (Propamocarb)	AgrEvo	◆				
Banrot (Etridiazole plus Thiophanate-m)	The Scotts Company	◆	◆	◆	◆	
Benefit (Thiophanate-m plus iprodione)	The Scotts Company		◆	◆		
Captan	Micro-Flo		◆			
Chipco 26019 (Vinclozolin)	Rhone-Poulenc		◆	◆	◆	◆
Cleary's 3336 (Thiophanate-m)	W.A. Cleary		◆	◆	◆	◆
Defend (PCNB or Quintozene)	W.A. Cleary		◆	◆	◆	◆

Table 19.1   continued

Product	Company	Water molds	Rhizoctonia	Fusarium	Thielaviopsis	Sclerotinia
Fungo (Thiophanate-m)	The Scotts Company		◆	◆	◆	◆
Mycostop (*Streptomyces* fungus)	Agbio	◆		◆		
SoilGuard (Gleocladium fungus)	Thermo Triligy Corp.	◆	◆			
Subdue (Metalaxyl)	Ciba	◆				
Systec 1998 (Thiophanate-m)	Regal		◆	◆	◆	◆
Terraclor (PCNB or Quintozene)	Uniroyal Chemical Co.		◆	◆	◆	◆
Terraguard (Triflumazole)	Uniroyal Chemical Co.		◆	◆	◆	
Terrazole (Etridiazole)	Uniroyal Chemical Co.	◆				
Truban (Etridiazole)	The Scotts Company	◆				

Table 19.2   Sprays for various diseases

Product	Company	Botrytis	General fungal leaf spots [a]	Rusts	Powdery mildews	Bacterial blights	Downy mildews
3336 (Thiophanate-m)	W.A. Cleary	✦	✦		✦		
Agrimycin (Streptomycin)	Merck					✦	
Aliette (Fosetyl-Al)	Rhone-Poulenc						✦
Benefit (Thiophanate-m plus iprodione)	The Scotts Company	✦	✦		✦		
Chipco 26019 (Iprodione)	Rhone- Poulenc	✦	✦				
Curalan (Vinclozolin)	BASF	✦	✦				
Daconil 2787 (Chlorothalonil)	ISK	✦	✦				
Dithane T/O (Mancozeb)	Rohm & Haas	✦	✦	✦			✦

Table 19.2 continued

Product	Company	*Botrytis*	General fungal leaf spots [a]	Rusts	Powdery mildews	Bacterial blights	Downy mildews
Fungo (Thiophanate-m)	The Scotts Company	◆	◆		◆		
Kocide 101/404 (Cupric hydroxide)	Griffin	◆	◆			◆	
Mycostop (*Streptomyces* fungus)	Agbio	◆					
Ornalin (Vinclozolin)	The Scotts Company	◆	◆				
Phyton-27 (Copper Pentahydrate)	Source Technology Biologicals	◆	◆	◆	◆	◆	◆
Pipron (Piperonyl)	SePRO				◆		
Plantvax (Oxycarboxin)	Uniroyal Chemical Co.			◆			
Protect T/O (Mancozeb)	W.A. Cleary	◆	◆	◆			
Rubigan EC (Fenarimol)	SePRO				◆		◆

Table 19.2   continued

Product	Company	Botrytis	General fungal leaf spots [a]	Rusts	Powdery mildews	Bacterial blights	Downy mildews
Strike (Triadimefon)	Olympic		◆	◆	◆		
Systec 1998 (Thiophanate-m)	Regal	◆	◆		◆		
Systhane (Myclobutanil)	Rohm & Haas			◆	◆		
Terraguard (Triflumazole)	Uniroyal Chemical Co.		◆	◆	◆		
Thalonil (Chlorothalonil)	Terra	◆	◆				
Thiolux (Sulfur)	Sandoz		◆	◆	◆		
Triact (Neem Oil)	Thermo Triligy Corp.	◆	◆	◆	◆		◆
Zyban (Thiophanate-m plus mancozeb)	The Scotts Company		◆	◆	◆		◆

[a]The category "General fungal leaf spots" is so diverse that all listed products will rarely control all the diseases in this category. Consult labels for more appropriate information.

SECTION FIVE

PUTTING IT ALL TOGETHER

Chapter 20

Writing Plant Protection Programs for Flower and Foliage Crops

T he primary goal of reading a book like this is to keep the crops you are producing healthy and free of pests. A secondary goal is to react quickly and properly when a problem arises. You accomplish the first goal by becoming aware of potential problems and planning operations to prevent their occurrence or development. You accomplish the second goal by correctly diagnosing the problem, determining its primary and secondary causes, and deciding upon and carrying out reactive or rescue health management (curative) programs.

Many people think that reactionary actions are the main objectives of gaining knowledge about diseases and pests. A problem occurs, the books are read, advisors are called, and curative actions are taken. Although this sort of after-the-fact knowledge can often save a grower from disaster, it more often results in a sad case of having to learn from hindsight what you should have done in the first place.

The purpose of this chapter is to show you how to write plant protection programs to keep plants healthy. It is really a three-step planning process. You must initially think about the crop you are growing. If it is one kind of plant, such as poinsettia or geranium, it is not too difficult to determine what diseases and insects might be present. The information given in this book can help you, but more detailed plant disease and pest dictionaries are available. Buy one and become familiar with the potential disease and insect problems of the various plant types you will be growing.

The second step in the plant protection planning process is the most difficult. After you have this great list of potential disease and insect problems in front of you, you must decide which of them are sufficient threats to warrant a preventive plant protection procedure. Actually, you must put each disease or pest into three categories. Is it definitely going to be a problem unless you take protective measures? Is it so rare that you can discount the problem as long as things go normally? Is it a problem that is relatively uncommon? Or will it have such a disastrous effect when it does occur that you need to always watch for it and be ready to take quick action if and when it shows up?

Where do you get help in getting through this second step? The individual crop programs in this chapter give you our opinion of those problems that are in the first category—as of this date! Notice how, as you read from crop to crop, many problems appear again and again. These are the basic plant protection concerns of our industry.

You may not agree with our inclusion of a particular problem on a particular plant. At least, you may not agree that the problem warrants the measure of protective activity we have suggested. There is nothing wrong with your feeling this way. Your knowledge and experience may have taught you that the problem in your case is not of great importance. However, it may be that you have been lucky or that some other health management practice that you routinely do secondarily prevents the problem we have mentioned. Watch out for these pitfalls!

This brings us to the third step in writing a plant protection program. Once we have decided that a particular disease or pest warrants some sort of protective practice, we must decide which practice to employ. In the various chapters of this book, we have shown you and emphasized how the use of integrated, holistic management practices is the cheapest, most successful way to prevent insect and disease problems. Again, we have suggested some practices in the following programs. How many of them can you employ? How economically can you do them, while still doing them effectively? There is only one hard-and-fast rule: Do not write plant protection programs based solely upon the use of pesticides. They simply will not work. Appreciate the role of secondary factors, such as environmental manipulation and sanitation. Include them in your plant protection programs.

Poinsettia programmed disease and pest control

Activity	Diseases and pests prevented

Crop stage: Propagation

Plant cuttings for stock plants in new potting mix in new containers. Place potted plants on disinfected surface of raised bench for growing on.	*Thielaviopsis* black root rot *Rhizoctonia* basal stem rot *Pythium* root rot Bacterial canker Bacterial soft rot
Organize a record-keeping system for pesticide applications, pest counts on sticky traps, and pest counts on plants. If stock plants are to be grown from cuttings, root the cuttings for stock plants on the disinfected surface of raised benches by sticking them into new propagating media in plastic bags, sterile flats, or containers, or use sterile propagating blocks following strict sanitation procedures.	Whiteflies, shore flies, and fungus gnats Root rots
Hang hose so nozzle does not touch floor.	Root rots
Fill bench or flats with propagating media. Place propagating tools and flats on bench, cover, and steam at 180F for one-half hour at coolest point. **OR** Use sterile propagating blocks.	Root rots, Bacterial soft rot
Do not allow dust to contaminate propagating media or sterile propagating blocks.	Root rots and crown rots
Wash hands thoroughly before taking cuttings from stock plants.	Bacterial soft rot
Remove cuttings from stock plant with a knife sterilized by dipping in 70 percent alcohol. Change knives between stock plants. **OR** Use a series of knives, changing between each stock plant. Use enough knives so that they can soak for at least 10 minutes in a quaternary ammonium salt or phenolic sanitizer before reuse.	Bacterial soft rot

Poinsettia continued

Activity	Diseases and pests prevented

Crop stage: Propagation

Activity	Diseases and pests prevented
Place cuttings immediately into a new plastic bag or sterile container.	Bacterial soft rot
Apply rooting hormones with a powder duster. Do not dip cuttings into any solution.	Bacterial soft rot
Stick rooted cuttings directly into new or steam-treated propagating media or sterile blocks from the plastic bags or sterile containers.	Root rots
If fungus gnat activity is seen, apply a drench application of an appropriate insecticide, insect growth regulator, or nematode for larval control.	Fungus gnats
If root or basal stem rot appears while the cuttings are rooting, discard affected plants and drench a 2- to 3-foot area around the affected cuttings with fungicides effective and labeled on poinsettia for *Rhizoctonia, Pythium,* and *Thielaviopsis.* This may require mixing together two fungicides. Apply 1 pint of suspension per square foot of bench area. Make one application only.	Root rots
If *Botrytis* blight appears, spray affected area with a registered fungicide or fumigate with Exotherm Termil. Make sure you turn mist off early enough in the evening to allow the leaves to dry prior to nightfall.	*Botrytis* blights
If bacterial soft rot appears, remove affected cuttings at once. If possible, lessen the amount of mist applied. Lower the nitrogen rate being given to the stock plants to correct the problem for the next batch of cuttings.	Bacterial soft rot
Make sure that *Encarsia* or other beneficial species shipments have been scheduled, if using biological control.	Biological whitefly control

Poinsettia continued

Activity	Diseases and pests prevented

Crop stage: Propagation

Inspect cuttings for presence of whitefly eggs or nymphs. If significant numbers are found, plan to make three to four applications of an appropriate insecticide as soon as plants are established. Use insecticides less harmful to beneficials if you plan to introduce beneficials.

Reducing whitefly problems

When cuttings have rooted, remove with sterilized tools or clean hands and place in sterile containers.

Root rots

Crop stage: Preparation for planting

Hang hose so nozzle does not touch the floor.

Thielaviopsis root rot
Rhizoctonia basal stem rot
Pythium root rot
Bacterial canker

Hang yellow sticky traps near tops of plants, and place some traps, sticky side up, on growing media surfaces. Use up to four traps per 1,000 square feet for best results If this trap number is too high for record keeping, use a number that is appropriate for you. Sticky traps and plant inspection is more effective than trapping alone for detecting whiteflies and thrips.

Whiteflies, thrips, and fungus gnats

Fungus gnat larvae can be detected in pots by placing potato slices or wedges on potting media surfaces.

Fungus gnats

Prepare potting mix for planting. Allow for good aeration. Adjust media pH to 5.0 to 6.0.

Pythium root rot

Fill pots with growing mix and place on greenhouse bench. Cover bench, pots, and potting tools, and steam at 180F for one-half hour at coolest point.
OR

Root rots

Poinsettia continued

Activity	Diseases and pests prevented

Fumigate or steam the batch of potting mix in a clean area a few days before use. Store it in an area where dust will not contaminate it.
OR
Use a sanitary medium directly from a container.

Crop stage: Planting

Plant rooted cuttings directly from sterile container, flats, or rooting blocks. Always wash hands thoroughly before planting rooted cuttings or pinching growing plants.

Thielaviopsis root rot
Rhizoctonia basal stem rot
Pythium root rot
Bacterial canker

Crop stage: Growing the plants

After the first watering, drench with soil fungicides, using a combination of products to protect against both *Rhizoctonia* and *Pythium*. Apply one-half pint of suspension per 6-inch pot. Plan for monthly fungicidal drenching.

Rhizoctonia basal stem rot
Pythium root rot
Erwinia stem canker
Botrytis blight

If using biological control, begin *Encarsia* or other beneficial species introductions during the first two weeks after potting. Be very careful with pesticide use. Note the *Encarsia* may not be effective against *Bemisia* whiteflies.

Whiteflies

Immediately after potting, begin a weekly plant scouting program for thrips, whiteflies, mealybugs, and aphids. Inspect plants in all areas of the greenhouse, but pay special attention to areas near open vents and doors. Inspect sticky traps weekly. Keep records. If whiteflies are detected and biological control is not being used, begin a pesticide application program.

Insect detection and population
  monitoring

Poinsettia continued

Activity	Diseases and pests prevented
If yellow traps indicate significant fungus gnat activity during the first week or two, apply an insecticide or insect growth regulator drench or "sprench." Nematodes can also be applied in this way.	Fungus gnat management
Water thoroughly, but only according to need.	
Apply a granular insecticide to the potting mix in late September to early October, or make sure that all high-volume sprays are applied before bracts begin to show color. If necessary to apply pesticides after bract coloration begins, use smokes, fogs, or aerosols.	Insect control with insecticides
If thrips are seen on sticky cards and damage is noted on foliage, apply a high-volume spray. One or two applications should be sufficient.	Thrips
After the pinch, spray plants every two weeks with mancozeb plus a spreader-sticker until bracts begin to form.	*Botrytis*
As the crop matures, guard against excessive humidity in the greenhouse. Never water late in the day. Keep air moving over the foliage at all times. If damp, rainy weather has been a problem, fumigate the greenhouse with Exotherm Termil, but do so only before the bracts begin to show color.	*Botrytis*
If *Botrytis* is noted on leaves, and bracts are just beginning to develop, treat with chlorothalonil to eradicate blight at once.	*Botrytis*
As the crop matures, make sure the nitrogen levels are decreased, especially if the weather is cloudy and warm. Ventilate vigorously to prevent the temperature from getting into the 80s. Make sure the plants get enough light.	*Botrytis*

Geranium programmed disease and pest control

Activity	Diseases and pests prevented

Crop stage: Propagation

Activity	Diseases and pests prevented
Purchase culture-indexed and virus-indexed cuttings for use as stock plants. Pot the cuttings into new containers in new or sanitized media.	Bacterial stem rot and leaf spot *Verticillium* wilt *Pythium* blackleg *Fusarium* blackleg Bacterial fasciation Viruses
Organize a record-keeping system for pesticide applications, pest counts on sticky traps, and pest counts on plants.	Insect pests
Use yellow sticky traps, placed horizontally on the growing media surfaces, to monitor for fungus gnat activity. If traps are catching more than a few adults per week during the first month, apply a drench.	Fungus gnats
Flower the stock plants only to verify variety. Remove and destroy other flowers in the bud stage.	*Botrytis*
Vent and heat at sundown to reduce the relative humidity during the spring and fall. Keep air moving over the plant at all times. Never water late in the day.	*Botrytis*
Treat stock plants at regular intervals with fungicides for *Botrytis*.	*Botrytis*
Hang hose so nozzle does not touch greenhouse floor.	Root rots
Do not allow visitors or employees not connected with the crop to go into the area where the stock plants are growing.	Bacterial wilt
Select a raised propagating bench away from other areas of geranium production.	Bacterial wilt

Geranium continued

Activity	Diseases and pests prevented
Crop stage: Propagation	
Place propagating media and tools on propagating bench and steam for one-half hour at 180F at coolest point.	Root rots Bacterial wilt
Wash hands thoroughly with a disinfectant soap. Break cuttings from stock plants and place in clean, sterile flats lined with new newspapers. Keep trays off floor. **OR** Remove cuttings with a knife disinfected by dipping in 70 percent alcohol. Use a series of knives, changing between each stock plant. Place cuttings in clean, sterile trays lined with new newspapers.	Bacterial wilt
Take cuttings from trays and stick directly in new or steamed propagating media or in new rooting cubes in benches, flats, trays, or pots. Do not dip cuttings into any solutions of any kind. If rooting hormone is to be used, dust it onto the cuttings.	Bacterial wilt Root rots
Do not allow dust to contaminate propagating medium or sterile propagating blocks.	Root rots
Make sure mist is turned off early enough in the evening to allow the leaves to dry prior to nightfall.	*Botrytis*
Crop stage: Planting	
Prepare planting mix, adding sphagnum peat moss, bark, perlite, or other amendments before steaming.	Root rots
Fill pots with soil mix and place on the production bench. Steam pots, bench, potting tools at 180F for one-half hour. **OR**	Root rots

Geranium continued

Activity	Diseases and pests prevented
Fumigate or steam the batch of potting mix in a clean area a few days before use. Store it in an area where dust will not contaminate it. Use only new or sanitized pots. **OR** Use a sanitary medium directly from a container.	
Wash hands thoroughly with a disinfectant soap.	Bacterial wilt
If culture-indexed rooted cuttings are purchased, plant from shipping container directly into steam-treated planting mix in pots on production bench. **OR** Remove rooted cuttings from propagating bench and place in clean, sterile flats lined with new newspapers. Plant from flats directly into steam-treated or new planting mix in pots on production bench.	Bacterial wilt
After the first watering, drench with soil fungicides, using a combination of products to protect against both *Rhizoctonia* and *Pythium*. Apply one-half pint of suspension per 6-inch pot.	Root rots
Hang yellow sticky traps near tops of plants, and place some traps, sticky side up, on growing media surfaces. Use up to four traps per 1,000 square feet for best results. For whitefly and thrips detection, traps plus weekly plant inspection is more effective than traps alone.	Whiteflies, thrips, and fungus gnats
If yellow traps indicate significant fungus gnat activity during rooting, an insecticide or insect growth regulator drench or "sprench" is required. You may also apply insect parasitic nematodes in this way. Potato slices or wedges placed on the potting mix surface will detect larvae.	Fungus gnats

Geranium continued

Activity	Diseases and pests prevented
Crop stage: Growing plants	
Hang hose so that nozzle does not touch the greenhouse floor. Avoid overhead watering.	Root rots
Wash hands thoroughly and rinse in diluted sanitizing agent before pinching plants.	Bacterial wilt
Remove and destroy flowers before they shatter and petals fall on leaves.	*Botrytis*
Thermal dust or spray at regular intervals with same materials as under "Propagation."	*Botrytis*
Vent and heat at sundown to reduce relative humidity. Space plants for good ventilation. Water only in morning; avoid overwatering when cool or cloudy. Keep air moving over the plants at all times.	*Botrytis*
Keep whiteflies and thrips under control. An established infestation of either pest group will require four to six applications of nonsystemic products at five- to seven-day intervals to obtain control.	Whiteflies and thrips
Watch for chewing and leaf-rolling injuries caused by caterpillars. Cutworms will be in the growing media at the bases of plants during daylight hours. Apply a pesticide or microbial product such as *Bacillus thuringiensis* or *Beauveria bassiana* late in the day, as these insects are active at night.	Leafrollers, beet armyworm, loopers, cutworms
In cool, cloudy weather, spray with Daconil 2787, Ornalin, Protect T/O, or Chipco 26019 according to labeled directions.	*Botrytis*
Drench monthly with fungicides for control of *Rhizoctonia* and *Phythium*.	Root rots

---

Easter lily programmed disease and pest control

Activity	Diseases and pests prevented

Crop stage: Preparation for planting

Prepare planting mix. Allow for good aeration.	*Rhizoctonia* root rot *Pythium* root rot
Organize a record-keeping system for pesticide applications, pest counts on sticky traps, and pest counts on plants.	Insect pests
Put soil mix, pots, and potting tools on raised bench and cover with steam cover. Steam this and other benches you plan to use for lily production at 180F for one-half hour at coolest point. **OR** Fumigate or steam the batch of potting mix in a clean area a few days before use. Store mix in an area where dust will not contaminate it. **OR** Use new potting mix directly from the container.	Root rots
Hang watering hose so nozzle does not touch greenhouse floor.	Root rots

Crop stage: Planting

Wash hands thoroughly before potting bulbs	Root rots
Plant bulbs directly from shipping container; pot directly on production bench.	Root rots
Using a hand lens, examine some bulbs for bulb mites. Low numbers will not be easily seen. If concerned about bulb mites, soak bulbs in a suspension of Kelthane 35 percent T&O and water (1⅓ lb per 100 gal) for 30 minutes.	Bulb mites
Set pots in place on steam-treated or disinfected production benches after potting bulbs. Do not set them on greenhouse floor.	Root rots

---

Easter lily continued

Activity	Diseases and pests prevented
After the first watering, drench with soil fungicides, using a combination of products to protect against both *Rhizoctonia* and *Pythium*. Apply one-half pint of suspension per 6-inch pot.	Root rots

Crop stage: Growing plants

Activity	Diseases and pests prevented
Water plants thoroughly, but let them dry slightly between waterings.	Root rots
Keep nitrogen levels high, relative to potassium and phosphorus, until plants are ready for market.	Root rots
Drench with soil fungicides once a month, using a combination of products to protect against both *Rhizoctonia* and *Pythium*. Apply one-half pint of suspension per 6-inch pot.	Root rots
Inspect plants regularly to detect aphids. Pay special attention when buds appear. If found, make at least two pesticide applications, seven days apart. If aphids are always problems late in the crop, Marathon applications to the potting mix about six to eight weeks prior to sale should control them.	Aphids

---

Bedding plant programmed disease and pest control

Activity	Diseases and pests prevented

Crop stage: Preparation for sowing seed and planting seedlings

Use only trays or flats that are new or that have been sanitized with a quaternary ammonium chloride or phenolic compound.	Damping-off
Prepare planting mix, adding sphagnum peat moss, bark, perlite, or other amendments before steaming.	Damping-off
Fumigate or steam the batch of potting mix in a clean area a few days before use. Store it in an area where dust will not contaminate it. **OR** Use a sanitary medium directly from a container.	Damping-off
Adjust media pH to 5.0 to 6.0.	Damping-off Root rots Bacterial blights
Organize a record-keeping system for pesticide applications, pest counts on sticky traps, and pest counts on plants.	Insect pests

Crop stage: Producing plugs or seedlings

Sanitize seeder machines each week or between each batch of seed.	Damping-off *Botrytis*
If sowing in rows, sow thinly.	*Botrytis*
Treat trays of petunias, pansies, or vinca with Terra-guard immediately after seeding.	*Thielaviopsis*
Germinate seed under high humidity and at the correct temperature for the plant species.	Damping-off
When seedlings have emerged, remove the trays from the high-humidity germination chamber and treat for water mold diseases. Also treat with a benzimidazole fungicide.	Damping-off

Bedding plant continued

Activity	**Diseases and pests prevented**
Crop stage: Producing plugs or seedlings	

If weather is damp and cloudy, spray seedlings lightly with Daconil 2787, Protect T/O, or Chipco 26019.	*Botrytis*
Hang yellow sticky traps near tops of plants and place some traps, sticky side up, on growing media surfaces. Use up to four traps per 1,000 square feet for best results. If this trap number is too high for record keeping, use a number appropriate for you. For whitefly and thrips detection, weekly plant inspection plus sticky traps are more effective than trapping alone. Fungus gnat larvae can be detected by placing potato slices or wedges on the potting mix surface.	Whiteflies, aphids, thrips, and fungus gnats

Crop stage: Transplanting and growing plants

Fumigate or steam the batch of transplanting mix in a clean area a few days before use. Store mix in an area where dust will not contaminate it. **OR** Use a clean transplanting mix directly from a bag or container.	Root and crown rots
Use only trays or flats that are new or that have been sanitized with a quaternary ammonium chloride or phenolic compound.	Root and crown rots
Adjust media pH to 5.0 to 6.0.	Root and crown rots *Botrytis* blights
Place flats only on disinfected surfaces for growing on.	Root and crown rots
Keep walkways clean and free of dust. Disinfect monthly.	Root and crown rots

Bedding plant continued

Activity	Diseases and pests prevented

Crop stage: Transplanting and growing plants

Immediately after potting, begin a weekly plant scouting program for whiteflies, aphids, and spider mites. Inspect plants in all areas of the greenhouse, but pay special attention to areas near open vents and doors. Inspect sticky traps weekly for whiteflies, fungus gnats, and thrips. Keep records. If an infestation of one or more pests is detected, begin a pesticide application program. The proper material and number of applications will depend on the pest and host plant.	Insect detection and population monitoring
After the first watering of transplanted seedlings, drench with soil fungicides, using a combination of products to protect against both *Rhizoctonia* and *Pythium*. Apply 100 gallons to whatever area of flats it takes to water the suspension well into the planting media. Make one application only.	Root and crown rots
Vent and heat at sundown to reduce relative humidity. Space plants for good ventilation. Water only in morning; avoid overwatering when cool or cloudy. Keep air moving over the plants at all times.	*Botrytis* Powdery mildews Fungal leaf spots
In cool, cloudy weather, spray with a fungicide for *Botrytis* according to labeled directions. Be particularly careful to avoid fungicide damage to plants in flower.	*Botrytis*
If virus symptoms are noted on some of the plants, begin a thrips management program.	Viruses
Spray with a properly labeled copper compound if oily or water-soaked leaf spots are seen.	Bacterial diseases

New Guinea or Rosebud impatiens programmed disease and insect control

Activity	Diseases and pests prevented
Organize a record-keeping system for pesticide applications, pest counts on sticky traps, and pest counts on plants.	Insect pests
Hang hose so nozzle does not touch floor.	Root rots

Crop stage: Propagation

Fill bench or flats with propagating media. Place propagating tools and flats on bench, cover, and steam at 180F for one-half hour at the coolest point. **OR** Use sterile propagating blocks.	Root and crown rots
Do not allow dust to contaminate propagating media or sterile propagating blocks.	Root and crown rots

Crop stage: Transplanting and growing on

Hang yellow sticky traps near tops of plants and place some traps, sticky side up, on growing media surfaces. Use up to four traps per 1,000 square feet for best results. For thrips detection, weekly plant inspection plus sticky traps are more effective than trapping alone. Fungus gnat larvae can be detected by placing potato slices or wedges on the potting mix surface. Mites are detected by plant inspection.	Aphids, thrips, mites, and fungus gnats
Fumigate or steam the batch of transplanting potting mix in a clean area a few days before use. Store it in an area where dust will not contaminate it. **OR** Use a clean transplanting mix directly from a bag or container.	Root and crown rots

New Guinea or Rosebud impatiens continued

Activity	Diseases and pests prevented

Crop stage: Transplanting and growing on

After the first watering of transplanted seedlings, drench with soil fungicides, using a combination of products to protect against both *Rhizoctonia* and *Pythium*. Apply 100 gallons of suspension over whatever area it takes to water the suspension well into the planting media. Drench monthly.	Root and crown rots
Immediately after potting, begin a weekly plant scouting program for thrips, aphids, and spider mites. Tarsonemid mites (e.g., broad mite, cyclamen mite) may also be problems. Inspect plants in all areas of the greenhouse, but pay special attention to areas near open vents and doors. Inspect sticky traps weekly for fungus gnats and thrips. Keep records. If an infestation of one or more pests is detected, begin a pesticide application program. The proper material and number of applications will depend on the pest and host plant. Thrips will be the most serious problem because of INSV transmission potential.	Aphids, thrips, mites, fungus gnats, and shore flies
If virus symptoms are noted on some of the plants, begin a thrips management program.	Viruses
Vent and heat at sundown to reduce relative humidity. Space plants for good ventilation. Water only in morning, avoid overwatering when cool or cloudy. Keep air moving over the plants at all times.	*Botrytis* Fungal leaf spots
In cool, cloudy weather, spray with a fungicide registered for *Botrytis* according to label directions. Be particularly careful to avoid fungicide damage to plants in flower.	*Botrytis*

Appendix I

Where to Write

Laboratories

Plant Diagnostic Laboratories

Many states have diagnostic laboratories associated with their State Department of Agriculture or with the United States Department of Agriculture (USDA) research facilities.

Alabama
Plant Disease Clinic
102 Extension Hall
Dept. of Plant Pathology
Auburn University
Auburn, AL 36849-5624
Contact: Jacqueline Mullen
Phone: 334/844-5508
Fax: 334/844-4072
E-mail: jmullen.@acenet.auburn.edu

Alaska
Dept. of Plant Pathology
University of Alaska
Ag. Forestry Experiment Station
Fairbanks, AK 99775-0080
Contact: Jenifer McBeath

Arizona
Plant Disease Clinic
Department of Plant Pathology
University of Arizona
Tucson, AR 85721

Arkansas
Plant Disease Clinic
Lonoke Agricultural Center
PO Drawer D; Hwy. 70 East

Lonoke, AR 72086
Contact: Stephen Van
Phone: 501/676-3124
Fax: 501/676-7847
E-mail: fungus@uaexsun.uaex.arknet.edu

California
Contact the local county farm advisor or extension specialist at the university nearest you.

Colorado
Plant Diagnostic Clinic
Jefferson County Extension
15200 W. 6th Ave.
Golden, CO 80401

Connecticut
Consumer Horticultural Ctr.
University of Connecticut
Storrs, CT 06269-4087
Phone: 860/486-3437
Fax: 860/486-0682
E-mail: emarrot@canrl.cag.uconn.edu

Connecticut Agriculture Experiment Sta.
Huntington Ave.
New Haven, CT 06512

Delaware

Extension Plant Pathologist
University of Delaware
136 Townsend Hall
Newark, DE 19717-1303

Florida

Nematode Assay Laboratory
Entomology & Nematology Dept.
Bldg. 78, Mowry Road
University of Florida
Gainesville, FL 32611
Contact: Frank Woods
Phone: 904/392-1994
Fax: 904/392-3438
E-mail: few@gnv.ifas.ufl.edu

Florida Extension Plant Disease Clinic
Bldg. 78, Mowry Road
University of Florida
Gainesville, FL 32611
Contact: G.W. Simone, R.E. Cullen
Phone: 904/392-1994
Fax: 904/392-3438

Florida Regional State Laboratories

Florida Extension Plant Disease Clinic
North Florida Research Ctr.
Route 3, PO Box 4370
Quincy, FL 32351
Contact: D. Chellami, H. Dantars
Phone: 904/627-9236
E-mail: doc@guv.ifas.ufl.edu

Florida Extension Plant Disease Clinic
SW Florida Research & Education Ctr.
PO Drawer 5127
Immokalee, FL 33934
Contact: R. McGovern, R. Urs
Phone: 941/751-7636
Fax: 941/751-7639
E-mail: rjm@gnv.ifas.ufl.edu

Florida Extension Plant Disease Clinic
Tropical Research & Education Ctr.
18905 SW 280th St.
Homestead, FL 33032-3314
Contact: R. Maxmillan, William Graves
Phone: 305/246-7000
E-mail: rtmcm@gvn.ifas.ufl.edu

Kentucky

(serving western Kentucky)
Plant Disease Diagnostic Laboratory
University of Kentucky
Research & Education Ctr.
Hwy. 91 South
Princeton, KY 42445
Contact: Paul Bachi
Phone: 502/365-7541
Fax: 502/365-2667
E-mail: pbachi@ca.uky.edu

(serving central and eastern Kentucky)
Plant Disease Diagnostic Laboratory
Dept. of Plant Pathology
University of Kentucky
Lexington, KY 40546-0091

Louisiana

Plant Disease Diagnostic Clinic
220 H.D. Wilson Bldg.
Louisiana State University
Baton Rouge, LA 70803-1900
Contact: Charles Overstreet, Clayton Hollier
Phone: 504/388-6195
Fax: 504/388-2478
E-mail: coverst@lsuvm.sncc.lsu.edu
    or chollie@lsuvm.sncc.lsu.edu

Maine

Pest Management Office
Cooperative Extension
University of Maine
491 College Avenue
Orono, ME 04473-1295
Contact: Bruce Watt
Phone: 207/581-3880
Fax: 207/581-3881
E-mail: jdill@umce.umext.maine.edu

Maryland

Plant Diagnostic Laboratory
Dept. of Plant Biology
University of Maryland
College Park, MD 20742
Contact: Ethel Dutky
Phone: 301/314-1611
Fax: 301/314-9082
E-mail: ed16@umail.umd.edu

Massachusetts

No disease diagnostic service is offered by a public agency to homeowners. Commercial samples are handled by individual extension specialists at the university.

Michigan

Plant Diagnostic Clinic
Dept. of Botany & Plant Pathology
Michigan State University
East Lansing, MI 48824-1312

New Hampshire

Plant Diagnostic Laboratory
322 Nesmith Hall
Plant Biology Dept.
Univ. of New Hampshire
Durham, NH 03824
Contact: Cheryl Smith
Phone: 603/862-3841
Fax: 603-862-4757
E-mail: c_smith@al@unhces

New Jersey

Plant Diagnostic Laboratory
Rutgers University
PO Box 550
Milltown, NJ 08850
Contact: Rich Buckley
Phone: 908/932-9140
Fax: 908-932-7070
E-mail: clinic@aesop.rutgers.edu

New Mexico

Extension Plant Pathologist
Box 3AE: Plant Science
Cooperative Extension Service
New Mexico State University
Las Cruces, NM 88003

New York

(homeowners and commercial samples)
Insect & Plant Disease Diagnostic
      Laboratory
Dept. of Plant Pathology
334 Plant Science Bldg.
Cornell University
Ithaca, NY 14853

Contact: Diane Karasevicz
Phone; 607/255-7850
Fax: 607/255-0939
E-mail: diane_karasevicz@cce.cornell.edu

(commercial ornamental samples only)
Long Island Horticultural Research
      Laboratory
Cornell University
39 Sound Ave.
Riverhead, NY 11901
Phone: 516/727-3595
Fax: 516/727-3611

North Carolina

Plant Disease & Insect Clinic
PO Box 7616
Williams Hall, Rm. 1104
North Carolina State Univ.
Raleigh, NC 27695-7616
Contact: Tom Creswell
Phone: 919/515-3619, 919/515-3825
Fax: 919/515-3670
E-mail: Tom_Creswell@ncsu.edu

South Carolina

Plant Problem Clinic
Cherry Road
Clemson University
Clemson, SC 29634-0377
Contact: James Blake
Phone: 803/656-3125
Fax: 803/656-2069
E-mail: ppclnc@clemson.edu
or jblake@clemson.edu

South Dakota

Plant Disease Clinic
Dept. of Plant Science
South Dakota State University
PO Box 2109
Brookings, SD 57007

Tennessee

Plant and Pest Diagnostic Ctr.
University of Tennessee
PO Box 110019
Nashville, TN 37222-0019

Texas

Texas Plant Disease Diagnostic Lab.
L.F. Peterson Bldg., Rm. 101
Texas A&M University
College Station, TX 77843-2132
Contact: Larry Barnes
Phone: 409/845-8033
Fax: 409/845-6499
E-mail: Barnes@ppserver.tamu.edu

Utah

Plant Pest Diagnostic Laboratory
Department of Biology
Utah State University
Logan, UT 84322-5305
Contact: Karen Flint
Phone: 801/797-2435
Fax: 801/797-1575
E-mail: KarenF@ext.usu.edu

Vermont

Plant Diagnostic Clinic
Dept. of Plant & Soil Science
University of Vermont
Hills Building
Burlington, VT 05405-0086
Contact: Ann Hazelrigg
Phone: 802/656-0493
Fax: 802/656-4656
E-mail: ahazelrigg@clover.uvm.edu

Virginia

Plant Disease Clinic
Dept. of Plant Pathology, Physiology &
   Weed Sci.
VPI and SU
Blacksburg, VA 24061

Canada

Manitoba

Crop Diagnostic Centre
201-545 University Cres.
Agricultural Science Complex
Winnipeg, Manitoba, R3T 5S6
Canada

New Brunswick

Pest Diagnostic Laboratory
New Brunswick Dept. of Agriculture &
   Rural Devel.
PO Box 6000
Fredericton, New Brunswick, E3B 5H1
Canada

Ontario

Pest Diagnostic Clinic
Agriculture & Food Service Ctr.
PO Box 3650
95 Stone Rd. W., Zone 2
Guelph, Ontario, N1H 8J7
Canada

Prince Edward Island

PEIDAFF
Plant Health Services
PO Box 1600
Charlottetown, Prince Edward Island C1A
   7N3
Canada
Phone: 902/368-5600
Fax: 902/368-5661
E-mail: mmpeters@gov.pe.ca

Quebec

Laboratoire de diagnostic
Le Service de Recherche en Phytotechnie
   de Quebec
2700, rue Einstein
Ste.-Foy, Quebec G1P 3W8
Canada

Alberta

Brooks Diagnostics LTD (a private laboratory) now does the testing for Alberta Special Crops and Horticultural Research Center.

Soil Testing Laboratories

Remember to contact your local county extension office for procedures on how to submit samples to your diagnostic laboratory.

Alabama

Auburn University
Soil Testing Laboratory
118 Funchess Hall
Auburn, AL 36849-5624
Contact: Hamilton Bryant
Phone: 334/844-3958
Fax: 334/844-4001
E-mail: hhbryant@acenet.auburn.edu
or
Contact: Charles Mitchell
Phone: 334/844-5489
Fax: 334/844-3945
E-mail: cmitchel@ag.auburn.edu

Alaska

University of Alaska
Soil Testing Laboratory
Agricultural Exp. Station
533 E. Firewood
Palmer, AK 99645

Arizona

University of Arizona
Dept. of Soils, Water & Engineering
Soil, Water & Plant Tissue Testing Lab.
Shantz (#38), Rm. 431
Tucson, AZ 85721
Phone: 602/621-9703
Fax: 602/621-3516

Arkansas

University of Arkansas
Soil Testing & Research Lab.
PO Drawer 767
Marianna, AR 72360

California

No testing service offered by a public agency.

Colorado

Colorado State University
Soil, Water, & Plant Testing Lab.
A319 NESB
Fort Collins, CO 80523

Connecticut

University of Connecticut
Plant Science Dept.
Soil Testing Laboratory
2019 Hillside Rd., U-102
Storrs, CT 06268
Contact: Erika Kares
Phone: 860/486-4274
Fax: 860/486-4562
E-mail: ekares@car1.cag.uconn.edu

Delaware

University of Delaware
Dept. of Plant & Soil Science
Soil Testing Laboratory
Newark, DE 19711

Florida

University of Florida
Soil Testing Laboratory
Wallace Bldg.
PO Box 110740
Gainesville, FL 32611-0740
Phone: 352/392-1950
Fax: 352/392-1960

Kentucky

University of Kentucky
103 Regulatory Services Bldg.
Soil Testing Laboratory
Lexington, KY 40546
Contact: Vern Case
Phone: 606/257-7355
Fax: 606/257-7351
E-mail: vcase@ca.uky.edu

Louisiana

Louisiana State University
Dept. of Agronomy
Soil Testing Laboratory
Baton Rouge, LA 70803
Contact: Rodney Henderson
Phone: 504/388-1219
Fax: 504/388-1403
E-mail: henderson@lanmail.lsu.edu

Maine

University of Maine
Maine Soil Testing Service
5722 Deering Hall
Orono, ME 04469-5722
Contact: Bruce Hoskins
Phone: 207/581-2945
Fax: 207/581-2999
E-mail: RPT910@maine.maine.edu

Maryland

The University of Maryland
Agronomy Dept.
Soil Testing Laboratory
College Park, MD 20742
Phone: 301/405-1349
Fax: 301/314-9049
E-mail: jb97@umail.umd.edu

Massachusetts

University of Massachusetts
Soil Testing
West Experiment Station
Amherst, MA 01003

Michigan

Michigan State University
Soil & Plant Nutrient Laboratory
A81 Plant & Soil Sciences
East Lansing, MI 48824
Contact: Donna Ellis
Phone: 517/355-0218
Fax: 517/355-1732
E-mail:
    ELLIS%staff%cssdept@banyan.msu.edu

New Hampshire

University of New Hampshire
Analytical Services Laboratory
Nesmith Hall

Durham, NH 03824
Contact: Stuart Blanchard
Phone: 603/862-3212
Fax: 603/862-4757
E-mail: stuart@christa.unh.edu

New Jersey

Rutgers University
Dept. of Environmental Sciences
Soil Testing Laboratory
PO Box 902
Milltown, NJ 08850
Contact: Stephanie Murphy
Phone: 908/932-9292 or 9295
Fax: 908/932-8644
E-mail: smurphy@aesop.rutgers.edu

New Mexico

New Mexico State University
Agronomy & Horticulture
SWAT Laboratory
Box 30003
Las Cruces, NM 88003
Contact: Andrew Bristol
Phone: 505/646-4422
Fax: 505/646-6041
E-mail: abristol@nmsu.edu

New York

Cornell University
SCAS Dept.
803 Bradfield Hall
Ithaca, NY 14853-1901
Contact: W. Shaw Reid
Phone: 607/255-1722
E-mail: wsrl@cornell.edu

North Carolina

North Carolina Dept. of Agriculture
Agronomic Division
Soil Testing Laboratory
4300 Reedy Creek Rd.
Raleigh, NC 27611
Contact: Ray Tucker
Phone: 919/733-2656
Fax: 919/733-2837
E-mail:
    Ray_Tucker@NCDAmail.agr.state.cm.us

South Carolina
Clemson University
Agricultural Service Laboratory
Soil Testing Laboratory
Clemson, SC 29634
Contact: Kathy Moore
Phone: 803/656-2300
Fax: 803/656-2069
E-mail: kmr@mail.clemson.edu

South Dakota
South Dakota State University
Plant Science Dept.
Soil Testing Laboratory
Box 2207-A, Ag Hall 06
Brookings, SD 57007-1096
Phone: 605/688-4766
Fax: 605/688-4602

Tennessee
University of Tennessee
Soil & Forage Testing Laboratory
PO Box 110019
Nashville, TN 37222-0019

Texas
Texas A&M University
Soil Testing Laboratory
Soil & Crop Sciences, Rm. 220
College Station, TX 77843

Utah
Utah State University
Dept. of Plant Soils & Biometeorology
Soil Testing Laboratory
Agricultural Sciences Bldg.
Logan, UT 84322-4830
Contact: Jan Kotuby-Amacher
Phone: 801/797-2217
Fax: 801/797-2117
E-mail: Jkotuby@mendel.usu.edu

Vermont
University of Vermont
Dept. of Plant & Soil Science
Soil Testing Laboratory
Hills Bldg.
Burlington, VT 05405-0086

Virginia
Virginia Tech Soil Testing
Laboratory 145, Smyth Hall
PO Box 10664
Blacksburg, VA 24062-0664
Contact: Steve Heckendorn
Phone: 504/231-9807 or 231-6893
Fax: 504/231-3431
E-mail: soiltest@vtvl1.cc.vt.edu
   or shckndrn@vt.edu

Canada

Manitoba
University of Manitoba
Dept. of Soil Science
Winnipeg, Manitoba R3T 2N2
Canada

New Brunswick
New Brunswick Dept. of Agriculture
Agricultural Soils Laboratory
PO Box 6000
Fredericton, New Brunswick E3B 5H1
Canada

Nova Scotia
Nova Scotia Agricultural College
Soil and Crops Branch
Truro, Nova Scotia B2N 5E3
Canada

Ontario
No provincial soil testing service offered.

Prince Edward Island
Dept. of Agriculture
Soil & Feed Testing Laboratory
Box 1600
Charlottetown, Prince Edward Island C1A
   7N3
Canada

Quebec
Canadian Industries Limited
Beloeil Works, Soil Laboratory
McMasterville, Quebec
Canada

Poison Control

Poison Control Centers

Alabama

Alabama Poison Ctr.
408-A Paul Bryant Dr.
Tuscaloosa, Al 35401
Emerg. phone: 800/462-0800
Admin. phone: 205/345-0600
Fax: 205/759-7994
E-mail: fisher3@aol.com
  or jfisher@ua1vm.ua.edu
AAPCC Certified Regional Poison Center

Regional Poison Control Ctr.
Children's Hospital of Alabama
1600 7th Ave. S.
Birmingham, AL 35233-1711
Emerg. phone: 205/939-9201,
  205/933-4050, 800/292-6678 (AL only)
Admin. phone: 205/939-9720
Fax: 205/939-9245
AAPCC Certified Regional Poison Center

Alaska

Anchorage Poison Control Ctr.
Providence Hospital Pharmacy
PO Box 196604
Anchorage, AK 95516-6604
Emerg. phone: 800/478-3193, 907/261-3193
Admin. phone: 907/261-3633
Fax: 907/261-3645

Arizona

Arizona Poison & Drug Info. Ctr.
Arizona Hlth. Sciences Ctr., Rm. 1156
1501 N. Campbell Ave.
Tucson, AZ 85724
Emerg. phone: 520/626-6016,
  800/362-0101 (AZ only)
Admin. phone: 520/626-7899
Fax: 520/626-2720
E-mail: mcnally@tonic.pharm.arizona.edu
Denes@tonic.pharm.arizona.edu
AAPCC Certified Regional Poison Center

Samaritan Regional Poison Ctr.
1111 E. McDowell Rd., Ancil. 1
Phoenix, AZ 85006
Emerg. phone: 602/253-3334,
  800/362-0101 (AZ only)
Admin. phone: 602/495-4884
Fax: 602/256-7579
E-mail: richardt@samaritan.edu
AAPCC Certified Regional Poison Center

Arkansas

Arkansas Poison & Drug Info. Ctr.
Univ. of Arkansas for Med. Sciences
4301 W. Markham, Slot 522
Little Rock, AR 72205
Emerg. phone: 800/376-4766
Admin. phone: 501/686-5540
Fax: 501/686-7357
E-mail: poison@poison.uams.edu

California

Central California Reg. Poison Control Ctr.
Valley Children's Hospital
3151 N. Millbrook
Fresno, CA 93703
Emerg. phone: 209/445-1222,
  800/346-5922
Admin. phone: 209/241-6040
Fax: 209/241-6050
AAPCC Certified Regional Poison Center

Los Angeles Reg. Drug & Poison Info. Ctr.
LAC+USC Medical Ctr.
GH Rm. 1107 A & B
1200 N. State St.
Los Angeles, CA 90033
Emerg. phone: 213/222-3212,
  800/777-6476
Admin. phone: 213/226-7741
Fax: 213/226-4194
E-mail: gthompso@hsc.usc.edu

San Diego Regional Poison Ctr.
UCSD Medical Ctr.
200 West Arbor Dr.
San Diego, CA 92103-8925
Emerg. phone: 619/543-6000,
　800/876-4766 (619 only)
Admin. phone: 619/543-3666
Fax: 619/692-1867
E-mail: amanoguerra@ucsd.edu
AAPCC Certified Regional Poison Center

San Francisco Bay Area Reg. Poison
　Control Ctr.
San Francisco General Hosp.
1001 Potrero Ave., Bldg. 80, Rm. 230
San Francisco, CA 94110
Emerg. phone: 800/523-2222
Admin. phone: 415/206-5524
Fax: 415/206-5480
AAPCC Certified Regional Poison Center

Santa Clara Valley Med. Ctr. Regional
　Poison Ctr.
750 S. Bascom Ave., Ste. 310
San Jose, CA 95128
Emerg. phone: 408/885-6000,
　800/662-9886 (CA only)
Admin. phone: 408/885-6002
Fax: 408/885-6015
E-mail:
　weilamic@wpgate.hhs.co.santa-clara.ca.us
　collimic@wpgate.hhs.co.santa-clara.ca.us
AAPCC Certified Regional Poison Center

Univ. of California at Davis Medical Ctr.
Regional Poison Control Ctr.
2315 Stockton Blvd.
House Staff Facility, Rm. 1024
Sacramento, CA 95817
Emerg. phone: 916/734-3692, 800/342-
　9293 (northern CA only)
Admin. phone: 916/734-3415
Fax: 916/734-7796
AAPCC Certified Regional Poison Center

Colorado
Rocky Mountain Poison & Drug Ctr.
8802 E. 9th Ave.
Denver, CO 80220-6800
Emerg. phone: 303/629-1123, CO WATTS
　800/332-3073; TTY 303/739-1127
Admin. phone: 303/739-1100
Fax: 303/739-1119
AAPCC Certified Regional Poison Center

Connecticut
Connecticut Poison Control Ctr.
Univ. of Connecticut Health Ctr.
263 Farmington Ave.
Farmington, CT 06030
Emerg. phone: 800/343-2722 (CT only),
　203/679-3056
Admin. phone: 203/679-3473,
　203/679-4540
Fax: 203/679-1991
AAPCC Certified Regional Poison Center

Delaware
The Poison Control Ctr.
3600 Sciences Ctr., Ste. 220
Philadelphia, PA 19104-2641
Emerg. phone: 215/386-2100,
　800/722-7112
Admin. phone: 215/590-2003,
　215/386-2066
Fax: 215/590-4419
AAPCC Certified Regional Poison Center

District of Columbia
National Capitol Poison Ctr.
3201 New Mexico Ave. N.W., Ste. 310
Washington, D.C. 20016
Emerg. phone: 202/625-3333,
　TTY 202/362-8563
Admin. phone: 202/362-3867
Fax: 202/362-8377
AAPCC Certified Regional Poison Center

Florida

Florida Poison Info. Ctr., Jacksonville
University Medical Ctr.
Univ. of Florida Health Sci. Ctr.,
    Jacksonville
655 West 8th St.
Jacksonville, FL 32209
Emerg. phone: 800/282-3171 (FL only);
    904/549-4465
Admin. phone: 904/549-4063
Fax: 904/549-4063
E-mail: schauben.pcc@mail.health.ufl.edu
AAPCC Certified Regional Poison Center

Florida Poison Info. Ctr., Miami
Univ. of Miami/Jackson Memorial Hosp.
1611 NW 12th Ave.
Urgent Care Ctr., Bldg., Rm. 219
Miami, FL 33136
Emerg. phone: 800/282-3171(FL only)
Admin. phone: 305/585-5250
Fax: 305/545-9762
E-Mail: rweisman@mednet.med.miami.edu

Florida Poison Info. Ctr. & Toxicology
    Resource
Tampa General Hospital
PO Box 1289
Tampa, FL 33601
Emerg. phone: 813/256-4444 (Tampa),
    800/282-3171 (FL only)
Admin. phone: 813/254-7044
Fax: 813/253-4443
E-mail: sven.normann@ashp.com
AAPCC Certified Regional Poison Center

Georgia

Georgia Poison Ctr.
Hughes Spalding Children's Hosp.
Grady Health Systems
80 Butler St. S.E.
PO Box 26066
Atlanta GA 30335-3801
Emerg. phone: 404/616-9000, 800/282-5846
    (GA only), 404/616-9287 (TDD)
Admin. phone: 404/616-9237
Fax: 404/616-6657
E-mail: lopez_g@mercer.edu
AAPCC Certified Regional Poison Center

Hawaii

Hawaii Poison Ctr.
1500 S. Beretania St., Rm. 113
Honolulu, HI 96826
Emerg. phone: 808/941-4411
Admin. phone: 808/973-3008
Fax: 808/973-8085

Idaho

Idaho Poison Ctr.
3092 Elder St.
Boise, ID 83720-0036
Emerg. phone: 208/334-4570,
    800/632-8000 (ID only)
Admin. phone: 208/334-4013
Fax: 208/334-4595

Illinois

Bromenn Poison Control Ctr.
Bromenn Regional Med. Ctr.
Franklin at Virginia
Normal, IL 61761
Emerg. phone: 309/454-6666
Admin. phone: 309/454-0738
Fax: 309/888-0902

Chicago & NE Illinois Reg. Poison
    Control Ctr.
Rush-Presbyterian-St. Luke's Medical Ctr.
1653 W. Congress Pkwy.
Chicago, IL 60612
Emerg. phone: 312/942-5969, 800/942-5969
Admin. phone: 312/942-7064
Fax: 312/942-4260

Indiana

Indiana Poison Center
Methodist Hospital of Indiana
I-65 & 21st St.
PO Box 1367
Indianapolis, IN 46206-1367
Emerg. phone: 317/929-2323,
    800/382-9097 (IN only)
Admin. phone: 317/929-2335
Fax: 317/929-2337
E-mail: jmowry@mhi.com
AAPCC Certified Regional Poison Center

Iowa

St. Luke's Poison Center
St. Luke's Regional Medical Ctr.
2720 Stone Park Blvd.
Sioux City, IA 51104
Emerg. phone: 712/277-2222, 800/352-2222
Admin. phone: 712/279-3710
Fax: 712/279-1852

Mid-Iowa Poison & Drug Info. Ctr.
Variety Club Poison & Drug Info. Ctr.
Iowa Methodist Medical Center
1200 Pleasant St.
Des Moines, IA 50309
Emerg. phone: 515/241-6254,
    800/362-2327 (IA only)
Admin. phone: 515/241-8211
Fax: 515/241-5085

Poison Control Center
Univ. of Iowa Hospitals & Clinics
Pharmacy Dept.
200 Hawkins Dr.
Iowa City, IA 52242
Emerg. phone: 800/272-6477
Admin. phone: 319/356-2600
Fax: 319/356-4545

Kansas

Mid-America Poison Control Ctr.
Univ. of Kansas Medical Ctr.
3901 Rainbow Blvd., Rm. B-400
Kansas City, KS 66160-7231
Emerg. phone: 913/588-6633,
    800/332-6633 (KS & KC metro only)
Admin. phone: 913/558-6638
Fax: 913/588-2350

Kentucky

Kentucky Reg. Poison Ctr. of Kosair's
    Children's Hosp.
Medical Towers South, Ste. 572
PO Box 35070
Louisville, KY 40232-5070
Emerg. phone: 502/589-8222,
    800/722-5725 (KY only)
Admin. phone: 502/629-5326, 502/629-7264
Fax: 502/629-7277
AAPCC Certified Regional Poison Center

Louisiana

Louisiana Drug & Poison Info. Ctr.
Northeast Louisiana Univ.
Sugar Hall
Monroe, LA 71209-6430
Emerg. phone: 800/256-9822 (LA only),
    318/362-5393
Admin.istration phone: 318/342-1710
Fax: 318/342-1744
E-mail: pydick@alpha.nlu.edu
AAPCC Certified Regional Poison Center

Maine

Maine Poison Control Ctr.
Maine Medical Ctr.
Dept. of Emerg. Medicine
22 Bramhall St.
Portland, ME 04102
Emerg. phone: 207/871-2950,
    800/442-6305 (ME only)
Admin. phone: 207/871-2664
Fax: 207/871-6226

Maryland

Maryland Poison Ctr.
Univ. of Maryland School of Pharm.
20 N. Pine St.
Baltimore, MD 21201
Emerg. phone: 410/528-7701, 800/492-
    2414 (MD only)
Admin. phone: 410/706-7604
Fax: 410/706-7184
AAPCC Certified Regional Poison Center

Massachusetts

Massachusetts Poison Control Sys.
300 Longwood Ave.
Boston, MA 02115
Emerg. phone: 617/232-2120,
    800/682-9211, TDD 617/735-6089
Admin. phone: 617/735-6609
Fax: 617/738-0032
AAPCC Certified Regional Poison Center

Michigan

Blodgett Regional Poison Ctr.
1840 Wealthy S.E.
Grand Rapids, MI 49506-2968
Emerg. phone: 800/POISON-1,
   TTY 800/356-3232
Admin. phone: 616/774-7851
Fax: 616/774-7204
E-mail: johntres@delphi.com

Poison Control Center
Children's Hosp. of Michigan
Harper Prof. Office Bldg.
4160 John R., Ste. 425
Detroit, MI 48201
Emerg. phone: 313/745-5711, 800/764-7661
Admin. phone: 313/745-5335
Fax: 313/745-5493
E-mail: Scsmoli@CMS.CC.Wayne.edu
AAPCC Certified Regional Poison Center

Marquette General Hospital
420 W. Magnetic St.
Marquette, MI 49855
Emerg. phone: 906/225-3497, 800/562-9781
Admin. phone: 906/225-3495
Fax: 906/225-3499

Minnesota

Hennepin Regional Poison Ctr.
Hennepin County Medical Ctr.
701 Park Ave.
Minneapolis, MN 55415
Emerg. phone: 612/347-3141,
   TDD 612/337-7474
Admin. phone: 612/347-3144
Fax: 612/904-4289
E-mail: deb.anderson@co.hennepin.mn.us
AAPCC Certified Regional Poison Center

Minnesota Regional Poison Ctr.
8100 34th Ave. S.
PO Box 1309
Minneapolis, MN 55440-1309
Emerg. phone: 612/221-2113
Admin. phone: 612/851-8100
Fax: 612/851-8166, 612/851-8160
E-mail:
   Lsioris@poison1.sprmc.healthpartners.com
AAPCC Certified Regional Poison Center

Mississippi

Mississippi Reg. Poison Control Ctr.
Univ. of Mississippi Medical Ctr.
2500 N. State St.
Jackson, MS 39216-4505
Emerg. phone: 601/354-7660
Admin. phone: 601/984-1675
Fax: 601/984-1676

Missouri

Cardinal Glennon Children's Hosp.
Regional Poison Ctr.
1465 S. Grand Blvd.
St. Louis, MO 63104
Emerg. phone: 314/772-5200,
   800/366-8888, 800/392-9111
Admin. phone: 314/772-8300
Fax: 314/577-5355
E-mail: mike@pcc.slu.edu
AAPCC Certified Regional Poison Center

Children's Mercy Hospital
2401 Gillham Rd.
Kansas City, MO 64108
Emerg. phone: 816/234-3430
Admin. phone: 816/234-3053
Fax: 816/234-3421

Montana

Serviced by: Rocky Mtn. Poison & Drug Ctr.
8802 E. 9th Ave.
Denver, CO 80220-6800
Emerg. phone: 303/629-1123; MT WATTS
   800/525-5042; TTY 303/739-1127
Admin. phone: 303/739-1100
Fax: 303/739-1119
AAPCC Certified Regional Poison Center

Nebraska

The Poison Center
8301 Dodge St.
Omaha, NE 68114
Emerg. phone: 402/390-5555 (Omaha),
   800/955-9119 (NE &WY)
Admin. phone: 402/390-5467
Fax: 402/390-3049
AAPCC Certified Regional Poison Center

Nevada

Serviced by: Rocky Mtn. Poison & Drug Ctr.
8802 E. 9th Ave.
Denver, CO 80220-6800
Emerg. phone: 303/629-1123; NV WATTS
    800/446-6179; TTY 303/739-1127
Admin. phone: 303/739-1100
Fax: 303/739-1119
AAPCC Certified Regional Poison Center

New Hampshire

New Hampshire Poison Info. Ctr.
Dartmouth-Hitchcock Medical Ctr.
One Medical Center Dr.
Lebanon, NH 03756
Emerg. phone: 603/650-8000, 603/650-5000
    (11 pm-8 am), 800/562-8236 (NH only)
Admin. phone: 603/650-6318
Fax: 603/650-8986
E-mail: l.courtemanche@dartmouth.edu

New Jersey

New Jersey Poison Info. & Education Sys.
201 Lyons Ave.
Newark, NJ 07112
Emerg. phone: 800/POISON1
    (800/764-7661)
Admin. phone: 201/926-7443
Fax: 201/926-0013
E-mail: toxdoc@IBM.net
AAPCC Certified Regional Poison Center

New Mexico

New Mexico Poison & Drug Info. Ctr.
Univ. of New Mexico
Health Science Ctr. Library, Rm. 125
Albuquerque, NM 87131-1076
Emerg. phone: 505/843-2551,
    800/432-6866 (NM only)
Admin. phone: 505/277-4261
Fax: 505/277-5892
E-mail: troutman@medusa.unm.edu
AAPCC Certified Regional Poison Center

New York

Central New York Poison Control Ctr.
SUNY Health Science Ctr.
750 E. Adams St.
Syracuse, NY 13210
Emerg. phone: 315/476-4766, 800/252-5655
Admin. phone: 315/464-7078
Fax: 315/464-7077

Finger Lakes Regional Poison Ctr.
Univ. of Rochester Medical Ctr.
601 Elmwood Ave., Box 321, Rm. G-3275
Rochester, NY 14642
Emerg. phone: 716/275-5151, 800/333-0542
Admin. phone: 716/273-4155
Fax: 716/244-1677
E-mail: dljc@troi.cc.rochester.edu
AAPCC Certified Regional Poison Center

Husdon Valley Poison Ctr.
Phelps Memorial Hosp. Ctr.
701 N. Broadway
North Tarrytown, NY 10591
Emerg. phone: 800/336-6997, 914/336-3030
Admin. phone: 914/366-3031
Fax: 914/366-1400
AAPCC Certified Regional Poison Center

Long Island Reg. Poison Control Ctr.
Winthrop Univ. Hospital
259 First St.
Mineola, NY 11501
Emerg. phone: 516/542-2323
Admin. phone: 516/739-2066, 516/542-6317
Fax: 516/739-2070
AAPCC Certified Regional Poison Center

New York City Poison Control Ctr.
N.Y.C. Dept. of Health
455 First Ave., Rm. 123
New York, NY 10016
Emerg. phone: 212/340-4494,
    212/POISONS, TDD 212/689-9014
Admin. phone: 212/447-8154
Fax: 212/447-8223
AAPCC Certified Regional Poison Center

Western New York Reg. Poison Control Ctr.
Children's Hospital of Buffalo
219 Bryant St.
Buffalo, NY 14222
Emerg. phone: 716/878-7654, 7655, 7856,
    7857
Admin. phone: 716/878-7657
Fax: 716/878-7857
E-mail: daq11537@ov.chob.edu

North Carolina

Carolinas Poison Ctr.
1000 Blythe Blvd.
PO Box 32861
Charlotte, NC 28232-2861
Emerg. phone: 704/355-4000,
    800/84-TOXIN
Admin. phone: 704/355-3054
Fax: 704/355-4051
E-mail: wahoo@med.unc.edu
AAPCC Certified Regional Poison Center

Catawba Mem. Hosp. Poison Control Ctr.
Pharmacy Dept.
810 Fairgrove Church Rd.
Hickory, NC 28602
Emerg. phone: 704/322-6649
Admin. phone: 704/326-3385
Fax: 704/326-3324

Duke Poison Control Ctr.
North Carolina Regional Ctr.
Duke University
Box 3007
Durham, NC 27710
Emerg. phone: 919/684-8111,
    800/672-1697 (NC only)
Admin. phone: 919/684-4438, 919/477-4297
Fax: 919/681-7336

Triad Poison Center
1200 N. Elm St.
Greensboro, NC 27401-1020
Emerg. phone: 910/574-8105,
    800/953-4001 (NC only)
Admin. phone: 910/574-8108
Fax: 910/574-7910

North Dakota

North Dakota Poison Info. Ctr.
Meritcare Medical Ctr.
720 4th St. North
Fargo, ND 58122
Emerg. phone: 701/234-5575,
    800/732-2200 (ND, MN, SD only)
Admin. phone: 701/234-6062
Fax: 701/234-5090

Ohio

Akron Regional Poison Ctr.
1 Perkins Square
Akron, OH 44308
Emerg. phone: 216/379-8562, 800/362-9922
    (OH only), TTY 216/379-8446
Admin. phone: 216/258-3066
Fax: 216/379-8447

Bethesda Poison Control Ctr.
2951 Maple Ave.
Zanesville, OH 43701
Emerg. phone: 614/454-4221
Admin. phone: 614/454-4246
Fax: 614/454-4059
E-mail: pusher1@delphi.com

Central Ohio Poison Ctr.
700 Children's Dr.
Columbus, OH 43205-2696
Emerg. phone: 614/228-1323,
    800/682-7625, TTY 614/228-2272
Admin. phone: 614/722-2635
Fax: 614/221-2672
AAPCC Certified Regional Poison Center

Cincinnati Drug & Poison Info. Ctr. & Reg.
    Poison Control Sys.
PO Box 670144
Cincinnati, OH 45267-0144
Emerg. phone: 513/558-5111, 800/872-5111
    (OH only), TTY 800/253-7955
Admin. phone: 513/558-0230
Fax: 513/558-5301
AAPCC Certified Regional Poison Center

Greater Cleveland Poison Control Ctr.
11100 Euclid Ave.
Cleveland, OH 44106
Emerg. phone: 216/231-4455
Admin. phone: 216/844-1573
Fax: 216/844-3242

Medical College of Ohio Poison & Drug
Info. Ctr.
3000 Arlington Ave.
Toledo, OH 43614
Emerg. phone: 419/381-3897,
800/589-3897 (419 only)
Admin. phone: 419/381-3898
Fax: 419/381-2818

Northeast Ohio Poison Education
& Info. Ctr.
1320 Timken Mercy Dr. N.W.
Canton, OH 44708
Emerg. phone: 800/456-8662 (OH only)
Admin. phone: 216/489-1304
Fax: 216/489-1267

Oklahoma
Oklahoma Poison Control Ctr.
940 N.E. 13th St., Rm. 3N118
Oklahoma City, OK 73104
Emerg. phone: 405/271-5454,
800/522-4611 (OK only)
Admin. phone: None
Fax: 405/271-1816

Oregon
Oregon Poison Ctr.
Oregon Health Sciences Univ.
CB550 3181 S.W. Sam Jackson Park Rd.
Portland, OR 97201
Emerg. phone: 503/494-8968,
800/452-7165 (OR only)
Admin. phone: 503/494-7799
Fax: 503/494-4980
E-mail: lastname@OHSU.EDU
AAPCC Certified Regional Poison Center

Pennsylvania
Central Pennsylvania Poison Ctr.
University Hospital

Milton S. Hershey Medical Ctr.
Hershey, PA 17033-0850
Emerg. phone: 800/521-6110, 717/531-6111
Admin. phone: 717/531-8955
Fax: 717/531-6932
AAPCC Certified Regional Poison Center

Lehigh Valley Hosp. Poison Prevention
Prog.
17th & Chew Sts.
PO Box 7017
Allentown, PA 18105-7017
Admin. phone: 610/402-2536
Fax: 610/402-2696

Poison Control Ctr.
3600 Sciences Ctr., Ste. 220
Philadelphia, PA 19104-2641
Emerg. phone: 215/386-2100, 800/722-7112
Admin. phone: 215/590-2003, 215/386-2066
Fax: 215/590-4419
AAPCC Certified Regional Poison Center

Pittsburgh Poison Ctr.
3705 Fifth Ave.
Pittsburgh, PA 15213
Emerg. phone: 412/681-6669
Admin. phone: 412/692-5600
Fax: 412/692-5793, 5868, 7497
E-mail: Krenzee@CHPLINK.EDU
AAPCC Certified Regional Poison Center

Regional Poison Prevention Ed. Ctr.
Mercy Regional Health Sys.
2500 Seventh Ave.
Altoona, PA 16602
Admin. phone: 814/949-4197
Fax: 814/949-4872

Rhode Island
Rhode Island Poison Ctr.
593 Eddy St.
Providence, RI 02903
Emerg. phone: 401/444-5727
Admin. phone: 401/444-5906
Fax: 401/444-8062
AAPCC Certified Regional Poison Center

South Carolina

Palmetto Poison Ctr.
Univ. of South Carolina
College of Pharmacy
Columbia, SC 29208
Emerg. phone: 803/765-7359, 800/922-1117
   (SC only), 706/724-5050, 803/777-1117
Admin. phone: 803/777-7909
Fax: 803/777-6127
E-mail: Metts@phar2.pharm.scarolina.edu

South Dakota

McKennan Poison Control Ctr.
800 E. 21st St.
PO Box 5045
Sioux Falls, SD 57117-5045
Emerg. phone: 605/336-3894, 800/952-0123,
   800/843-0505
Admin. phone: 605/339-7873
Fax: 605/333-8206

Tennessee

Middle Tennessee Poison Ctr.
Center for Clinical Toxicology
Vanderbilt Univ. Medical Ctr.
1161 21st Ave. S.
501 Oxford House
Nashville, TN 37232-4632
Emerg. phone: 615/936-2034 (local),
   800/288-9999 (regional),
   TDD 615/322-0157
Admin. phone: 615/936-0760
Fax: 615/936-2046
AAPCC Certified Regional Poison Center

Southern Poison Ctr., Inc.
847 Monroe Ave., Ste. 230
Memphis, TN 38163
Emerg. phone: 901/528-6048;
   800/228-9999 (TN only)
Admin. phone: 901/448-6800
Fax: 901/448-5419
E-mail: pchyka@utmem1.utmem.edu

Texas

Central Texas Poison Ctr.
Scott & White Memorial Clinic & Hosp.
2401 S. 31st St.
Temple, TX 76508
Emerg. phone: 817/774-2005, 800/764-7661
Admin. phone: 817/724-7403
Fax: 813/724-7408

North Texas Poison Ctr.
Texas Poison Ctr. Net. at Parkland
   Mem. Hosp.
5201 Harry Hines Blvd.
PO Box 35926
Dallas, TX 75235
Emerg. phone: 800/746-7661
Admin. phone: 214/590-6625
Fax: 214/590-5008
AAPCC Certified Regional Poison Center

South Texas Poison Ctr.
7703 Floyd Curl Dr.
San Antonio, TX 78284-7834
Emerg. phone: 800/764-7661 (TX only)
Admin. phone: 210/567-5762
Fax: 210/567-8718

Texas Poison Control Net. at Amarillo
1501 S. Coulter
PO Box 1110
Amarillo, TX 79175
Emerg. phone: 800/764-7661
Admin. phone: 806/354-1630
Fax: 806/354-1667

Texas Poison Control Net. at Galveston
Southeast Texas Poison Ctr.
Univ. of Texas Medical Branch
301 University Blvd.
Galveston, TX 77555-1175
Emerg. phone: 409/765-1420 (Galveston),
   (713) 654-1701 (Houston),
   800/764-7661 (TX only)
Admin. phone: 409/772-3332
Fax: 409/772-3917
E-mail: mellis @mspo1.med.utmb.edu
AAPCC Certified Regional Poison Center

West Texas Reg. Poison Ctr.
4815 Alameda Ave.
El Paso, TX 79905
Emerg. phone: 800/764-7661 (TX only)
Admin. phone: 915/521-7661
Fax: 915/521-7978

Utah

Utah Poison Control Ctr.
410 Chipeta Way, Ste. 230
Salt Lake City, UT 84108
Emerg. phone: 801/581-2151,
  800/456-7707 (UT only)
Admin. phone: 801/581-7504
Fax: 801/581-4199
E-mail: barbara.crouch@hsc.utah.edu
AAPCC Certified Regional Poison Center

Vermont

Vermont Poison Ctr.
Fletcher Allen Health Care
111 Colchester Ave.
Burlington, VT 05401
Emerg. phone: 802/658-3456
Admin. phone: 802/656-2439
Fax: 802/656-4802
E-mail: ruphold@moose.uvm.edu

Virginia

Blue Ridge Poison Ctr.
University of Virginia
Box 67
Blue Ridge Hospital
Charlottesville, VA 22901
Emerg. phone: 804/924-5543, 800/451-1428
Admin. phone: 804/924-5308
Fax: 804/243-6335
AAPCC Certified Regional Poison Center

Virginia Poison Ctr.
Virginia Commonwealth Univ.
401 N. 12th St.
Richmond, VA 23298-0522
Emerg. phone: 804/828-9123 (Richmond),
  800/552-6337 (VA only)
Admin. phone: 804/828-4780
Fax: 804/828-5291
E-mail: sliner@gems.vcu.edu

Washington

Washington Poison Ctr.
155 NE 100th St., Ste. 400
Seattle, WA 98125
Emerg. phone: 206/526-2121,
  800/732-6985 (WA only)
Emerg. TDD: 206/517-2394, 800/572-0638
  (WA only)
Admin. phone: 206/517-2350
Fax: 206/526-8490
AAPCC Certified Regional Poison Center

West Virginia

West Virginia Poison Center
3110 MacCorkle Ave. S.E.
Charleston, WV 25304
Emerg. phone: 304/348-4211,
  800/642-3625 (WV only)
Admin. phone: 304/347-1212
Fax: 304/348-9560
AAPCC Certified Regional Poison Center

Wisconsin

Poison Ctr. of Eastern Wisconsin
Children's Hosp. of Wisconsin
PO Box 1997
Milwaukee, WI 53201
Emerg. phone: 414/266-2222,
  800/815-8855 (WI only)
Admin. phone: 414/226-2221
Fax: 414/266-2820

Univ. of Wisconsin Hosp. Regional
  Poison Ctr.
E5/238 CSC
600 Highland Ave.
Madison, WI 53792
Emerg. phone: 608/262-3702, 800/815-8855
Admin. phone: 608/262-7537
Fax: 608/263-9424
E-mail: lc.vermeulen@hosp.wisc.edu

Wyoming

Serviced by: The Poison Ctr.
8301 Dodge St.
Omaha, NE 68114
Emerg. phone: 402/390-5555 (Omaha),
  800/955-9119 (NE &WY)
Admin. phone: 402/390-5467
Fax: 402/390-3049
AAPCC Certified Regional Poison Center

Canada

British Columbia

B.C. Drug & Poison Info. Ctr.
1081 Burrard St.
Vancouver B.C. V6Z 1Y6
Canada
Emerg. phone: 800/567-8911, 604/682-5050
Admin. phone: 604/682-2344, ext. 2126
Fax: 604/631-5262
E-mail: daws@dpk.bc ca

Ontario

Ontario Reg. Poison Control Ctr.
Hospital for Sick Children
555 University Ave.
Toronto, Ontario M5G 1X8
Canada
Emerg. phone: 416/813-5900,
    800/268-9017 (Ontario only)
Admin. phone: 416/813-6474
Fax: 416/813-7489

Nova Scotia

Poison Information Ctr.
1 WK Children's Hospital
PO Box 3070
5850 University Ave.
Halifax, Nova Scotia, B3J3G9
Canada
Emerg. phone: 800/565-8161 (PEI),
    902/428-8161(NS)
Admin. phone: 902/428-8132
Fax: 902/428-3213

Quebec

Quebec Poison Control Ctr.
2705 Blvd. Laurier, J782
Sainte-Foy; Quebec G1V 4G2
Canada
Emerg. phone: 418/656-8090
Admin. phone: 418/654-2731
Fax: 418/654-2747

Appendix II

Math and Conversion Tables

British measurement system

Linear measure

Unit	Equivalent values
Chain (engineers)	100 feet
Chain (surveyors)	66 feet
Fathom	72 inches or 6 feet
Foot	12 inches
Furlong	660 feet or 220 yards or 40 rods
Inch	0.0833 feet or 0.02778 yards
League	15,840 feet or 5,280 yards or 3 miles
Mil	0.001 inch
Mile	5,280 feet or 1,760 yards or 320 rods or 8 furlongs
Rod	16½ feet or 5½ yards
Yard	36 inches or 3 feet

Square measure

Unit	Equivalent values
Square acre	43,560 square feet or 4,840 sq. yards or 160 square rods
Square foot	144 square inches
Square mile	102,400 square rods or 640 acres
Square rod	272¼ square feet or 30¼ square yards
Square yard	1,296 square inches or 9 square feet

Calculating parts per million

In the horticulture industry, when we speak of fertilizing crops, we generally think in terms of pounds of actual element per acre or per 1,000 square feet, or in terms of spoonfuls of a particular fertilizer per 3- or 5-gallon container. This approach is fine as long as we're dealing only with the application of dry fertilizers or nutrient elements. A serious problem develops, however, when we change over, either by choice or necessity, to liquid fertilizers. Suddenly we're faced with having to think in terms of parts per million (ppm). In addition, recommendations for applications of growth promoting compounds, chemical pinching and branching agents, growth retardants, and root promoting compounds are all given in parts per million. Accurate applications can be made only if the grower has a working knowledge of what is meant by parts per million and how to make some basic calculations. Once these are understood, it becomes relatively simple to work out those problems concerning ppm.

Parts per million refers to concentration of a material for any specific unit of weight (mass) or volume. For example, one blonde-haired person living in a city with 999,999 brown-haired people would represent 0.0001 percent of that population or 1 ppm; one-quarter ounce of lead shot mixed in with 249,999 ounces of steel shot would represent 0.0001 percent or 1 ppm. Although not scientifically accurate, growers use the rule of thumb that 1 ounce of a material in 100 gallons of water is equal to 75 ppm. For example, 1 ounce of pure nitrogen dissolved in 100 gallons of water is equivalent to 75 ppm nitrogen. Using this rule of thumb, calculating ppm becomes simple. Consider the following:

Problem 1: A grower wants to apply 225 ppm N to a crop of Japanese holly liners. The soluble fertilizer available is 20-20-20. How much 20-20-20 should he dissolve per 100 gallons of water?

Solution:

1 ounce per 100 gallons = 75 ppm
225 ppm ÷ 75 ppm = 3
3 ounces supplies 225 ppm
but
20-20-20 = 20 percent N
5 ounces 20-20-20 = 1 ounce N (20 percent of 5)
therefore
3×5 ounces 20-20-20 = 15 ounces of 20-20-20 needed

The grower should dissolve 15 ounces of 20-20-20 in 100 gallons of water to apply 225 ppm N. Of course the solution would also contain 225 ppm of P_2O_5 and 225 ppm of K_2O.

The procedure may also be reversed to determine the concentration of a fertilizer solution. Problem 2 illustrates this.

Problem 2: A 15-45-5 fertilizer is recommended for use at the rate of 3 pounds per 100 gallons of water. How much N, P, and K are being applied by the solution?

Solution:

1 pound = 16 ounces
3 pounds = 48 ounces
48 ounces $\times$ 0.15 N $\times$ 75 ppm/ounce = 540 ppm N
48 ounces $\times$ 0.45 P_2O_5 $\times$ 75 ppm/ounce = 1,620 ppm P_2O_5
48 ounces $\times$ 0.05 K_2O $\times$ 75 ppm/ounce = 180 ppm K_2O

Problem 3: A grower would like to fertilize his crop of photinia liners with 225 ppm N using a 20-20-20 fertilizer and he would like to apply it through a proportioner that has a dilution ration of 1:15. How much 20-20-20 should be dissolved per gallon of concentrated stock solution?

Solution:

> 15 ounces 20-20-20 per 100 gallons water = 225 ppm N
> 1:15 proportioner = 1 gallon stock solution per 15 gallons water
> Total volume = 16 gallons
> 100 gallons ÷ 16 gallons = 6.25
> 15 ounces ÷ 6.25 = 2.4 ounces per gallon

To apply 225 ppm N through the 1:15 proportioner, dissolve 2.4 ounces of 20-20-20 in each gallon of stock solution.

Problem 4: A grower would like to spray a particular growth regulator on his azalea crop at a concentration of 2,000 ppm. The growth regulator as purchased from the supplier contains 18.5 percent active ingredients (ai). How much growth regulator should he use per gallon of spray?

Solution:

> 2,000 ppm = 0.2 percent = 0.002
> 1 gallon = 128 ounces
> 128 ounces × 0.002 = 0.256 ounces
> Divide 100 percent purity by actual rates of ai.
> 100 percent ÷ 18.5 percent = 5.4
> 5.4 ounces material = 1 ounce ai
> 5.4 × 0.256 = 1.38 ounces per gallon = 2,000 ppm

Conversion factors

Multiply	By	To obtain
Acres	43,560	Square feet
Acres	0.4047	Hectares
Acres	4,047	Square meters
Acres	0.001562	Square miles
Acres	160	Square rods
Acres	4,840	Square yards
Acre feet	12	Acre inches
Acre feet	43,560	Cubic feet
Acre feet	325,872	Gallons
Acre inches	3,630	Cubic feet
Acre inches	6,272,640	Cubic inches
Acre inches	27,154	Gallons
Board feet	144	Cubic inches
Bushels	1.244	Cubic feet
Bushels	2,150	Cubic inches
Bushels	0.03524	Cubic meters
Bushels	0.04545	Cubic yards
Bushels	35.238	Liters
Bushels	4	Pecks
Bushels	64	Pints (dry)
Bushels	32	Quarts (dry)
Centigrams	0.01	Grams
Centiliters	0.01	Liters
Centimeters	0.03281	Feet
Centimeters	0.3937	Inches
Centimeters	0.01	Meters
Centimeters	393.7	Mils
Centimeters per second	1.969	Feet per minute
Centimeters per second	0.03281	Feet per second
Centimeters per second	0.036	Kilometers per hour
Centimeters per second	0.6	Meters per minute
Centimeters per second	0.02237	Miles per hour
Centimeters per second	0.0003728	Miles per minute
Cords	128	Cubic feet
Cubic centimeters	0.0000353	Cubic feet
Cubic centimeters	0.06102	Cubic inches
Cubic centimeters	0.00001	Cubic meters
Cubic centimeters	0.000001308	Cubic yards
Cubic centimeters	0.0002642	Gallons
Cubic centimeters	0.001	Liters
Cubic centimeters	1	Milliliters
Cubic centimeters	0.03382	Ounces (fluid)
Cubic centimeters	0.002113	Pints (fluid)
Cubic centimeters	0.001057	Quarts (fluid)
Cubic feet	0.8	Bushels
Cubic feet	0.0078	Cords
Cubic feet	28,316.84	Cubic centimeters
Cubic feet	1,728	Cubic inches

Multiply	By	To obtain
Cubic feet	0.02832	Cubic meters
Cubic feet	0.03704	Cubic yards
Cubic feet	7.481	Gallons
Cubic feet	28.32	Liters
Cubic feet	51.42	Pints (dry)
Cubic feet	59.84	Pints (fluid)
Cubic feet	25.71	Quarts (dry)
Cubic feet	29.92	Quarts (fluid)
Cubic feet per minute	472	Cubic centimeters per second
Cubic feet per minute	448.8	Gallons per hour
Cubic feet per minute	0.1247	Gallons per second
Cubic feet per minute	1,698.74	Liters per hour
Cubic feet per minute	0.4720	Liters per second
Cubic feet per minute	62.4	Pounds of water per minute
Cubic inches	0.000465	Bushels
Cubic inches	16.387	Cubic centimeters
Cubic inches	0.0005787	Cubic feet
Cubic inches	0.00001639	Cubic meters
Cubic inches	0.00002143	Cubic yards
Cubic inches	0.004329	Gallons
Cubic inches	0.01639	Liters
Cubic inches	0.5541	Ounces (fluid)
Cubic inches	0.02976	Pints (dry)
Cubic inches	0.03463	Pints (fluid)
Cubic inches	0.01488	Quarts (dry)
Cubic inches	0.01732	Quarts (fluid)
Cubic meters	1,000,000	Cubic centimeters
Cubic meters	35.31	Cubic feet
Cubic meters	61,023	Cubic inches
Cubic meters	1.308	Cubic yards
Cubic meters	264.2	Gallons
Cubic meters	1,000	Liters
Cubic meters	2,113	Pints (fluid)
Cubic meters	1,057	Quarts (fluid)
Cubic yards	22	Bushels
Cubic yards	764,600	Cubic centimeters
Cubic yards	27	Cubic feet
Cubic yards	46,656	Cubic inches
Cubic yards	0.7646	Cubic meters
Cubic yards	202	Gallons
Cubic yards	764.6	Liters
Cubic yards	1,616	Pints (fluid)
Cubic yards	807.9	Quarts (fluid)
Cubic yards per minute	0.45	Cubic feet per second
Cubic yards per minute	3.367	Gallons per second
Cubic yards per minute	12.74	Liters per second
Cups (dry)	0.5	Pints (dry)
Cups (dry)	0.25	Quarts (dry)
Cups (dry)	16	Tablespoons (dry)
Cups (dry)	48	Teaspoons (dry)
Cups (fluid)	0.5	Pints (fluid)

Multiply	By	To obtain
Cups (fluid)	0.25	Quarts (fluid)
Cups (fluid)	16	Tablespoons (fluid)
Cups (fluid)	48	Teaspoons (fluid)
Days	24	Hours
Days	1,440	Minutes
Days	86,400	Seconds
Decigrams	0.1	Grams
Deciliters	0.1	Liters
Decimeters	10	Meters
Dekagrams	10	Grams
Dekaliters	10	Liters
Dekameters	10	Meters
Drams	27.343	Grains
Drams	1.772	Grams
Drams	0.0625	Ounces
Fathoms	6	Feet
Feet	30.48	Centimeters
Feet	12	Inches
Feet	0.3048	Meters
Feet	0.0606	Rods
Feet	0.333	Yards
Feet of water	0.02950	Atmospheres
Feet of water	0.8826	Inches of mercury
Feet of water	304.8	Kilograms per square meter
Feet of water	62.43	Pounds per square foot
Feet of water	0.4335	Pounds per square inch
Feet per minute	0.5080	Centimeters per second
Feet per minute	0.01667	Feet per second
Feet per minute	0.01829	Kilometers per hour
Feet per minute	0.3048	Meters per minute
Feet per minute	0.01136	Miles per hour
Feet per second	30.48	Centimeters per second
Feet per second	1.097	Kilometers per hour
Feet per second	0.5921	Knots per hour
Feet per second	18.29	Meters per minute
Feet per second	0.6818	Miles per hour
Feet per second	0.01136	Miles per minute
Feet of rise per 100 feet	1	Percent grade
Footcandles	10.76	Lux
Furlongs	4	Rods
Gallons	3,785	Cubic centimeters
Gallons	0.1337	Cubic feet
Gallons	231	Cubic inches
Gallons	0.003785	Cubic meters
Gallons	0.004951	Cubic yards
Gallons	3.785	Liters
Gallons	128	Ounces (fluid)
Gallons	8	Pints (fluid)
Gallons	4	Quarts (fluid)
Gallons of water	8.3453	Pounds of water
Gallons per minute	0.134	Cubic feet per minute

Multiply	By	To obtain
Gallons per minute	0.002228	Cubic feet per second
Gallons per minute	0.06308	Liters per second
Gills	2	Cups (fluid)
Gills	0.1183	Liters
Gills	4	Ounces (fluid)
Gills	0.25	Pints (fluid)
Grains (troy)	1	Grains (avoir.)
Grains (troy)	0.0648	Grams
Grains (troy)	0.4167	Pennyweights (troy)
Grams	15.43	Grains (troy)
Grams	0.001	Kilograms
Grams	1000	Milligrams
Grams	0.03527	Ounces (avoir.)
Grams	0.03215	Ounces (troy)
Grams	0.002205	Pounds
Grams per liter	1,000	Parts per million
Grams per liter	0.1336	Ounces per gallon
Grams per liter	0.0334	Ounces per quart
Hectares	2.471	Acres
Hectares	107,000	Square feet
Hectograms	100	Grams
Hectoliters	100	Liters
Hectometers	100	Meters
Horsepower	42.44	BTUs per minute
Horsepower	0.7457	Kilowatts
Horsepower	745.7	Watts
Horsepower (boiler)	33,520	BTUs per hour
Horsepower (boiler)	9.804	Kilowatts
Horsepower (boiler)	9,804	Watts
Horsepower hours	2,547	BTUs
Horsepower hours	0.7457	Kilowatt hours
Hours	60	Minutes
Hours	3,600	Seconds
Inches	2.540	Centimeters
Inches	0.08333	Feet
Inches	0.0254	Meters
Inches	0.02778	Yards
Inches of water	0.002458	Atmospheres
Inches of water	0.07355	Inches of mercury
Inches of water	25.4	Kilograms per square meter
Inches of water	0.5781	Ounces per square inch
Inches of water	5.204	Pounds per square foot
Inches of water	0.03613	Pounds per square inch
Kilograms	1,000	Grams
Kilograms	35.27	Ounces (avoir.)
Kilograms	2.2046	Pounds
Kilograms	0.001102	Tons (short)
Kilogram meters	7.233	Foot pounds
Kilograms per hectare	0.8929	Pounds per acre
Kilograms per cubic meter	0.001	Grams per cubic centimeter
Kilograms per cubic meter	0.06243	Pounds per cubic foot

Multiply	By	To obtain
Kilograms per cubic meter	0.00003613	Pounds per cubic inch
Kilograms per square meter	0.001422	Pounds per square inch
Kiloliters	1,000	Liters
Kilometers	100,000	Centimeters
Kilometers	3,281	Feet
Kilometers	1,000	Meters
Kilometers	0.6214	Miles
Kilometers	1,093.6	Yards
Kilometers per hour	27.78	Centimeters per second
Kilometers per hour	54.68	Feet per minute
Kilometers per hour	0.9114	Feet per second
Kilometers per hour	0.5396	Knots per hour
Kilometers per hour	16.67	Meters per minute
Kilometers per hour	0.6214	Miles per hour
Kilowatts	56.92	BTUs per minute
Kilowatts	1.341	Horsepower
Kilowatts	1,000	Watts
Kilowatt hours	3.415	BTUs
Kilowatt hours	1.341	Horsepower hours
Knots	6,080	Feet
Knots	1.853	Kilometers
Knots	1.152	Miles
Knots	2,027	Yards
Knots per hour	51.48	Centimeters per second
Knots per hour	1.689	Feet per second
Knots per hour	1.853	Kilometers per hour
Knots per hour	1.152	Miles per hour
Liters	1,000	Cubic centimeters
Liters	0.03531	Cubic feet
Liters	61.02	Cubic inches
Liters	0.001	Cubic meters
Liters	0.001308	Cubic yards
Liters	0.2642	Gallons
Liters	1,000	Milliliters
Liters	2.113	Pints (fluid)
Liters	1.057	Quarts (fluid)
Lux	0.0929	Footcandles
Meters	100	Centimeters
Meters	3.2808	Feet
Meters	39.37	Inches
Meters	0.001	Kilometers
Meters	1,000,000	Microns
Meters	1,000	Millimeters
Meters	1.0936	Yards
Meters per minute	1.667	Centimeters
Meters per minute	3.281	Feet per minute
Meters per minute	0.5468	Feet per second
Meters per minute	0.06	Kilometers per hour
Meters per minute	0.03728	Miles per hour
Meters per second	1,968	Feet per minute
Meters per second	32.84	Feet per second

Multiply	By	To obtain
Meters per second	3.0	Kilometers per hour
Meters per second	0.06	Kilometers per minute
Meters per second	2.237	Miles per hour
Meters per second	0.03728	Miles per minute
Microns	0.0001	Centimeters
Microns	0.00003937	Inches
Microns	0.000001	Meters
Microns	0.001	Millimeters
Mils	0.00254	Centimeters
Mils	0.001	Inches
Miles	160,900	Centimeters
Miles	5,280	Feet
Miles	63,360	Inches
Miles	1.6093	Kilometers
Miles	1,609.3	Meters
Miles	320	Rods
Miles	1,760	Yards
Miles per hour	44.7	Centimeters per second
Miles per hour	88	Feet per minute
Miles per hour	1.467	Feet per second
Miles per hour	1.6093	Kilometers per hour
Miles per hour	0.8684	Knots per hour
Miles per hour	26.82	Meters per minute
Milligrams	0.001	Grams
Milligrams	0.000001	Kilograms
Milligrams per liter	1	Parts per million
Milligrams per liter	0.0001	Percent
Milliliters	1	Cubic centimeters
Milliliters	0.001	Liters
Millimeters	1	Centimeters
Millimeters	0.03937	Inches
Millimeters	0.001	Meters
Millimeters	39.37	Mils
Months	30.42	Days
Months	730	Hours
Months	43,800	Minutes
Months	2,628,000	Seconds
Ounces (avoir.)	16	Drams
Ounces (avoir.)	437.5	Grains
Ounces (avoir.)	28.35	Grams
Ounces (avoir.)	0.9115	Ounces (troy)
Ounces (avoir.)	3	Tablespoons (dry)
Ounces (avoir.)	9	Teaspoons (dry)
Ounces (fluid)	1.80	Cubic inches
Ounces (fluid)	0.0078125	Gallons
Ounces (fluid)	0.02957	Liters
Ounces (fluid)	29.57	Milliliters
Ounces (fluid)	2	Tablespoons (fluid)
Ounces (fluid)	6	Teaspoons (fluid)
Ounces (troy)	480	Grains (troy)
Ounces (troy)	31.10	Grams

Multiply	By	To obtain
Ounces (troy)	1.097	Ounces (avoir.)
Ounces (troy)	20	Pennyweights (troy)
Ounces (troy)	0.8333	Pounds (troy)
Ounces per gallon	7.812	Milliliters per liter
Ounces per square inch	0.625	Pounds per square inch
Parts per million	0.001	Grams per liter
Parts per million	1	Milligrams per kilogram
Parts per million	1	Milligrams per liter
Parts per million	0.013	Ounces per 100 gallons
Parts per million	0.0001	Percent
Parts per million	0.0083	Pounds per 1,000 gallons
Pennyweights (troy)	24	Grains (troy)
Pennyweights (troy)	1.555	Grams
Pennyweights (troy)	0.05	Ounces (troy)
Percent	10	Grams per kilogram
Percent	10	Grams per liter
Percent	1.33	Ounces by weight per gallon of water
Percent	10,000	Parts per million
Percent	8.34	Pounds per 100 gallons of water
Pints (dry)	0.015625	Bushels
Pints (dry)	0.0194	Cubic feet
Pints (dry)	33.6	Cubic inches
Pints (dry)	0.0625	Pecks
Pints (dry)	0.5	Quarts (dry)
Pints (fluid)	473.167	Cubic centimeters
Pints (fluid)	0.0167	Cubic feet
Pints (fluid)	28.875	Cubic inches
Pints (fluid)	0.125	Gallons
Pints (fluid)	0.4732	Liters
Pints (fluid)	16	Ounces (fluid)
Pints (fluid)	0.5	Quarts (fluid)
Pounds	256	Drams
Pounds	7,000	Grains
Pounds	453.594	Grams
Pounds	0.453494	Kilograms
Pounds	16	Ounces
Pounds	14.583	Ounces (troy)
Pounds	1,215	Pounds (troy)
Pounds	0.0005	Tons (short)
Pounds of water	0.01602	Cubic feet
Pounds of water	27.68	Cubic inches
Pounds of water	0.1198	Gallons
Pounds per acre	1.12	Kilograms per hectare
Pounds per cubic foot	0.01602	Cubic feet
Pounds per cubic foot	16.02	Kilograms per cubic meter
Pounds per cubic foot	0.005787	Pounds per cubic inch
Pounds per cubic inch	27.68	Pounds per cubic centimeter
Pounds per cubic inch	27,680	Kilograms per cubic meter
Pounds per cubic inch	1,728	Pounds per cubic foot
Pounds per foot	1,488	Kilograms per meter

Multiply	By	To obtain
Pounds per inch	178.6	Grams per centimeter
Pounds per square foot	0.01602	Cubic feet of water
Pounds per square foot	4.882	Kilograms per square meter
Pounds per square foot	0.006994	Pounds per square inch
Pounds per square inch	0.06804	Atmospheres
Pounds per square inch	2.307	Cubic feet of water
Pounds per square inch	2.036	Inches of mercury
Pounds per square inch	0.070307	Kilograms per square centimeter
Pounds per square inch	703.1	Kilograms per square meter
Pounds per square inch	144	Pounds per square foot
Quarts (dry)	0.03125	Bushels
Quarts (dry)	0.0389	Cubic feet
Quarts (dry)	67.20	Cubic inches
Quarts (dry)	0.125	Pecks
Quarts (dry)	2	Pints (dry)
Quarts (fluid)	0.0334	Cubic feet
Quarts (fluid)	57.75	Cubic inches
Quarts (fluid)	0.25	Gallons
Quarts (fluid)	0.9463	Liters
Quarts (fluid)	946.3	Milliliters
Quarts (fluid)	32	Ounces (fluid)
Quarts (fluid)	2	Pints (fluid)
Rods	16.5	Feet
Rods	198	Inches
Rods	5.029	Meters
Rods	5.5	Yards
Square centimeters	0.00107	Square feet
Square centimeters	0.1550	Square inches
Square centimeters	0.0001	Square meters
Square centimeters	100	Square millimeters
Square feet	0.00002296	Acres
Square feet	929	Square centimeters
Square feet	144	Square inches
Square feet	0.0929	Square meters
Square feet	0.0000000357	Square miles
Square feet	0.111	Square yards
Square inches	6.452	Square centimeters
Square inches	0.006944	Square feet
Square inches	645.163	Square millimeters
Square kilometers	247.1	Acres
Square kilometers	10,764,961	Square feet
Square kilometers	1,000,000	Square meters
Square kilometers	0.3861	Square miles
Square kilometers	1,196,107	Square yards
Square meters	0.000247	Acres
Square meters	10.764	Square feet
Square meters	0.0000003861	Square miles
Square meters	1.196	Square yards
Square miles	640	Acres
Square miles	27,878,400	Square feet

Multiply	By	To obtain
Square miles	2.59	Square kilometers
Square miles	102,400	Square rods
Square miles	3,097,600	Square yards
Square millimeters	0.01	Square centimeters
Square millimeters	0.00155	Square inches
Square millimeters	0.000001	Square meters
Square yards	0.0002066	Acres
Square yards	9	Square feet
Square yards	1,296	Square inches
Square yards	0.8361	Square meters
Square yards	0.000000322	Square miles
Tablespoons (dry)	0.0625	Cups (dry)
Tablespoons (dry)	0.333	Ounces (dry)
Tablespoons (dry)	3	Teaspoons (dry)
Tablespoons (fluid)	0.0625	Cups (fluid)
Tablespoons (fluid)	15	Milliliters
Tablespoons (fluid)	0.5	Ounces (fluid)
Teaspoons (dry)	0.111	Ounces (dry)
Teaspoons (dry)	0.333	Tablespoons (dry)
Teaspoons (fluid)	0.0208	Cups (fluid)
Teaspoons (fluid)	5	Milliliters
Teaspoons (fluid)	0.1666	Ounces (fluid)
Temperature (0C) +17.8	1.8	Temperature 0F
Temperature (0F) -32	0.55	Temperature 0C
Tons (long)	1,016	Kilograms
Tons (long)	2,240	Pounds
Tons (long)	1.016	Tons (long)
Tons (long)	1.1199	Tons (short)
Tons (metric)	1,000	Kilograms
Tons (metric)	2,205	Pounds
Tons (metric)	0.9843	Tons (long)
Tons (metric)	1.1023	Tons (short)
Tons (short)	907.2	Kilograms
Tons (short)	2,000	Pounds
Tons (short)	0.8929	Tons (long)
Tons (short)	0.9072	Tons (metric)
Watts	0.05692	BTUs per minute
Watts	0.001341	Horsepower
Watts	0.001	Kilowatts
Weeks	168	Hours
Weeks	10,080	Minutes
Weeks	604,800	Seconds
Yards	0.009144	Centimeters
Yards	3	Feet
Yards	36	Inches
Yards	0.9144	Meters
Yards	0.000568	Miles
Yards	0.01818	Rods
Years (common)	365	Days
Years (common)	8.760	Hours
Years (leap)	366	Days

Fraction, decimal and millimeter equivalents

Fraction of an inch	Inches in decimal	Millimeter equivalent
$1/64$	0.015625	0.397
$1/32$	0.03125	0.794
$3/64$	0.046875	1.191
$1/16$	0.0625	1.588
$5/64$	0.078125	1.984
$3/32$	0.09375	2.381
$7/64$	0.109375	2.778
$1/8$	0.1250	3.572
$5/32$	0.15625	3.969
$11/64$	0.171875	4.366
$3/16$	0.1875	4.762
$13/64$	0.203125	5.159
$7/32$	0.21875	5.556
$15/64$	0.234375	5.593
$1/4$	0.2500	6.350
$17/64$	0.265625	6.747
$9/32$	0.28125	7.144
$19/64$	0.296875	7.541
$5/16$	0.3125	7.938
$21/64$	0.328125	8.334
$11/32$	0.34375	8.731
$23/64$	0.359375	9.128
$3/8$	0.3750	9.525
$25/64$	0.390625	9.922
$13/32$	0.40625	10.319
$27/64$	0.421875	10.716
$7/16$	0.4375	11.112
$29/64$	0.453125	11.509
$15/32$	0.46875	11.906
$31/64$	0.484375	12.303
$1/2$	0.5000	12.700
$33/64$	0.515625	13.097
$17/32$	0.53125	13.494
$35/64$	0.546875	13.891
$9/16$	0.5625	14.288
$37/64$	0.578125	14.684
$19/32$	0.59375	15.081
$39/64$	0.609375	15.478
$5/8$	0.6250	15.875
$41/64$	0.640625	16.272
$21/32$	0.65625	16.669
$43/64$	0.671875	17.066

Fraction of an inch	Inches in decimal	Millimeter equivalent
$^{11}/_{16}$	0.6875	17.462
$^{45}/_{64}$	0.703125	17.859
$^{23}/_{32}$	0.71875	18.256
$^{47}/_{64}$	0.734375	18.653
$^{3}/_{4}$	0.7500	19.050
$^{49}/_{64}$	0.765625	19.447
$^{25}/_{32}$	0.78125	19.844
$^{51}/_{64}$	0.796875	20.241
$^{13}/_{16}$	0.8125	20.638
$^{53}/_{64}$	0.828125	21.034
$^{27}/_{32}$	0.84375	21.431
$^{55}/_{64}$	0.859375	21.828
$^{7}/_{8}$	0.8750	22.225
$^{57}/_{64}$	0.890625	22.622
$^{29}/_{32}$	0.90625	23.019
$^{59}/_{64}$	0.921875	23.416
$^{15}/_{16}$	0.9375	23.812
$^{61}/_{64}$	0.953125	24.209
$^{31}/_{32}$	0.96875	24.606
$^{63}/_{64}$	0.984375	25.003
1	1.000	25.400

Metric system

The metric system is based on three basic units of measure: the meter, liter, and gram. Multiples of fractions of the three basic units are denoted by adding specific prefixes to the basic unit:

Metric prefix	Exponential multiplier	Numeric multiplier	Increment of basic unit
—	10	1	One
Deka	10	10	Ten
Hecto	10	100	One hundred
Kilo	10	1,000	One thousand
Mega	10	1,000,000	One million
Giga	10	1,000,000,000	One billion
Tera	10	1,000,000,000,000	One trillion
—	10	1	One
Deci	10	0.1	One tenth
Centi	10	0.01	One hundredth
Milli	10	0.001	One thousandth
Micro*	10	0.000001	One millionth
Nano	10	0.000000001	One billionth
Pico	10	0.000000000001	One trillionth

* An exception to the rule of metric prefixes is that one millionth of a meter is referred to as a micron rather than a micrometer.

Linear measure (basic unit is the meter)

Unit	Abbreviation	Equivalent values
Kilometer	km	1,000 meters
Hectometer	hm	100 meters
Dekameter	dkm	10 meters
Meter	m	1,000 millimeters
Decimeter	dm	0.1 meters
Centimeter	cm	0.01 meters
Millimeter	mm	0.001 meters
Micron		0.000001 meters
Millimicron		0.000000001 meters

Square measure (basic unit is the meter)

Unit	Equivalent value
Kilometer	1,000,000 square meters
Meter	10,000 square centimeters
Centimeter	100 square millimeters
Millimeter	0.01 square centimeters

Determining number of plants required per acre

1. $$\frac{\text{Plants per acre}}{\text{Row spacing (in feet)} \times \text{plant spacing (in feet)}} = 43{,}560$$

   OR

2. $$\frac{\text{Plants per acre}}{\text{Row spacing (in inches)} \times \text{plant spacing (in inches)}} = 43{,}560 \times 144$$

Distance between rows (in inches)	Distance between plants in the row (in inches)				
	12	24	36	48	60
1	43,560	21,780	14,520	10,890	8,712
2	21,780	10,890	7,260	5,445	4,356
3	14,520	7,260	4,840	3,630	2,904
4	10,890	5,445	3,630	2,722	2,178
5	8,712	4,356	2,904	2,178	1,742
6	7,260	3,630	2,420	1,815	1,452
7	6,223	3,111	2,074	1,556	1,245
8	5,445	2,722	1,815	1,361	1,089
9	4,840	2,420	1,613	1,210	968
10	4,356	2,178	1,452	1,089	871
12	3,620	1,810	1,210	907	726
14	3,111	1,555	1,037	778	622
16	2,722	1,361	907	680	544
18	2,420	1,210	807	605	484
20	2,178	1,089	726	544	436

Conversions and rules of thumb for pesticide application

1. Surface

1 square inch = 6.5 square centimeters
1 square foot = 929 square centimeters = 0.0929 square meters
1 square yard = 0.84 square meters
43,560 square feet = 1 acre
2.5 acres = 1 hectare = 10,000 square meters
1 quart per 100 square feet = 100 gallons per acre

2. Dry weight

1 ounce = 28.35 grams
1 pound = 454 grams = 16 ounces
1 pound of most wettable powders per 100 gallons is approximately 1 tablespoon per gallon
1 tablespoon = 3 teaspoons
1 ounce active per 100 gallons = 75 ppm
1 ppm = 1 mg per 100 gms = 0.001 ml per liter
1 gram per 100 square feet = 1 pound per acre

3. Liquid

1 ounce = 29.6 mls = 2 tablespoons = 6 teaspoons
8 ounces = 1 cup
2 cups = 1 pint
2 pints = 1 quart
4 quarts = 1 gallon
10 liters = 2.64 gallons
1 gallon = 128 ounces = 3800 ml = 8.34 pounds of water
1 gallon of concentrate per 100 gallons of spray = $2\frac{1}{2}$ tablespoons per gallon
1 quart per 100 gallons = $\frac{5}{8}$ tablespoons per gallon
1 pint = 1 pound of water

Pesticide dilutions

The recommended rate for many commercial products is given in either gallons or pounds of product per 100 gallons of water. The following table can be used to determine the amount of commercial product to use when mixing less than 100 gallons of material.

Product needed to mix						
100 gallons	25 gallons	20 gallons	15 gallons	10 gallons	5 gallons	1 gallon
Liquid formulations						
2 gals.	64 oz.	$51^3/_{16}$ oz.	$38^1/_2$ oz.	$25^1/_2$ oz.	$12^7/_8$ oz.	$2^1/_2$ oz.
1 gal.	32 oz.	$25^9/_{16}$ oz.	$19^3/_{16}$ oz.	$12^3/_4$ oz.	$6^1/_2$ oz.	$1^1/_4$ oz.
2 qts.	16 oz.	$12^{13}/_{16}$ oz.	$9^9/_{16}$ oz.	$6^3/_8$ oz.	$3^1/_4$ oz.	$^5/_8$ oz.
1 qt.	8 oz.	$6^3/_8$ oz.	$4^{13}/_{16}$ oz.	$3^3/_{16}$ oz.	$1^9/_{16}$ oz.	$^5/_{16}$ oz.
$1^1/_2$ pts.	6 oz.	$4^{13}/_{16}$ oz.	$3^9/_{16}$ oz.	$2^3/_8$ oz.	$1^1/_4$ oz.	$^1/_4$ oz.
1 pt.	4 oz.	$3^3/_{16}$ oz.	$2^3/_8$ oz.	$1^9/_{16}$ oz.	$^7/_8$ oz.	$^3/_{16}$ oz.
8 oz.	2 oz.	$1^9/_{16}$ oz.	$1^3/_{16}$ oz.	$^{13}/_{16}$ oz.	$^7/_{16}$ oz.	$^1/_2$ tsp.
4 oz.	1 oz.	$^{13}/_{16}$ oz.	$^9/_{16}$ oz.	$^3/_8$ oz.	$^1/_4$ oz.	$^1/_4$ tsp.
Solid formulations						
5 lbs.	20 oz.	16 oz.	12 oz.	8 oz.	4 oz.	$4^4/_5$ tsp.
4 lbs.	16 oz.	$12^{13}/_{16}$ oz.	$9^9/_{16}$ oz.	$6^3/_8$ oz.	$3^1/_4$ oz.	$3^4/_5$ tsp.
3 lbs.	12 oz.	$9^9/_{16}$ oz.	$7^3/_{16}$ oz.	$4^{13}/_{16}$ oz.	$2^3/_8$ oz.	$2^2/_5$ tsp.
2 lbs.	8 oz.	$6^3/_8$ oz.	$4^3/_8$ oz.	$3^3/_{16}$ oz.	$1^3/_4$ oz.	2 tsp.
1 lb.	4 oz.	$3^3/_{16}$ oz.	$2^3/_8$ oz.	$1^9/_{16}$ oz.	$^7/_8$ oz.	1 tsp.
8 oz.	2 oz.	$1^9/_{16}$ oz.	$1^{13}/_{16}$ oz.	$^{13}/_{16}$ oz.	$^3/_8$ oz.	$^1/_2$ tsp.
4 oz.	1 oz.	$^{13}/_{16}$ oz.	$^9/_{16}$ oz.	$^3/_8$ oz.	$^3/_{16}$ oz.	$^1/_4$ tsp.

Pots: volume and measurement

Pot diameter	Pot height	Trade designation	Actual dimensions (diameter × height)	Pot volume in cubic inches
6"	5"	1 gal. std.	$6^1/_2$" × 6"	140
6" tub	—	6" tub	$6^1/_2$" × 5"	—
8"	7"	2 gal.	8" × 7"	350
9"	8"	—	—	512
10"	9"	3 gal.	10" × $9^1/_2$"	711
11"	10"	—	—	950
12"	—	4 gal.	11" × $10^1/_2$"	—
13"	11"	—	—	1,463
14"	—	7 gal.	$13^1/_2$" × 12"	—
17"	14"	10 gal.	17" × 15"	3,178

Cubic inches to cubic feet

Cubic inches	Cubic feet
1,728 =	1
1,296 =	$^3/_4$
864 =	$^1/_2$
519 =	$^1/_3$
432 =	$^1/_4$

Potted plants required per 100 square feet (various spacings on center*)

Pot spacing	Plants per 100 sq. ft.	Pot spacing	Plants per 100 sq. ft.
4 × 4	900	18 × 18	45
6 × 6	400	24 × 24	25
8 × 8	225	30 × 30	16
9 × 9	178	36 × 36	11.11
10 × 10*	144*	48 × 48	6.25
12 × 12	100	72 × 72	2.78

* Example: If you measure and mark every 10 inches and place and center a plant right on top of each spot, it would take 144 plants to fill 100 square feet.

Application rates of media or surface-applied fertilizers or pesticides

Rate per acre	Rate per 1,000 sq. ft.	Rate per 100 sq. ft.
100 pounds	2 pounds 4 ounces	3 $1/2$ ounces
200 pounds	4 pounds 8 ounces	7 $1/4$ ounces
300 pounds	6 pounds 14 ounces	11 ounces
400 pounds	9 pounds	14 $1/2$ ounces
500 pounds	11 pounds 8 ounces	1 pound 2 ounces
600 pounds	13 pounds 12 ounces	1 pound 6 ounces
700 pounds	16 pounds	1 pound 9 ounces
800 pounds	18 pounds	1 pound 13 ounces
900 pounds	20 pounds 9 ounces	2 pounds 1 ounce
1,000 pounds	23 pounds	2 pounds 5 ounces
2,000 pounds	46 pounds	4 pounds 9 ounces
1 gallon	3 ounces (fluid)	$1/3$ ounce (fluid)
5 gallons	14$1/2$ ounces (fluid)	1$1/2$ ounces (fluid)
100 gallons	2$1/3$ gallons (fluid)	29$1/3$ ounces (fluid)
218 pounds	5 pounds	8 ounces
436 pounds	10 pounds	1 pound
2,178 pounds	50 pounds	5 pounds
4,356 pounds	100 pounds	10 pounds
43$1/2$ gallons	1 gallon	13 ounces (fluid)
5 gallons 3$1/2$ pints	1 pint	1$1/2$ ounces (fluid)
10 gallons 3$1/2$ quarts	1 quart	3 ounces (fluid)

Weight (mass) conversions

Unit	Equivalent values
Dram (avoirdupois)	27.34 grains
Dram (troy)	60 grains
Ounce (avoirdupois)	437.5 grains
Ounce (troy)	480 grains
Pennyweight (avoirdupois)	0.877 dram
Pennyweight (troy)	0.4 dram
Pound (avoirdupois)	7,000 grains or 16 ounces
Pound (troy)	5,760 grains or 12 ounces
Ton (long)	2,240 pounds
Ton (metric)	2,205 pounds
Ton (short)	2,000 pounds

Determining amount of soluble fertilizer or pesticide suspension for proportioner stock solutions to deliver 100 ppm

**Ounces of fertilizer to dissolve per
1 gallon of concentrate to deliver 100 ppm**

% N, P₂O₅ or K₂O in fertilizer	Proportioner dilution ration					
	1:15	**1:100**	**1:128**	**1:150**	**1:200**	**1:300**
5	4.05	27.0	34.6	40.5	54.0	81.0
7	2.89	19.3	24.7	28.9	38.6	57.9
10	2.02	13.5	17.3	20.3	27.0	40.5
15	1.35	9.0	11.5	13.5	18.0	27.0
20	1.01	6.8	8.6	10.1	13.6	20.3
21	0.96	6.4	8.2	9.6	12.9	19.3
25	0.81	5.4	6.9	8.1	10.8	16.2
30	0.68	4.5	5.8	6.8	9.0	13.5
35	0.58	3.9	4.9	5.8	7.7	11.6
40	0.51	3.4	4.3	5.1	6.8	10.1
45	0.45	3.0	3.8	4.5	6.0	9.0

Using the above table, you can readily determine how to mix a specific concentration of fertilizer stock solution for injection through most commercially available proportioners. Consider the following example:

You have a 1:200 proportioner and would like to apply 100 ppm N to juniper liners using 20-20-20 soluble fertilizer. How much 20-20-20 should you dissolve per gallon of stock solution in order to have 100 ppm N coming out of the proportioner delivery hose end? (Keep in mind that 20-20-20 contains 20 percent N, 20 percent P₂O₅, and 20 percent K₂O.)

Step 1. In the column labeled "percent N,P₂O₅ or K₂O in fertilizer," find 20 since there is 20 percent N in the fertilizer you're using.

Step 2. Go straight across to the column labeled "1:200" under the heading "Proportioner dilution ratio." Your finger should be on 13.6 ounces of soluble 20-20-20 in 1 gallon of water that when put on through the 1:200 proportioner would yield 100 ppm N. This solution would also contain 100 ppm P₂O₅ and 100 ppm K₂O. In this example, if you want to apply 200 ppm N using the same fertilizer and proportioner, double the fertilizer ounces required per gallon to dissolve 27.2 ounces of fertilizer per gallon of stock solution.

Volume: dry measure equivalents

Unit	Equivalent values
Acre foot	43,560 cubic feet or 1,163$^{1}/_{3}$ cubic yards
Acre inch	3,630 cubic feet or 134$^{1}/_{2}$ cubic yards
Barrel	7,056 cubic inches or 105 quarts dry or 4 cubic feet or 3$^{1}/_{4}$ bushels
Board foot	144 cubic inches (12 inches wide × 12 inches long × 1 inch thick)
Bushel	2,150 cubic inches or 4 pecks or 1$^{1}/_{4}$ cubic feet
Cord	128 cubic feet (4 feet wide × 4 feet high × 8 feet long)
Cubic foot	1,728 cubic inches
Cubic inch	0.00057 cubic feet
Cubic yard	21.6 bushels or 27 cubic feet
Cup	48 teaspoons or 16 tablespoons or 2 cups dry or $^{1}/_{2}$ quart dry
Quart	67.2 cubic inches or 4 cups dry or 2 pints dry
Tablespoon	3 teaspoons or 0.333 ounces
Teaspoon	$^{1}/_{3}$ tablespoons or 0.111 ounce

Volume: liquid measure equivalents

Unit	Equivalent values
Acre foot	325,151 gallons or 43,560 cubic feet
Acre inch	27,154 gallons or 3,630 cubic feet
Barrel	126 quarts or 31$^{1}/_{2}$ gallons
Cubic foot	953 fluid ounces or 59.84 pints or 29.9 quarts or 7.4 gallons
Cubic inch	0.554 fluid ounce or 0.034 pint
Cup	16 tablespoons or 8 fluid ounces or 2 gills or $^{1}/_{2}$ pint
Gallon	231 cubic inches or 128 fluid ounces or 8 pints or 4 quarts
Gill	4 fluid ounces or $^{1}/_{2}$ cup or $^{1}/_{4}$ pint
Hogshead	63 gallons or 2 barrels
Keg	62$^{1}/_{2}$ quarts or 15$^{2}/_{3}$ gallons
Ounce	6 teaspoons or 2 tablespoons or 1.8 cubic inches
Pint	28.87 cubic inches or 16 fluid ounces or 4 gills or 2 cups
Quart	57.75 cubic inches or 32 fluid ounces or 8 gills or 2 pints
Tablespoon	3 teaspoons or $^{1}/_{2}$ fluid ounce
Teaspoon	50 to 60 drops or $^{1}/_{3}$ tablespoon or 0.17 fluid ounce

Temperature conversions

The numbers in the center columns labeled "Reading" refer to the temperature that may be in either degrees Fahrenheit or degrees Celsius. If you want to convert from Celsius to Fahrenheit, the equivalent temperature in Fahrenheit will be on the corresponding line in the right hand column. If you want to convert from Fahrenheit to Celsius, the equivalent temperature will be on the corresponding line in the left hand column.

Example 1. To convert 20 degrees Fahrenheit to degrees Celsius, find 20 in the Reading column. The corresponding number in the Celsius column, -6.7, is the temperature in degrees Celsius.

Example 2. To convert 20 degrees Celsius to degrees Fahrenheit, find 20 in the Reading column. The corresponding number in the Fahrenheit column, 68.0, is the temperature in degrees Fahrenheit.
For temperatures not found in the table below, the following formulas can be used:

Celsius to Fahrenheit = (degrees $C \times \frac{9}{5}$) + 32 = degrees Fahrenheit

Fahrenheit to Celsius = (degrees F - 32) $\times \frac{5}{9}$ = degrees Celsius

Celsius	Reading	Fahrenheit
-17.8	0	32.0
-17.2	1	33.8
-16.7	2	35.6
-16.1	3	37.4
-15.6	4	39.2
-15.0	5	41.0
-14.4	6	42.8
-13.9	7	44.6
-13.3	8	46.6
-12.8	9	48.2
-12.2	10	50.0
-11.7	11	51.8
-11.1	12	53.6
-10.6	13	55.4
-10.0	14	57.2
-9.4	15	59.0
-8.9	16	60.8
-8.3	17	62.6
-7.8	18	64.4
-7.2	19	66.2
-6.7	20	68.0
-6.1	21	69.8
-5.6	22	71.6
-5.0	23	73.4
-4.4	24	75.2
-3.9	25	77.0

Celsius	Reading	Fahrenheit
-3.3	26	78.8
-2.8	27	80.6
-2.2	28	82.4
-1.7	29	84.2
-1.1	30	86.0
-0.6	31	87.8
0	32	89.6
0.6	33	91.4
1.1	34	93.2
1.7	35	95.0
2.2	36	96.8
2.8	37	98.6
3.3	38	100.4
3.9	39	102.2
4.4	40	104.0
5.0	41	105.8
5.6	42	107.6
6.1	43	109.4
6.7	44	111.2
7.2	45	113.0
7.8	46	114.8
8.3	47	116.6
8.9	48	118.4
9.4	49	120.2
10.0	50	122.0
10.6	51	123.8
11.1	52	125.6
11.7	53	127.4
12.2	54	129.2
12.8	55	131.0
13.3	56	132.8
13.9	57	134.6
14.4	58	136.4
15.0	59	138.2
15.6	60	140.0
16.1	61	141.8
16.7	62	143.6
17.2	63	145.4
17.8	64	147.2
18.3	65	149.0
18.9	66	150.8
19.4	67	152.6
20.0	68	154.4
20.6	69	156.2

Celsius	Reading	Fahrenheit
21.1	70	158.0
21.7	71	159.8
22.2	72	161.6
22.8	73	163.4
23.3	74	165.2
23.9	75	167.0
24.4	76	168.8
25.0	77	170.6
25.6	78	172.4
26.1	79	174.2
26.7	80	176.0
27.1	81	177.8
27.8	82	179.6
28.3	83	181.4
28.9	84	183.2
29.4	85	185.0
30.0	86	186.8
30.6	87	188.6
31.1	88	190.4
31.7	89	192.2
32.2	90	194.0
32.8	91	195.8
33.3	92	197.6
33.9	93	199.4
34.4	94	201.2
35.0	95	203.0
35.6	96	204.8
36.1	97	206.6
36.7	98	208.4
37.2	99	210.2
37.8	100	212.0
38.3	101	213.8
38.8	102	215.6
39.4	103	217.4
40.0	104	219.2
40.5	105	221.0
41.1	106	222.8
41.6	107	224.6
42.2	108	226.4
42.7	109	228.2
43.3	110	230.0
43.8	111	231.8
44.4	112	233.6
45.0	113	235.4

Celsius	Reading	Fahrenheit
45.5	114	237.2
46.1	115	239.0
46.6	116	240.8
47.2	117	242.6
48.3	118	244.4
48.3	119	246.2
48.8	120	248.0
54.4	130	266.0
60.0	140	284.0
65.5	150	302.0
71.1	160	320.0
76.6	170	338.0
82.2	180	356.0
87.7	190	374.0
93.3	200	392.0
98.8	210	410.0

Index of Host Plants, Diseases, and Insect and Mite Pests

T he following is a brief list of some of the major disease, insect, and mite pests of major flower and foliage crops. It is certainly not exhaustive of either plants or diseases and pests. Not all of the pests and diseases listed here were specifically discussed in the text. New pest and disease problems are constantly being recorded. Outdoor or Saran-produced crops may have different problems than the same plants produced in the greenhouse. Pest and disease problems differ according to geography and climate. Use this information as a guide to the types of problems you are likely to encounter with a plant type. In most cases with insects and mites, more than one aphid, mealybug, scale, etc. species can occur on a host plant, so the pest group is listed rather than all of the species known to occur on that plant. In some cases, examples are given.

Diseases	Pests

Ageratum

Botrytis blight	Aphids
Leaf spot	Caterpillars (e.g., cabbage looper, corn earworm, greenhouse leaf tier, tobacco budworm)
Root and crown rot	Cyclamen mites
	Greenhouse whiteflies
	Mealybugs
	Plant bugs
	Spider mites

Antirrhinum majus (**Snapdragon**)

Botrytis blight	Aphids
Crown rot	Caterpillars (e.g., cabbage looper, variegated cutworm)
Plant bugs	Cyclamen mites
Powdery mildew	Downy mildew
Root rot	Fungus gnats
Rust	Mealybugs
Stem rot	Spider mites
Tospoviruses	Thrips
	White grubs

Diseases	**Pests**

Aquilegia

Crown rot

Leaf spot

Rust

Aphids

Columbine borer (*Papaipema purpurifascia*)

Columbine leaf miner (*Phytomyza acqilegivora*)

Aster

Blight (*Rhizoctonia*)

Foot rot (*Phytophthora*)

Fusarium wilt

Leaf spots–several

Rust

Yellows

Aphids

Beetles (blister beetle, Japanese beetle)

Leafhoppers

Leaf miners (*Agromyza, Phytomyza*)

Plant bugs

Stalk borers

Azalea

Cylindroaladium blight

Leaf gall

Leaf spots–several

Petal blight

Phytophthora blight

Phytophtora wilt and root rot

Stem canker

Web blight (*Rhizoctonia*)

Ambrosia beetles

Aphids

Azalea leaf miners

Black vine weevils

Lace bugs

Leaf tier

Mealybugs

Rhododendron borers

Scales

Spider mites

Thrips

Whiteflies

Begonia

Bacterial leaf spot and wilt

Powdery mildew

Root rot

Tospoviruses

Aphids

Black vine weevils

Fungus gnats

Mealybugs

Scales

Thrips

Tarsonemid mites

Whiteflies

Diseases	Pests

Camellia

Canker and dieback	Aphids
Flower blight	Beetles
	Lepidoptera
	Mealybugs
	Scales
	Thrips
	Whiteflies

Cineraria

Botrytis blight	Aphids
Powdery mildew	Fungus gnats
Root rot	Leaf miners
Tospoviruses	Mealybugs
	Other caterpillars (e.g., cabbage looper)
	Spider mites
	Thrips
	Variegated cutworms
	Whiteflies

Coleus

Botrytis blight	Fungus gnats
Root rot	Mealybugs
Viruses	Plant bugs
	Slugs
	Spider mites
	Whiteflies

Cyclamen

Bacterial soft rot	Aphids
Botrytis blight	Black vine weevils
Fusarium wilt	Fungus gnats
Leaf spot and blight	Scales
Stunt (*Ramularia*)	Tarsonemid mites
Tospoviruses	Thrips
	White grubs

Diseases	Pests

Dahlia

Bacterial stem rot	Aphids
Bacterial wilt	Caterpillars (e.g., European corn borer, stalk borer)
Botrytis blight	Cyclamen mites
Fusarium and *Verticillium* wilt	Leafhoppers
Leaf spot	Plant bugs
Powdery mildew	Spider mites
Stem rot	Thrips
Viruses	

Delphinium

Aster yellow	Aphids
Bacterial leaf spot	Spider mites
Bacterial rot	Leaf miners
Crown and root rots–several	Stalk borers
Diaporthe blight	Tarsonemid mites
Fusarium wilt	
Powdery mildew	

Dendranthema (**Chrysanthemum**)

Ascochyta blight	Aphids
Bacterial blight	Beetles (e.g., blister beetles, rose chafer)
Bacterial leaf spot	Fungus gnats
Crown rot (*Rhizoctonia*)	Leaf miners
Fusarium wilt	Mealybugs
Leaf spots–several	Caterpillars (e.g., beet armyworm, cabbage looper, corn earworm, European corn borer, variegated cutworm)
Powdery mildew	Plant bugs
Root rot (*Pythium*)	Spider mites
Rust	Thrips
Verticillium wilt	Whiteflies
Viruses	White grubs

Dianthus (**Carnation**)

Alternaria blight	Aphids
Bacterial leaf spot	Beetles (e.g., Fuller's rose beetle)
Bacterial leaf wilt	Fungus gnats
Botrytis blight	Leaf miners (*Liriomyza* spp.)
Fairy ring spot (*Heterosporium*)	Caterpillars (e.g., cabbage looper, leafroller variegated cutworm)
Fusarium stem rot	Plant bugs
Fusarium wilt	Spider mites
Petal blight	
Rust	
Septoria leaf spot	
Viruses	

Diseases	**Pests**

Digitalis

Leaf spot	Aphids
Root and stem rot	Beetles
	Mealybugs

Euphorbia pulcherrima (**Poinsettia**)

Bacterial canker	Aphids
Black root rot	Caterpillars (e.g., leafroller)
Powdery mildew	Fungus gnats
Root rot	Mealybugs
Scab	Scales
Soft rot (*Erwinia*)	Spider mites
Stem rot	Thrips
	Whiteflies

Freesia

Bacterial scab	Aphids
Fusarium wilt	Bulb mites
Leaf spot	Thrips

Fuchsia

Botrytis blight	Aphids
Crown rot	Beetles
Pythium root rot	Mealybugs
Rust	Scales
Viruses	Spider mites
	Tarsonemid mites
	Thrips
	Whiteflies

Gerbera

Phytophthora	Aphids
Powdery mildew	Leaf miners
	Spider mites
	Tarsonemid mites
	Thrips
	Whiteflies

Diseases	**Pests**

Gladiolus

Botrytis blight
Corn rots–several
Leaf blight (*Stephylium*)
Leaf spots–several
Neck rot (*Rhizoctonia*)
Scab
Viruses

Aphids (bulb and foliar)
Bulb mites
Caterpillars
Mealybugs
Plant bugs
Spider mites
Thrips

Gloxinia

Myrotherium rot
Phytophthora leaf and stem rot
Viruses

Aphids
Black vine weevils
Cyclamen mites
Mealybugs
Thrips

Hibiscus

Leaf spots–several
Nectria canker
Rust

Aphids
Beetles
Whiteflies (esp. *Bemisia* whitefly)

Hydrangea

Botrytis blight
Powdery mildew
Viruses

Aphids
Beetles (e.g., rose chafer)
Plant bugs
Scales
Spider mites
Thrips

Impatiens

Botrytis
Root rot
Viruses

Aphids
Beetles (e.g., spotted cucumber beetle)
Cyclamen mites
Spider mites
Tarnished plant bugs
Thrips

Iris

Bacterial leaf spot
Crown rot
Fusarium wilt
Viruses

Aphids, including bulb aphids
Bulb mites
Florida red scales
Iris borers
Iris weevils
Lesser bulb flies
Thrips

Diseases	Pests

Kalanchoe

Crown rot (*Phytophthora*)
Powdery mildew

Aphids
Mealybugs
Tarsonemid mites
Thrips

Lantana

Black mildew
Fusarium wilt
Rust

Aphids
Caterpillars
Cyclamen mites
Mealybugs
Whiteflies

Lilium (**Lily**)

Botrytis blight
Root rot
Viruses

Aphids
Beetles
Bulb mites
Stalk borers

Lupinus (**Lupine**)

Crown rot (*Pellicularia*)
Leaf blights and spots–several
Powdery mildew
Rust

Aphids
Caterpillars
Fungus gnats
Plant bugs
Slugs, snails
Spider mites

Orchidaceae (**Orchid family**)

Bacterial soft rot
Botrytis blight
Leaf spots and blights–several
Rust
Viruses

Aphids
Beetles (borers and weevils)
Mealybugs
Orchid flies
Plant bugs
Scales
Slugs, snails
Thrips

Diseases	Pests

Pelargonium (Geranium)

Alternaria leaf spot	Aphids
Bacterial leaf spot and blight	Beetles
Blackleg (*Pythium*)	Fungus gnats
Botrytis blight	Mealybugs
Root rot	Caterpillars (e.g., cabbage looper, geranium
Rust	plume moth, leafroller variegated cutworm)
Viruses	Plant bugs
	Slugs
	Spider mites
	Tarsonemid mites
	Thrips
	Whiteflies

Petunia

Alternaria leaf spot	Aphids
Botrytis blight	Caterpillars (e.g., hornworm, variegated cutworms,
Crown rot (*Phytophthora*)	woolybear)
Pythium root rot	Cyclamen mites
Viruses	Flea beetles
	Leaf miners
	Plant bugs
	Thrips

Rosa (Rose)

Black spot	Aphids
Botrytis blight	Beetles (e.g., Fuller rose beetle, Japanese
Cane cankers	beetle, rose chafer)
Crown gall	Bristly rose-slugs
Downy mildew	Caterpillars (e.g., cutworms, leafrollers)
Nematodes	Leafhoppers
Powdery mildew	Plant bugs
Rust	Rose midges
Verticillium wilt	Scales
Viruses	Spider mites
	Thrips
	Whiteflies
	White grubs

Diseases	**Pests**

Saintpaulia (African Violet)

Botrytis blight	Aphids
Powdery mildew	Fungus gnats
Root and crown rot	Mealybugs
Root knot nematode	Springtails
	Tarsonemid mites
	Thrips
	White grubs

Salvia

Botrytis blight	Aphids
Root rot	Scales
	Whiteflies

Tagetes (Marigold)

Botrytis blight	Aphids
Leaf spot	Japanese beetles
Wilt and stem rot (*Phytophthora*)	Leafhoppers
	Leaf miners
	Plant bugs
	Spider mites
	Thrips

Tulipa (Tulip)

Botrytis blight	Aphids
Bulb rot	Bulb mites
Viruses	Narcissus bulb flies

Verbena

Bacterial wilt	Aphids
Botrytis blight	Caterpillars (e.g., leafroller, woolybear)
Root rot	Fungus gnats
Viruses	Spider mites
	Tarsonemid mites
	Thrips
	Whiteflies

Viola (Pansy)

Bacterial leaf spot	Aphids
Black root rot	Cutworms
Botrytis blight	Mealybugs
Pythium root rot	Spider mites

Diseases	**Pests**

Zinnia

Alternaria blight
Bacterial leaf spot
Powdery mildew

Aphids
Beetles
Leaf miners
Plant bugs
Spider mites
Thrips
Whiteflies

Glossary

Abdomen: The last body region of an insect or mite; the "tail" end.

Acaricide (miticide): An agent that destroys mites and ticks.

Acidic: A chemical condition consisting of more hydrogen ions than hydroxyl ions, measured in pH units. A pH less than 7 is considered acidic.

Active ingredient (a.i. or AI): Chemicals in a product that are responsible for the pesticidal effect.

Acute toxicity: The immediate toxicity of a material; to cause injury or death from a single exposure.

Adjuvant: A material mixed with pesticides in order to improve contact with leaves or improve pest control. Examples include wetting agents, spreaders, emulsifiers, stickers, penetrants, buffers, and dispersing agents.

Aerosol: A spray consisting of drops less than 50 microns in diameter; colloidal suspension of solids or liquids in air.

Aestivate: To become dormant or inactive during the summer.

Algae: Microscopic plants without true stems, leaves, or roots, but which contain chlorophyll. Algae are found on the growing medium surface, on irrigation matting, and in other poorly drained areas.

Alkaline: A chemical condition consisting of a higher concentration of hydroxyl ions than hydrogen ions, measured in pH units. A pH greater than 7 is considered alkaline or basic.

Arthropod: An animal having a segmented body, an exoskeleton, and jointed legs.

Bacterium (plural bacteria): A microscopic, one-celled microorganism that lacks chlorophyll.

Biological control: The use of one living organism to control another.

Blight: A disease symptom that results in the sudden death of leaves.

Blotch: A leaf disease symptom that appears as a large, irregular shaped, yellow or brown area.

Botanical pesticide: A pesticide produced from naturally occurring chemicals found in some plants. Examples are nicotine, pyrethrum, and rotenone. Botanical materials may or may not be highly toxic to mammals.

Broad-spectrum insecticide: Nonselective; having about the same toxicity to most insects.

Canker: The infected area of a stem, branch, or main root that is often swollen or sunken and discolored.

Capillary action: The upward movement of water through tiny pores, such as in growing media or plant stem.

Carbamate insecticide: One of a class of insecticides derived from carbamic acid.

Carrier: An inert material that serves as a diluent or vehicle for the active ingredient or toxicant.

Cast skin: The old, outer skeleton (exoskeleton) left behind after the insect (e.g., aphid) molts.

Caterpillar: The wormlike larva of a moth, butterfly, or skipper that usually has three pairs of jointed legs on the thorax and two or more pairs of legs on the abdomen.

Caudal: At or near the tail.

Centimeter: A metric unit of length; 0.394 inches.

Chlorosis: Yellowing of normally green plant tissues; a common symptom of insect damage, disease, or nutrient deficiency.

Chronic toxicity: The toxicity of a material determined beyond 24 hours and usually after several weeks of exposure.

Compatible chemicals: Chemicals that can be mixed together without losing their effectiveness.

Cocoon: A silken or fibrous case spun by a larva to provide protection during its pupal period.

Coldfogger: A low-volume pesticide applicator that produces mainly aerosol-sized drops by mechanical methods, without heat.

Common pesticide name: A common chemical name given to a pesticide. Many pesticides are known by a number of trade brand names but have only one recognized common name. For example, the common name for Orthene insecticide is acephate.

Conidium (see **Spore**).

Cornicle: One of a pair of "honey tubes" (siphunculi) that extend from the abdomen of an aphid.

Crawler: The mobile, first-instar nymph of a scale insect or whitefly.

Crown rot: Disease that affects the plant stem at the soil line or crown.

Cultivar: A variety of a cultivated plant that differs from others in the same species and keeps the distinguishing features when reproduced.

Cultural control: The use of resistant cultivars, crop rotation, fertilization levels, and irrigation practices as a pest management method.

Disease: Any disturbance to a plant that interferes with its health. Any deviation from the normal, healthy growth or development. Diseases can be caused by fungi, bacteria, viruses, or environmental imbalances.

Dispersible granule: A dry formulation of small particle size designed to be mixed with water prior to use.

Dorsal: Top or uppermost; pertaining to the back or upper side.

Dose, dosage: Same as rate. The amount of toxicant given or applied per unit of plant, animal, or surface.

Drench: A thorough soaking of growing media using a chemical pesticide and water.

Dry flowable: A type of granular pesticide formulation. It is mixed with water and becomes a sprayable suspension; also known as water-dispersible granules.

Dust: A dry pesticide formulation mixed with finely ground talc, clay, or powdered nut shells. Dusts are applied dry, never with water.

Economic injury level: The pest level at which additional management practices must be employed to prevent economic losses.

Electrostatic sprayer: A low-volume or ultra-low-volume applicator that applies sprays containing electrically charged spray drops.

Elytra: Thickened, leathery forewings that cover the hind wings; common to beetles and earwigs.

Emulsifiable concentrate: Concentrated pesticide formulation containing organic solvents and emulsifiers used to make an emulsion when mixed with water. An emulsion is not a solution, it is a mixture of one liquid dispersed in another.

Environmental Protection Agency (EPA): The federal agency responsible for pesticide rules and regulations and all pesticide registrations.

EPA establishment number: A number assigned to each pesticide production plant by the EPA. The number indicates the plant where the pesticide product was produced and must appear on all labels of that product.

EPA registration number: A number assigned to a pesticide product by the EPA when the product is registered by the manufacturer or his designated agent. The number must appear on all labels for a particular product.

Eradicant: Applies to fungicides in which a chemical is used to eliminate a pathogen from its host or environment.

Eradicate: To eliminate a particular pest species from a designated area.

Exclusion: Control of a disease or insect by preventing infected plants, insects, or mites from entering an area free of these problems.

Exhaust fan: A large diameter fan used to exhaust air from the greenhouse.

Flowable: A liquid pesticide formulation in which a very finely ground, solid particle is mixed in a liquid carrier.

Fly speck: A tiny spot of excrement left by a fly, such as a shore fly.

Formulation: Referring to pesticides, a toxic chemical combined with other ingredients to create a product that can be used to control a pest. A formulation may contain one or more active ingredients. Examples are dusts, wettable powders, emulsifiable concentrates.

Fumigant: A gaseous pesticide form.

Fumigation: To kill pests by pesticide vapor action.

Fungicide: A chemical that kills, inactivates, or inhibits fungi.

Fungistatic: Chemical action that inhibits the fungal spore germination.

Granule: A pesticide formulation containing an active ingredient impregnated on particles of fired clay, walnut shells, corn cobs, or other porous material.

Growing medium or media: Usually, a mixture of several organic and/or inorganic materials in which plants are grown.

Grub: Usually refers to a slow-moving, C-shaped larva of the Coleoptera (beetle) family Scarabaeidae having three pairs of forelegs and a fat, whitish body; sometimes also used to refer to many growing medium-inhabiting larvae of Coleoptera and Hymenoptera.

Hectare (ha): A metric unit of area; approximately 2.5 acres.

High-volume spray (HV): Generally, a "wet" spray applying more than 50 gallons per acre (500 l/ ha).

Holistic health management: An approach to maintaining plant health that considers all aspects of the plant's environment.

Honeydew: A sticky, sugary liquid excreted by certain insects of the order Homoptera, including aphids, soft scales, mealybugs, and whiteflies.

Host: The plant or animal upon which a parasite lives or which a predator consumes.

Humidity: The amount of moisture in the air, usually given in an amount relative to air temperature: relative humidity.

Hydraulic sprayer: A power sprayer used to apply high-volume sprays.

Hygrometer: An instrument used to determine the relative humidity.

Hypha: A thread of fungal cells; many hyphae together form a mycelium or fungal colony.

Inert ingredient: Material added to chemical pesticides that carry and dilute the active ingredients. They generally have no direct pesticidal activity, but rather influence the behavior of the toxic ingredient(s).

Infectious disease: A fungus, bacteria, or virus-caused disease that can be transferred to other plants.

Infestation: As related to insects and mites, the presence of large numbers of an animal pest species where they are likely to cause plant injury and/or annoyance.

Inhalation: Exposure of test animals either to vapor or dust for a predetermined time.

Inhalation toxicity: Poisonous to man or animals when breathed into the lungs.

Inoculum: A material containing microorganisms that is associated with the spread of the pathogen from plant to plant.

Inoculum potential: The ability of a fungus or bacteria to infect other plants in any given situation.

Insect: A six-legged arthropod that has three distinct body regions (head, thorax, abdomen) as an adult and often has one or two pairs of wings.

Insect-growth regulator (IGR): Chemical substance that disrupts the action of insect hormones controlling molting, maturity from pupal stage to adult and others.

Instar: The life stage of an arthropod between successive molts.

Integrated pest management (IPM): Using multiple tactics to control a pest or pathogen.

Larva (plural larvae): In insects with complete metamorphosis, the immature form occurring between the egg and pupal stages (e.g., egg, larva, pupa, adult); in mites, the six-legged first instar.

LD 50: A lethal dose for 50 percent of a population of test animals, expressed as milligrams of toxicant per kilogram of body weight (mg/kg). The higher the LD 50, the more chemical it takes to cause the 50 percent mortality and the safer the chemical.

Leach watering: The process of thoroughly watering plants to dissolve and wash fertilizer nutrients (salts) out of the media.

Life cycle: The development of an insect or mite from the egg (or live birth) to the reproductive stage.

Low-volume spray (LV): A spray, usually with a large portion of the volume consisting of aerosol-sized drops, with a total volume less than 50 gallons per acre (500 l/ha).

Maggot: Usually refers to fly larvae without distinct heads or legs.

Metamorphosis: Change in form and function during the development of an insect or mite.

Meter: A metric unit of length; 1.094 yards.

Microbial pesticide: Bacteria, fungi, or viruses formulated as pesticides and normally applied with conventional application equipment.

Micron: 1/1,000 (0.001) millimeter; commonly used to classify spray drops.

Millimeter: A metric unit of length; 0.034 inches.

Mite: A tiny arthropod, eight-legged as an adult and closely related to ticks.

Molt: The process of replacing the skin with a new skin; shedding.

Mycelium: A mass of hyphal; a fungal colony.

Natural enemies: Often used to describe parasites, predators, nematodes, and pathogenic microorganisms used in biological control.

Nematode: A tiny roundworm that generally cannot be seen without a microscope. Many are parasitic on plants or insects.

Noninfectious disease: A disease that is caused by an environmental imbalance.

Nymph: In reference to insects with simple or no metamorphosis, the immature form between egg and adult; in reference to mites and ticks, the eight-legged, immature form.

Oral toxicity: Toxicity of a compound when given by mouth in a single dose. Usually expressed in milligrams of chemical per kilogram of body weight that kills 50 percent of the test animals. The smaller the number, the greater the toxicity.

Organism: A life form in its entirety.

Organochlorine insecticide: One of the many chlorinated insecticides (e.g., DDT, dieldrin, chlordane, BHC, Lindane).

Organophosphate: Class of insecticides (also one or two herbicides and fungicides) derived from phosphoric acid esters.

Oviposition: The process of laying eggs.

pH: A measure of acidity or alkalinity, measured on a scale of 1 to 14. A pH of 7 is neutral, less than 7 is acidic, greater than 7 is basic.

Parasite: Any plant or animal that lives in or on another organism to the detriment of the host.

Parthenogenetic: Capable of reproduction without mating (without male fertilization of the eggs).

Pasteurization: A process in which substances are heated to 140 to 160F for one hour to kill disease-causing and other harmful pathogens and insects, but retain beneficial pathogens. Often used on soil mixes using aerated steam.

Pathogen: Any disease-producing microorganism, such as a fungus, bacterium, or virus.

Pest: An unwanted bacterium, fungus, virus, insect, mite, or other living organism.

Pest scouting: An organized program to detect and monitor for the occurrence of pests.

Pesticide: An "economic poison," defined in most state and federal laws as any substance used for controlling, preventing, destroying, repelling, or mitigating any pest. Includes fungicides, herbicides, insecticides, nematicides, rodenticides, desiccants, defoliants, and plant growth regulators.

Physical control: The use of screens, traps, barriers, etc., to reduce or prevent pest infestations.

Phytotoxic: Injurious to plants.

Poison control center: Information sources for human poisoning cases, including pesticides, usually located at major hospitals.

Pore space: The space between the particles of growing media.

Predator: A natural enemy that preys on and consumes all or part of its host.

Protectant: Fungicide applied to plant surface before pathogen attack to prevent penetration and subsequent infection.

Pseudopupa: A nonfeeding stage in thrips development intermediate between the nymph and adult.

Pupa (plural pupae): In insects with complete metamorphosis, the life stage between larva and adult; also, the next to the last developmental stage in thrips, male scales, and whiteflies is often referred to as a pupa.

Rate: Refers to the amount of active ingredient material applied to a unit area regardless of percentage of chemical in the carrier (dilution).

Registered pesticides: Pesticide products that have been approved by the EPA for the uses listed on the label.

Resistance (insecticide): Natural or genetic ability of an organism to tolerate the poisonous effects of a toxicant.

Restricted entry interval (REI): Waiting interval required by federal law between application of certain hazardous pesticides to crops and the entrance of workers into those crops without having to wear protective clothing. May also be referred to as the waiting period.

Rotary atomizer: A pesticide applicator that disperses pesticide off of a rapidly rotating, notched disc. A fan may be attached to provide additional forward momentum to spray drops.

Secondary pest: A pest that usually does little if any damage but can become a serious pest under certain conditions (e.g., when insecticide applications destroy a given insect's predators and parasites).

Selective pesticide: One that, while killing the pest individuals, spares much or most of the other fauna or flora, including beneficial species, either through differential toxic action or through the manner in which the pesticide is used (formulation, dosage, timing, placement, etc.).

Signal word: A required word that appears on every pesticide label to denote the product's relative toxicity. The signal words are either **Danger—Poison** for highly toxic compounds, **Warning** for moderately toxic, or **Caution** for slightly toxic.

Smoke generator: A pesticide combined with an oxidizing agent in a container that is ignited to produce a toxic vapor or tiny particles.

Soil application: Application of pesticide made primarily to soil surface rather than to vegetation.

Soluble powder: A dry powder pesticide formulation that dissolves in water.

Sooty mold: A dark fungal growth that develops on foliage covered with honeydew.

Spore: A tiny reproductive body produced by a plant. For fungi and ferns, spores are a major means of reproduction and spread. Often called conidia.

Spreader: Ingredient added to spray mixture to improve contact between pesticide and plant surface. Spreaders generally increase the area that a given volume of liquid will cover on a leaf.

Sticker: Ingredient added to spray or dust to improve its adherence to plants.

Surfactant: Ingredient that aids or enhances the surface modifying properties of a pesticide formulation (wetting agent, emulsifier, or spreader).

Symptom: A visible or otherwise detectable abnormality caused by a disease or disorder. A condition that indicates a health problem.

Systemic: A material such as a bacterium or pesticide that is absorbed and translocated throughout the plant or animal.

Target: The plants, animals, structures, areas, or pests to be treated with a pesticide application.

Thermal pulse-jet applicator: A type of low-volume pesticide application equipment in which a pesticide is mixed with an oil or water and is injected into a very hot air stream where it condenses into a fog and is carried throughout the area to be treated.

Thorax: The middle region of an insect's body; if present, the wings are found here.

Ultra-low-volume (ULV): Sprays, diluted or undiluted, that are applied at 0.5 gallon or less per acre.

Vector: An agent that transmits or spreads a disease-causing pathogen. For example, certain thrips species are vectors of tomato spotted wilt virus.

Wettable powder: Pesticide formulation of toxicant mixed with inert dust and a wetting agent that mixes readily with water and forms a short-term suspension (requires tank agitation).

Wetting agent: A compound that causes spray solutions to contact plant surfaces more thoroughly.

Suggested Reading

Cornell Cooperative Extension. 1993. *IPM for poinsettias in New York: a scouting and pest management guide.* New York State IPM Program Pub. No. 403. Ithaca, N.Y.

Baker, James A., ed. 1994. *Insect and related pests of flowers and foliage plants.* Raleigh, N.C.: North Carolina State University Cooperative Extension Service.

Daughtrey, Margery, and A.R. Chase. 1992. *Ball field guide to diseases of greenhouse ornamentals.* Batavia, Ill.: Ball Publishing.

Gaston, Michelle L., Stephen A. Carver, and Cheryl A. Irwin. 1995. *Tips on the use and safety of chemicals, biologicals, and the environment on floriculture crops.* Columbus, Ohio: Ohio Florists' Association.

Hara, Arnold H. 1994. Ornamentals and flowers. *In Insect pests and fresh horticultural products: treatments and responses.* Edited by R.E. Pauli and J.W. Armstrong. Wallingford, England: CAB International.

Hunter, Charles D. 1994. *Suppliers of beneficial organisms in North America.* Sacramento, Calif.: California Environmental Protection Agency.

Matthews, G.A., and E.C. Hislop, eds. 1993. *Application technology for crop protection.* Wallingford, England: CAB International.

Society of American Florists (SAF). 1984-96. *Proceedings of Insect and Disease Management Conferences.* Alexandria, Vir.: Society of American Florists.

Ware, George W. 1991. *Fundamentals of pesticides.* 3rd ed. Fresno, Calif.: Thomson Publications.

Some useful World Wide Web sites. (Many of the addresses below are cross-linked to each other, as well as many other addresses.)

http://www.yahoo.com (for searching the World Wide Web)

http://www.webcrawler.com (for searching the World Wide Web)

http://www.yahoo.com/science/agriculture/horticulture

http://www.cdpr.ca.gov/docs/dprodoes/goodbug/organism.htm (beneficials suppliers in North America)

http://wwwl.ag.ohio-state.edu/~ohioline/ (Ohio State University Extension)

http://www2.ncsu.edu/ncsu/cals/hort.sci (North Carolina State University)

http://www.aggie-horticulture.tamu.edu (Texas A&M University)

http://www.134.84.58.52/comflor.html (University of Minnesota)

http://www.weather.com (The Weather Channel)

http://www.ofa.org (Ohio Florists Association)

http://www.growertalks.com (Floriculture Worldwide Network: *GrowerTalks* and *FloraCulture International* magazines)

http://www.branchsmith.com (*GMPro* magazine)

Index